AF787227

China and the EU in the Era of Regional and Interregional Cooperation

PETER LANG

Bruxelles · Bern · Berlin · New York · Oxford · Wien

« International Issues »

Studies in international relations, particularly historical, stem from the changing face of diplomacy over time, where the deeper forces at play, such as those once defined by Pierre Renouvin, are taken into account. Individual states, and those who define and implement their policies, are placed at the heart of global life. According to this concept, countries pursue a course of action by taking advantage of the most diverse range of tools they can rely on, such as economic or cultural resources, which act alone or interact with others.

The study of international relations grew into different fields of analysis during the twentieth century, but it is now subject to a new scrutiny in this era of globalisation. This concept, which coincides with the development of neo-liberal analysis since the 1980s, reveals a new awareness about the increased number of actors – NGOs and multinational companies, for example – but also the large autonomy they enjoy when it comes to action.

This series aims to portray these new perspectives and their impact on current research. Without casting aside studies in international relations that focus on states, it tries to better understand the diverse range of factors that play out on the world stage and how they relate to each other – from the high stakes in sport to the use of colonial memory. This series targets academics and analysts who wish to apply twentieth-century history to contemporary thought.

Series Editors

M. Éric BUSSIÈRE, *Professeur à l'Université de Paris IV-Sorbonne*

M. Michel DUMOULIN, *Professeur ordinaire émérite de l'Université catholique de Louvain*

M. Sylvain SCHIRMANN, *Professeur d'histoire contemporaine, directeur de l'Institut d'études politiques de Strasbourg*

Mario Telò / Yuan Feng (eds.)

China and the EU in the Era of Regional and Interregional Cooperation

International Issues
Vol. 49

This publication is funded by EU-CHINA People to People Association and the "GEM-STONES research and doctoral project", funded by the EU Commission, DG Research, in the context of Horizon 2020 and coordinated by ULB-IEE.

This publication has been peer reviewed.

No part of this book may be reproduced in any form, by print, photocopy, microfilm or any other means, without prior written permission from the publisher. All rights reserved.

© P.I.E. PETER LANG s.a.
International Academic Publishers
Brussels, 2020
1 avenue Maurice, B-1050 Brussels, Belgium
brussels@peterlang.com; www.peterlang.com

ISSN 2030-3688
ISBN 978-2-8076-1396-6
ePDF 978-2-8076-1397-3
ePUB 978-2-8076-1398-0
MOBI 978-2-8076-1399-7
DOI 10.3726/b16864
D/2020/5678/17

Bibliographic information published by "Die Deutsche Nationalbibliothek".

"Die Deutsche National Bibliothek" lists this publication in the "Deutsche Nationalbibliografie"; detailed bibliographic data is available on the Internet at <http://dnb.de>.

Table of Contents

List of Contributors

Guy Burton is a visiting fellow at the LSE Middle East Centre and (as of January 2019) an adjunct professor of international relations at Vesalius College in Brussels. Previously, he was an assistant professor at the Mohammed bin Rashid School of Government (2016–2018). Before that, he was an assistant professor at the School of Politics, History and International Relations at the University of Nottingham, Malaysia Campus (2013–2016); a lecturer at the University of Kurdistan-Hewler in the Kurdistan Region of Iraq (2012–2013); and a research fellow (2010–2012) and acting director (2011–2012) at the Center for Development Studies at Birzeit University in occupied Palestine. Dr. Burton's research interests are wide ranging. He covers comparative politics, international relations, the politics of development and public policy and has regional specialism in the Middle East and Latin American areas. He is the author, most recently, of *Rising Powers and the Arab–Israeli Conflict since 1947* (Lexington Books, 2018). His publications also include co-authorship and authorship of *Presidential Leadership in the Americas since Independence* (Lexington Books, 2016) and *Policy-Making and Education Reform in the Development of Latin American Social Democracy* (Edwin Mellen, 2011), respectively. His work has also been published in peer-reviewed journals such as *Third World Quarterly, Conflict Security & Development, Middle East Critique, International Review of Education* and *Latin American Perspectives*. He received his PhD from the London School of Economics in 2009.

Jean François Di Meglio is the president of the Asia Centre, Paris. An alumnus of the École normale supérieure and Beijing University, Jean-François Di Meglio has spent 20 years of investment banking in connection with, or posted in, Asia-Pacific region. From 2005 to 2008, he led BNP Paribas' energy and raw materials division in China. He joined the Asia Centre in 2008, and became its president in 2009. He takes part on a regular basis in high-level EU-China debate about strategic and business cooperation.

Yuan Feng obtained her PhD in political and social sciences from the Université libre de Bruxelles, and PhD in political theory from Luis Guido Carli. She is currently associated researcher at the Institut des études européennes of ULB. Her research interests include multilateralism, institutionalism, EU-China relations and China's foreign policy. Her PhD thesis on past, present and future of China's regional and global multilateralism is forthcoming by Routledge.

Geoffrey Harris is a former official of the European Parliament (1976–2016). He is also a former visiting scholar at Fudan Development Institute, Shanghai, 2017, and a visiting professor at Xi'an Jiaotong-Liverpool University, Suzhou. He is the author of numerous essays and articles on EU-China relations and global order and takes part on a regular basis in EU-China strategic debate.

Hongyu Lin is the dean of the College of International Relations at Huaqiao University. He is also a standing councillor of China Association of International Studies (CAIS), senior fellow of China Pacific Studies Academy and one of the distinguished scholars of Peking social science theory studies. Prof. Lin earned his PhD from Peking University and once was a visiting scholar at Hoover Institution at Stanford University and director of the Department of International Politics at the China University of International Relations. He specialized in the studies of Sino-US relations, IPE, big powers' gaming and international security and has published several books including *Political Analysis of American Presidential Elections* (2017), *General Studies of BRICS* (2016), *Rise of China and World Governance* (2014), *Rise of China and International System* (2013), *Review of China National Security* in 2012 and *Methodology of International Studies* (2006).

P. Rodrigues, Assistant Professor, has a PhD in international politics from the University of Freiburg, Germany. His scientific interests focus on south-south and China-Brazil interregional relations, notably in the fields of environment and energy policies. After a bachelors in Pearson College, UWC and Trent University, Canada, he studied at the Freiburg University (Arnold-Bergstraesser-Institute). His publications deal with development policy in Guatemala and China's relations with South America.

Jürgen Rüland (1953) studied political science, history and German literature at the University of Freiburg, Germany. He earned a PhD in political science from the University of Freiburg in 1981 and his habilitation degree at the same university in 1989. From 1978 to 1991 he worked as a research fellow at the Arnold-Bergstraesser-Institute, Freiburg. He was a professor *pro tempore* of political science at the University Passau (1991–1993) and professor of political science at the University of Rostock (1993–1998). From 1998 to 2019 Rüland was full time professor of international relations at the University of Freiburg. From 2000 to 2002 he served as a dean of the Faculty of Humanities IV. Since November 2009 Prof. Rüland has been the chairperson of the Freiburg University's Southeast Asia Program, which is sponsored by the German Federal Ministry of Education and Research (BMBF). His numerous books on regional cooperation and interregional relations are considered as reference by the international epistemic community.

Ruixia Jia (1971) holds a PhD in law from Graduate School of Chinese Academy of Social Sciences. She has been a researcher of Institute of European Studies of Chinese Academy of Social Sciences since 1999. Her researches mainly focus on central and eastern European countries. Jia Ruixia is an associate research fellow, EU Science and Technology Policy Division Institute of European Studies, Chinese Academy of Social Sciences. She is currently a researcher at the Institute of European Studies,

Sebastian Santander is a full time professor, head of the Political Science Department and in-charge of the Center for International Relations Studies (CEFIR) of the Faculty of Law, Political Science and Criminology at the University of Liège (ULg). He is also an associate member of the Centre d'études sur l'intégration et la mondialisation from the Université du Québec à Montréal (UQAM) and of the Institute of European Studies of the Université libre de Bruxelles (ULB). He received a PhD from the ULB where he worked nine years as a lecturer and did a one-year post-doc at the Faculty of Art and Social Science of the University of Maastricht. He has been a visiting scholar at the College of Europe (European Interdisciplinary Studies Department, Natolin Campus) and in many other universities (Brasilia, Brussels, Hangzhou, Le Havre, Leuven, Lubumbashi, Lima, Maastricht, Rouen, etc.). He publishes on the topics of regionalism, interregionalism, emerging and established powers, and about the external relations of the European Union and Latin America. His articles have appeared in: *European Foreign Affairs Review, Foreign Affairs Latinoamerica, Journal of European Integration, Relations internationals, Études internationales, Politique européenne, Relazioni Internazionali*, and *Cuadernos sobre relaciones internacionales, regionalismo y desarrollo* (Venezuela). Recent books include: (ed.) *Concurrences régionales dans un monde multipolaire émergent*, (Brussels, Peter Lang, 2016, 358 p.); (ed.) *L'Afrique, terrain de jeu des émergents* (Paris, Karthala, 2014, 319 p.); (ed.) *Puissances émergentes: un défi pour l'Europe?* (Paris, Ellipses, 2012, 384 p.) and (ed.) *Relations internationales et régionalisme. Entre dynamiques internes et projections mondiales* (Liège, Presses universitaires de Liège, 2012, 381 p.).

Gerhard Stahl was born in Ludwigsburg, Germany, in 1950. He graduated in economics and became a research assistant to the chair of public finance at Technical University in Berlin. After joining the Federal Ministry of Finance in Bonn and working there for some years, he occupied several positions in the regional administration and in the European Parliament. He then worked for years in the European Commission (EC), namely in regional policy and in economic and monetary affairs. His last position in the EC was Deputy Head of

Cabinet of the Commissioner responsible for Economic and Monetary Affairs. He then joined the EU Committee of the Regions (CoR). Gerhard Stahl was Secretary General of the CoR for more than 10 years. His second mandate as CoR Secretary General came to an end in April 2014. Gerhard Stahl is a member of the IFO-Advisory Committee, and he was also a member of the Management Board of the IFO-Research Institute in Munchen for more than 12 years. He is a member of the Scientific Council of the Foundation for European Progressive Studies (FEPS), a member of the Administrative Council of the Madariaga – College of Europe Foundation, a member of the European Statistical Advisory Committee (ESAC) and a member of the Institute of Public Finance, a world-wide scientific association of economists. Since August 2012 he is a visiting professor at the College of Europe in the Economics Department, teaching a seminar on the Reality of Policy Implementation: EU2020 at Regional and Local Level. Since August 2014 he is a professor at the Peking University HSBC Business School, Shenzhen, teaching transition economics in the Master's program.

Shiwei Shi is a professor for international economics and director of Centre for European Studies at University of International Business and Economics (UIBE). He studied in Berlin and Potsdam between 1990 and 1998 and received his doctor title of Dr. rer. Pol. He worked in Beijing since then. He came back to Berlin in 2017 and is teaching at Institute of Sinology (OAS) in the framework of the Confucius China Studies Program (CCSP). Prof. Dr. Shi is a member of the Council of Chinese Association for Germany Studies, research fellow of Research Department of International Cooperation Center of National Development and Reform Commission and research fellow of Zentrum für Deutschlandstudien (ZDS), Peking University.

Jisheng Sun Prof. Sun is currently the vice president of China Foreign Affairs University (CFAU) and secretary general of China National Association for International Studies, deputy editor in Chief of Foreign Affairs Review. Before that, she was the director of the Department of Academic Affairs and dean of Department of English and International Studies, CFAU. She joined CFAU in 1996. From August 2006 to July 2007, she was an appointed research fellow of the Fellows Program, Weatherhead Center of International Affairs, Harvard University. From September 1999 to July 2000, she was invited to Marietta College, Ohio, as a visiting professor teaching Chinese culture and society and relevant courses. She holds a Master of Arts degree in English linguistics and literature and a PhD in international relations.

Mario Telò, a doctor in philosophy at Florence University, professor of international relations and "J. Monnet Chair", Université libre de Bruxelles and at LUISS University, Rome: he was a visiting scholar in CFAU Beijin, IEEM Macau, Renmin, Tsingua, Wuhan, Fudan, as well as in Fondaçao G. Vargas, Rio de Janeiro. He is an emeritus president of the IEE, ULB, and member of The Royal Academy of Sciences. He served as consultant for the EU Commission (2001–2006), the Presidency of the European Council (2000, 2007) as well as for the European Parliament and the Belgian House of representatives. He published 34 books and more than a hundred scientific articles in seven languages. The most relevant topics for this book are: *Europe. A Civilian Power?*, Palgrave, 2005; *European Union and New Regionalism*, (ed.) Ashgate, 2001, 2007 and 2014; *International Relations. A European Perspective,* Foreword by R.O. Keohane, Ashgate 2009 (in French in 2008 Greek, 2012, and Mandarin in 2013); *The EU and Global Governance*, Routledge 2009 and *EU Foreign Policy*, 2013; *Politics of Transatlantic Trade Negotiations*, Ashgate 2014; *Interregionalism and the EU*, Ashgate, 2014. In 2016/2017 he published: *Regionalism in Hard Times*, Routledge *L'Europe en crise et le monde*, Bruxelles, and *Deepening the EU-China Partnership* (Routledge). His next book with A. Weyenbergh will focus on Supranationality at stake, Routledge 2019. He served as Senior scholar of the global research networks GARNET (FP6) and GR:EEN (FP7) and still is coordinator of the Erasmus Mundus doctoral program GEM ("Globalization Europe multilateralism", 2010–2020).

He takes part in the public debate about the future of the EU and international relations since many decades.

Jin Wang is a Chinese PhD student at the University of Haifa. With a bachelor's degree in history and master's degree in international relations, he made his first foray into the field of Middle Eastern Studies by enrolling in a one-year master's program in international security and conflict management at University of Haifa in 2011. Wang Jin's intellectual curiosity in the Middle East and Israel arose while he was studying at Henan University in the city of Kaifeng, home to the ancient Jewish community from Persia. His interest in Israel was kindled further by the influence of the Institute of Jewish Studies at Henan University, one of China's leading academic centers in Middle Eastern studies. Associate professor in the Institute of Middle East Studies, Northwest University of China; research fellow, Syria Research Center, Northwest University of China (warmjohn@live.com).

Ling Wei is a full time professor at the China Foreign Affairs University where she obtained her PhD under the supervision of Professor Qin Yaqing. She was a visiting scholar to Oakland University (Michigan, the US, 2003) and French Institute of International Relations (IFIR, 2007), and a fulbright visiting research scholar at Cornell University (2012–2013). Her research interests include international relations theory and East Asian regionalism. She is China's Country coordinator for NEAT (the Network of East Asian Think-tanks), NACT (the Network of ASEAN-China Think-tanks), and NTCT (the Network of Trilateral Cooperation Think-tanks). She is on the editorial board of *Foreign Affairs Review* (*Waijiao Pinglun*).

Uwe Wissenbach is a diplomat and senior official with the European External Action Service in Brussels as well as associated researcher at the IEE-ULB, Brussels. He published a book by Palgrave on EU-China relations in collaboration with E. Kirchner and T. Christiansen in 2018. He is a scientific collaborator of the Institute for European studies, Free university of Brussels (IEE–ULB).

Min Zhang holds M.Sc. in regional geography, East China Normal University, Shanghai, China. She is a winner of Special Government Allowance from the State Council of China. At present she is the senior research fellow at the Institute of European Studies and director of the Center for Spanish Studies, Chinese Academy of Social Science (CASS). She also serves as a doctoral tutor at CASS University and City University of Macao and the executive director (Chinese side) of CASS University of Coimbra Chinese Research Center CASS. Prof. Zhang has conducted researches for decades in European economic and innovative policy studies, meanwhile specializing in Spain and Portugal countries studies, her major monographs including *Contemporary Economic and political studies of Spain, EU's Economic Reform and Policy Studies, series of Portugal country policy studies etc.* She has experiences as a visiting scholar in Spain, UK, Belgium, Finland, Germany, etc., and attended many high-level academic international conferences as a keynote speaker.

Jiakun Zhao is a Master candidate at the Department of Political Science, University of Chicago. He graduated from Tsinghua University, majored in International Politics and Economics, and studied in Johns Hopkins SAIS and Yale University.

List of Abbreviations

ACP	Africa, Caribbean and Pacific Group of States
AD	anno domini
ADB	Asia Development Bank
AIIB	Asian Infrastructure and Investment Bank
ALBA	the Bolivarian Alliance for the Peoples of Our America
Alfa	Academic Training in Latin America
AL-Invest	Latin America investment programme
APEC	Asia-Pacific Economic Cooperation
ASEAN	Association of Southeast Asian Nations
ASEM	Asia-Europe Forum
ASEP	Asia-Europe Parliamentary Partnership
BASF	Badische Anilin-und-Soda-Fabrik
BBVA	Banco Bilbao Vizcaya Argentaria
BC	Before Christ
BIT	Bilateral Investment Treaty (its new acronym is CAI, Comprehensive Arrangement on Investments)
BMENA	Middle East and North Africa Initiative
BREXIT	British Exit from the EU
BRI	Belt and Road Initiative
BRICS	Brazil, Russia, India, China, South Africa
BSCH	Banco Santander Central Hispano
CAFTA-DR	Dominican Republic-Central America-United States Free Trade Agreement
CAI	Comprehensive Agreement on Investment
CAN	The Andean Community
CARICOM	Caribbean Community
CASCF	China and the Pacific Island Countries and the China-Arab States Cooperation Forum
CASS	China Academy of Social Sciences
CEEC	Central and Eastern European Countries
CELAC	Community of Latin American and Caribbean States
CFAU	China Foreign Affairs University
CFM	CoFunding Mechanism
COP21	The 21st Conference of the Parties

Copolad	Cooperation Programme between Latin America, the Caribbean and the European Union on Drugs Policies
COSBAN	High-Level Coordination and Cooperation Committee
CPC	Communist Party of China
DAC	Development Assistance Committee
DG	Direction General
DPRK	Democratic People's Republic of Korea
ECLAC	Economic Commission for Latin America and the Caribbean
ECOWAS	Economic Community of West African States
EEAS	European External Action Service
EGTC	European Grouping of Territorial Cooperation
EP	European Parliament
ETESA	East Turkistan Educational and Solidarity Association
ETIM	East Turkistan Islamic Movement
EU	European Union
EU EIS	European Union Economic Information System
EUR	EURO
FDI	Foreign Direct Investment
FEALAC	Forum of East Asia-Latin America Cooperation
FIR	Fourth Industrial Revolution
FOCAC	Forum on China-Africa Cooperation
FP	Framework Programmes
FP	Framework Plan
FTA	Free Trade Agreement
FTAA	Free Trade Area of the Americas
GCC	Gulf Cooperation Council
GDP	Gross Domestic Product
GEM	Globalization, Europe and Multilateralism
GSD	Global Strategic Dialogue
IBSA	India, Brazil, South Africa Forum
ICT	Information and Communication Technology
IDB	Inter-American Development Bank
ILO	The International Labour Organization
IMF	International Monetary Fund
INCO	International Cooperation Specific
IORA	Indian Ocean Rim Association
IoT	Internet of Things
IPE	International Political Economy
IR	International Relations

ISIS	Islamic State
JPY	Japanese Yen
LA	Latin America
LAC	Latin American Countries
LAIF	Latin America Investment Facility
LIS	Alliance for the Information Society
MEPI	Middle East Partnership Initiative
MERCOSUR	Mercado Común del Sur (Southern Common Market)
MNC	Multi-national Company
NAFTA	North American Free Trade Agreement
NATO	The North Atlantic Treaty Organization
NE	North East
NGO	Non-governmental Organization
NLL	Northern Limit Line
NSC	National Security Council
NSS	National Security Strategy
OAS	Organization of American States
OECD	Organization for Economic Co-operation and Development
OIC	Organization of Islamic Cooperation
OPEC	Organization of Petroleum Exporting Countries
PA	Pacific Alliance
PDCA	Political Dialogue and Cooperation Agreement
PM	Prime Minister
PRC	People's Republic of China
R&D	Research and Development
Ralcea	Latin American Network of Knowledge Centres in the Water Sector
RCEP	Regional Cooperation Economic Partnership
ROK	Republic of Korea
RSC	Regional Security Complex
SADC	South African Development Community
SCO	Shanghai Cooperation Organization
SDR	Special Drawing Rights
SICA	Central American Integration System
SII	Summary Innovation Index
TAP	Air Portugal
TIKA	Turkish Cooperation and Coordination Agency
TPP	The Trans-Pacific Partnership
TPS	Temporary Protected Status

UAE	United Arab Emirates
UK	The United Kingdom
UN	The United Nations
UNACLA	UN Advisory Committee of Local Authorities
UNASUR	Union of South American Nations
UNCLOS	The United Nations Convention on the Law of the Sea
UNESCO	The United Nations Educational, Scientific and Cultural Organization
UNSC	The United Nations Security Council
URB-AL	Urban planning in Latin America
US	The United States
USD	US Dollar
USMCA	United States-Mexico-Canada Agreement
USSR	The Soviet Union
VAT	Value Added Tax
WITS	World Integrated Trade Solution
WTO	World Trade Organization

List of Figures

List of Tables

Mario Telò and Yuan Feng

Introduction

A Long-Term Research Endeavour

The IEE-ULB began developing research into the Europe-China relationship in 1987 when Prof. Telò was on his first lecturing tour in China, visiting Beijing University, the Shanghai Institute for International affairs and Canton University. China's opening up policy was launched in 1978 under the leadership of Deng Xiao Ping, and the World Trade Organisation (WTO) membership (2001) made it possible to deepen and widen China's multilateral cooperative network, including for the development of research cooperation, not only in European studies but also in global studies.

More recently, our cooperation, which has been mainly funded by the European Union (EU) research framework programmes (via the European Commission's DG Research), has become so strong that Chinese universities and research institutes, firstly FUDAN in Shanghai and then CASS and CFAU in Beijing, have become our regular partners via various institutionalised channels. One of the main research outcomes, an edited book entitled *Deepening EU-China Partnership, Bridging Ideational and Institutional Differences*, co-edited by M. Telò with Ding Chun, Fudan University, and Zhang Xiaotong, Wuhan (Routledge 2018), was an important milestone for two main reasons. On the one hand, it confirmed the efficiency of our method through the even and balanced participation of Chinese and European authors. On the other, during a scientific workshop open to policymakers, practitioners, diplomats, representatives of the European institutions, think tanks and high-level research centres, the first drafts of each chapter were discussed and then finalised by the authors according to the critical remarks emerged during the workshops.

The GEM project (Globalisation, Europe and Multilateralism, 2010–2019), continued by GEM STONES (2016–2020), respectively funded by DG Research and Marie Curie EU programmes[1], provided our research with two new substantial inputs[1]: firstly, research on regional and interregional cooperation within the current global governance was upgraded via relevant edited books, among them

1 We express our thanks to the GEM-STONES research and doctoral project, funded by the EU Commission, DG Research, in the context of Horizon 2020, for its generous support. We also express our thanks to Julian Hale for well revising the English language of non-native authors.

Interregionalism and EU. A Post-Revisionist Approach to Europe's Place in the World, ed. by M. Telò, L. Fawcett and F. Ponjaert (Ashgate-Routledge 2015); and secondly, the bottom-up fresh contribution of a qualified and dynamic new generation of PhD students, conducting their research and theses on several aspects of the EU-China relationship[2]. They played relevant roles as authors, discussants and even editors, such as Yuan Feng, of our collective books.

All in all, our strong commitment for the years to come to the research project framing this book will stick to this consolidated free and critical research method based on frank and even discussion and cooperation between European and Chinese scholars, in spite of the various regrettable signs of a new kind of Cold War.

In October 2019, China celebrated the 70th anniversary of the foundation of the People's Republic of China (PRC). The boom in the number of books about China and the world often focus, on the one hand, on the unique economic development of the last 40 years, following the major change in the country's direction after the death of Chairman Mao. On the other hand, the focus of international research is on the recent political developments under Xi Jinping's new style of internal and international leadership, announced at the 19th Chinese Communist Party (CCP) congress, going beyond the 'China's peaceful rise' theory of Deng and Hu and towards an assertive vision and, in practice, becoming an emerging global power.

There are exaggerations and paradoxes in the current literature about China, shifting from the acritical enthusiasm of 2007 about the G2 (a proposed informal special relationship between the PRC and the United States of America) towards a consideration of China's growth and the Belt and Road Initiative (BRI) no longer as opportunities, but only as imperial threats for the surrounding world and the West. However, the reality is more complex according to multidisciplinary critical research. On the one hand, China is already a major actor in the regional and global economy and politics, covering all policy fields, notably via economic investments and global chains spreading across every continent[2]. On the other hand, it is well known that China's expansion, notably the BRI, is not always welcomed but meets obstacles, resistance, criticism and opposition in every continent.

This book focuses on China's emergence as a regional and global power and its problematic expansion and partnerships, including with the EU. It has a more

2 The total value of traded goods rose 22-fold from US$12 billion in 2000 to US$275 billion in 2013.

global perspective than in the first book, mentioned above, and focuses on both the interregional and global dimensions of China's external relations with various continents.

The Relevance of the BRI as a Test for China's Multilateralism as well as for China-EU Relations: An Evolving and Convergent Research Agenda

What about China's global emergence and interregional relations in the Xi era? The BRI is the best case study for understanding the scope and aims of an interregional global project of historic magnitude. This interregional project has been presented as an opportunity for all, including Africa, Asia, Latin America, the Arctic and the EU. Defined by Xi Jinping as the 'project of the century', it is one of the pillars of 'China's Third Revolution' (after Mao and Deng, according to the definition proposed by Elisabeth Economy, 2018), beyond the period of economic growth and 'peaceful rise'. According to many authors of this volume, it will also be a key challenge for China to strike a balance between bilateralism and multilateralism 'with Chinese characteristics'.

A relevant thread linking many chapters of this collective book together is whether China's regional and interregional policies in Asia, the Middle East, Africa, Europe and Latin America are evolving towards a multilateral or hierarchical/asymmetric pattern. Firstly, are they respecting the two multilateral principles set out by the scientific literature (Ruggie 1993, Keohane 1984): 'reciprocity' and 'general principle of conduct'? Secondly, are they uniting or dividing the various regional/continental partners? Thirdly, whatever the aims and the rhetoric, does the political implication of China's economic initiative stabilise peaceful cooperation or create new competition and potential conflicts?

The book is divided into four complementary parts. The first part addresses the theoretical implication of a new conceptualisation coming from empirical comparative politics regarding China's external relations. On the one hand, regionalism and interregionalism (the chapters by Telò and Sun) and on the other, the interplay between traditional diplomacy and subnational actors – both are components of a new multilayered multilateralism which is de facto already emerging but needs to be better conceptualised. The second part focuses on the regional dimension of China's external policies, firstly on the neighbourhood of China, by addressing, on the one hand, the political stakes (Wei, Feng and Wissenbach) and, on the other hand, the economic achievements and challenges for the 'China model' and its network of global chains (Di Meglio and Shi).

The third part offers a comprehensive vision of China's interregional policies and focuses on some relevant and very different case studies in Latin America and the Middle East. The opening chapter, by Rüland and Rodrigues, acts as a general introduction to this structural feature of global governance, a new dimension of an increasingly multilevel global governance; while Santander focuses on China and Latin America from a different perspective: the triangular and competitive relationship with the EU and the USA. The chapters by Burton and Wang Jin address the recently enhanced economic and notably political presence of China in the Middle East.

The final part revives to the original aim of this multiannual research programme: How are EU-China relations evolving in the current multipolar, unpredictable and dangerous context? The balanced and complementary (political and economic) assessments by two eminent European experts (Harris and Stahl) on the one hand, and, on the other hand, by two Chinese scholars (Ruixia and Zhang) offer the reader a pluralist, comprehensive and even controversial perception of the evolution of the interregional strategic partnership, 16 years after it was signed in Beijing on 31 October 2003.

As we come to the end of 2019, we cannot ignore the diversity of signals provided to public opinion: at the beginning of the year, the very concerned European Commission Communication of March (mentioning partnership, competition and rivalry with China); less than one month later, the joint Brussels EU-China summit Declaration of 9 April strongly committed to deeper convergence at the bilateral/interregional level (Bilateral Investment Treaty [BIT] negotiations to be finalised in 2020) as well as at the multilateral level (Conference of the Parties [COP 21] of the UN's Climate Change Convention Framework and WTO), which is consistent with the optimistic atmosphere of the 4 November 2019 Shanghai meeting between France's President Emmanuel Macron (and EU Trade Commissioner Phil Hogan) and China's President Xi Jinping. The year 2019 is a year of confused transition, which calls for more in-depth research.

Comparative Regionalism and Theoretical Implications

When looking at the main focus of the authors of the first section, the book's comparative approach inevitably stimulates a theoretical development: since both the EU and China are developing regional and interregional partnerships with the near and far abroad (including the BRI, between China and the European continent), testing and upgrading our consolidated theoretical framework is needed. The essays of Sun and Telò offer an updated review of regionalist theories, deepening the linkages between regional cooperation and interregional partnerships.

The main theoretical issue is whether, in the context of the emergence of power politics and the return of old realist thought, regional cooperation and actorship are resilient, providing global governance with a multilayered structure beyond the mere inter-state Westphalian paradigm. Power politics and fragmentation are the main challenges: but the research prediction about the increasing importance of regional and interregional cooperation has been confirmed, even in the event of declining hegemonic power. Prof. Sun proposes an innovative step beyond Western rational choice theory towards a more pluralist understanding of International Relations (IR) theory, taking into account alternative background cultures[3]: for regionalism and regional cooperation, theories developed from different regions also have different features and connotations, bearing an influence from different local culture and experiences, even if very far from any concept of regional 'fortresses' (and 'clash of civilisations') or 'deglobalisation'. In a pluralist context, confirming how far the European-Chinese dialogue has allowed for excellent progress in terms of sharing concepts and literature, there are still major and different appreciations, notably as regards the evaluation of regionalism in the post-soviet space (Russian President Putin's 'Eurasian Community'): Is it a specific form of new regionalism or, rather, a competitive, authoritarian and hierarchical alternative model?

The Ling Hongyu/Zhao Jakun contribution is along the same post-realist lines. They argue in favour of the enhanced relevance of substate agents as international actors, which may change the traditional vision of diplomacy towards a multiactor and multidimensional conceptualisation of it. All the authors have done research that leads in the direction of features and structures of a new multilateralism.

A challenge for the future that is both political and theoretical is that multilateralism is becoming more pluralist, participative and more 'institutionalised', according to a broader understanding of institutionalisation, going from interconnectivity, informal fora, networks and arrangements up to intergovernmental regimes and to formal organisations (as the cases of climate change and trade clearly show). The Chinese understanding of this necessary innovation of interregionalism is inspiring, according to Sun and Wei, the 'Silk Road spirit' and the BRI. However, in the EU's perception, more intrusive interregionalism and multilateralism means de facto or de jure more (self-) binding (in a voluntary

3 "In China, IR theories developed such as Qin Yaqing's relational theory, Zhao Tingyang's Tianxia concept and Yan Xuetong's moral realism are also closely related with Chinese tradition, culture and history".

and not coercive way, of course) cooperation. In this new context, the interaction with new ways of cooperation (outside State cooperation) is becoming a major political and cultural issue, including for free multidimensional interregional relations, as we can see by comparatively analysing Europe and east Asia and notably the EU and China.

EU-east/Asia interregional relations are at a crucial juncture. With US President Donald Trump's new trade tariffs policy and the uncertain future of NATO after the mid-July 2018 summit in Brussels and the respective declarations of Trump and Macron, the EU is undertaking two important deals with two major Asian countries: Japan and China. These new agreements add to the existing economic relations between the EU and other key regional actors in Asia, such as India. The finalisation (or not) of BIT negotiations is a fundamental test.

The impact on the domestic polities and policies of multilateral and bilateral cooperation is becoming extremely relevant, as the examples of the EU and east Asia show, notably in the case of China. The EU is being encouraged by the US's inward-looking and protectionist trade policy and by the aggressive trade wars to become a more proactive actor in the reshaping of global and interregional trade rules. However, evolutions in the EU since the Lisbon Treaty, on the one hand (the veto power of the European Parliament in trade policy and the inclusion of trade within a single 'comprehensive' approach to external relations, based on EU values), and, on the other hand, the intrusion of national and subnational majoritarian politics and pressures by NGOs in relation to transparency and consistency with values show possible evidence of a contradiction between external effectiveness and internal legitimacy. Why? Because the standard-setting established by the Treaty and the 'Trade for all' strategy (2015) is a path of no return (due to internal legitimacy and transparency requirements). No trade arrangement can now be signed by the EU due to internal and demanding legitimacy constraints. In many relevant cases, this orientation has proved difficult but eventually successful (Canada, Japan, Vietnam, South Korea, Mexico and MERCOSUR[4]). How will China react to this challenge to upgrading investments and trade arrangements? This issue has evident theoretical implications and may broaden and deepen the common research agenda.

4 EU Trade Commissioner, Cecilia Malmström, said that "negotiations are more complex and difficult, but the current positive record in East Asia and South America says that they are possible"[6] and that other trading actors like Canada have also upgraded their standard requirements by trade negotiations.

Free Trade Agreement (FTA) negotiations with India are in deadlock and will not be resumed in the event that India sticks to environmental and social protection standards that are too low. Furthermore, the EU has a legal obligation to withdraw from negotiations for free trade in case of the systematic violation of values, notably of sustainable development and human rights protection. This very much matters in the context of the future of trade relations with, for example Myanmar (2016, Rohingya persecution) and Cambodia (government limiting the opposition's rights), while this did not stop the EU from signing and ratifying the trade treaty with Vietnam and starting negotiations with the Association of South East Asian nations (ASEAN) as a regional bloc. The European Commission is mounting a legal challenge against South Korea for not implementing the bilateral clause of the trade arrangement, including ratification of the International Labour Organization (ILO) Convention. This comprehensive approach may have an influence in terms of finalising complex negotiations with China on a BIT in the event that ILO conventions on labour rights are rejected. Of course, the EU needs to act with prudence and flexibility. It is obvious that, according to a rigid 'normative power Europe' approach (Manners 1992), the EU can only bargain with Norway, Canada, Switzerland and a few other countries in the world as things currently stand. That is why Europeans and the Chinese need an intercultural dialogue about fundamental values, as Prof. Sun is also calling for. A serious intercultural dialogue at the level of civil societies would be essential and must be combined with trade and diplomatic negotiations.

For its part, China is evolving towards a controversial situation that is likely to give rise to dilemmas. On the one hand, it is committed to defending the multilateral trade system that it has benefitted so much from since 2001, which implies increasingly implementing respect for the domestic rule of law and making its commitment to multilateral and interregional cooperation both sustainable and credible. On the other hand, the implication of multilateral cooperation in terms of respect for the rule of law may have domestic consequences in terms of pressures for domestic change, including in terms of labour standards (right of free association of workers and right to strike) and qualified standard-setting, which are not yet included in the government agenda, as established by the Chinese Communist Party (CCP) in its 19th congress of 2017.

The EU is not a single agent addressing the challenging question of the enhanced even if pluralist (institutionalised or 'relational', according to Qin Y. 2018) institutionalisation of governance 'beyond the state'. Other international organisations, such as the UN and the WTO, individual states, transnational social movements and regional consensus-based organisations like ASEAN are also focusing on the need to strengthen multilateral governance efficiency and its legitimacy: for example the role of the international courts, the implementation of the then UN Secretary General Kofi Annan's 'responsibility to protect' (2005), even if revised after controversial performances and the proposal by the former Brazilian government of the international community being involved in 'responsibility while protecting'.

Some of the Book's Main Comparative Findings and Research Avenues: Neighbourhood, Latin America, Africa and the Middle East

From the second to its third part, the book provides fresh research and innovative theoretical hypotheses regarding regional, interregional and global examples of China's emergence. In the second part, the tendency towards regional cooperation and networking is focused, as far as China's neighbourhood is concerned, from north east (Wissenbach) to south east Asia and central Asia (Feng), while Wei Ling deepens 'developmental regionalism' as an original approach with a special reference to the case of the Mekong region. Power politics and bottom-up networking interact in a critical way within an unstable context where there is still a security dilemma and where there are still huge development needs.

The book very much benefits from the skills of political scientists such as Wissenbach, Feng and Wei, all of whom are able to connect their empirical work with the theoretical issues addressed above. The concept of multilateral regionalism is critically addressed by Feng while the originality of Wei's chapter is notably on the deep link between regionalism and development. This explains to a large extent why developing States are interested in regional cooperation with China and notably in the BRI. Finally, Wissenbach underlines the "importance of historical grievances, critical junctures and how they relate to moralisation gaps and present distrust and emotionally charged perceptions and decisions impeding attempts at integration and co-operation despite rational 'incentives' ". His post-realist, historical institutionalist theoretical framework makes it possible to frame the main challenge of nationalism in North East Asia and the decline of the Confucian common cultural background via an open final forecast.

The second question addressed by this part of the volume is the economic impact of China through global chains, on the one hand (see the very well-documented Shi chapter), and the influence of the recently assertive 'Model China', on the other. Professor Di Meglio's comprehensive chapter addresses the extremely relevant question of the rapidly evolving economic side of China's presence in the Asia-Pacific and in the global economy, which is enhanced due to the trade wars with USA, as explained also by Shi's contribution.

China looks seriously committed to regional cooperation beyond the traditional concept of spheres of influence. However, its way of shaping and negotiating regional cooperation varies according to the nature of its partners: the triangular dialogue in NEA, 'ASEAN plus 3' and 'ASEAN plus 6' (including, respectively, the Chang Mai initiative and Regional Comprehensive Economic Partnership [RCEP]) and the partnership (not alliance!) with Russia in the Central Asian Shanghai Cooperation Organization.

For several decades now, China has also been officially committed to multilateralism, as many chapters of this part of the volume clearly show. However, by upgrading its ambitions as a global actor compared with the pre-Xi Jinping era, China is developing its own idea and characteristics and practices of global multilateralism and regionalism, both in the neighbourhood and by setting interregional relations with Africa, Europe and Latin America which are profoundly shaped by the BRI.

The chapter by Rüland and Rodrigues is to a large extent a reference contribution for the book, elaborating the concept of China's complex and hybrid interregionalism, its functions (institutionalising, agenda setting, rationalising and collective identity building, carrying out a kind of soft balancing of the US and EU presence in the region) and problems, via an original theoretical input, and connecting it with empirical reference to South America (which was not initially included in the BRI scheme). The interregional relations and notably the BRI and the relationship with South America are part of an "increasingly vertically and horizontally differentiated system of global governance". The China-Mercosur partnership (2003) established, along with the China-CELAC (Community of Latin American and Caribbean States) Forum (2016), a platform for a long-term commitment to the region as well as the Pacific Alliance members, Chile and Peru.

The main problems identified by Rüland and Rodrigues focus on the critical interplay between China's hybrid interregionalism (mainly bilateral, mercantilist, instrumental and state-centric) with multilateralism as well as the missing participation of civil society, with the single exception of the business community. A similar criticism is addressed by the Santander contribution, combining, in a critical way, the research legacy on the historically competitive Atlantic triangle (USA, EU and South America) with the question of the impact of a new external actor like China. Over the past 15 years, trade between China and Latin America has multiplied by a factor of 25, from USD 10 billion to USD 250 billion. The boom in trade and investment, which is often asymmetrical, in the context of a diplomacy that is about 'striving for achievement' and of a new form of rivalry, entails some political engagement as the multiple break with Taiwan and the Venezuela crisis clearly show. Donald Trump's 'America first' policy does not only consider that China's presence in Latin America is a "threat to the interests of the countries of the Western Hemisphere" but is supporting Latin American right-wing populist critics to China. The EU's reaction to the new game is epitomised by the 2019 EU-Mercosur agreement. Finally, the extremely relevant question is addressed as to whether external interregional ties are uniting or dividing Latin American partners and increasing the fragmentation of Latin American regionalism, contrary to the EU-Mercosur agreement.

This change of China's global policy, from a peaceful rise to global assertiveness, is part of a general question as to where, for example bilateral relations with individual African, Asian or Latin American or European countries risk weakening regional cooperation within the partner region, for example among African countries. Some scholars compare this bias with European trade arrangements with individual African countries started by the then EU Commissioner Peter Mandelson in 2006.

The case of a region in the Middle East that is burning, analysed by both Burton and Wang Jin's chapters from different perspectives, is different. Wang Jin remembers the old roots of China's interregional relations with the Arab region (2nd century BC). Both authors show that China has a growing interest in defending its relevant interests in this region and is tempted by *Realpolitik* combined with bilateralism, also because both regionalisation and regionalism are weak, in spite of Arab rhetoric and given the fact that the national regimes are authoritarian in nature. According to Burton, in interaction with the Gulf Cooperation Council (GCC) and the Maghreb Arab Union, the Arab League prepared a big step forwards towards China in 2014. Xi opened the first 'China Arab States Cooperation Forum', proposing a '1+2+3' formula of China-Arab cooperation in energy, trade and investment and the development of new (nuclear, energy and satellite) technology[5]. However, intra-GCC conflicts and splits mean that the FTA proposal has been stagnating, which is leading in the direction of the current return to bilateralism.

Politically, as Wang Jin writes, China is providing relevant contributions to fight terrorism and Islamic extremism through its 'selective commitment' to peacekeeping missions, notably in Lebanon, while in other cases, as in Syria, it

5 Trade between China and the bloc was worth $10 billion in 2000. By 2016, it had grown to $115 billion.

often converges with Russia by vetoing UN interventions in the United Nations Security Council (UNSC) (without being an ally of Russia). His conclusion about China's 'strategic logic of equilibrium' deserves to be deepened, but not only as far as this region is concerned.

Even if China's presence in the Middle East is relatively new (compared with the Western powers and Russia), the Middle East is an important region for China for three main reasons. First, Beijing hopes to diversify its oil imports and find a reliable energy partner in the Middle East. Second, Beijing hopes to receive support and understanding from the Middle East, especially from Muslim and Arab States, over China's counterterrorism and counter-extremism policies (the Uyghurs issue in China's far-west province of Xinjiang). Third, China hopes to deepen and widen its areas of cooperation with Middle Eastern states, especially to encourage and improve cooperation in high-tech areas. However, China is still keeping a low profile and will face several challenges in the future.

Since the China-Africa partnership is not directly addressed by the chapters in the book, let us make some observations about it. China's engagement in Africa has developed considerably since 2010 and even official scholars argue that economic ties there are supported by political objectives[6]. Since China started its BRI in 2013, China's interests and influence in the developing world have been growing rapidly, particularly in Africa and Latin America. While partially driven by its need for economic growth, China's diplomatic expansion in Africa cannot be fully understood without taking into consideration the strategic push that is accompanying its accelerating emergence as a global political power. Africa's interregional partnership is one of China's diplomatic 'new frontiers', as exemplified by the new Chinese leader Xi Jinping's many visits to Africa.

However, most analyses about China's diplomacy offensive in Africa and the Middle East focus on Beijing's quest for energy, Arab land and raw materials, and for economic profits and advantages. That is why it is often called 'energy diplomacy' or 'economic diplomacy', as if China, just like Japan in the 1980s, has become another 'geo-economic power'. But if one looks at the history of China's foreign policy, Beijing has seldom pursued its diplomacy for purely economic considerations. China's interests in Latin America and Africa are as follows: first, both of these regions fit into China's formal diplomatic framework as 'developing country' regions which have gained increasing attention for Chinese foreign

6 From a strategic and political perspective such as geo-strategic calculations (Wang Jiwei 2018), political and security ties with African countries, peacekeeping and anti-piracy efforts in the region, support for African regionalism, etc.

policymakers in recent years with Beijing wishing to use south-south relations to provide certain leverage in dealing with pressure from the USA. Second, Latin America and Africa are both clear matches for China's foreign policy of peaceful development since both regions have numerous commodity-rich countries that can both supply China with needed natural resources and also offer markets for Chinese investors – a 'win-win' situation of a complementary nature. The population of Africa and Latin America is nearly 2 billion, which means great market potential for China's excessive production capacity and capital exports. China's domestic needs also require more imports of oil, gas and mineral resources like iron ore from the two regions. Chinese leaders increasingly hope that countries in these regions may appreciate the 'China model' in their own development as an alternative to the 'Western model'. Governments and the general public in both regions are also happy to see Chinese capital coming into the region without any political terms and conditions that often come with Western financial institutions and the EU's democratic and human rights conditionality.

As Latin American and African countries have intensified commercial and diplomatic ties with China, countries in both regions share a common concern that they do not repeat past cycles of economic or political dependency, as risked in the case of asymmetric BRI projects (e.g. Djibouti, Kenya and Panama). China seems, in some cases, to understand local concerns and is using regional organisations such as the Forum on China-Africa Cooperation (FOCAC) to meet these concerns.

More recently, as the US-China trade dispute has escalated, the African and Latin American markets have also become much needed for Chinese products. However, the huge FDI and BRI plans for Africa are interpreted by the international community as an excellent opportunity but also as a risk of division and geopolitical domination (*The Economist*, September 2018).

China-EU Partnership: A New Debate about New Questions

The final part of the book focuses on the evolving and to some extent uncertain China-EU interregional partnership. By conceptualising this partnership, the official papers and many students use the concept of bilateralism while we share the Söderbaum, Rüland and Fawcett approach and define it as an interregional partnership, because one of the two partners is not a State but a regional entity (which also implies an internal multilateral negotiation combined with the external negotiation).

Beyond our abovementioned 2018 edited volume focusing on the policy dimensions of the EU-China strategic partnership signed in 2003, this book firstly adds that, according to Zhang Min, China's internal modernisation provides a new opportunity for deepening relations between China and the world's innovative countries, including EU Member States in first place. Recently, relations between China and EU countries in the field of scientific and technological innovation have tended to be diversified, innovative and forward-looking. Zhang Min analyses the new trends and developments from various different perspectives: Horizon 2020 with the EU and the Sino-British science and technology cooperation and even the innovative strategic partnership with Switzerland. These three cooperation models present the dilemma of the new directions of science and technology innovation development between China and Europe: i.e. opposing single countries to the EU.

It is obvious to EU scholars that these bilateral partnerships with individual countries raise some problems, as is clearly shown by the BRI arrangement with Greece, Portugal and Italy or the 17+1 process started in Budapest five years ago. In the case of the EU, we are witnessing, according to many authors and observers, a paradox: for many decades China looked to every observer as if it were strongly supporting EU unity and further integration with the purpose of balancing the EU against the Soviet Union and the USA. Xi Jinping's visit to Brussels in 2018 and 2019 seems to confirm this policy (contrary to the Trump and Putin approaches in favour of the EU's disintegration), which has deep roots not only in the Deng Xiaoping but also in the Mao Zedong vision of a multipolar world and of a politically united Europe having a balancing role, both in transatlantic and pan-European relations. The April 2019 joint declaration calls for a concentration of the partnership with China within the common EU institutions against this potential fragmentation of the EU. This integrating approach runs in parallel with China's political and financial support to the African Union (offer to Addis Abeba for the African Union headquarters building) and to Mercosur.

Regarding Europe, what is happening is that, according to Jia Ruxia, since its launch in 2012, the '16+1' (now 17+1 with the membership of Greece) cooperation has made significant progress in various fields and at various levels, irrespective of the EU-China global partnership (*EC-China S&T Agreement* as well as the participation in *Horizon 2020* analysed by Zhang Min). China and the Central and Eastern European Countries (CEECs) have continuously deepened their mutual understanding. However, the CEEC is not a regional entity. Seen from Brussels and the western capital cities, by consolidating its relationship with 17 EU and non-EU eastern European countries, China is de facto dividing the EU, much to the dismay of the EU institutions. The doubts expressed by G. Stahl and G. Harris in their complementary and critical contributions are quite robust and worrying. The EU respects China's unity and will never look for a special arrangement with Tibet or Taiwan. Does China currently work for EU unity or, as the USA and Putin's Russia have been proactively and openly doing for several years, is it working, via its 'interregionalism with Chinese characteristics', in a direction that will lead to the EU becoming weaker, disunited and possibly collapsing?

This question has both political and theoretical relevance. The theoretical issue is the impact of interregionalism on multilateralism: towards 'new multilateralism' or towards 'diminished multilateralism' (Rüland and Rodríguez's chapter)? The political issue relates to the fragmenting tendencies within the EU, which are often guided by the CEEC countries' leaderships, which are protectionist, right-wing populists and politically oppose both the EU and also China (because they are only interested in welcoming China's investments). Recent events are obliging neutral observers to address the general question of the nature, scope and aims of China's interregionalism as an open research question. This book started a mutual clarification. Chinese scholars and policymakers should be aware that the institutionalised partnership between China and the 17 European countries of eastern Europe, including EU Member States (12 out of 27), as well as the bilateral BRI arrangements with Italy, Portugal and Greece (2019) are, according to Harris and others, de facto weakening the EU institutions' role as a coordinator of EU external cooperation, trade and partnerships. They are also de facto strengthening eurosceptic and far right governments (Orban, Kacinsky and Di Majo–Salvini – in early 2019). Secondly, in the context of the economic decline of southern EU Member States after the 2009–2017 financial crisis, China's priority for individual relations with single EU countries, notably with the weakest, like Greece, raises concerns with regard to its hierarchical rather than multilateral and reciprocal nature as well as with regard to its possible political implications. This volume's approach is open to mutual understanding beyond any generalised Cold War attitude: we need to look at the detailed performances via a case by case comparative study without any prejudice and by trying to jointly elaborate a shared research agenda.

Comparing the BRI with the Marshall Plan: Risks and Opportunities

Many authors underline the historical relevance of the BRI for a correct understanding of China's global ambitions. The USA opposes the BRI as a major competitor and rival to US global influence and a threat for weak states. The EU is unhappy about a one-way BRI. Is the BRI serving a new form of multilateralism or does it run the risk of opening conflicts between multiple and competing projects of spheres of influence? In case its implementation is openly serving the geopolitical interests of one single great player, of a one-sided understanding of globalisation, it will give rise to resistance, criticism and 'containment policies'.

Several authors in this volume, notably Wang Jin, present a broad review of the academic debate about the BRI and suggest that it is providing the world with 'international common goods'. Comparison with the US Marshall Plan of 1947–1957 may be useful because the same concept was in application. The Marshall Plan's inspiration was innovative and enlightening, Keynesian in terms of an understanding of economic international relations: - the failure of the 1919 Versailles conference- was due to the rejection of the recommendation by Keynes (Keynes, 1919), who is to a large extent responsible of the success of Bretton Woods in 1944 and the next multilateral cooperation. However, in 1947, also because of Stalin's opposition, it became de facto an instrument of the Cold War and 'containment policy' (G. Kennan). The coexistence of these two aims and two pillars clearly explain what is defined as a 'hegemonic approach' by many scholars (see Keohane 1984, Ruggie, 1993 and Patrick, 2007). Their main features were:

- providing international public goods via a new multilateral method (European organisation for economic cooperation [including aid and loans to 16 States]);
- a power logic in the context of the emerging bipolar confrontation with the Union of Soviet Socialist Republics (USSR), making it impossible for recipients of aid to reject the US demand to become NATO members in 1949.

The second dimension became extremely relevant after the Prague coup of February 1948 and Stalin putting a stop to any participation by Prague and Belgrade.

In 2019 we are not (not yet) in a period of bipolar confrontation and even the leader of the Chinese realist school, Yan Xuetong, argues that there is no 'Thucydides trap', that is risk of war, between China and the West, around the corner (G. Allison, *Destined to War*, Melbourne 2017 and Yan X., *Leadership and the Rise of Great Powers*, Princeton 2019).

But what continues to be inspiring from these troubled times with regard to a potential new hegemonic project is that the former US multilateral approach survived the Cold War thanks to both its link to global economic growth and the attractiveness of the 'American way of life' as a relevant form of soft power. If the BRI wants to limit the impact of the multiple current negative comments, obstacles and containment policies, even without looking for a hegemonic model, it has to expand the nature of its international provision of public goods, the growth opportunities for autonomous partners, its support for sustainable development and its soft power dimension, thereby fostering shared leadership and reciprocity within a revived interregional and multilateral network.

The quality of the partnership with the EU[4] and the possible convergence both at global level (WTO reform, COP 21 implementation) and interregional level (BIT negotiation) will be crucial and is the key variable for this potentially virtuous interregional and multilateral scenario. In this virtuous scenario, a triangular partnership with Africa as a third partner, according to the Romano Prodi proposal, would also be a relevant test.

The chapters by Harris and Wissenbach and similar other chapters focus on both China's good relations and controversies with its south and north east Asian neighbours, for example in the south and east China seas. In an unstable international context in which Donald Trump is deepening economic, trade and political conflicts, Taiwan is shifting towards more independence from the mainland and Hong Kong is becoming a seriously critical issue, many authors are posing questions about the future global order, not just for China but also for other global actors, including European States and the EU. Contrary to China's perceptions of a revived Atlantic alliance, Harris wonders whether the "US is pushing Europe into an alliance with China". A formal alliance is to be excluded, but a 'rapprochement' is possible, provided that China and the EU are consistent with their respective multilateral discourse and are able to take this strategic opportunity.

As G. Stahl argues, "the future of EU-China cooperation will depend very much on an open international economy and the answers to the Fourth Industrial Revolution. This will affect all parts of the economy and society. With the help of artificial intelligence and big data, new methods of production will be developed, new services will be delivered and as a consequence restructuring of economies will take place".

The EU new leadership (Ursual Von der Leyen, Josep Borrell and Charles Michel), with support from national leaders such as Emmanuel Macron[7], is not only looking for trade investment and individual bilateral arrangements but for an authentic strategic partnership for multilateralism with China, which explains why China has never been explicitly considered as the cause of international tensions but as an actor that is convergent on essential issues, such as the environment and trade. Upgrading a controversial strategic partnership requires more trust and widespread reciprocity on crucial issues, not only in terms of trade, environment and investments but also in the areas of cyberspace, artificial intelligence, the digital economy and security challenges.

---

7 E. Macron: *The Economist* interview, November 2019 and Speech at 'Shanghai forum', November 2019.

Part One: Theorizing Regionalism, Interregionalism and International Relation

Mario Telò

Comparative Regionalism/Interregionalism and International Relations Theory

Innovating International Relations Theory via Comparative Regionalism

Comparative regionalism and interregionalism are bridging area studies (like EU studies or East-Asia studies) with International Relations (IR) theory. The first point is that we need to update the comparative method. In recent decades, the IEE-ULB has developed the hypothesis that the EU should not be considered as a teleological project towards a super state or even a federal state like the 'United States of Europe' but as a regional organisation, a regional association of states and societies. Comparing the enlarged EU-27 unification with the building process of the USA's federal model is much less useful in the 21st century than in the 20th, when the European Community of six member states was still a vague and open-ended project. The EU has some relevant federal features (a single currency, a single market, exclusive competences, an elected parliament and supranational law) but is not a federal state in the making. Some features are and remain typical of an international organisation based on an international treaty: unanimity for Treaty reform, unanimous voting in the Council for the main Common Foreign Security Policy (CFSP) decisions, etc.: the definition proposed by the author, based on Hegel, Montesquieu and, in parallel to N. Bobbio and J.L. Quermonne, for the EU polity is: 'a mixed constitution', including intergovernmental features, a democratic side and technocratic governance (Telò 2015).

However, the EU is not a unique and isolated case study in the current world. Regional cooperation and integration among neighbouring states and societies is growing in every continent. The EU is the most developed and institutionally sophisticated regional organisation, comparable, mutatis mutandis, with regional organisations in Asia, Africa and the Americas: looking at both differences and similarities is a way of approaching comparative studies, according to Max Weber.

The Asia/Pacific region is particularly interesting for a broad interdisciplinary comparative literature. China is at the centre of several regional cooperation organisations, both in the Asia-Pacific and central Asia regions: the Association of South East Asian Nations (ASEAN) plus 1, ASEAN plus 3, ASEAN plus

6, North-East Asian triangular cooperation and the Shanghai Cooperation Organisation (SCO).

The future of the EU will probably be a distinctive chapter in the global future of multilevel global governance, based not only on states but also on regional and global multilateral organisations.

Several definitions of regionalism have been proposed since the first comparative book published by Joseph Nye in 1971. Currently, international literature considers 'regionalism' as a structural feature of multilevel global governance. According to Nye, "regionalism means a limited number of states linked by geographic proximity and reciprocal complex interdependence" (Nye 1968, *International Regionalism*). After 20 years of research, several new regionalist scholars came to the conclusion that this definition should be completed and revised to some extent: "Regionalism is a various (alternative paths) and multi-dimensional (not only about trade) institutionalized (not only informal arrangements) set of multilateral cooperation among interdependent neighboring states and societies (social networks matter)". Furthermore, successful regionalism always includes a certain degree of 'regionness' (historical and cultural background) as well as trade-regionalisation (variously interplaying with globalisation) (see Telò 2001, 2014 "EU and new regionalism", Hettne 2001, Fawcett/Hurrell 1995, Milner/Mansfield 1997, Gamble/Paine 1996).

Why Is Regionalism Resilient? Various Driving Factors

What are the common causes that have made it possible for regional cooperation to emerge and to succeed for several decades? The new regionalist literature underlines the structural and enduring endogenous causes explaining the expansion and resilience of regionalism (Hettne 2001, Fawcett/Hurrell 1995, Milner/Mansfield 1997, van Langenhove 2009, Telò 2001, 2014). Since 2000, they have been classified either as endogenous or as exogenous factors. The main endogenous driving factors are:

1. Trade expansion beyond the national market: regional free trade areas or markets are a first step towards global openness combining in different ways, building blocks and stepping stones as far as their relationship with global liberalisation is concerned (Bhagwathi-Summers debate of 1992).
2. Economic cooperation: the role of the transnational business community and of interest groups as driving forces is not only studied by functionalist scholars. Furthermore, regional policies matter, contributing to regional convergence through coordination among EU Member States.

3. Social factors matter too: the role of civil society networks in coping with legitimacy challenges is a typical and shared feature of new regional entities. Moreover, the role of NGOs, cities, advocacy groups and their networking activities is increasingly studied by the literature.
4. The cultural dimension has been defined as a 'cognitive' factor of regionalism, according to Higgott and Acharya: shared perception of the other, feelings of common belonging and identity needs increasingly matter in several continents and support regionalism in a bottom-up way.
5. The political and security factors are extremely relevant provided that regionalism emerges beyond the form of mere trade regionalisation: member states who want to win back their lost sovereignty (because of globalisation) look, through regional organisations, at preventing or managing regional conflicts as well as at peace-building by supporting domestic democratic consolidation. In some cases, regionalism is also a way to better negotiate at interregional and global levels. Secondly, in the last ten years, the political implications of trade have become so significant that trade arrangements with friends, in the near or far abroad, look like becoming the new rule.

In spite of differences, regional cooperation/integration paths generally also share structural and long-term exogenous causes. The main systemic (in the sense of the global system) driving factors are economic and political:

1. The globalisation process as well as its uncertainties. Problems relating to global governance: first of all, the efficiency gaps and legitimacy deficits of global multilateral organisations (the United Nations [UN], the World Trade Organisation [WTO], the International Monetary Fund [IMF], the Food and Agriculture Organisation [FAO], etc.) when they are looking for complementarity with regional organisations.
2. The end of the bipolar world in 1991 opened up the space for the emergence of new actors; furthermore, the failures of the USA's unipolar ambitions (2001–2008) and the resulting political instability increase the need for a regional project as a second best option.
3. The domino effect is also historically relevant: the spread of information about and emulation of the success stories of other regional entities matter as drivers of regional institutional projects.

An open question is whether regionalism is compatible with the global multipolar power structure that has recently emerged. Part of the literature addresses the question as to whether and as to how China, Russia, India, Brazil and South Africa, Indonesia and Saudi Arabia, the most relevant emerging powers, are truly interested in new forms of regionalism. There are several assertions that one can make and several open questions: On the one hand, there is no doubt that ASEAN plus 1, ASEAN plus 3 and ASEAN plus 6 are multilateral regional entities; the same can be said for the Brazilian commitment to Mercosur (the Mercado Común del Sur or, in English, the Common Market of the South) and of South Africa to the Southern African Development Community (SADC) and the African Union (AU). On the other hand, several lines of questioning have been opened up by the literature regarding the nature of regional cooperation entities such as: the Eurasian Economic Community, the Gulf Cooperation Council and the Shanghai Cooperation Organisation. Are some BRICS (Brazil, Russia, India, China and South Africa) accepting the need for regional cooperation while changing the nature of regionalism?

We will come back to this new research agenda.

Second Conceptualisation: Interregional Relations

Regionalism and interregionalism are interconnected phenomena: regional organisations foster interregional cooperation or are the target of interregional projects started by great powers like the USA or China. Interregional relations are also very much developed and disseminated within the current framework of global governance (Rüland, Soederbaum, Fawcett/Telò).

In the early stages, interregionalism was limited to bi-regionalism, that is partnerships between two different blocs, such as EU-ASEAN or EU-Mercosur. However, based on my research and after a lengthy dialogue and cooperation with L. Fawcett and F. Söderbaum, the author arrived at the following definition: interregionalism defines multidimensional relations between, on the one hand, a regional organisation and, on the other hand, either another regional organisation or a large state, or a group of states, belonging to two (or more) different continents. Examples are:

1. The BRI is a comprehensive project for a double interregional partnership linking China and Europe (not only) by land and by sea. Its implementation has provoked controversy and debate, with some highlighting the underlying gains for everyone and others focusing on the resulting imbalances and risks. There is no mature midpoint between these sets of views.
2. The China-Africa summits can also be considered as part of an interregional framework for a series of Chinese and African policies.
3. As far as US interregionalism is concerned, the failed Bill Clinton/George Bush initiative of a pan-American Free Trade Area of the Americas (FTAA)

(1994–2005), the declining Asia-Pacific Economic Cooperation (APEC) (1994), the abandoned Transatlantic Trade Partnership (TTP) (signed by Obama in 2015, but withdrawn by the Trump administration in 2017) and the frozen and never signed Transatlantic Trade and Investment Partnership (TTIP) (negotiated between the USA and the EU between 2013 and 2016) are interregional projects driven by US administrations. There is no need to underline that they have met with a low level of success!
4. As regards the EU's interregionalism: the first one was the African People's Convention (APC), which began in 1973 (Yaoundé, Lomé and Cotonou) with former colonies transformed into cooperation partners; secondly, Asia-Europe Meeting (ASEM), which was launched in 1996; thirdly, the EU-CELAC (Community of Latin American and Caribbean States) which began in 1999 and fourthly the 'Barcelona process', which began in 1996. We have to note that, even if we have to recognise that the EU's record has been mixed, interregionalism is at the heart of the EU's global role.
5. Even other regional organisations are supporting interregional ties and arrangements: the ASEAN, for example, via the ASEAN+6, the Regional Comprehensive Economic Partnership (RCEP), ASEAN-Mercosur and so on.

We can conclude that both regionalism and interregionalism are already structural features of the current framework of global governance: it is becoming a multilayered, multiactor and multipurpose form of global governance.

From Comparative Research to an Innovative Theoretical Context

Is it possible to draw some theoretical input from the empirical comparative research for the purposes of theoretical innovation? It would be not convincing if the empirical basis were to be isolated and limited to a single case study, for example to the EU success story for a period of 70 years. We assert that it is legitimate in the case of several case studies that come to similar conclusions:

1. The growth and expansion of regional and interregional relations in number and scope are contributing evidence to a consolidation of cooperation/interdependence theories (Keohane) versus international anarchy theories (K. Waltz, J. Mearsheimer): these processes are part of a wider tendency towards the institutionalisation of international life.
2. We could consider regional organisation in the context of the international regime theory (S. Krasner 1993): it is a matter of fact that there are sets of multiple intergovernmental regimes. There are numerous examples. In the

case of ASEAN: a political/security regime, an economic and trade regime and a cultural and social regime. The EU also includes a monetary cooperation regime (the eurozone) while ASEAN plus 3 started, in 2000, a financial cooperation regime (the Chang Mai initiative). The RCEP is a trade regime, whereas the ASEAN regional forum included an incipient and fledgling security regime (Code of Conduct regarding the South China Sea). All regimes have the effect of reducing, sometimes drastically, security dilemmas between neighbouring and distant states. Institutionalisation provides elites with socialisation, mutual information about respective intentions and spill-over effects.

3. In many cases, regional entities contribute evidence confirming pluralist multiactor theories of 'multiplex global governance' (Acharya, 2011) of a participatory and various forms of multilateralism (Qin, 2018) versus the legacy of mainstream State-centred paradigm (Westphalian) as well as versus the old understanding of hegemonic multilateralism.
4. As far as the exogenous factors are concerned, regionalism and interregionalism contribute evidence in terms of the shift of the global system from bipolarity to unipolarity and then to multipolarity. However, this does not apply in the way meant by K. Waltz (1979) and of Mearsheimer (1989): first of all, the system changes and is not eternal and unchangeable; secondly, systemic change after 1991 (end of bipolarity) fosters a type of world politics that is characterised by both more cooperation and competition; and not only by more anarchy.
5. As far as relations between regionalism/interregionalism and the global order are concerned, we are clearly in the realm of post-hegemonic theories: Was regionalism part of US hegemonic system (Gamble, 2015)? To some extent, it was a component of the bipolar confrontation system (European Community, the ASEAN, Pan-Americana); however, there is considerable evidence that it was, at the same time, one of the driving forces of the process overcoming a hegemonic world order and building a more pluralistic and cooperative international system. It is extremely useful to mention the thesis of post-hegemonic 'régime resilience' (Keohane, 1984) versus hegemonic stability theory (Gilpin, 1990). Régimes can survive the defection of the main driver and may expand beyond its declining, or failing, hegemonic role. Look, for example at the continuation of Trans-Pacific Partnership, in spite of the USA's defection. Contrary to the hegemonic stability thesis, regimes are not at all a mere instrument of the hegemonic power. They do not follow the cycle of the emergence and decline of the hegemonic power. They can gradually, partially or largely function autonomously from the states who are at their origins.

6. Furthermore, contrary to the functionalist (Rosenau/Czempiel, 1992) approach focusing on cybernetic governance, decentralisation and economic governance and contrary to new medievalist (H. Bull) theories emphasizing the decline of the role of the territorial state, the territorial dimension of governance (as well as the dimension of politically and legally formalised government) is making a comeback.

The first conclusion is that the regionalist and interregionalist comparative research agenda can better be framed by cooperation/interdependence/régime theories and clearly goes beyond mainstream US theory: neo-realism. We may add that this comparative agenda converges with new institutionalist theories to a large extent. The second question to be answered is how and to what extent are neo-institutionalist theories able to grasp regional and interregional cooperation regimes, organisations and arrangements.

This is a highly controversial issue within the current neo-institutionalist debate:

Is rational choice, based on cost benefit analysis, a sufficient explanation for the construction of regional and interregional arrangements? There is no doubt that the weight of rational choice factors is very relevant: the shared interest in reducing 'transaction costs' is the main point here. The dominant rational choice motivation, notably trade interests, has been considered since the 1990s (see the literature in International Political Economy and, notably, J. Bagwathi). The interest in joining regional entities can be also based on the expectation of reaching the average, in terms of regional macroeconomic indicators, more quickly.

However, the driving role of other (non-rational choice) factors that we have mentioned above is fostering a deeper theoretical explanation.

Historical Neo-institutionalism

Historical neo-institutionalism (Peter Hall, 1992) allows for a better balance between systemic and domestic factors, and exogenous and endogenous driving forces. Secondly, a dyachronic approach to the history of regionalism is complementary to the comparative synchronic approach. Thirdly, historical neo-institutionalism is not only about considering the weight of history in the research agenda of regional entities: it takes open distance from the mainstream theory of the eternal anarchical global system and focuses on change through historical turning points. These changes not only affect the cost and benefit calculations of states but their ideas, principle, values, strategies and institutional constructions. Institutional construction, after critical turning points, evolves according to 'path dependency'. Let us focus on the main critical junctures affecting the history of regional cooperation from the 20th to the 21st century. The three main eras considered in my research (Telò, 2016) are:

1) The 1930s–1940s: authoritarian regionalism;
2) From 1944/1947 to the 1970s: regional cooperation/integration under US hegemony;
3) From 1989/1991 to the 2000s: emergence and spread of 'new regionalism' in every continent
4) The open question is whether a new fourth era is about to begin in the 21st century.

1) The first era was defined by the famous historian K. Polanyi as the 'Great transformation' of the first half of the 20th century. The first '*belle époque*' was softly regulated by the multipolar Concert of European power (only including Japan and the USA at the end of the 19th century), fostering the first forms of multilateral cooperation and the big wave of globalisation, including the spread of free trade arrangements (and the pivotal role of Britain from 1871 to 1929/1931). The first historical juncture exploded in 1914 with the outbreak of World War I and continued with the deeper economic crisis from 1929 to 1936. With the crisis of the pre-existing global order, regional projects emerged in many continents: we define these first regional projects and soft institutions as 'authoritarian/hierarchical regionalism' (1930s–1940s). The main case studies are:

a) *Neue Europäische Ordnung*, centred on Nazi Germany;
b) *Greater East Asia Co-Prosperity Sphere*, centred on Japanese militarism.

These historical examples, characterised by 'leonine pacts' (the opposite of multilateral arrangements) with members, should not be underestimated because they entailed ideational drivers. In spite of a hypercentralised and uneven decision-making system of resource allocation, they were able to mobilise in terms of convergence, alliances and expectations. However, they collapsed in 1945 after the victory of the allied forces.

Several (and various) regional associations from the same period were to some extent similar to the hierarchical and anti-multilateral way of taking decisions: the *Pan-Americana*, centred on the USA and inspired by Theodore Roosevelt's revision of the 'Monroe doctrine'; as well as the British Commonwealth, the *Empire colonial français* and, after 1945–1949, the Council for Mutual Economic Assistance (COMECON) under the iron leadership of the Union of Soviet Socialist Republics (USSR). Contrary to fascist regionalism, they could continue working for a while until the next historical juncture by combining economic asymmetric cooperation modes and ideational factors. The two key principles of multilateralism were not applicable: reciprocity and the general principle of conduct.

2) The second era of regionalism was triggered by a second historical juncture: the USA's new role after victory in World War II and the emergence of a bipolar (USA-USSR) world. Regional cooperation was either revived or invented between 1950 and the 1980s; however, it was structurally framed (and limited) by the new US hegemony and the global multilateral institutions founded in Bretton Woods (1944) and San Francisco in 1945 (1950s–1980s). As historians, we may speak about a kind of second '*belle époque*': the golden 30 years of 'embedded capitalism' (Ruggie) were framed by global multilateralism in the context of the Cold War confrontation. This new hegemonic system was compatible with both Keynesian national capitalisms and regional cooperation at the economic level (notably in western Europe and South America). Relevant examples are the European Community and NATO, the first era of ASEAN and South East Asia Treaty Organisation (SEATO), the new version of the *Pan-Americana* and the Organisation of American States (OAS).

However, the bipolar order ended in 1989–1991: the USSR collapsed dramatically in 1991 and the USA, which had been declining since the end of the Bretton Woods monetary system (1944–1971), became the centre of a unipolar global system only after the ambitious agenda of G.W. Bush and the neo-conservative intellectuals (Bolton, Wolfowitz, etc.). Obama recognised the multipolar world power structure in 2008. This major international system change may be considered as a third historical juncture influencing the future of regionalism.

3) The emergence of a multipolar world came at the same time as a huge wave of globalisation. The third era of regionalism has been defined by a large body of the international literature as 'new regionalism' with the aim of underlining its differences from previous eras. The economic context evolved from the decades of growth to the economic crisis of 2008: a third '*belle époque*' was marked by a continuous increase in international trade as the main driver of economic growth. Globalisation took place in parallel with regionalisation while, in the new context, the space was opening up for new global and regional actors to emerge.

It is extremely impressive how simultaneous the process of foundation, revival and consolidation of new regional organisations has been: the European Community was transformed into the EU with the Maastricht Treaty (1992), the ASEAN was re-founded with the Singapore Summit (1992), Mercosur was founded (the Asunción Treaty, 1991) as well as SADC (Windhoek Summit in

1992) and other subcontinental organisations like the Economic Community of West African States (ECOWAS), while the Organization of African Unity (OAU) (1963) was transformed into the African Union (2001, Addis Abeba Summit).

The new regionalist organisations shared several significant features (Hettne, 2001, Fawcett/Hurrel; Mansfield/Miller 1997, Telò 2001 and 2014, Acharya, 2007):

- They were post-hegemonic and more internationally autonomous than in the previous era;
- They were increasingly multipurpose oriented and not only limited to Free Trade Agreements (FTAs);
- They were driven by bottom-up forces, the business community, social networks, cultural and identity needs and shared hopes and fears;
- They tended to institutionalise their bodies beyond the previous merely diplomatic modes;
- Very often they worked in parallel with a domestic democratic transition and consolidation (the ASEAN Charter, the Ouro Preto protocol, the EU Charter of Fundamental Rights and the Copenhagen Criteria).

A relevant international research program including 44 universities, GARNET, focused on the new regionalism for a period of five years, and the conclusion was: new regionalism is a structural feature of global governance and is developing on every continent; however, it is developing according to alternative paths. Professor Qin confirmed this analysis, even if focusing only on the ASEAN and the EU. International scholars such as Gamble (2017) addressed the question: To what extent were they depending on the atmosphere of liberal peace and the illusion of the 'end of the history'? The dreams of overcoming power politics and of an evolution towards a pluri-regional post-hegemonic democratic order are over. To my mind, the true test for the new regional organisations will be their ability to cope with the challenge of the next critical juncture and to survive the tendencies towards internal fragmentation and external power politics.

Since the wave of globalisation and the economic and financial crisis of 2008–2016, multipolarity has been associated with a significant economic power shift from the West to the BRICS. Is this new critical juncture provoking a change in regional cooperation/integration? Is a fourth era about to start? What are its features?

4. Are we about to experience a kind of fourth historical juncture characterised by 'competitive regionalisms'? Regionalism has experienced hard times for a decade now. The similarities with the 1930s–1940s are superficial because the legacy of global and regional democratic institutionalisation is so relevant that a

return to the second part of the Polanyi theory, which talks of conflicting security interests paving the way to military confrontation, is far from a realistic forecast. However, new regionalism is being challenged by alternative models, which are clearly threatening its principles, values and rules.

Historical institutionalism may, more than rational choice considerations, offer an explanation of the multidimensional change which is taking place.

On the one hand, new regionalist organisations are affected by internal challenges: multiple forms of nationalism provoking internal disintegration (Brexit and populist nationalism are the European symptoms of this). The definition of these new political phenomena by Qin, 'populist realism', is quite relevant for research purposes. The global economic crisis and the increased immigration flows have provoked both efficiency and legitimacy deficits in the global multilateral network. This has demanded more regional cooperation. But regions have often been unable to cope with this demand because of inward-looking policies, nationalist isolationism, protectionist policies and xenophobic demands called for by far-right parties.

Internal nationalism, on the one hand, and the multipolar world structure with the emergence of the BRICS, on the other hand, are in many cases challenging the very features of new regionalist organisations through the revival of power politics and arrogant policies. Is the Westphalian paradigm about to be restored?

This does not seem to be the case. In the new context of the multipolar 21st century, new regionalism looks to many comparative scholars neither as heading for inevitable decline nor as being as stable as it used to be in the previous decade. It is changing in various directions, either because of competing instrumental projects or because the resilience is upgrading the degree of cooperation/integration (EU, ASEAN). Some great powers, for example the USA and the BRICS, are fostering their own understanding of regional cooperation.

a) New instrumental, regional and interregional forms of cooperation are emerging, which are looking at alternatives in terms of their aims and scope: the Eurasian community and the Gulf Cooperation Council (GCC) are the main examples where leading states foster a new kind of authoritarian regional cooperation beyond the realist concept of 'sphere of influence' but far from multilateral rules and principles. The SCO should be investigated in a comparative way. Could regionalism be transformed into a mere instrument of power politics led by regional hegemons?
b) The US looked, under President Obama, at establishing trade arrangements with allies (securitisation and geopolitical interregionalism), for example

the TTIP and the Trans-Pacific Partnership (TPP). Trade became a political issue. Containing China should have been, according to Obama, a precondition for negotiating better with China about trade standards and so on.

c) Contrary to Obama, the current US President, Donald Trump, is oscillating between general hostility to regional (EU and North American Free Trade Agreement [NAFTA]) and global (UN, WTO and the UN Framework Convention on Climate Change Conference of the Parties [COP] 21) cooperation regimes, on the one hand, and the transformation of regions into authoritarian transactional arrangements, on the other (the US-Mexico-Canada Agreement [USMCA] replacing NAFTA in 2018): these are not only far from multilateral criteria but also from the model of traditional FTAs. Nationalism, protectionism and trade wars (notably against China and the EU) are in conflict with both regional and global multilateralism; moreover, they are, de facto, supporting a zero sum game with regard to the interests and common goods of the planet. It is not just about withdrawing from a position where the US held global leadership for a long period. Trump's 'America first' rhetoric openly challenges the core tenets of multilateralism. The vacuum created by the Trump Pacific policy is, to a large extent, providing the EU with an opportunity of initiative. A new generation of EU-centred trade arrangements are being signed or are under negotiation: EU-South Korea; EU-Japan Treaty (2019), EU-Vietnam (signed in 2018) as well as negotiations with the ASEAN, China (BIT) and Australia/New Zealand.

China's Approach to Multilateralism: A Crucial Research Agenda with Theoretical Implications

China is the first power to take advantage of the USA's withdrawal from its global moral and political responsibilities, notably in the Asia-Pacific, via a proactive, multiple and subtle regional strategy.

Contrary to the USA, China is very much paying attention to the development and consolidation of regional cooperation: many Sino-centric arrangements have been consolidated in the last two decades.

There are two possible interpretations of this dynamic approach: a) An interpretation of China's national interest as not only being compatible but needing stronger and more innovative multilateral cooperation: in this context, regionalism is an excellent way forward, including as a way to revive and transform global multilateralism (Qin-Zhu, 2005 and Qin, 2018); b). As an opposite interpretation, China's regionalism can be seen as an instrument of national foreign policy in the context of a global bipolar confrontation with the USA (Yan, 2019). In both cases, the critical juncture mentioned above fosters path dependencies. The open question for the first approach is: To what extent will China accept the domestic implications of stronger multilateral institutions at global and regional levels? The open question for the second, realist, approach is: How can a form of instrumental regional cooperation that is far from multilateral rules be sustainable in attracting free and democratic countries?

Let us look at the empirical basis of China's approach to multilateralism:

- The 'Belt and Road' not only represents an interregional project with Europe but also a series of multiple projects concerning Central Asia, Africa, the Arctic, South America, etc. (worth around 1,000 billion dollars and competing with the new India-Japan 'Road of Freedom' project and not yet converging with the EU investment plan known as the 'Juncker plan'); and there is a controversy as to whether it is unilateral and whether it is compatible with the two basic principles of multilateralism: widespread reciprocity and general principles of conduct. In the event that it divides the EU (see 17+1, limited to eastern European states), this initiative is seen as a threat to the unity of the EU and an instrumental tool.
- The Asian Infrastructure Investment Bank (AIIB) is a multilateral bank including more than 80 partners with the exception of the USA (which has boycotted it); it is competing with the IMF and the Asian regional bank: That is why it has been defined as an example of 'counter-multilateralism' by Robert Keohane (2015). This is also an open issue: counter-multilateralism may or may not share the basic principles of multilateralism.
- The RCEP is a large project (29.5 % of global GDP)[1]. However, it is still very limited in scope and has not yet overcome comparatively low standards in terms of trade arrangements because of the protectionism displayed by India and other countries. It takes place in the context of the ASEAN + 6 (Japan, South Korea, China, Australia, New Zealand and India) as an alternative to the (currently changing) TPP, with Japanese leadership. It is to be noted that the TPP is divisive for the ASEAN (e.g. Vietnam is a member whereas Indonesia is not) and the RCEP is not only keeping the ASEAN united, but is also, apparently, in the driving seat.

1 RCEP is the single arrangement including India, Japan and China as well as the ASEAN (Australia, China, India, Japan, South Korea and New Zealand). The RCEP has been upgraded by China as a strategic reaction to TPP and TTIP.

- The ASEAN plus 1, plus 3, plus 6 and the ASEAN Regional Forum are multilateral cooperation arrangements, and China welcomes ASEAN with its headquarters in Jakarta. This architecture makes it possible to deepen the ASEAN (founding its political, economic and cultural community via the Kuala Lumpur Declaration of 22 November 2015) and approving the 'ASEAN 2025 Declaration' ('Forging ahead together').

There are two strong arguments in favour of the thesis above.

- The China-Africa partnership and the China-South America partnership are extremely significant and are competing with the legacy of, respectively, the US and the EU influence in these continents. This is an argument in favour of the realist approach above.
- The SCO is an extremely significant organisation as far as strategic competition and conflict prevention are concerned: it includes all the countries of central Asia and both the leading powers, Russia and China. It entails many intergovernmental cooperation regimes, from energy to transport and from education to military cooperation. However, its very nature is still to be clarified: multilateralism needs reciprocity and a general principle of conduct as well as a dynamic role of bottom-up participation, which is missing. There are similarities, in terms of a top-down nature, with the Eurasian community, even if strategic competition could emerge: the Eurasian community also includes (beyond the dictatorship of Belarus and the weak Armenia, which is being blackmailed) Russia and Kazakhstan in the same region. The main difference between the SCO and the Eurasian community is the internal balance of power, which is totally missing in the hierarchical Eurasian economic community dominated by Russia.
- China-centred 'six party talks' about the Korea peninsula are de facto over, and the trilateral dialogue in North East Asia is being challenged by Trump/Kim bilateralism, again an argument in favour of the realist interpretation so far.

All in all, when considering these memberships of regional organisations, and after adding the relevant role of co-leadership of the COP 21 and the UN Security Council (UNSC), any observer must recognise that China presents itself as being genuinely committed, at least in terms of its rhetoric, to regionalism, interregionalism and various kind of multilateralism, which confirms the Qin-Zhu interpretation; however, not only is the implementation of some policies more controversial but so are developments in terms of the increasing bipolar confrontation with the USA's Trump administration.

New Trends in Regional Cooperation/Integration

In current unpredictable times, two main scenarios have been set out by the research community. The first global governance scenario (No. 1): Decline and disintegration of regionalism and multilateralism within a multipolar post-hegemonic and fragmented world is a dangerous scenario for the reasons mentioned above underlining the positive *win-win* effects of regimes based on cooperation. Some of the regions will converge with the bias towards contingent, instrumental cooperation/confrontation and welcome the return of power politics/spheres of influence (e.g. USA, China and Russia). The progress towards this first scenario will certainly ease the revival and updating of realist approaches.

As a consequence, competitive regionalism and instrumental interregionalism could provoke a fragmented and conflicting global order (or disorder). The EU and the ASEAN (but also the AU and the regional cooperation regimes in South America) would be the victims of this trend, fuelling trade wars, fragmentation, inward-looking policies and spheres of influence.

What about an alternative scenario? Could new regional organisations successfully cope with this new and highly competitive context? The ASEAN, Mercosur and the EU (and other regional entities) have very little choice but to enhance their political unity and relevance. They are experiencing a difficult transition due to both internal and external challenges: widening and fragmenting, disintegration and integration tendencies are currently creating conflict within each regional organisation. To cope with them, economic success, social cohesion, new leadership and the reorganisation of regional governance should be on the agenda for the next few years. Regarding this last point, several macro-regional cooperation entities are evolving towards a new institutional architecture based on concentric circles, surrounding leading political hard cores (look at the example offered by the concentric circles of cooperation surrounding the deepening ASEAN). Concentric circles are also emerging on the European continent, complete with hard cores within the EU (the Defense Union, eurozone, etc.). In the EU jargon, this evolution is defined as a path towards 'differentiated integration'. Notwithstanding significant opposition, it was set up by the EU Council of Rome (Declaration of March 2017).

A prospect of five concentric circles has already emerged as the evolving architecture of the European continent:

a) Consolidating (and democratising) the eurozone (19 countries);

b) Creating hard cores of '9 plus' countries: 1) via 'enhanced cooperation' (Article 20) or 2) or via 'structured cooperation' (Article 46): the Defense Union started in 2017;
c) Deepening the EU-27 (and possible enlargement to a list of applicant countries): the EU's single market, a regional and in particular a globally proactive common commercial policy based on deeper democratic legitimacy;
d) Special and flexible relationships with, for example the UK, Ukraine and Turkey;
e) Shaping the EU's neighbourhood policy via various partnerships, which are alternatives to enlargement, regarding neighbours at the east and the south.

This second scenario is to a large extent not only open but already on the way and confirms the one consolidated in South East Asia. A positive evolution in these two parts of the world would suggest theoretical implications in favour of neo-institutionalist approaches against the revival of old thinking.

> Under these conditions, regionalism could foster an innovation in global studies: the concept of multilayered global governance and of new multilateralism need research about the scope and quality of convergence and divergence among member states. Examples of convergence with China in relation to public and common goods address the demand about the best way to implement effective policies. Do they need more supranational governance beyond the classical Westphalian understanding of sovereignty and non-interference? This should include the problematic implementation of the successful COP21 in Paris (the December 2015 conference about limiting climate change), the controversies about WTO reform and a better trade conflict regulation after the Trump attacks on its 'supranationality'. The trade issues also include the scope and quality of the new trade arrangements, the so-called second generation trade arrangements, including social, environmental and other sensitive issues. Finally, new multilateralism should be more pluralistic, involve more participation by civil society actors and also be more effective in fostering innovation at domestic level.

Conclusions: Theoretical Challenges for Our Shared Research Agenda

How could regionalism/interregionalism provide relevant steps for a pluralist innovation of IR theory?

Beyond the conservative approach of sticking to a merely rational choice calculation of costs and benefits, research confirms the relevance of other factors explaining cooperation both at regional and interregional levels.

First of all, even in trade we are witnessing steps from specific reciprocity to diffuse reciprocity via the second-generation arrangements.

Secondly, security and conflict prevention is playing a growing role not only in Africa but also as far as the ASEAN and the EU are concerned, which explains the politicisation of regional cooperation. This evolution is not only strengthening the multilateral approach to security challenges (terrorism, Islamic fundamentalism and so on) but is also fostering a new balance between regional and global conflict prevention beyond the UN Charter of 1945, providing the regions with a subordinated and marginal role. Political-security factors are often linked to regime-boosting factors (Risse Boerzel, 2016).

Thirdly, ideas matter much more than rational choice scholars expected. The weight of subjective factors (like projects, identities, cultural backgrounds, collective perceptions of hopes and fears, discourses and communication – see Sun Jisheng's chapter) on institution building and consolidating should be a focus for new and innovative research. Researchers can work on the solid basis of the achievements of Katzenstein (2005), Acharya (2009) and the notion of cognitive regionalism by Higgott. This is also linked to the balance between efficiency and legitimacy. The role of civil society is crucial before and after multilateral arrangements; it is the precondition for efficiency (input versus output legitimacy, according to F.W. Scharpf). Region building addresses the question of a future multilevel democracy, local, national, regional and global.

Last but not least, we started by addressing the methodological and epistemological question of the complex interlink between area studies and global studies. There is a convergence when looking for examples in the ASEAN and the EU. As far as the multiple links between area studies and global studies are concerned, the EU and new regional organisations like the ASEAN can only survive within a more pluralist global governance, including a large array of different approaches to multilateral multilevel cooperation (binding and instrumental, multidimensional and contingent, ad hoc and strategic), regional and interregional, but looking for convergent multilateral agendas regarding at least some transnational challenges and the related provisions of public goods:denuclearisation, financial stability, climate change, the fight against poverty, infectious diseases, criminality, terrorism, civil wars, etc.

New multilateralism is, thanks to Professor Qin and others (Qin, 2018), a shared research agenda: in my opinion, combining Multilateralism A (Westphalian) with Multilateralism B (post-Westphalian) is a major theoretical challenge. Between old realism and the cosmopolitan utopia of a global government, the best possible normative scenario is: regionalism and interregionalism as building blocks of a new post-hegemonic form of multilateral cooperation and a pluralist theory of international relations[2].

References

Acharya, A. (2001). *Constructing a Security Community in Southeast Asia*. New York: Routledge.

Acharya, A. (2011). *Whose Ideas Matter? Agency and power in Asian regionalism*. Ithaca, NY & London: Cornell University Press.

Acharya, A. (2013). *The Making of South East Asia*. Ithaca, NY: Cornell University Press.

Acharya A. and B. Buzan (2007) "Why Is There No Non-Western International Relations Theory? An Introduction", *International Relations of the Asia-Pacific* 7(3), 1 September.

Allison, G. (2017). *Destined for War*. Melbourne: Scribe.

Annan, K. (1999). "Two Concepts of Sovereignty", *The Economist*, September 18, p. 49. Available at www.economist.com/node/324795.

Baldwin, R. (2001). *A Domino Theory of Regionalism*. Working Paper No. w4465. Cambridge, MA: NBER.

Berger, S. (2016). "Resilient Europe", Paper delivered at Conference of European Studies, Philadelphia, PA, April.

Bhagwati, J. (1992). "Regionalism versus Multilateralism", *World Economy 15*(5): 535–555.

Braudel, F. (1958). "La Longue Durée", *Annales 13*(4): 725–753.

Caffarena, A. (2014). "Couples and Trust-building in International Society: A Social Capital Perspective". In B. Vasort-Rousset (ed.), *Building Sustainable Couples in International Relations: A Strategy towards Peaceful Cooperation*. Basingstoke: Palgrave Macmillan

Cerutti, F. (2017). *Conceptualizing Politics: An Introduction to Political Philosophy*. London: Routledge.

Cerutti, F., Lucarelli, S., & Schmidt, V.A. (eds.) (2011). *Debating Political Identity and Legitimacy in the EU*. London: Routledge.

2 See CFAU conference, April 2018, promoted by Professor Qin Y., with participation of Yan X. Zhao T., P. Katzenstein, A. Acharya, B. Buzan and M. Telò, first panel chaired by Professor Sun J.

Eco, U. (2007). "Transcultura", Paper presented at EU and India conference, Pondicherry.

Fawcett, L., & Hurrell, A. (1995). *Regionalism and World Politics*. Oxford: Oxford University Press.

Fawcett, L., Telò, M., & Ponjaert, F. (eds.). (2015). *Interregionnalism and the EU*. Abingdon: Routledge.

Gamble, A. (2014). "Regional Blocs, World Order and the New Medievalism". In Telò M. (ed.), *EU and New Regionalism*. Farnham: Ashgate, pp. 25–42.

Gamble, A. (2015). "The Power of Market Fundamentalism: Karl Polanyi's Critique", .*Cambridge Review of International Affairs 28*(1), July.

Gamble, A., & Payne, A. (eds.). (1996). *Regionalism and World Order*. London: Red Globe.

Gamble, A. (2017). "Regional Blocs, World Order and New Medievalism". In M. Telo'(ed.), *EU and New Regionalism*, Farnham: Ashgate, pp. 25–41.

Gilpin, R. (2000). *The Challenge of Global Capitalism*, Princeton: Princeton University Press.

Haass, R. (2008). "The Age of Nonpolarity: What Will Follow US Dominance", *Foreign Affairs 3*(87). Available at www.foreignaffairs.com/articles/united-states/2008-05-03/age-nonpolarity.

Habermas, J. (2004). *Der gespaltene Westen*. Frankfurt am Main: Suhrkamp.

Hall, P., & Taylor, R. (1996). "Political Science and the Three New Institutionalisms", *Political Studies 44*(5): 936–957.

Huntington, S. (1996). *The Clash of Civilizations and the Remaking of World Order*. New York: Simon & Schuster.

van Langenhove, L. (2011). *Building Regions. The Regionalization of the World Order*, Farnham: Ashgate.

Judis, J. (2016). *The Populist Explosion: How the Great Recession transformed American and European politics*. New York: Columbia Global Reports.

Jullien, F. (2017). *L'Invention de l'Idéal et le Destin de L'Europe*. Paris: Gallimard.

Katzenstein, P. (2005). *A World of Regions*, Ithaca, NY: Cornell University Press.

Keohane, R. (1986). "Reciprocity in International Relations", *International Organization 40*(1): 1–27.

Keohane. (2014). *After Hegemony*. Princeton: Princeton University Press (1984, 1st edition).

Keohane, R. (2015). "Contested Multilateralism". In Morin, Novotna, Ponjaert, Telo' et al. (eds.), *The Politics of Transatlantic Trade Negotiations*. Burlington, VT: Routledge, pp. 17–27.

Krasner, S. (ed). (1983). *International Regimes*, Ithaca, NY: Cornell University Press.

Manners, I., & Lucarelli, S. (2006). *Values and Principles in EU Foreign Policy*. London: Routledge.

Mauss, M. (2001). *The Gift: The form and reason for exchange in archaic societies*, 2nd edition. New York: Routledge Classics.

Mearsheimer, J. (1990). "Back to the Future. Instability in Europe after the Cold War", *International Security 15*(1), 5–56, MIT Press.

Milner, H., & Mansfield, E. (1997). *The Political Economy of Regionalism*. New York: Columbia University Press.

Nye, J. (1968). *International Regionalism*. Boston, MA: Little, Brown & Co.

Polanyi, K. (1944). *The Great Transformation*. Boston, MA: Beacon Press.

Qin, Y. (2019). "A multiverse of knowledge: Cultures and IR Theory" in *Globalizing IR Theory, Qin, Y ed.*, New York: Routledge

Qin, Y., & Zhu, L. (2005). "Neo-Internationalism and China's Diplomacy", *Foreign Affairs Review*, October 2005.

Risse, T. & Börzel, T. (eds.). (2016). *The Oxford Handbook of Comparative Regionalism*. Oxford, UK: Oxford University Press.

Rosenau, J. and Czempiel, E. O. (eds.). (1992). *Governance without Government*, Cambridge: Cambridge University Press.

Scharpf, F., & Schmitter, P. (1995). *Governance in the EU*. London: Sage.

SIPRI. (2017). *Report*. Stockholm: Stockholm International Peace Research Institute.

Steinmo, S., Thelen, K., & Longstreth, F. (1992). *Structuring Politics: Historical Institutionalism in Comparative Analysis*. Cambridge: Cambridge University Press.

Telò, M. (ed.). (2001 and 2014). *EU and New Regionalism*. Farnham: Ashgate.

Telò, M. (2015). "Three Reasons for Reasserting the Autonomy of a Regionalist and Interregionalist Research Agenda". In *Interregionalism and EU. A Post-Revisionist Approach to the Europe's Place in the World* (in cooperation with L.Fawcett and F.Ponjaert), Ashgate, pp. 67–85.

Telò, M. (2016). *Regionalism in Hard Times*. London: Routledge.

Telò, M. (2018). "The Past & Present of Europe's Intercultural Dialogue: Beyond a 'Normative Power' Approach to Two-Way Cooperation". In T. Meyer and de Sales Marques J. (eds.), *Multiple Modernities and Good Governance*. Abingdon: Routledge, pp. 101–117.

Telò, M., Sapir, A., & Sassoon, D. (2017). *La place de l'Europe dans le monde du 21e siècle*. Brussels: L'Académie en poche.

Yan, X. (2019). *Leadership and the Rise of Great Powers*, Princeton: Princeton University Press.

Wendt, A. (1999). *Social Theory of International Politics*. Cambridge: Cambridge University Press.

Waltz, K. (1979). *Theory of International politics*, New York: Newbery Awards Record.

Jisheng Sun

Observing the Belt and Road Initiative from the Perspective of Regional and Interregional Cooperation: A Theoretical Perspective

After the Chinese President Xi Jinping proposed to build an 'economic belt along the Silk Road' and a '21st-Century Maritime Silk Road' when visiting Kazakhstan and Indonesia in 2013, the Belt and Road Initiative (BRI) soon became the most important platform and mechanism for China to further its cooperation with the rest of the world, and the BRI has also become a major Chinese discourse across the world. According to official Chinese documentation, the aim of the BRI is to strengthen the connectivity of the Asian, European and African continents and their adjacent seas and strengthen partnerships among the countries along the 'Belt and Road', to set up all-dimensional, multitiered and composite connectivity networks and to achieve diversified, independent, balanced and sustainable development in these countries.[1] It emphasises the principle of extensive consultation, joint contribution and shared benefits.[2] All the participating countries carry out consultation as equals, jointly shoulder responsibilities and enjoy the benefits together. From what the BRI has advocated, we can see that it not only follows the basic rules for traditional means of international cooperation, but also reflects the Chinese way of promoting regional and interregional cooperation, which is also of theoretical significance for us to rethink international cooperation. Following such an observation, this chapter aims to view the BRI from a theoretical perspective, to see how it can promote regional and interregional cooperation differently and to see what it can contribute, in terms of theory, to the study of international cooperation. Accordingly, the first part of this chapter will analyse the factors influencing the development and creation of

---

1 "Vision and Proposed Actions Outlined on Jointly Building Silk Road Economic Belt and 21st-Century Maritime Silk Road", China daily, March 30, 2015, http://language.chinadaily.com.cn/2015-03/30/content_19950951.htm (accessed May 2, 2019).

2 Jinping Xi, "Remarks by H.E. Xi Jinping President of the People's Republic of China at the Press Conference of the Second Belt and Road Forum for International Cooperation", *Ministry of Foreign Affairs of the People's Republic of China*, April 27, 2019, https://www.fmprc.gov.cn/mfa_eng/wjdt_665385/zyjh_665391/t1659452.shtml (accessed May 2, 2019).

theory, the second part will review regionalism and regional cooperation from a theoretical perspective, the third part will focus on Chinese culture and its influence on the Chinese approach to regionalism and regional cooperation and the last part will further explore the BRI in relation to regional and interregional cooperation and its theoretical contribution in this regard.

Three Main Factors Influencing the Development and Creation of International Relations Theory

From the very beginning of International Relations (IR) studies in 1919, IR theories, as an important component of IR studies, have been in a process of development for one hundred years. If we review the creation process and general development of IR theories, we can see that culture and tradition; the world situation and big global changes and foreign policy and relevant practices are the three main factors influencing the creation and development of IR theory.

Culture and tradition are very important sources in the creation and development of theory. Culture, which is accumulated and formed throughout a nation's development and history, can be reflected through a series of tradition and customs, shaping not only ideas and thoughts, but also norms and habits. In this sense, the creation and development of theory are, on the one hand, influenced by local culture and tradition and, on the other hand, reflect local features, making theories bear the mark of local influence.

Culture directly influences a country's world view, its way of thinking and behaviour and habits. As a backdrop of behaviour and action, culture exerts considerable influence on people's values and helps to shape national character. People with similar cultural backgrounds are very likely to form a shared cultural community. For those with different cultures, their social practices and ways of interacting are likely to be different. According to social theorists, social structures are the primary source of habits through socialisation. Culture in this case serves as part of the social structure and shapes habit. This is why, theoretically speaking, there is not only logic of rationalism and logic of appropriateness,[3] but also logic of habit and logic of practice.[4] That is to say, people's behaviour and

3 For the logic of rationalism and appropriateness, see Peter Katzenstein, Robert Keohane and Stephen Krasner (eds.), *Exploration and Contestation in the Study of World Politics*, translated by Qin Yaqing *et al.* (Shanghai: Shanghai People's Publishing House), 367–71.

4 Ted Hopf, "The Logic of Habit", *European Journal of International Relations* 16, No. 4 (2010), 539–61, 540.

actions are quite often a kind of habit without rational reflection. John Searle's analysis of background knowledge, Pierre Bourdieu's social theory and concept of '*habitus*' and Michel Foucault's historical *a priori* all provide similar explanation for the influence of culture and background knowledge. According to Searle, people often do things unconsciously, although they do follow certain rules. If they are very familiar with the rules, when they obey them, they are not even aware of their existence and make their behaviour appear unconscious. This kind of unconsciousness is actually behaviour guided by background knowledge.[5] Similarly, Bourdieu argues that *habitus*, as a system of embodied dispositions and tendencies that organise the ways in which individuals perceive the social world around them and react to it, represents the way that group culture and personal experience shape the body and the mind and, as a result, social action in the present.[6] For Foucault, historical *a priori* is the prior knowledge derived from history and no one can avoid influence from such knowledge.[7] As a result, people with similar cultural backgrounds are likely to interpret discourse and action in a similar fashion and vice versa. In practice, people often unconsciously use their own standards to interpret or judge the behaviour or action of others. As a result, what one country considers normal may be considered abnormal by other countries. People who lack a sufficient understanding of the history and culture of other countries do not have the background knowledge, which may lead to frequent misunderstanding and inefficient communication.

Culture is a very important source for the development of theory. The theorizing process is a practice that necessarily draws from diverse symbolic, cultural and historical resources. Countries or regions from different cultures may nurture different preferences and different norms, which are formed prior to the influence of the external international system. As theorists all live at a certain time and within a certain cultural space, the theories that they develop also

---

5 About the influence of background and how it influences behaviour, see John R. Searle, *The Construction of Social Reality* (New York: The Free Press, 1995). Chapter 6 provides a detailed analysis of how background knowledge influences the construction and interpretation of social phenomena.

6 *Wikipedia*, https://en.wikipedia.org/wiki/Habitus_(sociology) (accessed March 2, 2019).

7 Maurice Blanchot, "Michel Foucault in My Imagination", *Amazon*, July 8, 2015, https://www.amazon.cn/dp/B00I2KOEHK/ref=sr_1_1?s=digital-text&ie=UTF8&qid=1485311092&sr=1-1&keywords=%E7%A6%8F%E6%9F%AF (accessed May 2, 2019).

reflect local influence.[8] For instance, many concepts proposed and developed by American scholars such as power transition, structural conflicts, tragedy of great powers, etc., are mostly based on the American experiences since the end of World War II. The English School represented by Barry Buzan proposes the core concept of 'international society', which is based on the history and practice of Europe. However, because of the academic and discursive hegemony of the English language and the Western world, these theories are often universalised and used to explain the diplomatic practice of the whole world. For a long time, it has been Anglo-Saxon scholars who have dominated the IR discourse.[9] Hitherto, IR theories have been Western-centric and are far from being really global ones and cannot therefore offer a comprehensive picture of IR. This is one of the reasons behind Amitav Acharya's proposal to develop global IR so as to cover more perspectives from different regions and cultures, thus making IR theories more objective and pluralistic, or truly global.[10] In recent years, with the increasing awareness of the need to develop national schools of IR from non-Western countries, more and more voices have begun to be heard against such hegemony. For instance, in Russian academia, many have emphasised the uniqueness of Russia as a country that operates according to a set of different and unique rules of engagement and therefore cannot be understood through the lens of Western IR theory.[11] In China, IR theories that have been developed, such as Qin Yaqing's relational theory, Zhao Tingyang's Tianxia concept and Yan Xuetong's moral realism, are also closely related with Chinese tradition, culture and history.[12] It can be clearly seen that countries or regions from different

8 About culture and theory development, see Yaqing Qin, *Relation and Process, the Cultural Construction of China's IR Theories* (Shanghai: Shanghai People's Press, 2012), 12–25.

9 John Mearsheimer, "A Global Discipline of IR: Benign Hegemony", *International Studies Review* 18, No. 1 (2016), 147–149, 147.

10 On global IR, see Amitav Acharya, "Advancing Global IR: Challenges, Contentions, and Contribution", *International Studies Review* 18, No. 1 (2016), 4–15.

11 Maria Y. Omelicheva and Lidiya Zubytska, "An Unending Quest for Russia's Place in the World: The Discursive Co-evolution of the Study and Practice of International Relations in Russia", *New Perspective* 24, No. 1 (2016), 19–51, 20.

12 See Yaqing Qin, *A Relational Theory of World Politics* (Cambridge: Cambridge University Press, 2018); Tingyang Zhao, *Tianxia System* (Nanjing: Jiangsu Education Press, 2005); Xuetong Yan, *The Transfer of World Power: Political Leadership and Strategic Competition* (Beijing: Peking University Press, 2015).

cultures may nurture different preferences and different norms, which exist prior to any influence from the international system.[13]

Besides culture and tradition, theoretical development is also influenced by the structure and big changes in the international situation. Theories are the systematic and conceptualised ideas used to explain, describe and predict reality.[14] The world itself is the most important source and provides constant momentum and dynamism for theorists to reflect on and create new theories. For instance, in the 1970s, living in a bipolar world composed of the two camps led by the two powers of the United States and the Soviet Union, Kenneth Waltz developed very parsimonious neorealism, with the international system analogised to a market.[15] A country's choice has to be determined by the international structure. In the late 1980s, along with the questioning towards the main IR theories of neo-realism and neo-liberalism for their failure to predict the end of the Cold War, many new concepts and perspectives entered the IR research agenda from the 1990s, such as identity, gender, discourse, emotion, etc. which leads to a pluralistic development period of IR in the 1990s and early 21st century. Now many people hold that the current international order and system is faced with profound changes caused by the redistribution of power between developed countries and emerging developing countries, and the fast development of new technology. Meanwhile, the global governance system is also facing increasing failure and deficits in terms of governance. The world has been witnessing ideological changes as well, such as the rise of populism, antiglobalisation, nationalism, etc. All of these elements provide new empirical sources for rethinking current IR theories.

The development and creation of theory are also influenced by a country's foreign policy and relevant practice. For any country, while absorbing theories from other countries, its foreign policy often reflects its own national culture and tradition. For countries with different cultures, the national characteristics of their foreign policies are also different in terms of diplomatic style, approaches and measures.[16] For instance, with regard to the ideas and foreign policy of the

13 Majia Zehfuss, *Constructivism in International Relations: The Politics of Reality* (Cambridge: Cambridge University Press, 2002).

14 See Steve Smith, "Introduction: Diversity and Disciplinarity in International Relations Theory", in Tim Dunne (ed.) *International Relations Theories: Disciplines and Diversity* (New York: Oxford University Press, 2007), 1–12.

15 Kenneth Waltz, *Theory of International Politics* (New York: McGraw Hill, 1979).

16 Jisheng Sun, "Traditional Culture and the Construction of the Chinese Diplomatic Discursive System since the 18th Party Congress", *Foreign Affairs Review*, No. 4 (2017), 2.

United States, democracy and freedom are core values. From their pioneering days, Americans have formed the idea of being God's chosen people with a sense of mission, believing that the United States shoulders the responsibility for exporting its ideals of freedom, its democratic system and associated values to other countries. This is one of the rationales for many US external actions such as the war on Iraq, etc. In line with such a mindset, it is not surprising that 'democratic peace' theory was developed in the United States. Similarly, China's cultural tradition also shapes China's unique world view, values and the ways of thinking and acting. Dating back a long way into the past, China values peace, respects differences and diversity and encourages inclusiveness and tolerance. Such a tradition also influences China's foreign policy. It prevents China from imposing its own ideas and systems on other countries or exporting them to other countries or making anyone else Chinese.[17] One of the underlying reasons for this is that China, throughout its long history, has always considered the world as a whole, with itself being the centre of the world. There is no clear division between the 'Self' and the 'Other'. By contrast with the expansion of Western civilisation, "China's perception towards its own civilization doesn't include the idea of expansion. It will not seek to improve the other and adds an extra burden for itself".[18] All of these characteristics show the inward and non-expansionist features of China's cultural tradition. According to the Ministry of Foreign Affairs of China, China has formed its own diplomatic theory, with peaceful development as the basic approach and win-win cooperation as the core principle.[19] Similarly, Russia's foreign policy is often related to its great power identity derived from its material capacities and its intellectual, cultural and spiritual potential.[20] Such an identity influences its perceptions and responses to international events, regardless of its internal condition.[21] Thus, regarding Ukraine,

17 Daniel McCarthy, "Whose Civilization? Which Clash?" *Modern Age* 60, No. 4 (2018), 10.

18 Mark Mancall, *China at the Center: 300 Years of Foreign Policy* (New York: The Free Press, 1984), 11.

19 The Party Committee of the Chinese Ministry of Foreign Affairs, "Innovation of the Diplomatic Theory and Practice of a Major Country with Chinese Characteristics since the 18th CPC National Congress", *Renminwang*, March 17, 2016, http://theory.people.com.cn/n1/2016/0317/c40531-28207116.html (accessed May 2, 2019).

20 Maria Y. Omelicheva and Lidiya Zubytska, "An Unending Quest for Russia's Place in the World: The Discursive Co-evolution of the Study and Practice of International Relations in Russia", *New Perspective* 24, No. 1 (2016), 36.

21 *Ibid.*, 36.

Russia sees itself as a heroic nation on a mission to safeguard the Russian world and restore 'fairness' in international relations, which have been long abused by the West.[22] For regionalism and regional cooperation, theories developed from different regions also have different features and connotations, bearing an influence from different local cultures and experiences.

Theoretical Review of Regionalism and Regional Cooperation: Old, New and Open Regionalism

Theoretically speaking, cooperation within the framework of regionalism gained considerable momentum after World War II and, in the 1950s and 1960s, a great deal of attention was paid to international regionalism and cooperation. Regionalism can be divided into three main categories: old, new and open regionalism, each having different focuses in both theory and practice regarding cooperation.

The first kind is old regionalism, starting from the end of World War II and running until the 1970s. In 1958, the European Community was established, based on the early European Coal and Steel Community, on the one hand, to prevent war in Europe between major powers and to promote cooperation and, on the other hand, to promote cooperation and to start the regional integration process of western Europe, although the idea of European integration has existed in Europe throughout history. The idea of community is a breakthrough term both in concept and practice. In 1963, the Organization of African Unity was established, aiming to promote African unity and integration, and cooperation between African countries in the field of politics, diplomacy, economy, culture and military affairs. In 1967, the Association of South East Asian Nations (ASEAN) was established with the aim of promoting regional integration regarding politics, economy and security so as to build a peaceful and stable ASEAN community. During this period, although different regional integration institutions have been established in different regions, people pay quite a lot of attention to European experience, economic activities and intergovernmental organisation. Functionalism, neo-functionalism, intergovernmentalism, etc. are the main theories people use to explain European integration, that is the cooperation and integration processes starting from a single small area gradually spill over into other areas. The EU has been considered to be the most successful model for such cooperation and regionalism for quite a long time. The core of regionalism,

---

22 *Ibid.*, 37.

based on EU experience, is mainly institutionalised regionalism. Countries that have not reached the relevant standard are not allowed to join the EU and, after becoming a member, all the rules and norms have to be followed. By the 1970s, the slowdown in regional institutionalism combined with the obsolescence of regional theory marked the end of old regionalism.[23]

The second kind is new regionalism. The late 1970s and 1980s saw a remarkable revival in regionalism. With the end of the Cold War and the development of globalisation, new regionalism gradually attracted more attention. In 1991, American scholar Norman D. Palmer put forward the idea of new regionalism for the first time so as to differentiate it from old regionalism.[24] By comparison with old regionalism, new regionalism emphasises interregional or transregional aspects, which means that regional cooperation should go beyond a single region and efforts should be made to realise the cooperation and integration across regions. Transregional dimensions seemed to be one of its most distinctive features.[25] Later, Bjorn Hettne defined new regionalism as a multidimensional integration process, including social, political and cultural dimensions apart from the economic dimension, which has traditionally been the focus.[26] It can therefore be seen that the prominent feature of new regionalism is the transregional and multidimensional feature of cooperation and the final goal is still an organisation or institution that goes beyond the nation state. Non-state actors such as economic and social forces have been given more weight, the ideological differences between countries have been weakened and new liberal economic policies have been widely accepted. With regard to cooperation, it is still strict institutionalism, which goes beyond the region and extends to interregional cooperation.

In 1997, after the Asian financial crisis, the new regionalism of East Asia based on ASEAN 10+1, 10+3 and +3 gained fresh momentum. However, the new regionalism of East Asia is not the simple type of new regionalism. It also has its own features. The first priority is still within the region and the establishment of institutions within the region to promote cooperation and the integration process. Meanwhile, efforts were also made to build coordinating

---

23 Norman D. Palmer, *The New Regionalism in Asia and the Pacific* (Mass: Lexington Books, 1991), 9.

24 *Ibid.*, 12.

25 *Ibid.*, 2.

26 Bjorn Hettne, "Globalism and New Regionalism: The Second Great Transformation", in Bjorn Hettne *et al.* (eds.) *Globalism and New Regionalism* (London: Palgrave Macmillan, 1999), 1.

institutions between different regions. In this sense it is a kind of combination of open regionalism and new regionalism.

Different IR theories provide different reasons for the need for regionalism and ways to achieve cooperation. According to neo-realism, both economic and political regionalism are designed to deal with different challenges. Within a certain region, the beginning of regionalism can be brought about by a regional hegemon, with small and weak states forming an alliance to counterbalance the influence of the regional hegemon. For instance, one of the reasons for starting the ASEAN was fear of Vietnam. A regional institution can restrict the power of a regional hegemon. Weak and small states can join the regional process dominated by the hegemon. A hegemon in decline can also use regional institutions to share responsibility. During the process, regional institutions that are set up also play a very important role for regional cooperation in different fields.

According to neo-liberalism, interdependence between states increases the need for cooperation and, through cooperative institutions, states can form common interests and solve common problems. Effective regional institutions can reduce uncertainty during the interaction and make the results of cooperation more predictable. Regional institutions can manage regional cooperation. Besides, regional institutions can enhance exchanges of information and increase transparency between states and reduce the security dilemma, just like two business people after signing a business contract have a clear expectation about the benefits and gains from the deal, knowing that it is the same for their counterpart. Institutions will continue to work once they are formed. Such roles that institutions play have been well illustrated by scholars such as Robert Keohane in his publication entitled *After Hegemony: Cooperation and Discord in the World Political Economy*, which emphasises that, once formed, rules and institutions will continue to produce binding effects even when the hegemon has declined.[27]

According to constructivism, the interaction and negotiating process among states during the cooperation and integration process can gradually change national identity, interest and mutual perception and strengthen 'we-ness' among states, and even change the habits or culture of the region. For instance, the ASEAN is a typical example of this kind. During the integration process, the identity of the ASEAN becomes stronger for each ASEAN member and the approach and style towards regional integration gradually takes shape. The ASEAN

27 Robert O. Keohane, *After Hegemony: Cooperation and Discord in the World Political Economy* (Princeton: Princeton University Press, 2005).

gradually forms a habit of mutual consultation and non-interference and ensures that all sides feel comfortable, which is quite different from the EU method of strict institutionalism. In such a case, it is not only the result of cooperation that is important but also the process, which can play an essential constructive role in shaping identity and interest and thus the final action.

From the above it can be seen that although regional integration is a very effective way to promote regional cooperation, it does not mean that the way to achieve it is the same for all countries and regions. Rules are important factors in guaranteeing successful cooperation. However, the process of formulating and making rules also varies between different countries and regions. For instance, for EU integration or European regionalism, big regional powers such as Germany and France have played an essential role in promoting the process. For East Asian regionalism, it is the small states working together, which is ASEAN, to play the dominant role, not regional powers such as China and Japan. That is to say, local culture, tradition and experience play a very important role in nurturing national and regional preferences and differences, which leads to different paths and processes towards a certain goal.

Chinese Culture and Its Influence on the Chinese Approach to Regionalism and Regional Cooperation

China is a country with a long history of several thousand years and Chinese culture has been accumulated and shaped from generation to generation throughout this long history, which inevitably influences the Chinese way of thinking and acting.

The first feature of Chinese culture is a holistic and long-term way of thinking. Chinese culture is a culture that values collectivism and often emphasises viewing things from an overall perspective and tendency rather than from individual perspective. Chinese history is often viewed with dynasty as a unit, with some dynasties lasting hundreds of years. Such a form of long-term thinking can also be reflected in Chinese policies. For instance, the Chinese government often sets long-term goals or plans, such as a five-year plan, a three-step strategy or two Centennial Goals. After the goals have been set, relevant policies will be adopted and the relevant measures will be taken to reach them. Similarly, China's foreign policy also often emphasises the general and overall trend and long-term and systematic thinking. In practice, before doing concrete things, an analysis of the overall situation, such as that of the world or the country, was always carried out. For example, in 1984, after Deng Xiaoping just began China's reform and opening up, his judgement of the world then was that peace and development was the main theme and that a third world war could be avoided.[28] The world today is described as "multi-polar, economically globalised, digitalised and culturally diversified". After assessing the overall situation, specific strategies or policies are adopted, which is called '*shun shi er wei*', meaning following the general trend of the times. In addition, China often tries to integrate the individual parts to form a whole and then proceed in an integrated framework. For instance, in recent years, quite a few mechanisms have been formed, such as the creation of the '16+1' cooperation between China and the central and eastern European countries, the Forum of China African Cooperation (FOCAC) between China and African countries and the Lancang-Mekong Cooperation mechanism for countries along the Langcang and Mekong river. When dealing with concrete issues such as a crisis or conflicts, the emphasis is always on coordinating relations smoothly first, through consultation or negotiation, so as to establish a friendly environment or form a language of dialogue and conversation rather than to use force or sanctions directly.[29]

The second feature of Chinese culture is to stick to the golden means *(zhong yong)* and emphasise the interconnectivity between things. As distinct from the Western way of thinking of categorisation, the Chinese way of thinking emphasises connectivity, mutual tolerance and inclusiveness. Even when things are in opposition to or in conflict with each other, they are still interdependent and can change mutually and eventually form a harmonious whole, as can be seen from the 'Yin and Yang' in Chinese Taiji or the positive and negative poles of a battery. Therefore, the fact that things are different is a kind of natural state and differences should be respected. Besides, things cannot simply be divided into right or wrong, black or white, as they often switch to the opposite side and quite often the final result depends on the context. Things should therefore be viewed and treated dialectically, as should differences. Besides, Chinese culture always emphasises tolerance, inclusiveness and integration, which is also considered a very important reason why Chinese civilisation has lasted throughout history. Even when non-Han people dominated China, it could still remain inclusive and absorb the useful elements from other cultures and integrate them

---

28 "Deng Xiaoping's Four Historic Contribution", *Renminwang*, August 25, 2014, http://dangshi.people.com.cn/n/2014/0825/c85037-25534260.html (accessed May 1, 2019).

29 Jisheng Sun, "Traditional Culture and the Development of China's Diplomatic Discourse System since the 18th CPC National Congress", *Foreign Affairs Review*, No. 4 (2017), 8.

into its own. It is a kind of peaceful and harmonising mindset, which influences the very starting point of people's way of thinking and acting. With regard to China's foreign policy, this is one of the reasons why peace is always emphasised, no matter for the ends or as means. To build and maintain peace is always the goal of China's foreign policy, and the goal should also be reached in peaceful ways. Whether in relation to the Five Principles for Peaceful Coexistence proposed by China in the 1950s or peaceful development and harmonious world proposed at the beginning of the 21st century or the building of a human community with a shared future proposed after the 18th Communist Party of China (CPC) National Congress, such a logic and the goal for peace has always been emphasised.

The third feature of Chinese culture is the attitude towards differences and the emphasis of interchangeability between different things. Chinese culture always emphasises that differences should be respected and treated dialectically. Under certain conditions, the conflictual or different things can change and move in the opposite direction. This is why, for Chinese culture, the idea of 'the clash of civilisations' seldom exists, as this does not conform to the Chinese way of thinking.[30] In practice, when people come across differences or problems, they are encouraged to make efforts to move them towards a good direction. A harmonizing mindset is always emphasised. For instance, for some regional and international issues, it is always emphasised that measures should be taken to help move towards a good direction through dialogue, negotiation and consultation instead of simply imposing a sanction or using military force.

The above Chinese way of thinking and behaving also influences the Chinese approach to regionalism and regional cooperation. Based on China's culture and experience and the traditions of China's foreign policy, China has formed its own attitudes and approach towards regionalism and regional cooperation. This is also an important part of Asian regionalism, which has the following two main features: one is the emphasis on process, which is in sharp contrast with the EU approach, which is more results-oriented, as the interaction and integration process will help change the identity or interest perception among states or even change the political culture of Asia. The other is pluralism and looseness or flexibility of the operation process. EU regional integration displays more features of homogenisation. When the EU set the standard for membership, it had already set the standard for, for example the economic system, the political system, and

30 Regarding the clash of civilizations, see Samuel Huntington, *The Clash of Civilizations and the Remaking of World Order* (New York: Simon & Schuster, 2011).

social development while the Asian approach is much more pluralistic in terms of actors, concrete operation and the whole integration process. It is much looser and more flexible during the process.

Besides, China also emphasises open regionalism. On the one hand, China sticks to the opening up policy by itself. It hopes to rely on its own openness of the economy and its own economic influence to influence the development of a regional open economy and even go beyond the region so as to facilitate the operation of trade and investment within the region and beyond, and to promote an open global economy. Even today, when the world is faced with deglobalisation and antiglobalisation, China still emphasises its strong support for an open global regional and global economy. On the other hand, China always promotes the basic rules of open regionalism, which are mutual respect, reaching consensus through consultation and ensuring that all sides feel comfortable, which is also a very typical Asian way. This process involves three dimensions: general rules, an open region and specific issues. Any country or economic entity accepting such Asian ways and the facilitation of trade and investment can join the open Asian regionalism and regional cooperation process.

In recent years, with the development of China's economy and international influence, objectively China has gained more conditions and space to implement its own ideas, strategies and policies. Subjectively, China has become more confident in itself, proposing four types of confidence, which are confidence in the system, the institution, the development path and culture. Regarding foreign policy, China has become more proactive since the 18th CPC National Congress and has been trying to propose its own ideas and solutions. In practice, the Chinese government has begun to pay more attention to hosting international and multilateral events so as to show its sense of responsibility as a major country and to integrate more of its ideas and approaches into the process. China's discursive power in rule making and agenda setting can also be reflected through the process. Regarding cooperation, besides the regional cooperation within Asia, China began to promote regional and interregional cooperation in its own way, such as the creation of the '16+1' cooperation mechanism, the Lancang-Mekong cooperation mechanism and FOCAC. Among the initiatives proposed by China, the most important one is the BRI, based on the spirit of the old Silk Road, which has played a major role in promoting exchanges between China and the countries along the Silk Road through trade and other cooperation activities. In the past six years, the BRI has become a very important mechanism and platform for China to promote regional and interregional cooperation. China's approach to push it forward can also provide additional thoughts for the theoretical study on international cooperation.

The BRI and Regional and Interregional Cooperation

According to the current studies on regionalism and regional cooperation, especially neoliberal institutionalism, cooperation can be conducted between countries through institutions, international rules and norms. They emphasise the strict binding and regulating role of rules. That is to say, countries accepting the rules or joining the institutions have reached certain set conditions or standards; and after joining, all the members must follow the same rules and same procedures, which is more result-oriented and the process is a homogeneous one for the involving actors. The BRI first and foremost is a cooperation mechanism and platform, which aims to promote international cooperation, both regional and interregional, for joint development and common prosperity. It is also considered a Chinese concept or a network.[31] Since it was launched, it has become the most important initiative for China to further its cooperation with the rest of the world. It links the already existing regional cooperation of the ASEAN, the EU and the post-Soviet region. In the past six years, China has been taking concrete and active steps to bring this undertaking to fruition, which has led to the BRI to develop from ideas to expectation, from expectation to implementation and from implementation to harvesting results. Now it has entered the period of high-quality implementation.[32] From the main guiding principles as well as the practical experiences during the last six years since it was launched, it can be seen that, in addition to following the traditional way of cooperation, the BRI has also experienced new ways of cooperation between countries within the region and beyond. With regard to regionalism, it can be viewed as a kind of gradual and incremental open regionalism, or the new development of regionalism, which, from the theoretical perspective, also provides new ideas for regional and international cooperation and in some sense even for the new round of globalisation. The main reason is that the BRI sticks to its own values of equality, openness, inclusiveness and development promotion, which

31 Jim O'Neil, "Ambitious Concepts Needs Matching Tactics: China should Make Key Asian Countries Feel Empowered to Influence the BRI Path", in *Common Prosperity: Global Views on Belt and Road Initiative*, compiled by China Watch (Beijing: Wuzhou Communication Press, 2019), 32; Romano Prodi, "Forward", in *Common Prosperity: Global Views on Belt and Road Initiative*, compiled by China Watch (Beijing: Wuzhou Communication Press, 2019), 13.

32 Jinping Xi, "Promoting High-Quality Development of Belt and Road Cooperation", *Ministry of Foreign Affairs of the People's Republic of China*, April 27, 2019, https://www.fmprc.gov.cn/mfa_eng/wjdt_665385/zyjh_665391/t1659454.shtml (accessed May 2, 2019).

adds new content and elements to regionalism and international cooperation in the traditional sense.

Regarding equality, the very basic element of globalisation is to promote the flow of goods, information and capital around the globe, and the whole world is viewed as one entity. However, one of the major problems with the current round of globalisation is its stimulation of the concentration of capital and the increasing gap between the rich and the poor. The result is partial: not every country can join equally, and the benefit is also not shared equally, which has led to the division within a country and between different countries, producing marginalised groups and even marginalised countries. The world today is calling for a bridge that can better connect the developed and developing world. The BRI emphasises equality by connecting everyone. According to the BRI, the first step is to increase 'connectivity' in the five major areas, namely policy, infrastructure, trade, finance and people. From China's 40 years of experience after its reform and opening up, it can be seen quite clearly that connectivity has greatly promoted China's development and what is more important is that connectivity also helps to change people's way of life and sense of time and space. Similarly, connectivity within the framework of the BRI is also expected to play its due role in promoting international cooperation and development. Regarding participation, all countries, although with different needs, are equal no matter whether they are rich or poor, strong or weak. As described in the 2015 'Vision and Action', the 'Silk Road Spirit' is described as a "historic and cultural heritage shared by all countries around the world".[33] All countries can make a contribution and derive benefits from the platform equally. During the first China Import Expo in Shanghai in 2018, not only did enterprises and companies from developed countries attend, but also those from underdeveloped countries and, for those underdeveloped countries, the fees were waived. That means that all countries can benefit from the huge Chinese market. Among the five areas of connectivity, the first focus is the creation of shared transport links, which is expected to strengthen connectivity and partially solve the problem of fragmentation. Connectivity is able to not only better promote the flow of goods, better link the markets and promote more Chinese exports to Europe but also allows more exports to China. Efforts to strengthen 'connectivity' in the five

33 NDRC, FMPRC and MOFCOM, "Vision and Actions on Jointly Building Silk Road Economic Belt and 21st-Century Maritime Silk Road", *Ministry of Foreign Affairs of the People's Republic of China*, March 28, 2015, http://www.fmprc.gov.cn/ce/cevn/chn/sghkt/t1251121.html (accessed April 12, 2017).

major areas, namely policy, infrastructure, trade, finance and people, are expected to strengthen connectivity for today's world. The BRI serves more as a kind of public good and platform through which countries can cooperate via the principle of extensive consultation, joint contribution and shared benefits. It encourages parting countries and others to combine comparative advantages, narrow development gaps, accelerate regional integration and achieve common development.

The second feature is its openness. Originally, when the BRI was first proposed, it was often heard that 'countries along the Belt and Road…', and such expression seems to limit the scope of the countries that can participate. Although according to 'Vision and Action', five general routes are suggested, this does not mean that there are fixed notions about routes and participating partners. The suggested pathways are intended more as a broad organising notion, around which a series of bilateral and multilateral cooperative activities may be initiated with a variety of partners. Any country who would like to join is welcome. Besides the openness towards different actors, the content of the BRI remains open, which makes the BRI a project which can integrate new ideas and realities more than a program. That is why there are not only traditional land, maritime or air connections, but also a 'digital silk road' and a 'silk road on ice'. That is to say, the BRI is an open mechanism. For other countries who would like to join, it is also an opportunity to launch new cooperation under the BRI framework. In this sense, it would lead to the kind of integration of a Chinese style or even an Asian style, which puts more emphasis on connectivity and strategic synergy (*zhan lue dui jie*) between countries. Although most of the time when talking about the 'Belt and Road', people will first think of the connectivity of the Eurasian continent, the BRI goes beyond Asia and Europe. It extends to Africa and Latin America. During Chinese President Xi Jinping's meeting with US President Donald Trump in 2017, he said that China also welcomes the United States to participate in the cooperation under the framework of the BRI. It is a Chinese way to promote the new round of globalisation, in particular when the world is faced with the challenges of antiglobalisation and deglobalisation. From this perspective, it is also a kind of innovation for international cooperation.

The third one is inclusiveness. Chinese culture always emphasises harmony without uniformity, taking the existence of differences as a natural state and is always ready to accept differences. Different things put together can also form a harmonious whole. The current round of globalisation is mainly led by Western ideas and thoughts. The globalisation of trade and finance also led to the globalisation of Western ideas, and the direct result is the spread of Western values and standards, producing an exclusive order and even 'the clash of civilisations'. The implementation of the BRI can be a good supplement in this respect. Chinese culture always emphasises peaceful coexistence, seeking common ground while shelving differences, which means countries with different social and political systems, different religions and different civilisations can all join; different regional and international organisations can join as well. Regarding the means of cooperation under the framework of the BRI, there are also no fixed standards or rules. According to the understanding of Kerry Brown, there is clearly no set pattern for how projects under the BRI are meant to be run. There is also an embedded notion of flexibility.[34] The way to cooperate can be very diverse, flexible and inclusive, even one country one policy, taking the local conditions into full consideration.

The fourth one is its development promotion. The 'Silk Road Spirit' is described as a new way to promote world peace and development. No country has ever paid so much attention to development over the past four decades as China has done. Development has been the subject that China has been committed to in the past four decades. China, with its efforts since its reform and opening up, has successfully lifted over 800 million people out of poverty. In terms of development, China can be a good example for other low-income countries to learn from. The BRI can serve as a mechanism by which other countries and regions may benefit from the gains of China's development through win-win cooperation. From what has happened in the past six years, it can be seen that the BRI is in line with various development agendas at regional and national level, such as the 2030 Agenda for Sustainable Development, the China-Europe Land-Sea Express Route, the Paris Agreement on Climate Change and World Trade Organization (WTO) Trade Facilitation. During the 2016 G20 Hang Zhou Summit, development was, for the first time, put on the global governance agenda, which is a unique way for China to improve global governance.[35] According to the World Bank, about 19 countries along the 'Belt and Road' are middle- and low-income countries, whose total population is 2.4 billion, accounting for 82 % of the total such population and the average percentage of its manufacturing industry is only

---

34 Kerry Brown, "Looking for the 'China Model' ", in *Common Prosperity: Global Views on Belt and Road Initiative*, compiled by China Watch (Beijing: Wuzhou Communication Press, 2019), 47.

35 Jinping Xi, "A New Starting Point for China's Development a New Blueprint for Global Growth", *Ministry of Foreign Affairs of the People's Republic of China*, September 3, 2016, https://www.fmprc.gov.cn/mfa_eng/wjdt_665385/zyjh_665391/t1396112.shtml (accessed May 2, 2019).

14.8 %.[36] If the BRI can help to promote the development of these countries and turn them into middle-income countries, the total development landscape of the world will change. As said by President Xi Jinping at the opening ceremony of the first Belt and Road Forum for International Cooperation in 2018, "Development holds the master key to solving all problems. In pursuing the Belt and Road Initiative, we should focus on the fundamental issue of development, release the growth potential of various countries and achieve economic integration and interconnected development and deliver benefits to all".[37] If this happens, it will be a great contribution to the realisation of the 2030 UN Sustainable Development Goals, also an achievement that the current round of globalisation was not able to attain.

From the process of the BRI and its way of promoting regional and interregional cooperation, it can be seen that besides the similarities that it has shown with the traditional form of international cooperation based on strong institutionalism, it also carries some new features. Firstly, it has experienced a gradual process. In the past six years, the BRI has undergone a gradual process, moving from idea to action, from expectation to reality and from implementation to harvesting results. In this sense, the implementation of the BRI is also a learning and consensus-building process between participating countries. Secondly, the implementation is more flexible. As distinct from strong institutionalism, under which all actors must obey the same rules, for the BRI cooperation, under the general consensus, the implementation and ways to cooperate and areas in which to cooperate are determined by both sides. It is a process whereby participating countries work things out through consultation. In such a case, it is not only a strong institution that can promote cooperation but also a flexible institution in the making. That is to say, under the BRI framework, cooperation between different countries may be the same, or may vary as well. Thirdly, the BRI cooperation may nurture new cooperation norms. Since international cooperation within the framework of the BRI can also take place without very strict cooperation rules, such a cooperation-generating process can also produce new norms for cooperation.

---

36 Feiteng Zhong, "The Belt and Road Initiative, New Type Globalization and Major Country Relations", *Foreign Affairs Review*, No. 3 (2017), 6.

37 Jinping Xi, "Work Together to Build the Silk Road Economic Belt and the 21st-Century Maritime Silk Road", *Ministry of Foreign Affairs of the People's Republic of China*, May 14, 2017, https://www.fmprc.gov.cn/mfa_eng/wjdt_665385/zyjh_665391/t1465819.shtml (accessed May 5, 2019).

Conclusion

As can be seen, the development of IR theory is influenced by culture and tradition, the world situation and big global changes as well as foreign policy and relevant practices. Therefore, theories developed in different time and space also bear specific hallmarks. For regionalism and regional cooperation, it is the same, as can be seen from the different approaches towards regionalism and regional cooperation between the EU and the ASEAN. Over the years, China has also developed its own strategy, approach and policy for its interaction with the rest of the world, proposing its own ideas, initiatives and measures. The BRI is an initiative of this kind. Against the backdrop of the deglobalisation of the world, especially since 2016 after the occurrence of a series of 'black swans', the BRI can serve as an effective platform and mechanism to further the cooperation between China and other countries and between different regions, promoting the new round of globalisation in a Chinese way, with its emphasis on mutual consultation, joint effort and mutual benefit, with an aim of engineering better global governance as well. Its emphasis on equality, openness, inclusiveness and its special emphasis on development will add more benign, equal and equitable, more open and pluralistic elements to international cooperation and regionalism of the traditional sense, which provide us with a good source to rethink international cooperation. Meanwhile, for cooperation within the framework of the BRI, it has to be kept in mind that although the BRI has a great vision and is of great potential, it is not only up to the Chinese. It also needs the joint response and efforts of the countries involved to make it come true. The whole process needs the vision, wisdom and determination of everyone. The result and success of the BRI will not only depend on China but also on the interaction and the joint efforts of all participating countries. It is a mutual learning and mutual engagement process for everyone, during which the BRI may constantly evolve and change towards a better version. The engagement and cooperation process are as important as the final result.

Jiakun Zhao and Hongyu Lin

Regionality and Multilayered Diplomacy

Introduction

This chapter aims to connect the accumulated de jure analysis relating to substate agents' engagements in multilayered and multilateral diplomacy exercises with a more selective empirical domain so as to tentatively offer a de facto theory on the feasibility of these exercises within certain institutional contexts outside the conventional federalism approach–based observations, and to evaluate their long-term prospects in terms of geopolitical stability and connectivity. The ongoing 'One Belt, One Road' (OBOR) initiative is an economic agenda–oriented regional relationship integration process that is the subject of geopolitical concerns and anticipates limitations in relation to conventional diplomatic measures, as widely debated in open dialogues. It nevertheless provides an optimal experimental field for testing de facto theories of multilayered diplomacy engagements in pragmatic terms. Four reasons underpin our claim. To narrow down the topic, the notion of substate agents, or actants as we refer to them in our chapter, is exclusively concentrated on substate constituents or other devolution targets of state powers as diplomatic engagers; and the term 'multilayered diplomacy' is defined in conventional theoretical style as multilayered foreign engagements in political dimensions with formal rectifications. In general, the process and actors in our scenario work in a top-down manner, but their interaction environments and outcomes hinge on both governmental and bottom-up dynamics.

Firstly, the OBOR initiative elicits sufficient policy motivations for shareholders, especially the major investors and promoters, to adopt flexible channels and bodies of engagements in minimising potential suspicion about unilateral power projection or diplomatic oppression of minor states. Secondly, substate governments are closely positioned to enforcement levels of infrastructure programmes and play key roles in making transnational investment enterprises real, which has given them a non-negligible status in the overall objectives of the OBOR initiative. Thirdly, the availability of established platforms of 'city diplomacy' or other types of channels for accepting substate government bodies into international organisations alongside the coverage of the OBOR initiative is more sparse than that of Europe, which is typified as a matured regional atmosphere for substate diplomacy based on stable security environments and affluent dialogue platforms associated with structural links within the trajectory of European integration. This sharp regional contrast demonstrates an ideal opportunity to perceive domestically generated multilayered diplomacies as novel, explorative endeavours that are less susceptible to path dependence. Last but not least, the domestic regime comparability and overlapping between the People's Republic of China (PRC) and partner states along the OBOR initiative areas of coverage and within its 'peripheral diplomacy' ranges are, not surprisingly, limited. These contexts lead to further examinations about the adaptability of substate agents and their transnational interaction strategies as well as the domestic empowering mechanism for such endeavours. This disproportionality of domestic regimes, accompanied by differentiated geopolitical interest stances and disputes about China's real motivation, have elicited higher demands for multilayered diplomacies to address legitimisation concerns by balancing sovereign integrity and interventional engagements between constituent bodies. Compared with regions and settings with higher levels of socialisation on transborder communications between municipalities, the stage of the OBOR initiative demands stricter investigation relating to the pragmatist rationales of the legitimacy foundations of multilayered diplomacy and how engagers actively conform to them.

Our approach aims neither to deliberate on a universally applicable model of multilayered diplomacy with various substate agencies nor to substitute established theories on city diplomacy or 'substate diplomacy' normalisations regarding the specific regionality of China, east Asia or other areas of OBOR coverage. Rather, through the process of our rationale on the substate governments in multilayered diplomacy under specific contexts, we wish to emphasise the aspect of legitimacy consolidation, constitutional competence parity between agencies and how the domestic empowerment process of such engagers, driven by vertical ratifications of centralised states, strives to address them. We highlight these concerns as deterministic in multilayered diplomacy and focus on their domestic solutions through empowering agents instead of external solutions from well-established international organisations or dialogue frameworks, which had been largely and monotonously discussed in previous debates about substate diplomacy theories.

Sovereign Is Here to Stay: Legitimisation Evaluations of Multilayered Diplomacy

Since the early phases of conceptualisations of substate diplomacy by Hocking, Michelmann, Soldatos and Kincaid[1], legitimacy concerns have occupied a central theoretical front in defending this novel type of engagement that appears not to conform to Satowian definitions of diplomatic actants[2] or Westphalian/Vattelian conventions on sovereign jurisdictions[3]. The intensity of this contradiction partly hinges on narrations and topics of engagement focus. For instance, the discourses of 'paradiplomacy' went further in acknowledging the independent natures of constituents and their initiatives in promoting utilities independently[4]. When framed with more concentrations of a social constructive process such as communication[5] and norm transitions[6], the diplomatic practices do

---

1 Hocking, Brian. "Localizing foreign policy". In *Localizing Foreign Policy*, pp. 8–30. Palgrave Macmillan, London, 1993; Hocking, Brian. "Non-central Governments and Multilayered Diplomacy". In *Localizing Foreign Policy*, pp. 31–69. Palgrave Macmillan, London, 1993; Michelmann, Hans J., and Panayotis Soldatos, eds. *Federalism and International Relations: The Role of Subnational Units*. Oxford University Press, 1990; Kincaid, John. "Foreign Relations of Sub-national Units", *Federalism in a Changing World: Learning from Each Other* (2003): 74–96.

2 Satow, Ernest Mason. *Satow's Guide to Diplomatic Practice*. 5th ed./edited by Lord Gore-Booth, assistant editor, Desmond Pakenham.Longman, London; New York, 1979, 3, 67.

3 Papisca, Antonio. "International Law and Human Rights as a Legal Basis for the International Involvement of Local Governments", *City Diplomacy: The Role of Local Governments in Conflict Prevention, Peace-Building, Post-Conflict Reconstruction* (2008): 27–46; Wyn Jones, Richard, and Elin Royles. "Wales in the World: Intergovernmental Relations and Sub-state Diplomacy", *The British Journal of Politics and International Relations* 14, No. 2 (2012): 250–269.

4 Duchacek, Ivo. "Perforated Sovereignties: Towards a Typology of New Actors in International Relations", *Federalism and International Relations: The Role of Subnational Units* 1, No. 2 (1990); Cornago, Noe. "Paradiplomacy as International Custom: Sub-national Government and the Making of New Global Norms", *Global Norms for the Twenty-First Century*, Vol. 67, No. 81, pp. 67–81. Cambridge Scholars Publishing in association with GSE Research, 2006.

5 Wang, Jian. "Localising Public Diplomacy: The role of Sub-national Actors in Nation Branding", *Place Branding* 2, No. 1 (2006): 32–42.

6 Sevin, Efe. "A Multilayered Approach to Public Diplomacy Evaluation: Pathways of Connection", *Politics & Policy* 45, No. 5 (2017): 879–901; Cornago, Noe. "Paradiplomacy as International Custom: Sub-national Government and the Making of New Global Norms", *Global Norms for the Twenty-First Century*, Vol. 67, No. 81, pp. 67–81. Cambridge Scholars Publishing in association with GSE Research, 2006.

not necessarily challenge sovereign principles and could receive support from a wider range of International Relation scholars. Bull, for instance, describes the social trait underpinning the anarchy system as associated with human intercourse that can be traced back long before sovereign norms[7], which fortifies Keohane and Nye's proposition for 'thick' participation involving interactive units that densely cover multiple layers of information and resource flows[8]. The sensitivity of the topic also accounts for the necessity to address legitimacies. Within the perspectives of security maintenance and conflict management, for instance the role of subcentral constituents could ignite more debates on the sovereign jurisdictions than state-level humanitarian operations and clearly more variations on enforcing procedures[9].

In general, as long as the anarchy system composed of sovereigns, instead of other primary actors, is here to stay, researchers would have to explain how their accommodation of non-sovereign actants from both sides into direct diplomacies will not receive resistance from states that are highly sensitive to unalienable exclusive jurisdiction, let alone de jure points calling into question their rationales. The key is how they process the discourse of legitimisation arguments, which inevitably affects the narrations, signals and commensurate reactions received from cross-border counterparts. We review the intellectual trajectories of debates between conventional non-intervention principles and the 'revisions' of sovereignty in post-Cold War periods based on 'responsibility to protect' along with multiple versions of interventionism rationales, as legal bases for multilayered diplomatic engagements. We will explain why interventionism or humanitarianism-based legitimisation arguments for multilayered diplomacy implementation might not be optimal in regions with higher sovereign sensitivity for hosting transterritorial connections, and provide criteria

7 Bull, Hedley. *The Anarchical Society: A Study of Order in World Politics*. Macmillan International Higher Education, 2012.

8 Nye Jr, Joseph S. "Public Diplomacy and Soft Power", *The Annals of the American Academy of Political and Social Science* 616, No. 1 (2008): 94–109.; Keohane, Robert O., and Joseph S. Nye Jr. "Power and Interdependence in the Information Age", *Foreign Affairs* 77 (1998): 81.

9 Sizoo, Alexandra, and Arne Musch. "City Diplomacy, the Role of Local Governments in Conflict Prevention, Peace-Building and Post-Conflict Reconstruction", *W: City Diplomacy. Red. A. Musch, Ch. van der Valk, A. Sizoo, K. Tajbakhsh. VNG International, The Hague* (2008); Bush, Kenneth. "The Peace-Building Role of Local Governments", *City Diplomacy: The Role of Local Governments in Conflict Prevention, Peace-Building, and Post-Conflict Reconstruction* (2008): 105–122.

to preliminarily evaluate that sensitivity as a part of locality in the following chapters of this chapter.

Taking Issue with Sovereignty?

Firstly, the conventional principles of exclusionist territorial jurisdiction for undertaking transborder engagements is neither historically coherent nor practically bearable and at least not sustainable in the strictest terms. The Westphalian/Vattelian concept of sovereign conceives of two primary theorems as self-evident: the first one is the unicentric trait of jurisdiction authority within the domain[10], and the second one is de jure immunity from foreign intervention and self-restraint from intervening in another sovereign's exclusive territorial jurisdictions[11]. The specific definitions vary from loose to strict. Narrations under international legal perspectives, for instance conceptualise 'constitutional insularity', which leaves the door open for flexibility of the principles to be enhanced by new norms[12]. However, one common corollary in foreign practice is the threshold for actors justified as entitled actors of international society, an identity limited to sovereign authorities with acknowledgments from counterparts or intergovernmental organisations[13]. To enlarge transnational roles for substate agents and entitle their interactions as diplomatically legitimate, the corollary of exclusive sovereignty would have to be loosened. Firstly, enabling non-central constituents of multiple levels to delegate or manage engagements with external political bodies, regardless of whether they are appropriate counterparts, might

10 Philpott, Daniel. "Sovereignty: An Introduction and Brief History", *Journal of international affairs* (1995): 353; Prokhovnik, Raia. "Hobbes, Sovereignty, and Politics: Rethinking International Political Space". In *International Political Theory after Hobbes*, pp. 189–212. Palgrave Macmillan, London, 2010.

11 Suganami, Hidemi. "Understanding Sovereignty through Kelsen/Schmitt", *Review of International Studies* 33, No. 3 (2007): 511; Biersteker, Thomas J., and Cynthia Weber, eds. *State Sovereignty as Social Construct*. Vol. 46. Cambridge University Press, 1996, 121; Krasner, Stephen D. *Sovereignty: Organized Hypocrisy*. Princeton University Press, 1999.

12 James, Alan. "Sovereignty: Ground Rule or Gibberish?", *Review of International Studies* 10, No. 1 (1984): 1–18; Suganami, Hidemi. "Understanding Sovereignty through Kelsen/Schmitt", *Review of International Studies* 33, No. 3 (2007): 511–530.

13 Martin, Stevie. "Sovereignty and the Responsibility to Protect: Mutually Exclusive or Codependent?", *Griffith Law Review* 20, No. 1 (2011): 153–187; Sarkees, Meredith Reid, and Frank Whelon Wayman. *Resort to War: A Data Guide to Inter-state, Extra-state, Intra-state, and Non-state Wars, 1816–2007*. Cq Pr, 2010, 18.

risk dispersing unicentric domestic jurisdictions, rendering other international actors to doubt the accountabilities of not only the substate agents, but also that sovereign state itself. Secondly, the recipient states might find it perplexing to correspond with multilayered diplomacy interactions while preserving their own sovereignty. When a foreign body engages a substate constituent directly, the non-intervention principle is called into question. When a non-sovereign actor seeks to be hosted by the sovereign itself, the interaction is non-reciprocal. Thirdly, when actants have reached a relationship parallel with conventional diplomacy, or 'protodiplomacy'[14], accompanied with unstable domestic constraints from central authorities to substate actants, the process of empowerment could be sensitive as the endeavours could be seen as autonomy-seeking or separatism-provoking[15]. In either respect, integral sovereignty is theoretically challenged. Luckily for multilayered diplomacy theorists, the contingency of the sovereignty norm is seldom free from these kinds of challenges.

As Glanville[16], Biersteker[17] and Adelman[18] pointed out, popular understandings of 'non-intervention' principles do not necessitate permanent values or rights of immunity from interventions under all circumstances. On the contrary, it is a candidly and socially constructed mentality. The 'impregnable' integrity of self-autonomous and unicentric sovereigns is a neoteric imagination that emerged shortly after the early emergences of Westphalian actors, was gradually enhanced during periods of conventional great power balancing and concerts of Europe and finally stabilised in its current shape, with legally binding endorsements, up until the period of the Cold War[19]. The progress of sovereign conceptualisation is based on remarkable resilience for regime changes and accommodating

---

14 Cornago, Noé. "On the Normalization of Sub-state Diplomacy", *The Hague Journal of Diplomacy* 5, No. 1–2 (2010): 31.

15 Wolff, Stefan. "Paradiplomacy: Scope, Opportunities and Challenges", *The Bologna Center Journal of International Affairs* 10, No. 1 (2007): 141–150; Cornago, N., 2013. *Plural Diplomacies: Normative Predicaments and Functional Imperatives*. Martinus Nijhoff Publishers, 125.

16 Glanville, Luke. "The Myth of 'Traditional' Sovereignty", *International Studies Quarterly* 57, No. 1 (2013): 87; Glanville, Luke. *Sovereignty and the Responsibility to Protect: A New History*. University of Chicago Press, 2013, 60.

17 Biersteker, Thomas J., and Cynthia Weber, eds. *State Sovereignty as Social Construct*. Vol. 46. Cambridge University Press, 1996.

18 Adelman, Jeremy. *Sovereignty and Revolution in the Iberian Atlantic*. Princeton University Press, 2009, 344.

19 Krasner, Stephen D. "Abiding Sovereignty", *International Political Science Review* 22, No. 3 (2001): 248.

major power desires, as well as downplaying discussions on the limitations or conditionalities of insular sovereignty[20]. As the revival of justified intervention and legal-based examinations on sovereign responsibility performances in the post–Cold War period shows, the enlargement of diplomatic engagers might be a milder departure and prudent revision.

Social constructivism approaches for norm evolutions of sovereignty also provide matured models for the insertion process of new diplomatic discourses into ongoing agendas. The pragmatism theory of norm alteration, as Schmidt noticed, allows actors to continuously deliberate and reflect[21] their customised patterns of behaviour according to environmental *stimuli*. Incidents that ignite sufficient willingness to enlarge interaction channels, such as a foreign investment opportunity that satisfies regional development layouts[22], a participation opportunity in a United Nations (UN) or North Atlantic Treaty Organisation (NATO) initiative in the neighbourhood[23] or novel frameworks providing valuable public goods like EGTC or UNACLA[24], could have environmental and systematical consequences in urging political elites to reassess topics of de-territorialisation and 'glocalisation' against their traditional perceptions of state interests and a sovereign's '*le domaine réservé*'. This essential step of adaptation composes the central mechanisms of major theories on multilayered diplomacy formation, including Cornago's four dimension rationales on the normalisation of sub-state diplomacy[25] and Gilboa's framework on analysing multidisciplinary public

---

20 Jahn, Beate. "Kant, Mill, and Illiberal Legacies in International Affairs", *International Organization* 59, No. 1 (2005): 177; Havercroft, Jonathan. "Was Westphalia 'All That'? Hobbes, Bellarmine, and the Norm of Non-intervention", *Global Constitutionalism* 1, No. 1 (2012): 120–140.

21 Schmidt, Sebastian. "Foreign Military Presence and the Changing Practice of Sovereignty: A Pragmatist Explanation of Norm Change", *American Political Science Review* 108, No. 4 (2014): 820.

22 Soong, Jenn-Jaw. "The Political Economy of the GMS Development between China and Southeast Asian Countries: Geo-economy and Strategy Nexus", *The Chinese Economy* 49, No. 6 (2016): 442–455.

23 Ruffert, Matthias. "The Administration of Kosovo and East-Timor by the International Community", *International & Comparative Law Quarterly* 50, No. 3 (2001): 613–631; O'Connell, Mary Ellen. "Continuing Limits on UN Intervention in Civil War", *Indiana Law Journal* 67 (1991): 903.

24 European Grouping of Territorial Cooperation, UN Advisory Committee of Local Authorities.

25 Cornago, Noé. "On the Normalization of Sub-state Diplomacy", *The Hague Journal of Diplomacy* 5, No. 1–2 (2010): 11.

diplomacy[26]. Aside from habitual adaptation, however, both theories also relied considerably on regionalisation aspects that distinguish socialisation levels and contexts of norm construction, which we will address in subsequent chapters.

Natural Human Rights and 'Responsibility to Protect': A Feasible Legitimisation?

Aside from the social constructive natures of unicentric sovereign norms and epidemiological barriers relating to entitling subnation actors as transborder actants, the legitimacy debates for multilayered diplomacy remained within the de jure trajectory concentrated on transnational legal personalities and conditionalities of 'non-intervention' principles. Despite the significant divergence between the justifiability of intervention and the legal basis of multilayered diplomacy in logic, scholars with progressive notions of substate diplomatic agents, including Duchacek and Kincaid[27], still resorted to the conventional sovereign debates, especially the interventionism topics, to demonstrate the comprehensiveness of diplomatic interactions among substate actors as well as the inevitability for them to be integrated into the current network of intergovernmental cooperation and anointed with legal status commensurate with their contributions.

Three sets of logic served as pillars for interventionism arguments for the legitimacy of multilayered diplomacy. The first one relates to sovereign responsibility arguments[28], requiring the sovereign's rights and intervention-free privileges

---

26 Gilboa, Eytan. "Searching for a Theory of Public Diplomacy", *The Annals of the American Academy of Political and Social Science* 616, No. 1 (2008): 55–77.

27 Duchacek, Ivo D., Latouche, Daniel, and Garth, Stevenson. *Perforated Sovereignties and International Relations: Trans-Sovereign Contacts of Subnational Governments*. No. 211. Greenwood Pub Group, 1988; Duchacek, Ivo D. "The International Dimension of Subnational Self-government", *Publius: the Journal of Federalism* 14, No. 4 (1984): 5; Kincaid, John and Soldatos, Panayotis. "Constituent Diplomacy in Federal Polities and the Nation-State: Conflict and Cooperation", *Federalism and International Relations. The Role of Subnational Units* (1990): 54–75.

28 Scheffer, David J. "Toward a Modern Doctrine of Humanitarian Intervention", *University of Toledo Law Review* 23 (1991): 253; Chopra, Jarat, and Weiss, Thomas G. "Sovereignty Is No Longer Sacrosanct: Codifying Humanitarian Intervention", *Ethics & International Affairs* 6 (1992): 95; Glanville, Luke. "The Myth of "Traditional" Sovereignty", *International Studies Quarterly* 57, No. 1 (2013): 86; Goldman, Steven E. "A Right of Intervention Based upon Impaired Sovereignty", *World Affairs* 156, No. 3 (1994): 124–129.

to be contingent on sovereign performances in satisfying the 'responsibility to protect', a principle endorsed by the UN summit of 2005[29] and followed by affirmations and institutional constructions[30]. Responsibility criteria do not only provide conditionality for unicentric jurisdictions (which does not necessitate the enlargement of diplomatic agents) but also, more importantly, prioritise the utilitarian effects of regional/global governance qualities. This rationale enabled scholars to internationalise local administrative responsibilities and build trans-border cooperation directly upon human development narrations[31], the target of protection responsibility ratified by the UN's General Assembly. The second source is the universality and priority of human rights, a progressive liberal argument supported by the Universal Declaration of Human Rights[32], which solidly underpins the 'responsibility to protect' declaration. It enabled a human-centric

29 United Nations 2005 World Summit, *Resolution adopted by the General Assembly on 16 September 2005*: paragraphs 138 and 139; Bellamy, Alex J. "Whither the Responsibility to Protect? Humanitarian Intervention and the 2005 World Summit", *Ethics & International Affairs* 20, No. 2 (2006): 143–169.

30 *2005 World Summit Outcome Summary* (retrieved from https://www.state.gov/documents/organization /74063.pdf), UNITED NATIONS 2005 World Summit, *Resolution adopted by the General Assembly on 16 September 2005*; Bellamy, Alex J. "The Responsibility to Protect and the Problem of Military Intervention", *International Affairs* 84, No. 4 (2008): 615–639.

31 Papisca, Antonio. "Relevance of Human Rights in the Glocal Space of Politics: How to Enlarge Democratic Practice beyond State Boundaries and Build up a Peaceful World Order?", *The Local Relevance of Human Rights* (2011); Sizoo, Alexandra, and Much, Arne. "City Diplomacy, the Role of Local Governments in Conflict Prevention, Peace-Building and Post-conflict Reconstruction", *W: City Diplomacy. Red. A. Musch, Ch. van der Valk, A. Sizoo, K. Tajbakhsh. VNG International, The Hague* (2008); Black, David R., MacLean, Sandra J., and Shaw, Timothy M. "Introduction: A Decade of Human Security: What Prospects for Global Governance and New Multilateralisms?". In *A Decade of Human Security*, pp. 19–34. Routledge, 2016.

32 Assembly, UN General. "Universal Declaration of Human Rights", *UN General Assembly* (1948); Hannum, Hurst. "The Status of the Universal Declaration of Human Rights in National and International Law", *Georgia Journal of International & Comparative Law* 25 (1995): 287; Papisca, Antonio. "International Law and Human Rights as a Legal Basis for the International Involvement of Local Governments", *City Diplomacy: The Role of Local Governments in Conflict Prevention, Peace-Building, Post-Conflict Reconstruction* (2008): 18; Buergenthal, Thomas, Shelton, Dinah L., and Stewart, David P. "International Human Rights in a Nutshell", *Thomas Buergenthal, Dinah Shelton & David P. Stewart, International Human Rights in a Nutshell 4th* (2009): 2013–34.

view of international interactions with alienable rights, as a systematic property, for all individual members to maximise their humanitarian welfare through all levels of de-territorialised platforms, including diversified urban partnerships and social transformation programmes[33]. The argument assumes nation states as instrumental entities derived from the responsibilities of protecting inherited human rights to peace and development, which could be readily substituted by alternative instruments according to relative performance. A third source for justifying substate governments' diplomatic engagements is their potential 'legal personalities', vaguely proposed by current international law developments through the International Court of Justice's frameworks. However, the enlarged scope of legal subjects could be the most approachable and practical avenue for progress for involving substate agents in broader enterprises of transfrontier collaborations in the short term.

The foresight values inherited in the liberal *Zeitgeist* is admittedly immeasurable. However, in practical terms, the current legal basis of multilayered diplomacy may not serve optimally in legitimising engagement endeavours between substate constituents due to our feasibility concerns. Firstly, aside from straightforward interventionism, intergovernmental coordination does not teleologically hamper the primary roles of sovereign units on international stages nor the subjective goals of maximising the utilities of their affiliated nation states, regardless of the domestic regimes. The 'responsibility to protect' rationale provoked a contradiction of unnecessary tensions between municipal or provincial connectivity with transborder counterparts and the conventional diplomacy on central levels. From classical cases of substate actants assisting third world counterparts[34], substate actants in delegating negotiations for treaty frameworks and implementing international provisions[35] and substate diplomacies in peace

---

33 Papisca, Antonio. "International Law and Human Rights as a Legal Basis for the International Involvement of Local Governments", *City Diplomacy: The Role of Local Governments in Conflict Prevention, Peace-Building, Post-Conflict Reconstruction* (2008).

34 Wyn Jones, Richard, and Royles, Elin. "Wales in the World: Intergovernmental Relations and Sub-state Diplomacy", *The British Journal of Politics and International Relations* 14, No. 2 (2012): 250; Alexander, Colin. "Sub-state Public Diplomacy in Africa: The Case of the Scottish Government's Engagement with Malawi", *Place Branding and Public Diplomacy* 10, No. 1 (2014): 70.

35 Paquin, Stéphane. "Federalism and Compliance with International Agreements: Belgium and Canada Compared", In *Regional Sub-State Diplomacy Today*, p. 183. Brill Nijhoff, 2010; Schiavon, Jorge A. "Sub-state Diplomacy in Mexico", *Regional Sub-State Diplomacy Today*, pp. 65–97. Brill Nijhoff, 2010; McMillan, Samuel. *The Involvement of State Governments in US Foreign Relations*. Springer, 2012: 187.

maintenance[36] and promoting transnational economic connectivities[37], we observed multilayered engagements that are highly susceptible to sovereign relationships and unicentric processes, with the deliberate sense of central-local coordination. 'Paradiplomacy', on the other hand, expressed a more theoretical scenario than actualised parallelness between regional and central levels of diplomacy[38].

In general, we do not expect a legal status that is comprehensively commensurate with sovereign states to be entitled to subnation governments as a prerequisite or foundation for legitimising multilayered diplomacy. Interventionism-based approaches actually burdened these moderate diplomatic attempts with tightened legal conventions and human rights–oriented stage settings, which reduced the flexibility of undertaking plural policy missions. Also, the multilayered diplomacy exercises scatter under highly diversified regionality. For international systems with less institutional assets and transborder interdependence from metropolis to community levels, the European experiences, which have been widely cited and employed[39], might not work.

Contextualizing Multilayered Diplomacy: Regionality and Sovereign Sensitivities in OBOR

The challenges for sovereign authorities of host states must be contained not only for reasons of theoretical prudence but also for practical reasons unique to the Eurasia and Indo-Pacific regions. Before classifying engagement conditions

---

36 Schiavon, Jorge A. "Sub-state Diplomacy in Mexico". In *Regional Sub-State Diplomacy Today*, p. 65. Brill Nijhoff, 2010; Bush, Kenneth. "The Peace-Building Role of Local Governments", *City Diplomacy: The Role of Local Governments in Conflict Prevention, Peace-Building, and Post-Conflict Reconstruction* (2008): 105.

37 Daksueva, Olga, and Juo-yu Lin, Joyce. "The Role of Provinces in Decision-Making Processes in China: The Case of Hainan Province". In *Enterprises, Localities, People, and Policy in the South China Sea*, pp. 77–96. Palgrave Macmillan, Cham, 2018; Paquin, Stéphane. "Federalism and the Governance of International Trade Negotiations in Canada: Comparing CUSFTA with CETA", *International Journal* 68, No. 4 (2013): 545.

38 Lecours, André, and Moreno, Luis. "Paradiplomacy: A Nation-Building Strategy? A Reference to the Basque Country", *The Conditions of Diversity in Multinational Democracies* (2003): 267.

39 Papisca, Antonio. "International Law and Human Rights as a Legal Basis for the International Involvement of Local Governments", *City Diplomacy: The Role of Local Governments in Conflict Prevention, Peace-Building, Post-Conflict Reconstruction* (2008): 43.

against regionality traits, we first explain why multilayered diplomacy specified for the OBOR initiative might entail an alternative source of legitimacy, how we identify the source from a wide choice of established policy pools and why it is differentiated from the unfeasible legal basis that we rejected. Critically reflecting on theoretical facilities from the point of view of pragmatic standards, we supplement de facto constitutional competency as a supportive source for legitimising substate governments in approaching each other under low socialisation contexts where information and mutual confidence are less stable across sovereign borders.

Regionality and Multilayered Diplomacy

The de-territorialisation objective of multilayered transborder interactions is frequently encountered with endogenous regionality. Regional contexts set fundamental institutional environments, subsystem interrelationships and interaction cultures for substate actors, which play key roles in multilayered diplomacy theories throughout their intellectual trajectories. For instance, Alagappa's layout for how sovereign-centred, regionalism-motivated and restrained instrumental transborder cooperation could provid a pioneering framework for reserved polylateralism participation[40], which is inherited by latter theories on substate diplomacy. Cornago's model incorporated regional integration schemes based on domestic bargains as the key variable differentiating the substate diplomacy performances across the EU, the North American Free Trade Agreement (NAFTA) trilateral relationships, the community cultivations of the Mercado Común del Sur (Mercosur, or Common Market of the South) market bloc and the integration of the post-Soviet space into the Asian-Pacific rim. These clashes of plural institutional backgrounds differentiated the feasible extent to which substate actants are empowered and drawn into multilateral interactions[41]. Nevertheless, the normalisation model predicts less about the outcomes of intercourse between substate actants with variant regionalities, such as the Japanese prefectures and Russian autonomous republics, which limited the regionality rationale to a domestic-determinate one. Criekemans[42],

40 Alagappa, Muthiah. "Regionalism and Conflict Management: A Framework for Analysis", *Review of International Studies* 21, No. 4 (1995): 359–387.

41 Cornago, Noé. "On the Normalization of Sub-state Diplomacy", *The Hague Journal of Diplomacy* 5, No. 1–2 (2010): 25.

42 Criekemans, David. "Regional Sub-state Diplomacy from a Comparative Perspective: Quebec, Scotland, Bavaria, Catalonia, Wallonia and Flanders". In *Regional Sub-State Diplomacy Today*, pp. 37. Brill Nijhoff, 2010; Criekemans, David. "The

Royles[43], Paquin[44] and Bursens[45] went on to account for state-centric regionality in different aspects, but due to the case-oriented tradition in this field, as Cornago and Royles admitted, the empirical coverage on multilayered diplomatic regionality exhibits path dependence in relation to regions with high-performance profile and favourable regimes, which limited the commonalities of frameworks. The networking approach adopted by Taylor[46] and Acuto[47] might yield higher explanatory power as an alternative paradigm for contextualising multilayered diplomatic engagements in subsystems, but the case concentration still has a limited coverage. In general, the polylateralist nature of multilayered diplomacy renders its outcomes sensitive to the suitability of the regional environment.

We accept regionality, following the approach suggested by Mansfield and Lauridsen[48], as based on politically constructed properties, including macro political mentalities and self-identified subsystems with a characteristic set of norms and interactional patterns. However, the objective respects of regionality have remained prominent since state and substate actors' affiliation to multidimensional international subsystems are equally stable, especially to the regional economic networks that their domestic prosperities are based on[49]. The case

---

Geopolitics of Renewable Energy: Different or Similar to the Geopolitics of Conventional Energy". In *ISA Annual Convention*, pp. 16–19. 2011.

43 Royles, Elin. "Substate Diplomacy, Culture, and Wales: Investigating a Historical Institutionalist Approach", *Publius: The Journal of Federalism* 46, No. 2 (2016): 247.

44 Paquin, Stéphane. "Federalism and Compliance with International Agreements: Belgium and Canada Compared". In *Regional Sub-State Diplomacy Today*, p. 177. Brill Nijhoff, 2010.

45 Bursens, Peter, and Deforche, Jana. "Going beyond Paradiplomacy? Adding Historical Institutionalism to Account for Regional Foreign Policy Competences". In *Regional Sub-State Diplomacy Today*, pp. 151–171. Brill Nijhoff, 2010.

46 Taylor, Peter J. "New Political Geographies: Global Civil Society and Global Governance through World City Networks", *Political Geography* 24, No. 6 (2005): 703–730.

47 Acuto, Michele. *Global Cities, Governance and Diplomacy: The Urban Link*, p. 171. Routledge, Abingdon, Oxon; New York, 2013.

48 Mansfield, Edward D., and Solingen, Etel. "Regionalism", *Annual Review of Political Science* 13 (2010): 145; Lauridsen, Laurids S. "Changing Regional Order and Railway Diplomacy in Southeast Asia with a Case Study of Thailand". In *Mapping China's 'One Belt One Road' Initiative*, p. 221. Palgrave Macmillan, Cham, 2019.

49 Ruggie, John Gerard. "International Regimes, Transactions, and Change: Embedded Liberalism in the Postwar Economic Order", *International Organization* 36, No. 2 (1982): 379.

might be more noteworthy in the Asian-Pacific region given the historical link[50] between intrinsically political agendas of regional governance cooperation and capital/industrial market integrations, especially for south east Asian developing economies simultaneously embracing unilateral trade liberalisation and mercantilist causes for developmentalist motivations. Aside from the dynamics between domestic coalitions representing different trade sectors, as Jayasuriya mentioned, the frequent cohesion of political and economical integration agendas elicit more intricacy in relation to regional conditions of multilayered diplomacy[51], some of which might cause both motivations and restraints for unilateral enlargement of agent access to diplomatic engagements.

As Wesley[52] pointed out, competitive aspects are deeply embedded in the regionality of east Asia. As China's thrifty regional economical influence expands in the form of regional infrastructure investment cooperation, host states who self-identified as minor subsystem members receive simultaneously increased motivations to introduce alternative partners into the negotiation process and to maintain a sustainable freedom of choice. Lauridsen[53] added that host states deliberate on the choice of a potential 'balancer' to minimise the regional rivalry and to maximise native manoeuverability over investment and political agendas. The competition aspect of regionality is not limited to project levels such as high-speed railways in Thailand, economic corridors across Pakistan[54] and container ports in Singapore[55], but also influences configurated systematic level tensions between organisations. The OBOR initiative and the Asian Infrastructure Investment Bank received negative evaluations from leading states of the Association of South East Asian Nations (ASEAN) as revisioning regional

---

50 Jayasuriya, Kanishka. "Embedded Mercantilism and Open Regionalism: The Crisis of a Regional Political Project", *Third World Quarterly* 24, No. 2 (2003): 339.

51 Breslin, Shaun. "Comparative Theory, China, and the Future of East Asian Regionalism (s)", *Review of International Studies* 36, No. 3 (2010): 709.

52 Wesley, Michael. "Trade Agreements and Strategic Rivalry in Asia", *Australian Journal of International Affairs* 69, No. 5 (2015): 480.

53 Lauridsen, Laurids S. "Changing Regional Order and Railway Diplomacy in Southeast Asia with a Case Study of Thailand". In *Mapping China's 'One Belt One Road'Initiative*, p. 224. Palgrave Macmillan, Cham, 2019.

54 Shamsi, Syed Shahbaz, Umbreen Javaid, Pirzada Sami Ullah Sabri, Muhammad Ilyas, and Iffat Batool. "Compulsions of Sino-Pakistani Strategic Engagement in lieu of Security Constraints Engendered by the Anarchistic International Political System", *South Asian Studies* 29, No. 2 (2014): 597.

55 Lim, Alvin Cheng Hin. "China's "Belt and Road" and Southeast Asia: Challenges and Prospects", *JATI-Journal of Southeast Asian Studies* 20 (2015): 3–15.

orders[56]. Given the existing resistance to unilateral integration efforts, the introduction of multilayered diplomacy accompanied by the same set of initiatives could elicit unexpected dynamics considering the theoretical fractions between substate diplomatic channels and non-intervention sovereign norms that we have mentioned. Despite their reserved anticipations for functional utilities of multilayered diplomacy in promoting regional governance, scholars generally tend to underestimate host state anxiety. For instance, Cornago's model actually acclaims China's provincial international engagements as an effective innovation for bypassing diplomatic isolation and encirclement after 1989 and 1996, while simultaneously facilitating economic outward transformations[57]. Other comments on recent exercises of China's regional multilayered engagements along the OBOR areas of coverage treated substate actors as 'complexing'[58] in terms of tractability and 'domestic-driven' tools in terms of constituent level economic cooperation[59]. The acceptance positivity and geopolitical concerns from host states, nevertheless, have not been considered as a major hindrance for regional networking expansion or relationship facilitation[60] as major power competitions.

---

56 Yeoh, Kok-Kheng Emile. "Forward China: Foreign Relations and Maritime Conflict", *International Journal of China Studies* 2, No. 3 (2011): 551–553; Yu, Hong. "Motivation behind China's 'One Belt, One Road' Initiatives and Establishment of the Asian Infrastructure Investment Bank", *Journal of Contemporary China* 26, No. 105 (2017): 364.

57 Wei, Y. I. N. "The Role of Chinese State-Owned Investors and OBOR-Related Investments in Europe: The Implication of the China-EUBIT". In *The Belt and Road Initiative*, pp. 284–314. Brill Nijhoff, 2018; Cornago, Noé. "On the Normalization of Sub-state Diplomacy", *The Hague Journal of Diplomacy* 5, No. 1–2 (2010): 24.

58 Zhimin, Chen, and Jian Junbo. "Chinese Provinces as Foreign Policy Actors in Africa", *South African Institute of International Affairs (SAIIA)* (2009): 24.

59 Szczudlik-Tatar, Justyna. "China's New Silk Road Diplomacy", *Policy Paper* 34, No. 82 (2013): 4; Summers, Tim. "China's 'New Silk Roads': Sub-national Regions and Networks of Global Political Economy", *Third World Quarterly* 37, No. 9 (2016): 1628–1643.

60 Sternberg, Troy, Ahearn, Ariell, and McConnell, Fiona. "Central Asian 'Characteristics' on China's new Silk Road: The Role of Landscape and the Politics of Infrastructure", *Land* 6, No. 3 (2017): 55; Summers, Tim. "China's 'New Silk Roads': Sub-national Regions and Networks of Global Political Economy", *Third World Quarterly* 37, No. 9 (2016): 1628–1643; de Haan, Arjan, and Warmerdam, Ward. "New Donors and Old Practices: The Role of China in the Multilateral System". In *Multilateral Development Cooperation in a Changing Global Order*, p. 30. Palgrave Macmillan, London, 2013.

The regionally generated resistance for substate diplomatic contacts initiated by subsystem unipole or great powers, especially accompanied by overlapping economic and political integration agendas, might bring the theoretically unsolved legitimacy concerns of multilayered diplomacy into tension in practice. To clarify from other aspects of risk evaluation in the OBOR initiative or in non-state involvement in diplomacy, we identify this certain trait of regionality as 'sovereign sensitivity'. Deriving from similar sources of resistance in conventional agendas, this sensitivity also reflects suspicions about China's power projection motivations and Sino-centric sphere perception[61] behind infrastructure-aiding programmes and connectivity programmes for facilities, whilst this is further intensified by sovereign concerns associated with potentially stricter inspections toward the agents and forms of diplomatic engagement attempts in large volumes.

The Prioritisation of Sovereign Sensitivities

As a holistic concept that extends Chinese President Xi Jinping's comprehensive governance philosophy to the international level, the target-based risk evaluation of the Belt and Road Initiative (BRI) accordingly requires gross detections to nuances motivations of resistance. The salient reliance on provincial investment outputs and substate units, including state owned enterprises (SOEs) at central and provincial levels[62], to undertake project implementations also requires feasibility assessments for their foreign engagement with related constituents to provide flexible reaches accordant with their functions in BRI. Prudent accommodation of host states' sovereign geopolitical concerns has occupied a valued position in policy discourse and implementation of the initiative, even towards the targeted regions with stable security environments and diplomatic accountabilities in the legal provisions. As Shao[63],

61 Pop, Irina Ionela. "Strengths and Challenges of China's 'One Belt, One Road' Initiative", *Centre for Geopolitics and Security in Realism Studies* (2016); Yu, Hong. "Motivation behind China's 'One Belt, One Road' Initiatives and Establishment of the Asian Infrastructure Investment Bank", *Journal of Contemporary China* 26, No. 105 (2017): 363.

62 Johnson, Christopher K. "President Xi Jinping's 'Belt and Road Initiative' ", *Center for Strategic and International Studies* 2 (2016): 21.

63 Shao, Zeng-Zhen, Zu-Jun Ma, Jiuh-Biing Sheu, and Gao, H. Oliver. "Evaluation of Large-Scale Transnational High-Speed Railway Construction Priority in the Belt and Road Region", *Transportation Research Part E: Logistics and Transportation Review* 117 (2018): 45.

Rolland[64], He and Starostin[65] observed, despite the broad nominal coverage and open acceptance of BRI, the planned infrastructure projects along six major corridors underpinning the OBOR initiative showed geographical selectivity in terms of security conditions and stable diplomatic approachability to China. The high-speed railway network layouts, for instance, clearly reflect not only economic efficiency optimisation but also relational stabilities. However, regarding multilayered diplomatic engagements accompanied by the BRI, the risk assessment frameworks could not be theoretically completed without accounting for sovereign sensitivities. This aspect of regionality works as a conditional variable for each dyad of substate actants' connectivity and inevitably limits the quality and sustainability of multilateral cooperation. The conventional assessments of regional security and stability performance could hardly substitute for the effects of reserved sovereign sensitivity, which frequently varies across engagement targets in substate diplomacy and more markedly depend on the realities of bilateral relationships. However, we believe that certain commonalities exist among the patterns of sovereign sensitivities in OBOR regions towards China-initiated substate diplomacy.

Conventional literature on the risks and feasibilities of multilayered diplomacy have proposed very limited theorisation about the practical constraints of sovereign sensitivities. We believe that this partly results from the conventional interventionism rationale of legitimising substate actors' diplomatic access and partly due to the lack of frameworks for intergovernmental interactions above unit-level competence or domestic empowerment analysis[66]. However, in practice, sovereign sensitive concerns might take prior position relative to other dimensions of substate foreign relations, especially for the recipient constituents constrained by their central superiors.

Contrary to the expectations of constituent autonomy from paradiplomacy theories[67], expanding actor access to diplomatic connections necessitates the

---

64 Rolland, Nadège. "China's 'Belt and Road Initiative': Underwhelming or Game-Changer?", *The Washington Quarterly* 40, No. 1 (2017): 136.

65 He, Huang, and Starostin, N. "Political Risks and Controls of Oversea Investment by Chinese Enterprises: Based on the Countries along 'One Belt and One Road' ", *Journal of Shenzhen University (Humanities & Social Sciences)* 33, No. 1 (2016): 93–100.

66 Royles, Elin. "Substate Diplomacy, Culture, and Wales: Investigating a Historical Institutionalist Approach", *Publius: The Journal of Federalism* 46, No. 2 (2016): 228; Kincaid, John. "Foreign Relations of Sub-national Units", *Federalism in a Changing World: Learning from Each Other* (2003): 75.

67 Wolff, Stefan. "Paradiplomacy: Scope, Opportunities and Challenges", *The Bologna Center Journal of International Affairs* 10, No. 1 (2007): 142; Kuznetsov, Alexander

ratification process from the state level. The poliheuristic theories of modelling foreign policy deliberation could aptly demonstrate the superiority of sovereign considerations in regional integration, economic cooperation and attempts at reforming diplomacy norms. As Minz[68] and Simon[69] pointed out, trade-offs between multiple trajectories of policy utilities are frequently not feasible for decision-makers due to the non-compensatory natures (or principles) of policy choices. It rejects the conventional alternative-based decision model that allows interdimensional exchanges between one set of political goals and the other[70] and presume the hierarchical sequence of dimensions exogenous to the decision-making, usually determined by the domestic political process. The poliheuristic analysis is initially adapted to security studies and military decision-making[71] where the dimensional distinction is theoretically evident. The institutional negotiation and economic development topics emerged later on[72], with more diversified criteria in discriminating utility dimensions, incorporating domestic constituency groups, accountability to stakeholders and audience cost analysis into the process. The poliheuristic decision-making process still exists for atomised state actors given the multidimensional trait of state interests and foreign stakeholders. The ASEAN countries' decision-making scenario between

S. *Theory and Practice of Paradiplomacy: Subnational Governments in International Affairs*. Routledge, 2014.

68 Mintz, Alex. "The Decision to Attack Iraq: A Noncompensatory Theory of Decision Making", *Journal of Conflict Resolution* 37, No. 4 (1993): 595.

69 Simon, Herbert. "The Poliheuristic Theory of Foreign Policy Decision-Making", *Decision Making on War and Peace: The Cognitive-Rational Debate* 1 (1997): 81.

70 Redd, S.B., 2003. The Poliheuristic Theory of Foreign Policy Decision Making: Experimental Evidence. In *Integrating Cognitive and Rational Theories of Foreign Policy Decision Making* (p. 112). Palgrave Macmillan, New York.

71 Mintz, Alex. "The Decision to Attack Iraq: A Noncompensatory Theory of Decision Making", *Journal of Conflict Resolution* 37, No. 4 (1993): 595; Mintz, Alex, and Geva, Nehemia. "A Prospect-Based Analysis of War Termination", *Conflict in World Politics: Advances in the Study of Crisis, War and Peace* (1998): 288–305.

72 Simon, Herbert. "The Poliheuristic Theory of Foreign Policy Decision-Making", *Decision Making on War and Peace: The Cognitive-Rational Debate* 1 (1997): 81; Taylor-Robinson, Michelle M., and Redd, Steven B. "Framing and the Poliheuristic Theory of Decision: The United Fruit Company and the 1954 US-Led Coup in Guatemala". In *Integrating Cognitive and Rational Theories of Foreign Policy Decision Making*, pp. 77–100. Palgrave Macmillan, New York, 2003; Eisenband, Dori. "Application of the Poliheuristic Theory of Decision to the Political Negotiation Process". In *Conference on the Nexus between Domestic and International Relations, March*, Texas A&M University, College Station, TX, 2003.

infrastructure cooperation opportunities from China and Japan[73] exemplifies non-compensational relationships between utility dimensions, requiring prioritisation in political terms affiliated to investments, technique spillover and transfer potentials, bilateral trade and Foreign Direct Investment (FDI) flow along with security concerns. The poliheuristic process also influences acceptance of BRI engagements for Eurasian states such as Pakistan, Kyrgyzstan and Turkmenistan, where the great power competition for economic corridor and energy channel construction is less frequent. For instance, domestic nationalism and inclinations based on perceived Chinese ethnic dynamics occupy a policy level of Kyrgyzstan's reaction to BRI's Eurasian land bridge corridor, while the economic catalyst effects occupy the other[74]. A poliheuristic decision hinges on how further connectivity with China's regional network is politically tolerated by nationalist constituency groups. Economic realities assist the process as auxiliary factors.

Regarding multilayered diplomacy interplays, however, the complexity of utility dimensions is considerably reduced. The functional contributions of substate diplomatic actants have been proven supportive but not deterministic in contributing to (epistemological) global governance, order maintenance, humanitarian and developmental assistance or the multilateral process of municipal communications and community building. The risk related to multilayered engagement due to incomplete legitimacy and recognition of the accountability of substate actors as we mentioned is more obvious than perceived benefits. Expanding diplomatic qualifications for participants in an unbalanced subsystem without common consensus or unanimous ratifications might readily trigger the 'legitimacy weakness' of multilayered diplomacy and the sovereign sensitivity of the host state, which might significantly suppress inclination to foreign relations of the constituents, generate strategic misconceptions and misreading, in the end reducing the enforcement quality of regional negotiations and treaties. Although the conventional channels of diplomatic engagements have no prerogatives in relation to freeing themselves from certain

---

73 Yu, Hong. "Motivation behind China's 'One Belt, One Road' Initiatives and Establishment of the Asian Infrastructure Investment Bank", *Journal of Contemporary China* 26, No. 105 (2017): 365; Lauridsen, Laurids S. "Changing Regional Order and Railway Diplomacy in Southeast Asia with a Case Study of Thailand". In *Mapping China's 'One Belt One Road'Initiative*, p. 231. Palgrave Macmillan, Cham, 2019.

74 Laruelle, Marlène, and Peyrouse, Sébastien. *The Chinese Question in Central Asia: Domestic Order, Social Change, and the Chinese Factor*. Vol. 29.Columbia University Press, New York, 2012.

reservations due to sovereign concerns, especially from geopolitically subordinate recipients of regional integration plans, the precipitately launched substate actant relationships might provoke more severe anxieties of interventionism and 'imperialism' perceptions[75] despite their being accompanied by narrational or de facto egalitarian regional structures. In fact, the sovereign sensitivity-driven mentalities, as we proposed, might as well account for regionally based controversial reactions towards the expansion of inclusive infrastructure connectivity[76].

Several micro-mechanisms could exacerbate localised hostility and official dissatisfaction even in conditions where there are benign diplomatic ties at central levels. The subnationalism constituents and populists within the region might conceive localised interest preferences in a different way to central governments regarding foreign investment programmes as well as have incongruous perceptions about and sentiments towards the presence of foreign actors from substate levels. The unicentric sovereign boundaries yield protection to relatively minor states in maintaining socioeconomic independence while de-territorialisation diplomacy seeks to bypass the boundary limitations[77] and requires synchronous power devolution on both sides. In general, the attempts at multilayered diplomacy accompanied by regional integration projects might be highly liable to trigger the sovereign considerations of central and local administrators, which occupied a critical dimension of their poliheuristic considerations and cannot be fundamentally altered from economic dimensions. Failures to assess, address and accommodate such sovereign sensitivities might lead to unintended messages through substate interactions and negatively affect the transnational projects that they aim to assist.

---

75 Sidaway, James D., and Chih Yuan Woon. "Chinese Narratives on "One Belt, One Road" (一带一路) in Geopolitical and Imperial Contexts", *The Professional Geographer* 69, No. 4 (2017): 599.

76 Swaine, Michael D. "Chinese Views and Commentary on the 'One Belt, One Road' Initiative", *China Leadership Monitor* 47, No. 2 (2015): 47; Soong, Jenn-Jaw, and Khac Nghia Nguyen. "China's OBOR Initiative and Vietnam's Political Economy: Economic Integration with Political Conflict", *The Chinese Economy* 51, No. 4 (2018): 342–355; Zhu, Cuiping. "The South Asian Direction of 'OBOR' Strategy: Geopolitical Pattern, Indian Difficulties and Breakthrough Path". In *Annual Report on the Development of the Indian Ocean Region* (2017), p. 3. Springer, Singapore, 2018.

77 Papisca, Antonio. "International Law and Human Rights as a Legal Basis for the International Involvement of Local Governments", *City Diplomacy: The Role of Local Governments in Conflict Prevention, Peace-Building, Post-Conflict Reconstruction* (2008): 29.

Multilayered Diplomacy and Sovereign Sensitivity: Assessment and Accommodation

Sizoo and Musch have classified substate actants' diplomatic initiatives in stabilising missions into three levels: lobbying engagements with local publics, project implementation and dialogue promotion[78]. Corresponding with Berg and Den's theory of engagement sequences[79], multiple classifications of multi-layered diplomacy actions reflected a general theoretical understanding for the orders of policy goals. Firstly, approaching targeted regions for domestic support and strengthening inter-municipal/inter-constituency relationships assists the creation of solid legitimacy for transborder engagements so as to enable more frequent and embedded interactions. Secondly, the project enforcement phase delivers major functional objectives of the relationship. Thirdly, the establishment of channels for dialogue stabilises the outcome of collaborating projects and sustains the constructive substate relationship for future utilisation. Regionalities prone to high sovereign sensitivities, according to the theory, elevate the engagement thresholds for public acceptance and make the process of project facilitation tougher.

The region-based resistance for the BRI as an aspect of general geopolitical risk has been widely discussed. A major trajectory of risk evaluation relies on great power rivalry, including the balancing endeavours in relation to growing Chinese influence from conventional regional powers including Japan, India and maritime leading members of ASEAN[80]. The mixed reactions and attitudes toward the BRI and alternative Chinese initiations with outward postures in the economic realm, as received from Asia-Pacific countries[81], have been frequently

78 Sizoo, Alexandra, and Much, Arne. "City diplomacy, the Role of Local Governments in Conflict Prevention, Peace-Building and Post-conflict Reconstruction", *W: City Diplomacy. Red. A. Much, Ch. van der Valk, A. Sizoo, K. Tajbakhsh.* VNG International, The Hague (2008): 18.

79 Berg, Dion Van Den. "City Diplomacy Campaigns in the Netherlands: Lessons from Recent Times", *City Diplomacy: The Role of Local Governments in Conflict Prevention, Peace-Building, Post-Conflict Reconstruction*: 75.

80 Singh, Bhubhindar, Teo, Sarah, and Ho, Benjamin. "Rising Sino-Japanese Competition: Perspectives from South-East Asian Elites", *Australian Journal of International Affairs* 71, No. 1 (2017): 118; Yu, Hong. "Motivation behind China's 'One Belt, One Road' Initiatives and Establishment of the Asian Infrastructure Investment Bank", *Journal of Contemporary China* 26, No. 105 (2017): 366.

81 Emmers, Ralf, and Teo Sarah. "Regional Security Strategies of Middle Powers in the Asia-Pacific", *International Relations of the Asia-Pacific* 15, No. 2 (2014): 194; Cheng, Joseph YS, and Stephanie Paladini. "China's Ocean Development Strategy and Its

discussed within the context of regional security environment dynamics and even territorial dispute realities. Similar arguments derived from a balancing mentality also involve the fractions between south east Asian minor power's internationalist preference for multilateral stakeholder configuration in infrastructure and economic integration and the perceived unilaterally driven styles of the BRI programmes and funding. Another trajectory stresses the presence of extra-regional great powers[82] and brings the conventional dichotomy of revisionism and *status quo* rhetoric back in.

The frameworks of risk and resistance evaluation for regional integration agendas have not been formalised, and their application to the feasibility analysis of multilayered diplomacy is untested. In fact, a majority of scholars review substate diplomatic channels as ways to bypass these conventional geopolitical concerns and as alleviators for the host country's strategic suspicions and regional resistance, which is, as we discussed, neglecting localised sovereign sensitivities. Abundant empirical observations, including the case studies on Chinese provincial foreign relationships in relation to Hainan and Yunnan[83], have shown that projects driven by substate actants are more susceptible to state-level relationships and regionalities of targeted counterparts. The intergovernmental dialogues on subordinate levels occasionally encounter *débâcles* and contradictions that cannot be endogenously solved between multilayered actants. Hence, we present a feasibility and risk evaluation framework fixed on regional units and bilateral dyads of substate agents to separate the regionality assessments of multilayered diplomacy from other evaluations and factors of state-level relationships. We concluded major determinants for the sovereign sensibility environments for substate agents, which is the theoretical prerequisite for a potential policy solution of enhancing the adaptation of substate actants. Based on previous empirical approaches to the regional assimilation of

---

Handling of the Territorial Conflicts in the South China Sea", *Philippine Political Science Journal* 35, No. 2 (2014): 185.

82 Chan, Lai-Ha. "Soft Balancing against the US 'Pivot to Asia': China's Geostrategic Rationale for Establishing the Asian Infrastructure Investment Bank", *Australian Journal of International Affairs* 71, No. 6 (2017): 568.

83 Li, Mingjiang. "Local Liberalism: China's Provincial Approaches to Relations with Southeast Asia", *Journal of Contemporary China* 23, No. 86 (2014): 277; Dosch, Jörn, and Hensengerth, Oliver. "Sub-regional Cooperation in Southeast Asia: the Mekong Basin", *European Journal of East Asian Studies* 4, No. 2 (2005): 263; Junbo, Jian, Chen Zhimin, and Chen Diyu. "The Provinces and China's Multi-layered Diplomacy: The Cases of GMS and Africa", *The Hague Journal of Diplomacy* 5, No. 4 (2010): 331.

substate actors, the sources for sovereign sensitivity that they encountered could be addressed from three perspectives: power parity, symmetricity of domestic regimes and central-local vertical relationships under transregional contexts. Each of these perspectives alters the quality of lobby, project implementation and communication missions of substate actors, but the distribution of 'sensitivity' and subjective hindrance varies from engagers to precipitants according to cases.

Power Disparity and Transition Trends

The configuration of regional power distribution, we argue, is less influential than the simpler power comparison between two engagers at the state level. Lemke applied revised power transition theories of Organski to subsystem[84] and substate[85] interactions. He observed that regional power parities affect middle-level actors and subordinate political organisations in ways similar to great power rivalries and that the stable parity and parity as a process of power transcending both increase the chances of confrontation, which revised the previous accounts on balance of power dynamics by Morrow[86]. The key mechanisms under debate regarding the catalyst impacts of parity relationships, however, rely on perception and satisfaction mentalities around the systematic or regional *status quo*[87], a conceptualisation with controversial implications for policy behaviours[88]. Danilovic[89] and Benson[90] first revealed the omnipresence of the relationships between (relative) rising powers' dissatisfaction with the *status quo* and the power parities as a stage of power transition, in terms of synergistic effects on conflicts. Sample[91] further revisited multiple compositions and levels

84 Lemke, Douglas, and Werner, Suzanne. "Power Parity, Commitment to Change, and War", *International Studies Quarterly* 40, No. 2 (1996): 235.
85 Lemke, Douglas. "Power Politics and Wars without States", *American Journal of Political Science* 52, No. 4 (2008): 774–786.
86 Kim, Woosang, and Morrow, James D. "When Do Power Shifts Lead to War?", *American Journal of Political Science* (1992): 917.
87 Danilovic, Vesna, and Clare, Joe. "Global Power Transitions and Regional Interests", *International Interactions* 33, No. 3 (2007): 302.
88 Schweller, Randall L. "Neorealism's status-quo Bias: What Security Dilemma?", *Security Studies* 5, No. 3 (1996): 90.
89 Danilovic, Vesna, and Clare, Joe. "Global Power Transitions and Regional Interests", *International Interactions* 33, No. 3 (2007): 291.
90 Benson, Michelle. "Status quo Preferences and Disputes Short of War", *International Interactions* 33, No. 3 (2007): 271.
91 Sample, Susan G. "Power, Wealth, and Satisfaction: When Do Power Transitions Lead to Conflict?", *Journal of Conflict Resolution* 62, No. 9 (2018): 1905.

of *status quo* satisfactions and their conflict-promoting effects with modified operationalisation, which is applicable to parity actors of diversified power status and relative positions in the system.

Although the previous theories of power parity and conflict inclination thoroughly covered the targets from great powers to minor and non-state actors, the pictures of multilayered diplomatic interactions and the state-level power distributions involve more differentiation than power magnitudes of actors. Firstly, the satisfaction of rising power in conventional theories is more deterministic in transforming power parity, dynamic or static, to conflict. Under substate foreign relationships, the power perception and satisfaction of the recipient side, whether gaining relative growth or relative decline from the power transition process, is more sensitive to power parity and distributions at a bilateral level. Secondly, the power transition theories focus on systematic power distribution as well as dyadic power comparisons between potential conflict units. We propose that the sovereign sensitivity towards multilayered diplomacy should be analysed on the basis of dyad power parities instead of on the basis of systematic power distribution, because the theories of alliances, external balancing and multilateral interactions are far from applicable to the current levels of substate diplomacy developments. The limited empirical cases of cohesive multilateral substate actant systems were mostly from the European and north Atlantic regions[92], where the institutional environments and socialisation of interdependence norms are distinct from east Asia. Meanwhile, although relative status and hierarchies within the system matter for sovereign sensitivities, the evaluation of multilayered diplomacy in a bilateral context is more a reciprocal process concentrated on each other due to the relatively sparse opportunities and limited partners for substate governmental engagements for a given region in a given period.

Most importantly, the sovereign sensitivity and resistance for substate engagers is more readily triggered by relative decline in power and unfavourable power disparities instead of the approach relating to parity. How do the relatively minor positions at the state level produce the perception of vulnerability at the substate constituent level? Firstly, the aggravating disparity between state-level engagers

---

92 Kincaid, John. "Constituent Diplomacy in Federal Polities and the Nation-State: Conflict and Co-operation", *Federalism and International Relations: The Role of Subnational Units* (1990): 54; Criekemans, David. "Regional Sub-state Diplomacy from a Comparative Perspective: Quebec, Scotland, Bavaria, Catalonia, Wallonia and Flanders". In *Regional Sub-State Diplomacy Today*, pp. 37. Brill Nijhoff, 2010.

distinguishes their devolution potentials to subordinate constituents, causing the municipal, provincial or autonomous regional actors from each side to be placed on unequal positions in terms of regulatory leeway and administrative resources, in both material and policy versatility terms. Although the absence of security dimensions is temporarily (but not permanently[93]) outside the considerations of substate foreign relations, the gap in terms of administrative capacity and the state reach beyond general power parity is still empirically significant in affecting constituents' effectiveness[94], especially for prevalent latent-developing modes in the topic region[95]. Meanwhile, substate actants backed up with superior economic, industrial and intellectual strengths from home prefectures are more likely to be the engagers[96] while constituents based on less-developed regions are more frequently recipients. The fundamental excogitation of regional economic and infrastructure reconfiguration (or a 'spatial fix') in the BRI, on the other hand, exploits the compatibility between the distinct industrial backgrounds of China and the OBOR partners, with one side specialised on primary commodities and the other side dominating capitals, technical sectors and project supplies, especially on localised interconnection levels[97]. Hence, the disparity of

93 Kuznetsov, Alexander S. *Theory and Practice of Paradiplomacy: Subnational Governments in International Affairs*. Routledge, 2014: 78; Cornago, Noé. "Diplomacy and Paradiplomacy in the Redefinition of International Security: Dimensions of Conflict and Co-operation", *Regional & Federal Studies* 9, No. 1 (1999): 40–57.

94 Hooghe, Liesbet, and Marks, Gary. "Does Efficiency Shape the Territorial Structure of Government?", *Annual Review of Political Science* 12 (2009): 225–241; Powers, Kathy, and Goertz, Gary. "The Economic-Institutional Construction of Regions: Conceptualisation and Operationalisation", *Review of International Studies* 37, No. 5 (2011): 2387–2415.

95 Tilly, Charles. "Survey Article: Power–Top Down and Bottom Up", *Journal of Political Philosophy* 7, No. 3 (1999): 330–352; Crone, Donald K. "State, Social Elites, and Government Capacity in Southeast Asia", *World Politics* 40, No. 2 (1988): 252–268.

96 Kincaid, John. "Comparative Observations on the International Activities of Constituent Governments". In *Foreign Policy of Constituents Units at the Beginning of 21st Century*, p. 1528. Institut d'Estudis Autonòmics, 2010; Archer, Kevin, and Morici, Peter. "State Export Promotion Policies", *States and Provinces in the International Economy* (1993): 185.

97 Summers, Tim. "China's 'New Silk Roads': Sub-national Regions and Networks of Global Political Economy", *Third World Quarterly* 37, No. 9 (2016): 1628–1643; Wong, John. "A China-Centric Economic Order in East Asia", *Asia Pacific Business Review* 19, No. 2 (2013): 286–296; Ling, Jin. "The New Silk Road Initiative: China's Marshall Plan", *China International Studies* 50 (2015): 70.

complex powers might be more evident, instead of ameliorated, with regional cooperation initiated by substate actants in the BRI.

From the domestic perspectives of the recipient, singular relationships with foreign constituents on substate levels might lead the realities or perceptions for transregional inequality towards development opportunities and policy segmentation, in a context of great disparity at the state level. Unlike the policy segmentation theory of substate actants from federalist perspectives[98], the segmentation of the pace of regional development and economic integration based on unidirectionally subordinated foreign relationships, specifically with a foreign constituent with policy favours and leverages instead of Multi-national Companies (MNCs) under open market orders, might elicit reasonably severe sovereign sensitivities from central administrators and national counterparts. Meanwhile, the sovereign sensitivity in relation to the trajectory of general international political economy (IPE) realms, including the debates about economic independence and import/export substitution, should be distinguished from the localised reactions for substate actant approaches on their distinct sociopolitical levels, although two causal mechanisms have considerable overlaps in terms of regional foreign relations with great powers.

In general, we argue that power disparity and the transitional process at the state level still affects sovereign sensitivities in relation to foreign engagements and involvement in regional affairs through non-conventional diplomatic channels, and the substate actants might encounter extra sources of localised *débâcles* due to similar mechanisms. Thus, the requirement to deliberately avoid intervention impressions and seeking new rationales for the legitimacy of multilayered diplomacy is still prominent.

Symmetricity of Domestic Regimes

The term of (a)symmetricity on dyads of substate counterparts has many levels of interpretation. Kuznetsov[99] referred to the asymmetry between constituent units as disproportionate economic potentials, which we reviewed as a part of a disparity in terms of state background powers between substate engagers. Another dimension of symmetricity focuses on constitutional jurisdictions

---

98 Soldatos, Panayotis. "An Explanatory Framework for the Study of Federated States as Foreign-Policy Actors", *Federalism and International Relations: The Role of Subnational Units* (1990): 34–53.

99 Kuznetsov, Alexander S. *Theory and Practice of Paradiplomacy: Subnational Governments in International Affairs*. Routledge, 2014: 106.

and accountabilities of undertaking diplomatic endeavours, in terms of levels of negotiations, treaty provisions and commitments, which is closely related to the debate on the sources of legitimisation of substate governments as foreign negotiators throughout the domestic process[100]. Although the second rationale captures the complexity of addressing diplomatic status issues, we argue that symmetricity of domestic regimes should not be confined to the level of substate actants *per se* but confined to the structural background from which they receive empowerments and devolutions. Aside from the conventional debates regarding the feasibility of separating foreign affairs competency from alternative levels under a state-centric order of norms[101], we focus on the audience responses to substate engagers from asymmetric institutional and constitutional environments.

One might wonder, since domestic structures of prefectures and constituents are seldom consistent even among the regions sharing abundant culture, norms and historical or institutional connections[102], which together have a high profile in multilayered diplomacy, why we should consider regime diversity as a problem. It is absolutely feasible for substate actors to reach a reciprocal interaction with their inherent traits of governance and relative relationships with their central authorities. Actants with higher autonomous jurisdictions and broader diplomatic measures, such as the federal bodies of Belgium[103], could comfortably accommodate interactions with counterparts with diversified regime backgrounds or less independent policy manoeuvers. Admittedly, the substate actants have been progressively creating links and dyads among all

---

100 Wheatley, Steven. *The Democratic Legitimacy of International Law*. Bloomsbury Publishing, 2010: 311; Lecours, André. "Paradiplomacy: Reflections on the Foreign Policy and International Relations of Regions", *International Negotiation* 7, No. 1 (2002): 91–114.

101 Bernstein, Steven, and Cashore, Benjamin. "Can Non-state Global Governance Be Legitimate? An Analytical Framework", *Regulation & Governance* 1, No. 4 (2007): 352.

102 Paquin, Stéphane. "Federalism and Compliance with International Agreements: Belgium and Canada Compared". In *Regional Sub-State Diplomacy Today*, pp. 173–197. Brill Nijhoff, 2010; Criekemans, David. "Regional Sub-state Diplomacy from a Comparative Perspective: Quebec, Scotland, Bavaria, Catalonia, Wallonia and Flanders". In *Regional Sub-State Diplomacy Today*, pp. 37–64. Brill Nijhoff, 2010.

103 Bursens, Peter, and Deforche Jana. "Going beyond Paradiplomacy? Adding Historical Institutionalism to Account for Regional Foreign Policy Competences". In *Regional Sub-State Diplomacy Today*, pp. 151–171. Brill Nijhoff, 2010.

types of counterparts since the early phases[104], including the autonomous towns and cities, counties and arrondissement départemental/régions of Anglo-French multilayered relations, or the 53 cooperative international friendship cities listed by Beijing that cover capital municipalities such as Paris to sub-provincial municipalities such as Bucharest and Cologne. However, the procedures for both sides to fit in with the conformity and equality requirements in government coordination could entail adaptation costs when altering domestic regimes and enforcing vertical devolutions, which is a potential exacerbation for sovereign sensitivities elicited from other sources.

The pressures for empowering subordinate constituents to fit in interaction rules with unconventional foreign diplomatic engagers produce not only regional segmentation, as we discussed, but also subsequent additional policy costs[105] in relation to the stability of central-regional relationships. As the federalist system empirically favourable to multilayered governance occupies fewer spheres in the Asia-Pacific region than Europe, the flexibility of transborder actors to pursue counterpart relationships unhindered wanes, while their dependence on central devolutions to adjust foreign relations increases. The sole mentality of adjusting, even mildly, domestic constitutional arrangements in a way that imitates foreign counterparts or accommodates extra-border or extra-regional actors without adequate legitimacy as diplomatic principles could elicit sovereign sensitivities in relation to the self-consistency and self-autonomousness of domestic regimes. The convenience for engagers with higher levels of mobility in terms of participation and motivation to adopt diversified manners of substate diplomatic relationships could hardly compensate for, or substitute, the regime gaps that less internationalised constituents have to cope with. For multilayered diplomatic relationships together with infrastructure programmes of dense investments like container ports and pivotal corridors, the host state cannot confirm with a high certainty that its domestic empowerment potentials based on inherent constitutional norms are compatible with foreign counterparts in terms of higher administrative flexibilities. When perceiving foreign actants as being less accountable to judicial limitations or other forms of domestic institutional constraints, local authorities and native audiences may receive higher pressure

104 Hooghe, Liesbet, Marks, Gary and Marks, Gary Wolfe. *Multi-level Governance and European Integration*. Rowman & Littlefield, 2001.

105 Tatham, Michaël. "Devolution and EU Policy-Shaping: Bridging the Gap between Multi-level Governance and Liberal Intergovernmentalism", *European Political Science Review* 3, No. 1 (2011): 53–81.

regarding 'inequality' in bargaining power and jurisdictions in regionalised diplomatic relationships with these foreign counterparts, because they have unconventional preponderances in administrative resources for manoeuvring the agendas and projecting dominance. Hence, when the multilayered diplomatic process inevitably cuts into provoking domestic adjustments[106], the de facto constitutional competences between actors could be harder to accomplish, requiring efficient channels for not only devolutions and communications, but also moderate constraints.

Central-Local Vertical Relationships

The tractability and manoeuvrability of devolution in terms of diplomatic powers and their manipulations by regional constituents are prerequisites for securing central level endorsements for intergovernmental relationships between substate engagers. As Duchacek admitted in the early rationales for constituent diplomacy, subnational relationships with foreign regimes outside the framework of central supervision may lead to 'trans-sovereign-meddling'[107] due to the inexperience of provincial governors and possible segmentation within the territorial communities. The research into a centrifugal impetus accompanied by substate diplomacy has been covered by a broad range of the literature as the major source of risk generator and sovereign concerns and received more attention than the discussions regarding the theoretical legitimacy of substate diplomacy and sovereign orders. The sensitivity of the sovereign and central-local connections being violated by substate foreign discourses consists of two categories. The first one is vigilance in relation to interventional engagements from foreign actants upon native subjects and the second one is vigilance in relation to separatist endeavours within the border, seeking diplomatic status as a struggling approach or seeking to bolster a state/nation building[108]. The latter one has received more empirical attention since the central perception of regional stability determines the incentives for ratifying substate foreign engagements and devolutions,

---

106 Lecours, André. *Political Issues of Paradiplomacy: Lessons from the Developed World*. Netherlands Institute of International Relations 'Clingendael', The Hague, 2008: 13.

107 Duchacek, Ivo D. "The International Dimension of Subnational Self-government", *Publius: The Journal of Federalism* 14, No. 4 (1984): 5–31.

108 Bartmann, Barry. "In or Out: Sub-national Island Jurisdictions and the Antechamber of Para-diplomacy", *The Round Table* 95, No. 386 (2006): 556.

including observations on Catalonia[109], Tatarstan[110] or some paradoxical cases for federalist theories such as Indian substates[111].

Both issues could generate pressures in relation to vertical state reach, especially when the cross-border housekeeping necessities are geopolitically overlapping regional separatism or weak border controls. Supplementing the previous research on the tensions between centrifugal bodies and the constraints from unicentric sovereigns, we argue that the awareness of regional unrest and suspected separatist inclinations might reverse the effect on the sensitivity towards foreign interventions. The sensitivity might uniformly function as *débâcles* against substate engagers with political status or their projects with the potential of altering economic landscapes in adjacent territory. The accumulated theories on internal constraints of constituents' foreign relations, in that case, should incorporate the constraints or regulations on the relationships with centrifugal foreign counterparts, along with the sensitivities to the host country's signals for preferences in selecting subordinate actants. The emphasis on scrutinising homeland constituents' engagements with a detachment from the territorial integrity or security concerns of partners is thus insufficient to address the 'separatist' dimension of risks in multilayered diplomacy[112]; and the nature for such risks, unfortunately, could be exogenous and unpredictable. The fluctuation of border relationships between Yunnan, a provincial frontier of China's gateway and economic corridor, towards regional connections with south-east Asian nations, and Myanmar used to be considered as a result of periodic backgrounds during the Cold War[113], which prevented the land corridor of Yangon from being operational again until the 1990s. However, the normalised Sino-Myanmar (Burma) relationships had been established since the 1950s, far earlier than diplomatic relationships with several other ASEAN countries, and kept a stable course in the 1980s, especially after the 1988 crackdown on democratic movements and

109 Criekemans, David. "Regional Sub-state Diplomacy from a Comparative Perspective: Quebec, Scotland, Bavaria, Catalonia, Wallonia and Flanders". In *Regional Sub-State Diplomacy Today*, pp. 37–64. Brill Nijhoff, 2010.

110 Sharafutdinova, Gulnaz. "Paradiplomacy in the Russian Regions: Tatarstan's Search for Statehood", *Europe-Asia Studies* 55, No. 4 (2003): 613–629.

111 Sridharan, Kripa. "Federalism and Foreign Relations: The Nascent Role of the Indian States", *Asian Studies Review* 27, No. 4 (2003): 463–489.

112 Kuznetsov, Alexander S. *Theory and Practice of Paradiplomacy: Subnational Governments in International Affairs*. Routledge, 2014: 88.

113 Li, Mingjiang. "Local Liberalism: China's Provincial Approaches to Relations with Southeast Asia", *Journal of Contemporary China* 23, No. 86 (2014): 275–293.

subsequent sanctions from foreign countries[114]. The special ethnic relationships between Yunnan and the unrest in the north-east regions of Myanmar might offer an alternative account for Myanmar's hesitation in authorising the border corridor reconnections. Another apt example of high sensitivities in relation to domestic separatism within the area covered by the OBOR is Pakistan. The immense infrastructure investment projects touch on all five major provinces[115], their densely populated divisions and the federally administered tribal areas, all of which require perennial and localised cooperation in maintaining fragile energy transmission pipelines, motorways and railway tracks along the mountain regions, especially for the corridors crossing tribal areas and the port complex in the south Balochistan province. Both regions have intricate ethnic realities and polylateral connections with neighbouring countries, attracting reasonable sovereign sensitivities from Islamabad regarding their municipal or provincial foreign relationships, the reconfiguration of regional economic landscapes and their status of socioeconomic dependence relationships with central and foreign constituents. The spillover effects of multilayered programmes on assistance, intellectual property and sharing of techniques, infrastructure modernisation and integration of local resources into wider industrial networks could be beneficial and welcomed at regional levels, but reactions from the central level may become a conditional issue when the transborder enterprises are intertwined with substate political relationships, bypassing domestic hierarchies.

In general, the conventional wisdom of balancing the separatist endeavours or unendorsed subcentral initiations in multilayered diplomacy[116] through internal institutional restraints[117] reflected a prominent discourse about sovereign sensitivities. In addition, the outward developments of substate actors in seeking diplomatic relationships are also responsible for addressing domestic regional dynamics when choosing local constituents as partners, in a qualified sense

---

114 Seekins, Donald M. "Burma-China Relations: Playing with Fire", *Asian Survey* 37, No. 6 (1997): 525–539.

115 Hali, Shafei Moiz, Tan Shukui, and Sumera Iqbal. "One Belt and One Road: Impact on China-Pakistan Economic Corridor", *Strategic Studies* 34, No. 4 (2015): 147–164; Ibrar, Muhammad, Mi, Jianing, Rafiq, Muhammad and Lal Karn, Arodh. "The China-Pakistan Economic Corridor: Security Challenges". *DEStech Transactions on Economics, Business and Management, APME* (2016).

116 Kuznetsov, Alexander S. *Theory and Practice of Paradiplomacy: Subnational Governments in International Affairs*. Routledge, 2014: 89.

117 Cornago, Noé. "On the Normalization of Sub-state Diplomacy", *The Hague Journal of Diplomacy* 5, No. 1–2 (2010): 34.

depending on the sensitivity of target state and central-local relationships within its constitutional contexts. Our proposition is that sovereign sensitivity might derive not only from manifest centrifugal discourses or conflicts, but also a wide range of factors of instability, including ethnic and interterritorial relationships, autonomous status and historical connections with foreign entities, as well as transborder security conditions. To receive sufficient political support and a benign environment for constituent level interactions by fitting the engagements into the strategic interests of the host countries, substate actants are required to accommodate the primacy of central inclinations and policies above regional actors' motivations.

Conclusion

Throughout the discussions, we have proposed the contradictions and radicalness of the current legitimisation pillars of multilayered diplomacy, based on justifications relating to interventionism, as the theoretical hindrance to integrating substate actants into the current diplomatic system in a proper manner. We specifically focused on regional exercises with limited institutional assets and unfavourable levels of subsystem socialisation, which is distinct from mainstream empirical observations on matured regional networks for substate constituents in communications and collaborative governance. Applying the poliheuristic models of decision-making and its basic assumptions, we demonstrated why the engagements with foreign substate actants might touch on an independent dimension of state utility that could not be compensated or substituted by utilities associated with alternative schemes such as economic integration or facility assistance. Meanwhile, initiating constituent level engagements without primarily addressing the sovereign sensitivities of host states may elicit counterproductive disturbances in terms of the perceptions regarding parallel multilateral or bilateral projects at the state and regional levels. The sovereign sensitivity is far broader and more complicated than a mere function of the three contextualising factors that we mentioned above, but the three aspects of conditional terms for substate diplomatic engagers and their home/host countries could offer a practical fulcrum in assessing the risks and impediments derived from this specific dimension of the legitimacy status of multilayered diplomacy and its tensions with conventional norms of sovereign-based international relations. Admittedly, there are many alternative dimensions in evaluating the controversial impacts of multilayered diplomacy on social, cultural, interpersonal and identity recognition levels supported by abundant research; and the dynamics of the three dimensions of sovereign sensitivities within the relationship of substate actors could be equally prominent and deterministic outside the sphere of the BRI. However, we selectively focus on the sovereign-based reactions towards multilayered diplomacy within this particular geopolitical area for the current period because of the appallingly diversified interaction backgrounds for provincial, municipal or other constituent actors to imitate the multilayered governance routes of their European or north Atlantic counterparts. The massive economic infrastructure and institutional integration that are ongoing in the same context, which have been considered as prerequisites or at least as an impetus for multilayered governance in precursory empirical cases, have provided not only motivations and interconnection environments for the constituents of internationalism, but also a sensitive scale in measuring their interaction outcomes. Continued observation of the multilayered diplomatic engagements in this area might demonstrate if the high-profile experiences of multilayered diplomacy in the developed world still hold true in less institutionalised contexts, which is a 'minimum likelihood' examination case for the extent to which substate diplomatic norms have been accepted by the conventional international society of sovereigns.

In the end, the rationale for a legitimacy pillar of substate actants could not practically rely on interventionism oriented to humanitarian and protection obligation to engage foreign counterparts with higher sovereign sensitivities, especially when the statehood power disparity, regime asymmetricity and central-local tensions are simultaneously presented as the background of interaction dyads. Constituents engaged in foreign affairs, as we explained, are seldom freed from the conditionality and limitations of home/host state backgrounds, and could be even more susceptible to bilateral relationships and susceptible to localised antipathy or non-cooperation. Hence, the de facto political environment of multilayered diplomacy is far from mature enough to empower a detour or a network system in parallel to the imperfect reality of state-centric orders as paradiplomacy theories expected. For practical reasons, the practice of substate actors might as well utilise the localised properties of the subsystem, including developmentalism or transborder ties of assorted cultural heritage[118] to replace the interventionism legitimisation routes; but the durability of such models in substate governance collaboration and their effectiveness in offsetting objective or deliberate resistance from sovereign levels is still undetermined.

118 Winter, Tim. "Heritage Diplomacy along the One Belt One Road", *The Newsletter* 74 (2016): 8–10.

Part Two: China as a Regional and Global Power: The Political and Economic Dimensions

Ling Wei

Developmental regionalism and the Belt and Road Initiative

Introduction: Why the Belt and Road Initiative?

The Belt and Road Initiative (BRI) was developed by China's President Xi Jinping in 2013. It aims to build trade routes over land and sea connecting Asia, Europe and Africa and consists mainly of infrastructure projects, education programmes and the development of industrial and special economic zones. According to Chinese official data, by the end of March 2019, China had "signed 173 cooperation agreements with 125 countries and 29 international organisations" and the 'Belt and Road' "expanded from Asia and Europe to include more new participants in Africa, Latin America and the South Pacific" (BRI Office 2019). A study conducted by the World Bank shows that "Belt and Road transport corridors could substantially improve trade, foreign investment, and living conditions for citizens in participating countries – but only if China and corridor economies adopt deeper policy reforms that increase transparency, expand trade, improve debt sustainability, and mitigate environmental, social, and corruption risks" (World Bank 2019).

What is the logic behind the BRI? Why did China make such a proposal in the first place? How come it has made progress in some regions and areas despite controversies, practical challenges and potential risks? Scholars tend to focus on the geostrategic ambition and the geoeconomic effect of the BRI. A prevailing argument is that the BRI reflects China's ascendance in the global arena, economically, politically and strategically, which holds interconnectivity of infrastructure development at its core and has the potential to change the economic and political landscape of Asia (Yu 2017). Some argue that the BRI aims to break the perceived US 'encirclement' of China in the Asia-Pacific and counterbalance the Quad and the Indo-Pacific strategy (Tellis 2017). Some emphasise the economic underpinnings of the BRI and China's domestic development needs to redress economic imbalances between its coastal and interior provinces and to find outlets for excess production capacity, where the geopolitical gains that may come from the success of the BRI are of secondary importance (Cai 2017, Clarke 2017). Some point out Beijing's ambition to develop a 'soft power' narrative and to present China as an alternative leader to the global hegemony of the United States (Fukuyama 2016). However, few have studied why countries along the routes have chosen to cooperate with China.

This paper argues that what drives the BRI process and secures cooperation from countries along the routes can be called developmental regionalism. It means regional actors interact with each other to promote national and regional economic growth and strength. Development in this context mainly refers to economic growth, which takes place under the premise of basic social and political stability and is supported by two pillars, infrastructure building and foreign trade. Developmental regionalism can be regarded as international practice rooted in the background knowledge that economic growth has overriding importance and even generates the greatest amount of security. The BRI process is development-driven, development-oriented and development-focused, featuring pragmatism and flexibility. As an anchoring practice, development shapes norms and sets the agenda in regional processes and requires the basic stability of the region and cooperation among states. In due course, developmental regionalism helps nurture the habit of cooperation and has a significant impact on regional culture.

In the following pages, the chapter will first attempt to provide an analytical framework for developmental regionalism. The writer will then discuss one case that is taking place along the BRI routes and demonstrate how developmental regionalism has worked to promote cooperation. The BRI has five major routes. The Silk Road Economic Belt has three routes. The first runs from north-west China, north-east China, through Central Asia, Russia, to Europe and the Baltic Sea. The second runs from north-west China, through Central Asia, western Asia, to the Persian Gulf and the Mediterranean Sea. And the third runs from south-west China, through the Indo-China Peninsula to the Indian Ocean. The 21st-century Maritime Silk Road, starting from the coastal areas of China, proceeds along two routes. The first crosses the South China Sea, passes through the Malacca Strait and reaches the Indian Ocean, extending to Europe. The other crosses the South China Sea and extends to the South Pacific (BRI Office 2017). The case to be discussed in the chapter is China-Myanmar cooperation along the economic corridor. It takes place along the third route of the economic belt, and demonstrates why and how cooperation has been achieved in twists and turns.

Background Knowledge, Anchoring Practice and the Logic of Habit

This chapter argues for a distinctive form of regionalism practised in the BRI process, which can be called developmental regionalism. It is based on the following assumptions about background knowledge, anchoring practice and the logic of habit.

Locality and background knowledge matter. Partly tacit and partly reflexive, background knowledge consists mainly of 'intersubjective expectations and dispositions'. It does not necessarily "create uniformity of a group" but organises "their differences around a pervasive understanding of reality" (Adler and Pouliot 2011, 16). Locality refers to the specific geographic area where actors exist. It is the very context and important content of the background knowledge of the actors. Most developing countries had colonial or semi-colonial experiences in modern history and gained independence at the end of World War II. Moreover, many of them were exposed to the risks of the bipolar confrontation during the Cold War. Such shared experience is probably the core part of the background knowledge of China and many developing countries along the BRI routes. Thus, a pervasive understanding among them is that development carries overriding importance (Deng 1993, 377) and that development can even provide the greatest amount of security (Xi 2014).

Background knowledge is embedded in practice. A practice is competent performance, which tends to be based on a pattern, socially significant and recognisable (Adler and Pouliot 2011, 7). For a community of practices, the anchoring practice is one that renders other practices possible, embodies defining rules and principles for the community and provides the infrastructure for actors to go on and engage in other practices (Sending and Neumann 2011, 237). The anchoring practice in the BRI process is the practice of development, all-round efforts in promoting national strength and people's living standards and welfare. For many countries, a basic incentive to join the BRI is to obtain the necessary resources and investment for their economic development and social and political stability. Thus, it is the practice of development that has enabled and empowered the BRI process, established the defining rules and principles and provided the 'infrastructure' for regional cooperation.

The logic of habit tends to be predominant in an institutionalised environment, which reduces uncertainty and prolongs stability. Habits are automatic and unreflective reactions of actors to the world around them, including perceptions, attitudes, emotions and practices. Acquired from the social structures in which actors are situated and "maintained through use, utility, the absence of challenges, and the physiology of the brain", habits are broken or replaced only when actors become aware that "they are no longer working, instrumentally, normatively, or functionally" (Hopf 2010, 540–544). There are different kinds of logics, including the logics of consequentialism, appropriateness, effect, practice and habit. Institutionalised settings and durable relationships are favourable conditions for the logic of habit to work; and "even deliberate reflective decisions are still made on the background of structured habits" (Hopf 2010, 547). In areas of long-term relationships of cooperation and conflict, habit rationality tends to apply (Hopf 2010, 540).

Developmental Regionalism as an Analytical Framework

As 'a contested concept' (He 2017, 7), regionalism invokes different understandings of and approaches to a region and regional arrangements. According to Higgott, they fall into four categories, namely, de facto regionalism, de jure regionalism, instrumental regionalism and cognitive regionalism, referring, respectively, to market-led economic integration, state-led institutional cooperation, common policy based on common interest and shared culture (Higgott 2007a & b, He 2017, 8).

The existing literature about developmental regionalism tends to put the emphasis on states' inventions in markets for national development agendas. They often fail to identify economic development as the anchoring practice of regional processes and how regional structures and norms are defined and shaped by such an anchoring practice towards a more cooperative regional culture. Hettne and Söderbaum regard developmental regionalism as a new regionalism, referring to "concerted efforts from actors (i.e. state, market and civil society) within a geographical area to increase the economic development of the region as a whole and to improve its position in the world economy" (Hettne and Söderbaum 1998, 19). Nesadurai puts forward the concept of 'developmental regionalism' as a way to incorporate domestic politics into understanding the globalisation-regionalism relationship. Derived from the concept of 'developmental state', developmental regionalism is used to emphasise "state intervention in markets to promote national development agendas" (Nesadurai 2003, 235, 238). Dent points out the "strong 'developmental' characteristics of east Asia's new regionalism", where regional cooperation and integration activities "are particularly orientated to enhancing the economic capacity and prospects of less developed countries with the view of strengthening their integration into the regional economy, and thereby bringing greater coherence to regional community building overall" (Dent 2008, 767). In Elumbre's definition, developmental regionalism in ASEAN integration is "strategic and progressive ideas aimed at the economic convergence of member states" (Elumbre 2014, 83). Tønesson proposes 'developmental peace' and argues that the priority placed on economic development by leaders of regional states is the key to the long peace in east Asia. He also finds that there is a pattern in their foreign policies when east Asian states prioritise state-driven economic growth. They typically strive to maintain external and internal stability, accommodate the USA and adopt pragmatic policies towards their neighbours (Tønesson 2015, 10–13).

Developmental regionalism proposed in this chapter means regional actors that interact with each other to promote national and regional economic growth and strength. Regional processes are development-driven, development-oriented and development-focused. Economic development is the anchoring practice and core of the background knowledge for the region, which shapes norms and sets the agenda in regional processes, and defines the basic infrastructure for interaction among regional actors. Security challenges and disputes are typically resolved in regional consultative processes to facilitate development. Featuring pragmatism and flexibility, developmental regionalism, when sustained, can help nurture the habit of cooperation and have a significant impact on a regional culture in the long run.

Developmental regionalism proposed in this chapter emphasises the following points. Firstly, economic development carries significant political-security weight and embodies a shared understanding of its practical and strategic significance. The chapter follows an analytically eclectic approach (Sil and Katzenstein 2010, 441) by integrating elements from different theoretical traditions to build complex arguments and provide pragmatic solutions. Secondly, national governments are the main actors in developmental regionalism and domestic institutions, and political practices play a significant role in shaping the regional policy preferences of a state (Moravcsik 1997). Thirdly, developmental regionalism indicates that 'development' is the common background knowledge for agents involved in the regional process. Inclusive and sustainable development is the motive and the biggest common ground for regional cooperation. The legitimacy of such regional processes lies in steady growth, poverty reduction and continuous improvement of people's lives.

As economic development is the anchoring practice in developmental regionalism, structures and norms of regional processes are developed to facilitate growth. Firstly, connectivity and trade facilitation are two pillars for developmental regionalism. Connectivity mainly refers to the connectivity of physical infrastructure. Trade facilitation means opening local markets to the outside and obtaining development opportunities through the global free trade system. The BRI carries China's vision for the achievement of a multilateral opening-up process through multilateral cooperation. In fact, even before the BRI was set out, China was already an extremely important trading partner for many countries in the region (Zheng & Liu 2019). A study conducted by the World Bank shows that the BRI can significantly reduce times of shipments and trade costs. 'Belt and Road' economies located along the corridors where projects are built experience the largest gains. Time needed for shipments along these corridors falls up to 11.9 % and trade costs up to 10.2 % (De Soyres *et al.* 2018). Secondly, institutionalisation serves to promote cooperation in functional areas instead of being an end in itself. States will first try to maintain basic social and political stability at home so as to build a stable and friendly environment for investment and growth. States involved in developmental regionalism usually observe the norm of non-intervention and have mutual respect for each other's concerns. Institutionalisation first takes place in areas of economic and functional cooperation. Thirdly, peace and cooperation is to be enhanced by trade facilitation and growth-sharing (Mahbubani 2010, 37). On the one hand, states become stakeholders of regional processes and have more and more interest in maintaining a stable and cooperative regional culture. On the other hand, as practices are repeated, form patterns and become competent performances with social recognition, cooperation for development can help improve trust and build confidence among the states involved, and even help them develop a habit of cooperation and identification with regional processes for peace and development.

Developmental security is the security norm observed in developmental regionalism. It is a dominant norm and belief that security and development are indispensable from each other. On the one hand, development is promoted to preserve stability and peace. On the other, stability provides the necessary conditions for development. Developmental security also means that security challenges are typically tackled in a way which can best facilitate regional and domestic development. When involved in security disputes, states prefer engaging each other in consultation and dialogue in order to explore the possibilities and gradual steps for solutions or to put disputes aside for future settlement under extremely difficult circumstances in order to create favourable conditions for development. They typically avoid direct confrontation or seeking solutions at the cost of development.

Developmental regionalism features pragmatism and flexibility. The spirit of pragmatism is probably best captured in the late Deng Xiaoping's famous line: "It does not matter whether a cat is black or white; if it catches mice, it is a good cat", which is interpreted as "Results matter" by Mahbubani (Mahbubani 2010, 37). For instance, as distinct from the EU model of regional integration built on legally binding treaties, pragmatism in the BRI process is showcased by pragmatic institutions with a relatively low level of institutionalisation and considerable room for flexibility and autonomy. It often consists of politically attainable goals, a practical agenda tailored to the needs of members, decision-making by consensus which aims at seeking and expanding common ground through consultation and attention paid to how comfortable the parties concerned feel, and pragmatic agreements where voluntary implementation can be expected from all (Marić 2018). Flexibility means minimum institutionalism and flexible practices in regional processes. As Tianbiao Zhu argues, the acceleration of globalisation since the 1980s has given rise to a new development paradigm – compressed development, where "different stages and sequences of development are collapsed into one single point in time" (Zhu 2012, 101–102). As states in compressed development are confronted with multiple tasks and different challenges from different developmental stages simultaneously, they cannot exactly follow the examples of early developers in terms of institutionalisation, standardisation and rule-based bureaucratic operations. They tend to make flexible adaptations, experiment and improvise rather than to go for the preset goals. Hence, flexibility in policies and practices has become a prominent feature of developmental regionalism, where states bend rules, adapt quickly to new circumstances and learn quickly to "deploy new tactics and find practical solutions" when facing new challenges (Zhu 2012, 105–106).

Practices of cooperation in and for development can lead to the coevolution of agents and structures and of institutions and growth. Yuen Yuen Ang argues that successful development is a co-evolutionary process in which markets and governments mutually adapt and that it unfolds in a three-step sequence, weak institutions being harnessed to build markets, emerging markets stimulating strong institutions and strong institutions preserving markets (Ang 2016). Making a compelling case for China's rapid growth out of poverty, her argument actually applies to developmental regionalism as well. 'Weak institutions' can be established first to promote cooperation for long-term peace and sustainable development. Then, as regional integration grows, it can stimulate stronger institutions. Finally, strong institutions preserve the regionalisation process. In development-oriented regionalisation, practices and institutions, states and regional structures co-evolve. What drives such co-evolution is a community of practice of cooperation in and for development.

China-Myanmar Economic Corridor in the BRI Process

The China-Myanmar Economic Corridor (CMEC) is a good test case for developmental regionalism. China is Myanmar's largest investment partner. Between 1988 and May 2018, China invested (USD) $20.01 billion in Myanmar. Myanmar is regarded as an important partner in jointly building the 'Belt and Road'. However, China-Myanmar cooperation in the BRI process should not be taken for granted. After the 2011 political transition to democracy (Song 2011), China-Myanmar relations experienced a relatively low period. As the Myitsone hydropower project was suspended, some even argued that China had lost Myanmar. The annual approved foreign direct investment (FDI) from China dropped from $8.2 billion in the peak year of 2010/2011 to merely $56 million in 2013/2014 (Sun 2015). When the National League for Democracy (NLD) led by Aung San Suu Kyi won the national election in 2015, many perceived Myanmar as pro-Western and hence became even more pessimistic about bilateral relations (Li and Char 2015). In the first Chinese official document about the BRI released in 2015, there was no single programme under the CMEC, although Myanmar was included in the Bangladesh-China-India-Myanmar economic corridor and China-Indochina Peninsular economic corridor (NDRC 2015). In 2015, although a consortium led by China's International Trust and Investment Consortium (CITIC) won the international bidding for the development of the Kyauk Phyu Special Economic Zone (KPSEZ), no significant progress was made for several years. However, noticeable changes have taken place since 2017. Not only were the framework agreements on both the CMEC and the KPSEZ signed but also a national BRI steering committee was set up in Myanmar, chaired by Aung San Suu Kyi herself. Why did Myanmar take a proactive and cooperative turn towards China and the BRI?

Political and Development Challenges in Myanmar

In the past ten years, Myanmar has seen an end to its military regime, the establishment of a civilian government and the political transformation toward democracy. Shortly after gaining independence from British colonial rule in 1948, Prime Minister U Nu established a parliamentary system in Myanmar. In 1962, Ne Win launched a coup and established a military junta, which lasted for almost 50 years. In 2008, under both internal and external pressure, Myanmar developed a new Constitution and Election Law. In 2010, Myanmar held a general election, the first in 20 years. The Union Solidarity and Development Party (USDP), which was supported by the military junta, won an overwhelming victory. In March 2011, as the newly elected President U Thein Sein took office, Myanmar's military regime officially ended and its 'roadmap to democracy' was put into effect (Song 2011). U Thein Sein vowed to establish a government of justice and integrity and put the emphasis on promoting economic growth, establishing a market economy and inviting foreign investment. The election paved the way for further changes in Myanmar. But the new government still faced serious challenges, such as an economy that had crashed, domestic opposition, ethnic militants and sanctions imposed by the West.

In November 2015, the second election took place, where the NLD led by Aung San Suu Kyi won a majority of the total seats and the USDP, which was supported by the military, was defeated. This is a milestone in Myanmar's democratic transition although the Constitution still guarantees a lot of power and rights for the military and the military are still a parallel centre of power. Since the NLD took office in March 2016, there have been some positive changes in Myanmar politics. General stability was achieved in the country through the practice of civilian government and civilian-military governance. However, the NLD-led government still has to deal with complicated political, ethnic, religious, economic and social issues.

The Rohingya crisis broke out in 2016–2017, which reflects how serious domestic security challenges are in Myanmar and why development matters. The Rohingya crisis was an aggregation of a crisis of religious conflict, a security crisis, a refugee crisis and a diplomatic crisis. The UN, the USA and the EU increased sanctions against the Myanmar military and the pressure against the Myanmar government. But Suu Kyi held the Arakan Rohingya Salvation Army (ARSA) responsible for acts of terrorism and emphasised the delicate nature of Myanmar democracy and the little time her own party had been in power. She defined the crisis as a complex internal issue and contrasted the violence with the government's ongoing development agenda, specifically its efforts to deliver peace, stability, harmony and progress to the nation as a whole (Aung San Suu Kyi 2017). Some argue that Aung San Suu Kyi should not be fully blamed for the Rohingya crisis and that her silence, hesitation and indifference were actually a calculated move to avoid antagonising the military forces and Buddhist nationalists. As the military still held significant power in the country and Buddhist nationalists held sizeable influence in the legislature, Suu Kyi lacked the power to deal with the crisis effectively herself. She could not risk alienating the two powerful political constituencies. And, without the cooperation of the military or the support of neighbouring countries, Suu Kyi could not address the concerns of the Rohingya (Peng 2017). After the crisis, Suu Kyi identified three responsibilities of the Myanmar government – democratic transition, peace and stability, and development – and said that none of these challenges was easy or straightforward. She argued that development had to be achieved after nurturing democratic values, establishing peace and stability and achieving sustainable development (Aung San Suu Kyi 2017).

China supported the smooth development of Myanmar's peace progress. As the two countries share a land border of more than 2,000 kilometres, conflicts and crises in northern Myanmar can easily spill over the border and cause refugee problems and social instability in China's Yunnan Province, making it even more difficult for one of the least developed provinces to alleviate poverty and close the development gap between it and China's coastal region, and even causing damage to the overall domestic stability that is indispensable for China's sustainable growth. It is therefore in the interest of China to help maintain stability and peace in northern Myanmar. On his visit to Myanmar in November 2017, Chinese State Councillor Wang Yi made clear China's position on the Rohingya problem. He said that China respected the sovereignty, independence and territorial integrity of Myanmar and expected that the Myanmar government could conduct friendly negotiations with ethnic armed groups to reach a political consensus featuring national unity and a high degree of autonomy under the framework of the Myanmar Constitution for sustainable peace and lasting stability. He also expressed China's willingness to maintain communication and enhance cooperation with Myanmar in controlling the situation in northern Myanmar and safeguarding stability in the border region (Wang 2017a). China proposed a three-phase solution to the Rohingya problem. The first was to put in place an on-site ceasefire and to restore stability. The second phase was to encourage Myanmar and Bangladesh to strengthen communication and dialogue so that a repatriation agreement could be signed and implemented as soon as possible. In the third phase, Myanmar could seek help from the international community to address the root cause of the problem (Wang 2017b).

> China believes that poverty is the root cause of turbulence and conflicts. Although Rakhine State boasts rich resources, its development still lags behind. We call for the international community to increase support and investment to this area to promote development through poverty alleviation and achieve stability through development. (Wang 2017b)

It was under such circumstances that Wang Yi, on behalf of the Chinese government, made the official proposal to build a Y-shaped China-Myanmar Economic Corridor (Wang 2017c) when meeting with Aung San Suu Kyi in Nay Pyi Taw on the same visit.

China-Myanmar Economic Corridor and Kyauk Phyu Port

Myanmar is regarded as an important partner in the joint construction of the 'Belt and Road', with distinct complementary advantages. For China, the CMEC can help to both further consolidate the bilateral comprehensive strategic cooperative partnership and deepen practical cooperation. Running from Kunming, the capital city of China's Yunnan Province, to Myanmar's major economic checkpoints – first to Mandalay in central Myanmar, and then east to Yangon and west to the KPSEZ – the estimated 1,700-kilometre-long CMEC gives China access to the Indian Ocean and connects China's less-developed western inlands with the outside world. Moreover, the CMEC is an important energy route, and once completed and running smoothly, will add to the Malacca Strait and the South China Sea to significantly improve China's energy security to help it in its rise to great power status. In the long run, the CMEC will facilitate the expansion of China's presence and influence in the Indo-Pacific. Nonetheless, China has made it clear that the construction of the CMEC should be conducted on the basis of consultation and mutual benefits and priority should be given to the actual development needs of Myanmar. Such a consideration is both strategic and pragmatic because a stable and prosperous Myanmar is in China's interest in building a benign neighbourly environment to create and seize the strategic opportunity for China's rejuvenation.

Since the historic transition in 2011, Myanmar has become one of the fastest growing economies in the world. What it needs most, as identified by Suu Kyi in the above section, is peace, stability and development. In 2015, the Asian Development Bank (ADB) launched the East–West Economic Corridor Eindu to Kawkareik Road Improvement Project to improve connectivity within the isolated Kayin State and link Myanmar's 'rice bowl' with neighbouring Thailand and beyond. When meeting with the ADB President Takehiko Nakao in 2016, Suu Kyi emphasised the critical importance of infrastructure for sustainable and inclusive development and job creation in Myanmar. She said that it was of critical importance to connect villages with power and roads to improve lives in rural areas and that improved access would support education, health, women's social participation as well as peace and stability (ADB 2019). Therefore, the BRI, which attaches great importance to connectivity, trade and industrial cooperation, is a development opportunity of strategic importance for Myanmar. From August 2016 to the end of 2017, Suu Kyi visited China three times to meet with China's President Xi to facilitate bilateral cooperation and to seek development opportunities for Myanmar from the BRI. The Rohingya crisis deterred Western investment and made Myanmar more economically dependent on China. When China's initiative to build the CMEC was set out, Suu Kyi expressed her appreciation and said that it fitted well with Myanmar's development plan as Myanmar urgently needed to address its undeveloped traffic and electricity. She also expressed a willingness to talk with China about this initiative at an early date (Wang 2017d).

The CMEC is expected to open up new prospects for the joint construction of the 'Belt and Road' between China and Myanmar, and to boost the economy in the Mandalay-Yangon core zone and in impoverished Rakhine for more balanced development across the country. It is expected to start from the fields and projects needed most by Myanmar first and then gradually develop into a corridor of mutually beneficial cooperation (Wang 2017c). In December 2017, an agreement was reached on establishing the CMEC connecting Kyauk Phyu and Kunming. In September 2018, China and Myanmar signed memoranda of understanding (MOUs) on the joint construction of the CMEC. The corridor marks the largest foreign investment in Myanmar in years. It meets the development needs of both countries, allowing Myanmar to boost trade and connectivity with China and providing China with an alternative route of oil transportation from the Indian Ocean. In November 2018, the two sides had an in-depth exchange of views and reached extensive consensus on docking the economic development plans of the two countries, pushing forward the building of the China-Myanmar Economic Corridor in a pragmatic way, conducting cooperation in key projects such as New Yangon city project and striving for early harvests in terms of results achieved as soon as possible (Xinhua 2018). It is widely believed that the CMEC agreement is likely to bring tens of billions of dollars of investment into Myanmar from private and state-owned Chinese firms (Hammond 2018).

The CMEC has been making steady progress so far. Under the CMEC MOUs, China and Myanmar agree to cooperate on industry, transportation, energy, agriculture, the 'digital silk road', finance, tourism, environmental protection, people-to-people exchanges, science and technology, personnel training, water resources and flood prevention and control. Hence, it is not just a physical corridor, but also a conceptual corridor. It can bring about greater regional integration through initiatives such as industrial zones, trade quotas and tax breaks, and cooperation in areas not directly connected to the economy, such as disaster mitigation and public health (Hammond 2018). According to Myanmar sources, China has submitted proposals for 38 projects in total under the CMEC. When Suu Kyi attended the second Belt and Road Forum in Beijing in April 2019, Myanmar and China signed three agreements focused on strengthening cooperation on trade and technology. The two sides also signed a document outlining a list of nine early harvest projects (to achieve early results) for the CMEC to facilitate the implementation of infrastructure projects, including building economic zones and upgrading roads across the country, such as three economic cooperation zones in Kachin and Shan states, the KPSEZ and the Muse-Mandalay railway project. In October 2018, the China Railway Group Ltd and Myanmar Railways signed an MOU on a feasibility study for the proposed railway line from Muse to Mandalay. The two cities are envisioned as key hubs in a plan to improve connectivity in south-east Asia (Nan 2019).

China and Myanmar also signed a separate framework agreement in November 2018 for KPSEZ, a key strategic project under the BRI that is expected to provide China with direct access to the Indian Ocean, allowing its oil imports to bypass the Strait of Malacca. Kyauk Phyu is well endowed with a natural deep sea harbour and abundant natural resources in oil and gas, marine resources as well as unique scenic landscapes. It also has sufficient land and ample labour for industrial development and the expansion of residential areas. Strategically located at the geographic centre, Kyauk Phyu can serve as a unique trade corridor connecting the three dynamic economies of China, India and the ASEAN (BEAC Office 2019). A Singapore-based consortium led by CPG Consultants was assigned the development of the master plan for the KPSEZ, and international bidding for its development started in 2014. In December 2015, a consortium of six foreign group companies, led by China's CITIC, won the bid to implement two projects of the KPSEZ. The transnational consortium involves five Chinese firms and one Thai firm. The announcement was made by Myanmar's KPSEZ Bidding Evaluation and Awarding Committee (BEAC) following the approval by the government cabinet and parliament. The CITIC consortium established the project joint ventures together with Myanmar local enterprises for the construction and operation of the two projects which will be implemented under the framework of the Myanmar Special Economic Zone Law promulgated by the Myanmar government in 2014. The Industrial Park, which covers an area of about 1,000 hectares, was to enter into construction in February 2016. The Deep Sea Port project was to be constructed within 20 years and is planned to consist of the Made Island Terminal and Yanbye Island Terminal complete with ten berths, including the road and bridge connecting the Industrial Park and Deep Sea Port (Xinhua 2015).

Although the CITIC consortium won the international bid in 2015, the KPSEZ projects have not proceeded as smoothly as planned. Negotiations dragged on for years mainly because of disagreements over funding shares. Initially, the project was to be 85 % funded by the Chinese consortium. But, after the NDL government took office in 2016, it asked for a reduction in the Chinese companies' stake in the project to 70 %. Prolonged negotiations fuelled criticism of the BRI, which some foreign critics said could add to local debts and even threaten other countries' sovereignty. The Chair of the KPSEZ Management Committee U Set Aung insisted that the project would not amount to a debt burden for Myanmar. He said that negotiations were made to make the project sustainable, to avoid a debt burden and to ensure the transparency of the process. China has maintained that the BRI is an open platform to facilitate regional and global economic integration and to help countries along the routes with economic growth and job creation. In the meantime, China and Myanmar discussed three key points in negotiating the CMEC MOUs to avoid a 'debt trap' and to ensure that the project benefits both countries. Firstly, Myanmar is allowed to seek financing from international financial institutions to implement the projects. Secondly, the Myanmar government can invite international tenders so as to ensure international investment in the projects. And thirdly, the proposed projects shall be chosen by Myanmar while creating mutual benefits for both sides (Nan 2019). In October 2018, China agreed on a 70 % stake, at the lower end of a proposed range. In November 2018, The Framework Agreement on the KPSEZ Deep Sea Port Project was signed. Under the framework agreement, Myanmar will pitch in the remaining 30 %. The initial phase of the project will include two berths with a total investment of $1.3 billion. A joint venture will be set up to construct and run the port. The Kyauk Pyu project is estimated to deliver 100,000 jobs to the local community and will contribute as much as $15 billion in tax revenue to Myanmar. Once completed, the port will have an annual gross output of $3.2 billion (U Aung 2018). KPSEZ is of strategic importance to China as it is the terminal of the China-Myanmar oil and gas pipeline.

Developmental Regionalism in Practice

A review of China-Myanmar cooperation in the BRI processes demonstrates that developmental regionalism is at work. First and foremost, development is the centerpiece of the cooperation and is the anchoring practice. Meeting the development needs of Myanmar has been repeatedly emphasised on almost all occasions during China-Myanmar cooperation. Chinese government officials and business developers have made it clear time and again that cooperation will be prioritised on projects which can bring practical benefits to the people, improve infrastructure to provide basic services like roads and electricity and narrow the development gap by connecting the most-developed Yangon area and the least-developed northern area. According to the development plan disclosed in 2015, the KPSEZ Industrial Park will include technology and capital-intensive industries and labour-intensive industries such as textiles and garments, construction material processing industries, food processing industries and marine supply as well as services industries. The Deep Sea Port project consists not only of berths, but also of roads and bridges connecting the KPSEZ Industrial Park and the port. The Deep Sea Port is to be updated to complete the container terminal in due course. According to the plan, during the whole concession period, the Myanmar government will receive a total of $15 billion of tax revenue from the park and port projects. When the concession period expires, both projects will be handed over to the Myanmar government.

For China, the corridor and the port are of strategic significance to the country's peaceful development and to its rise to great power status. Development is based on internal and external stability and defined mainly as continued economic growth. The most significant element is to help build a stable, developing and friendly external environment. With a 2,000 kilometre land border, instability can easily spill over and interrupt China's own social and economic development. The corridor and the port can also significantly improve China's energy security to help with its continued development. The corridor also connects China's less-developed south-west better with the region and brings greater opportunities to close the development gap at home. Moreover, industrial cooperation is conducive to China's industrial restructuring and upgrading.

Secondly, developmental security is the norm. When Suu Kyi said that Myanmar was fragile, she meant both institutionally and economically. She agreed with the Chinese leadership that development is important to strengthen Myanmar in its political transition. From 2011 to 2015, there were some fluctuations in the China-Myanmar relationship. However, after the NLD took power, it became increasingly clear that Myanmar had to turn to China for help to satisfy its development needs. That is why Suu Kyi approached China and started to actively participate in the BRI process. The CMEC MOUs and the framework agreement for the port were only signed after Suu Kyi met and reached consensus with China's President Xi Jinping on developmental security. The reasons for the Rohingya conflict and crisis are complicated, but poor economic development and the scramble for resources, such as land and coal mines, are a key factor. Developing industries and better urban planning can create wealth and reduce dependence on natural resources. Doing so will help mitigate the conflict in northern Myanmar. Connecting the northern area with the three-end corridor is also a solution in terms of developmental peace, not only for Myanmar, but also for China.

Thirdly, China-Myanmar cooperation in the BRI process is pragmatic, flexible and open. It has been conducted in a down-to-earth manner, catering to each other's specific needs. Cooperation is based on consultation on an equal footing. There are no preset rules prior to consultation. The specific concerns and practical needs of the parties concerned are taken care of and accommodated. For instance, the design of the CMEC demonstrates due consideration for the development gap between different regions in Myanmar and the security concern in northern Myanmar. The negotiation of the framework agreement on the KP SEC Deep Sea Port also shows the pragmatic, flexible and open nature of developmental regionalism. The international bidding process was launched in 2014. But a preliminary agreement was not reached until late 2018. The project has involved actors of different nationalities and different natures of players, including governments, businesses and civil society. China's initial objective and desired share of the funding was 85 %. However, in the end, there was a compromise and it was reduced to the low point of the range, 70 %. It is not because China was not a tough negotiator, but because keeping the cooperation process going for continued growth and stability is the ultimate goal. Hence, the process is actually open. There are no preset specific material goals because the cooperation process is an end in itself.

Finally, we can also find evidence of co-evolution in the China-Myanmar case. Myanmar resumed active cooperation with China after several years of a relatively low level of cooperation, not only because it has developmental needs, but also because both have evolved to accommodate the changing context and to accommodate each other. A study of the investment activities of Chinese state-owned enterprises shows that practices and institutions have co-evolved in the course of Myanmar's political transition. The transition emboldened social activism expressed as protests regarding the injustices. Many of these protests were related to large-scale extractive investments. After the West lifted most of its sanctions, transnational capital actors returned to Myanmar and offered higher investment standards. In response to the 'push' of public pressure and the 'pull' of new investments, reformists in Myanmar have attempted to implement stronger investment regulatory frameworks. The new demands on foreign investments to comply with higher investment standards are strengthened by China's nascent efforts to curtail the excesses of Chinese enterprises globally. As a result, Chinese enterprises are being pressurised to adapt to the new operating environment, resulting in observable changes in investment behaviour (Mark & Zhang 2017). Such co-evolution has happened not only at the economic and business levels, but also and more significantly at the political and state levels. In other words, actors and practices co-evolve and so do institutions. They have accommodated and complemented each other to facilitate their coexistence.

Conclusion

Since the BRI process was initiated in 2013, despite doubts and scepticism, it has expanded rapidly in terms of participating members, cooperation mechanisms and projects and geographic regions. This chapter intended to find out why countries choose to engage and cooperate in the BRI process. The author has sought to develop a theory of developmental regionalism. Developmental regionalism means regional processes that are development-driven, development-focused and development-oriented. Actors engaged in such regional processes become a community of practice of cooperation and for development. In such processes, development mainly refers to sustainable economic growth, which serves as the anchoring practice for the community. As the anchoring practice, the practice of sustainable economic growth defines the norms, sets the agenda and builds the basic frameworks and infrastructure for the interaction of the actors involved. The main actors in developmental regionalism are nation states. Hence, sovereignty, non-intervention and respect for each other's major concerns are usually observed in the process. In practice, developmental regionalism features pragmatism, flexibility, openness and co-evolution of agents and structures. It is rolled out in three steps. Firstly, basic political and social stability has to be achieved as prerequisite for economic development activities. Secondly, infrastructure development, trade and investment are prioritised and promoted. Thirdly, economic growth and prosperity consolidates social stability, promotes the co-evolution of agents and institutions and hence produces favourable conditions for sustainable peace.

The chapter took the China-Myanmar Economic Corridor as a case study to find out why Myanmar has chosen to engage and cooperate in the BRI process. The background is that China-Myanmar bilateral relations were at a relatively low point when the BRI was initiated and Myanmar was perceived as pro-Western after its political transition towards democracy in 2011. After the NLD led by Ang Sang Suu Kyi won the second national election, people became even more sceptical and pessimistic about China-Myanmar relations. However, from 2015 to 2017, Suu Kyi made four visits to China and was received by China's President Xi each time. Not only has the agreement on building the CMEC been reached and implemented, but the stalled KPSEZ and deep water seaport projects have also witnessed significant progress. In late 2018, a national BRI steering committee chaired by Suu Kyi herself was established in Myanmar, a signal that the level of China-Myanmar cooperation in the BRI process had reached a new high. Myanmar chose cooperation because the BRI process followed developmental regionalism and satisfied Myanmar's development needs.

However, from the case study, we can also find out that the healthy and sustainable practice of developmental regionalism in the BRI process requires special attention to be paid to the following points. Firstly, the asymmetry between actors should be taken into consideration in the process. In the Myanmar case, the asymmetry between China and Myanmar is obvious in terms of size, economic power and their share of investment in the projects. Such asymmetry not only leads to sensitivity and vulnerability but also misperception (Keohane and

Nye 2001, Womack 2001). So, when asked for their opinion about the CMEC, the Myanmar people said that they would have to be very careful because they were too vulnerable (Hammond 2018). Therefore, it is very important for reassurance to be provided to the lesser agents all the time to reduce their suspicion and boost their confidence. Secondly, public consultation and information disclosure is very important in winning the support of the local people, without which major projects, especially infrastructure projects, cannot go smoothly. Although states are major actors and play a decisive role in the BRI process, the principle of 'extensive consultation' should also apply to state-society interaction and foreign investor-local community interaction. In the Myanmar case, some local people complained about talks behind closed doors. Because of the lack of information, some had fears that the CMEC might be a 'debt trap' and the fact that the corridor was cutting through conflict areas could be very risky (Hammond 2018). Thirdly, the mutual facilitation of development and security and co-evolution of practices and institutions should be promoted. The BRI and the CMEC have raised the expectations of many Myanmar people that the corridor would help to end Myanmar's civil conflicts, bringing economic development to those areas as a way of peacebuilding and that the CMEC was important for supporting Myanmar's economic development (Hammond 2018). However, in developmental regionalism, security and development only reinforce each other when co-evolution is at work. Therefore, social reconciliation and institution-building for better governance are important in consolidating security for continued growth and sustainable peace. Finally, although the ongoing BRI may verify the theory of developmental regionalism, we still have to collect more empirical evidence in a longer period of time to see if the BRI can stand the test of time or if developmental regionalism can be sustainable.

References

ADB (Asian Development Bank). 2019. "ADB's Work in Myanmar". https://www.adb.org/countries/myanmar/overview (Accessed 20 Jan. 2019)

Adler, Emanuel and Pouliot, Vincent. 2011. "International Practices: Introduction and Framework". In *International Practices*, edited by Emanuel Adler and Vincent Pouliot, 3–35. Cambridge: Cambridge University Press.

Ang, Yuen Yuen. 2016. *How China Escaped the Poverty Trap*. Ithaca: Cornell University Press.

Aung San Suu Kyi. 2017. "Aung San Suu Kyi's Full Speech on the Rohingya Crisis". 19 Sept. http://news.rediff.com/commentary/2017/sep/19/

aung-san-suu-kyis-full-speech-on-the-rohingya-crisis/833702ff2d11cf7681b36fdc456055aa (Accessed 20 Jan. 2019)

BEAC Office, Kyauk Phyu SEZ Management Committee. 2019. "About KP SEZ". http://kpsez.org/about-kp-sez/ (Accessed 20 Jan. 2019)

BRI Office (Office of the Leading Group for Promoting the Belt and Road Initiative). 2017. *Building the Belt and Road: Concept, Practice and China's Contribution*. Beijing: Foreign Language Press. https://eng.yidaiyilu.gov.cn/wcm.files/upload/CMSydylyw/201705/201705110537027.pdf (Accessed 20 Jan. 2019)

BRI Office (Office of the Leading Group for Promoting the Belt and Road Initiative). 2019. "The Belt and Road Initiative: Progress, Contributions and Prospects". 22 April. https://eng.yidaiyilu.gov.cn/zchj/qwfb/86739.htm (Accessed 20 Jan. 2019)

Cai, Peter. 2017. "Understanding China's Belt and Road Initiative", Lowy Institute for International Policy, Analysis, 22 March. https://www.lowyinstitute.org/publications/understanding-belt -and-road-initiative.

Clarke, Michael. 2017. "The Belt and Road Initiative: China's New Grand Strategy?", *Asia Policy*, 24: 71–79. DOI:https://doi.org/10.1353/asp.2017.0023.

Deng, Xiaoping. 1993. *Selected Works of Deng Xiaoping (Deng Xiaoping Wenxuan)*. Vol. 3. Beijing: People's Publishing House.

Dent, Christopher M. 2008. "The Asian Development Bank and Developmental Regionalism in East Asia", *Third World Quarterly*, 29(4): 767–786.

Dent, Christopher M. 2017. "East Asian Integration Towards an East Asian Economic Community". ADBI Working Paper 665. Tokyo: Asian Development Bank Institute. https://www.adb.org/publications/east-asian-integration-towards-east-asian-economic-community (Accessed 20 December 2018).

Dent, Christopher M., and Richter, Peter. 2011. "Sub-Regional Cooperation and Developmental Regionalism: The Case of BIMP-EAGA", *Contemporary Southeast Asia*, 33(1): 29–55.

Derudder, Ben, *et al.* 2018. "Connectivity along Overland Corridors of the Belt and Road Initiative". Discussion paper of the Macroeconomics, Trade, and Investment (MTI) Global Practice of the World Bank. http://documents.worldbank.org/curated/en/264651538637972468/pdf/ Connectivity-Along-Overland-Corridors-of-the-Belt-and-Road-Initiative.pdf. (Accessed 15 Feb. 2019)

De Soyres, François, *et al.* 2018. "How Much Will the Belt and Road Initiative Reduce Trade Costs?" World Bank Policy Research Working

Paper 8614. October. http://documents.worldbank.org/curated/en/592771539630482582/pdf/WPS8614.pdf.

Elumbre, Adonis L. 2014. "Interpreting ASEAN Developmental Regionalism through Discursive Institutionalism", *Kasarinlan: Philippine Journal of Third World Studies*, 29(1): 75–108.

Fukuyama, Francis. 2016. "One Belt, One Road: Exporting the Chinese Model to Eurasia", *Australian*. 4 Jan. http://www.theaustralian.com.au/news/world/one-belt-one-road-exporting-thechinese-model-to-eurasia/news-story/269016e0dd63ccca4da306b5869b9e1c.

Haas, Ernst B. 1980. "Why collaborate?: Issue-Linkage and International Regimes", *World Politics*, 32(3): 357–405.

Hammond, Clare. 2018. "The grand plan for the China-Myanmar Economic Corridor". *Frontier*. 26 Sept. https://frontiermyanmar.net/en/the-grand-plan-for-the-china-myanmar-economic-corridor.

He, Baogang. 2017. *Contested Ideas of Regionalism in Asia*. London and New York: Routledge.

Hettne, Björn and Söderbaum, Fredrik. 1998. "New Regionalism Approach". *Politeia*, 17(3): 6–21.

Higgott, Richard. 2007a. "The Theory and Practice of Regionalism in East Asia: Peter Katzenstein's Value Added", *Journal of East Asian Studies*, 7: 382–383.

Higgott, Richard. 2007b. "Alternative Models of Regional Cooperation? The Limits of Regional Institutionalisation in East Asia". In *European Union and New Regionalism: Regional Actors and Global Governance in a Post-Hegemonic Era*, edited by Mario Telò, 75–106. Aldershot: Ashgate.

Hopf, Ted. 2010. "The Logic of Habit in International Relations", *European Journal of International Relations*, 16(4): 539–561.

Keohane, Robert O. 1984. *After Hegemony: Cooperation and Discord in the World Political Economy*. Princeton: Princeton University Press.

Keohane, Robert, and Nye, Joseph. 2001. *Power and Interdependence*. 4th edition. Boston: Longman.

Li, Chenyang, and Char, James. 2015. "China-Myanmar Relations since Nay Pi Daw's Political Transition: How Beijing can Balance Short-term Interests and Long-term Values". 16 March. RSIS Working Paper No. 288. https://www.rsis.edu.sg/wp-content/uploads/2015/03/WP288_150316_China-Myanmar-Relations.pdf.

Mahbubani, Kishore. 2010. "Results Matter: Pragmatism Prevails in Asia", *Global Asia*, 5: 37–42.

Marić, Nataša. 2018. *Pragmatic Institutions and the Habit of Cooperation: China's Foreign Policy Mechanism and Its Implication in Central and Eastern Europe*. PhD dissertation. China Foreign Affairs University.

Mark, Siu Sue and Youyi, Zhang. 2017. "From Impediment to Adaptation: Chinese Investments in Myanmar's New Regulatory Environment", *Journal of Current Southeast Asian Affairs*, 36(2): 71–100.

Moravcsik, Andrew. 1997. "Taking Preferences Seriously: A Liberal Theory of International Politics", *International Organization*, 51(4): 513–553.

Nan, Lwin. 2019. "New Chinese Ambassador Vows to Seek 'Practical Cooperation' with Myanmar on BRI Projects", *The Irrawaddy*. 19 June. https://www.irrawaddy.com/ news/burma/new-chinese-ambassador-vows-seek-practical-cooperation-myanmar-bri-projects.html

Nesadurai, Helen E. S. 2003. "Attempting Developmental Regionalism through AFTA: the Domestic Sources of Regional Governance", *Third World Quarterly*, 24(2): 235–253.

NDRC (National Development and Reform Commission of the PRC). 2015. "Vision and Actions on Jointly Building Silk Road Economic Belt and 21st-Century Maritime Silk Road". 28 March. http://en.ndrc.gov.cn/newsrelease_8232/201503/t20150330_1193900.html.

Peng, Darwin. 2017. "Understanding Aung San Suu Kyi's Silence on the Rohingya". *Harvard Political Review*. 21 Feb. http://harvardpolitics.com/world/understanding-aung-san-suu-kyis-silence-rohingya/.

Sending, Ole Jacob and Neumann, Iver B. 2011. "Banking on Power: How Some Practices in an International Organization Anchor Others". In *International Practices*, edited by Emanuel Adler and Vincent Pouliot, 231–254. Cambridge: Cambridge University Press.

Sil, Rudra, and Katzenstein, Peter J. 2010. "Analytic Eclecticism in the Study of World Politics: Reconfiguring Problems and Mechanisms across Research Traditions", *Perspectives on Politics*, 8(2): 441–431.

Song, Qingrun. 2011. "Civilians Come to Power", *Beijing Review*, April 21, 14–15.

Sun, Yun. 2015. "China's relations with Myanmar: Does an NLD government mark a new era?" 8 Dec. https://www.stimson.org/2015/chinas-relations-myanmar-does-nld-government-mark-new-era.

Tellis, Ashley J. 2017. "Protecting American Primacy in the Indo-Pacific", testimony before the US Senate Armed Services Committee, 25 April.

Tønesson, Stein. 2015. "Explaining East Asia's Developmental Peace: The Dividends of Economic Growth", *Global Asia*, 10(4): 10–15.

U Aung. 2018. "China, Myanmar Sign Kyaukphyu SEZ Deep-Sea Port Deal after Years of Negotiations", *Global Times*, 9 Nov. https://eng.yidaiyilu.gov.cn/qwyw/rdxw/71209.htm.

Wang, Yi. 2017a. "China Supports Myanmar's Domestic Peace Process". Nay Pyi Taw, 23 Nov. http://mm.china-embassy.org/eng/sgxw/t1513327.htm.

Wang, Yi. 2017b. "China Proposes 3-Phase Solution to Address Issue of the Rakhine State of Myanmar". Nay Pyi Taw, 23 Nov. http://mm.china-embassy.org/eng/sgxw/t1513333.htm.

Wang, Yi. 2017c. "China Proposes to Build China-Myanmar Economic Corridor". Nay Pyi Taw, 23 Nov. http://mm.china-embassy.org/eng/sgxw/t1513330.htm.

Wang, Yi. 2017d. "Wang Yi Holds Talks with State Counsellor and Foreign Minister Aung San Suu Kyi of Myanmar". Nay Pyi Taw, 23 Nov. http://mm.china-embassy.org/eng/sgxw/t1513323.htm.

Womack, Brantly. 2001. "How Size Matters: the United States, China and Asymmetry", *Strategic Studies*, 24(4): 123–150.

World Bank. 2019. "Belt and Road Economics: Opportunities and Risks of Transport Corridors". Advance Edition. World Bank, Washington, DC. License: Creative Commons Attribution CC BY 3.0 IGO. https://openknowledge.worldbank.org/bitstream/handle/10986/31878/9781464813924.pdf.

Xi, Jinping. 2014. "New Asian Security Concept for New Progress in Security Cooperation: Remarks at the Fourth Summit of the Conference on Interaction and Confidence Building Measures in Asia". Shanghai, 3 June. http://www.china.org.cn/chinese/2014-06/03/content_32561159.htm.

Xinhua. 2015. "CITIC-led Consortium Wins Bid for Implementing SEZ in Myanmar". 31 Dec. http://www.chinadaily.com.cn/business/2015-12/31/content_22882073.htm.

Xinhua. 2018. "China, Myanmar Vow to Push Forward Building of China-Myanmar Economic Corridor". 28 Nov. https://eng.yidaiyilu.gov.cn/qwyw/rdxw/72921.htm.

Yu, Hong. 2017. "Motivation behind China's 'One Belt, One Road' Initiatives and Establishment of the Asian Infrastructure Investment Bank", *Journal of Contemporary China*, 26(105): 353–368, DOI: 10.1080/10670564.2016.1245894.

Zhang, Yuan. 2018. "B&R Interconnection Witnesses Great Breakthroughs in 5-year Development". *Xinhua Silk Road Information Service*. 23 Oct. https://eng.yidaiyilu.gov.cn/qwyw/rdxw/69500.htm.

Zheng, Yongnian, and Liu, Bojian. 2019. "Development Agenda of Belt and Road Initiative as an International Public Product", Paper presented at the "China Development Forum 2019". Beijing, 23–25 March. http://www.cdrf.org.cn//jjh/pdf/guojigonggongchanpindefazhan(yingwen).pdf.

Zhu, Tianbiao. 2012. "Compressed Development, Flexible Practices, and Multiple Traditions in China's Rise". In *Sinicization and the Rise of China: Civilizational Processes beyond East and West*, edited by Peter J. Katzenstein, 99–119. London and New York: Routledge.

Uwe Wissenbach[1]

North-East Asia's Conflicted Regionness

Introduction

The speed with which a switch to nationalism in the USA since 2016 has undermined multilateralism is disruptive – the US initiated Trans-Pacific Partnership (TPP) was buried immediately by the new president. His national security strategy (NSS; The White House 2017) is explicitly promoting 'principled realism', power politics and national sovereignty. US support to a multilateral order, regionalism or even US alliances can no longer be taken for granted. In December 2018, US Secretary of State Pompeo, speaking in Brussels, rode a frontal attack against multilateralism if it did not serve US interests and stated: "Our administration is thus lawfully *[sic!]* exiting or renegotiating outdated or harmful treaties, trade agreements, and other international arrangements that do not serve our sovereign interests, or the interests of our allies".[2] Through tax reductions and tariffs the USA is trying to repatriate US companies from investments abroad, and the national economy is conceived of as the second pillar of national security. More than a thousand economists earlier warned the president that his policies of withdrawing from economic agreements were the same kind of 'flat earth economics' that unbalanced the global economy in the 1930s and led to the Great Depression (Gowing and Langdon 2018:120) while Adam Tooze in his book about the global financial crisis calls the Trump administration's "declaration of independence from an interconnected and multipolar world" perilous (Tooze 2018:6). The NSS identifies China as America's global strategic rival and North Korea as a rogue state and threat to US national security. That did not stop Trump to declare he fell in love with the North Korean leader at the Singapore summit in 2018. The US also tries to mobilise other countries (the 'free world') against China, first and foremost its allies in the region, Japan and South Korea. America has ignited a new cold

1 The author writes in his private capacity. This chapter does not reflect EU policy or views.

2 US Department of State: Restoring the Role of the Nation-State in the Liberal International Order. *Remarks Michael R. Pompeo Secretary of State German Marshall Fund Brussels*, Belgium December 4, 2018 accessed at https://www.state.gov/secretary/remarks/2018/12/287770.htm on 13 December 2018.

war against China (Woodward 2017). At the same time those US allies have also felt the heat of 'America first' in terms of trade and burden-sharing for US military expenditure against China (Hahm 2017; Snyder 2019). Paradoxically too, to make the maximum pressure strategy to achieve North Korea's denuclearisation pay off, the USA needs China and Russia, which the NSS singles out as global rivals of the USA. North-east (NE) Asia is being shaped as the main battleground between the USA and China. This promotion of polarisation has implications for the relations between the EU and China and for the 'era of regional and interregional cooperation' that this book is investigating. This chapter is about China's regional neighbourhood which is affected by the competition with the USA, but also has its own dynamics. My focus here is on NE Asia including China (including Taiwan), South and North Korea and Japan. These countries in the last decade or so have escalated nationalistic disputes and deadly conflicts about insignificant islets, about disputed waters, about schoolbooks and even menus at state banquets[3]. These conflicts occur even between the liberal democracies there (Japan and South Korea or Taiwan; Selden 2011). Hahm (2017) sees NE Asia at a crossroads between regional integration and globalisation or trade wars, territorial disputes and an arms race undergirded by resurgent nationalism.

Beyond this layer of global rivalry between the USA and China, there is a deeper layer of NE Asia's own 'conflicted regionness' – a series of deep-seated conflicts that straddle the divide between political systems and do not fit into America's new narrative of a struggle between free and liberal democratic countries and countries which suppress liberty and their own people. While the conflicts between China and Japan are framed by Japan in this way (Hagström and Hanssen 2016), the conflicts between Japan and Korea or Taiwan over

3 *Japan anger at South Korea's shrimp surprise for Donald Trump, The Guardian* 10–11–2017 (https://www.theguardian.com/world/2017/nov/10/japan-anger-south-koreas-shrimp-surprise-menu-donald-trump-sex-slave?utm_source=esp&utm_medium=Email&utm_campaign=Morning+briefing&utm_term=251661&subid=8251405&CMP=ema-2793 (accessed November 10, 2017): "The menu at South Korea's state banquet for Donald Trump has left a nasty taste in Japan, after the president was served seafood caught off islands at the centre of a long-running territorial dispute between Seoul and Tokyo. Japanese officials have also complained about the decision to invite a former wartime sex slave to the event, held earlier this week during the second leg of Trump's five-nation tour of Asia. Conservative media in Japan labelled the banquet "anti-Japanese" for featuring shrimp from near Dokdo – a rocky outcrop known in Japan as Takeshima. Both countries claim sovereignty over the islands, which are administered by Seoul".

uninhabited islets, wartime atrocities and historical justice – moralisation gaps – obviously do not fit this new cold war narrative.

How can a region with which the EU trades more than two billion euros a day[4] be so conflicted? Will the new bipolar struggle between the USA and China further destabilise NE Asia? What are the dynamics of the regional security complex (RSC) that includes the external power US is such a crucial way?

This situation of conflicted regionness is astonishing, especially when contrasted with the region's more distant past, which until the 19th century was characterised by a long period of peaceful prosperity and a high degree of integration. The current lack of regionalisation dynamics is often explained with variables such as the Asian way (open regionalism), the political system differences between democracies and communist states, and the strategic designs of the USA or the rise of China. While all these factors are important, by themselves they are inadequate to explain the conflicted regionness of NE Asia. Nationalism and moralisation gaps resulting from critical junctures on historical pathways are better variables to explain the dynamics in the region (Hahm 2017). This is because nationalism can be considered as an ideological institution of international society with a transformative capacity on its constitutive institutions (sovereignty, international law and the economy). These ideological institutions have to be considered in the analysis of NE Asia's RSC (Buzan 2003) and regionalism.

The security literature is vast, anchored in paradigmatic approaches and often recycles and interprets policymakers' positions or advises them. The US NSS explicitly builds on the realist paradigm. The RSC approach pioneered by Buzan and Waever (2003) as part of a new approach to regionalism is a synthesis approach bridging realist and constructivist paradigms, but Buzan also reduces NE Asia's regional security to a power game between the USA and China. Beyond the RSC, 'New' Regionalism is searching for elusive regions while the 'Old' Regionalism focussed too much on the specific example of the EU (Söderbaum 2015). But whether old or new, these explanations for regionalism on their own offer few clues to explain the 'conflicted regionness' of NE Asia today.

A new analytical concept is needed to make sense of NE Asia's paradoxical pathway. This pathway leads us back to critical junctures in a distant past when – in contrast to today – it was NE Asia that was a tightly knit, peaceful, culturally

4 Calculated on the basis of 2017 figures for EU total trade with China, Japan and RoK (not including Taiwan and DPRK) http://trade.ec.europa.eu/doclib/docs/2006/september/tradoc_122530.pdf

and politically integrated community – the Confucian world (Kang 2010) – while Europe was defining itself through conflict. One of the problems is that countries in NE Asia 'disown' this shared past based on nationalist constructs of history which continue to this day.

The Regional Security Complex in NE Asia

Asia's security has spun an enormous literature and has long been a constant preoccupation of policymakers and analysts alike. This is because of the complexity of the situation, its constant evolution and the difficulty to analyse all this with the often simple paradigmatic approaches which characterise International Relations (IR) as an essentially American discipline of analysis. Buzan and Waever (2003) developed an approach that has successfully integrated realist, liberal and constructivist approaches to address RSCs, among them the 'security architecture' in Asia (Buzan 2003). The term 'architecture' is somewhat misleading, as architecture implies the presence of an architect, a plan and a final construction. Maybe NATO as an alliance can be captured with an architecture metaphor, but the situation in Asia is definitely not the product of someone's masterplan and has displayed a rather important fluidity beyond its apparent stability (or narrow band of security options as Buzan calls it; 2003:166). This being said, the concept of a RSC is a promising one. In a nutshell, Buzan argues that there is a global level of security structure and a regional level that are of more or less equal importance. He further divides the Asian region into a south Asian, a south-east Asian and a north-east Asian security complex arguing that they have been integrating after the end of the Cold War (in particular the south-east Asian and the north-east Asian one). While this was his main story in 2003, I remain focused on NE Asia as it has a very specific security complex which I call conflicted regionness (and that has revealed this conflictedness in the years since 2003).

In fact, the US presence in the region can be explained by several factors. It is in the region for its own national interest, that is both nationally and globally defined in an oscillation depending on the domestic priorities of the moment: 1) a left-over of the Cold War containment strategy against the communist camp and in particular the Soviet Union (as the Japanese focus on territorial defence in the north until recently also confirms); 2) a more general strategic necessity to protect its Pacific coast from any threats emanating from the Asia-Pacific region ('Pearl Harbour trauma'), which has been a constant since the 1900s (Green 2017); 3) an inherent attribute to define the USA as a global power (implying a global presence and a self-perception as an indispensable power with a universalist mission entitled to use violence as a means to advance its national cum universal interests – that is very clearly expressed in the NSS[5]); 4) a function of US economic interest in the Asia-Pacific region that had been a key motivation of its 1899/1900 open door policy and has continued to grow with the economic rise of the Asian countries throughout the 20th and 21st centuries (Green 2017) and 5) a demand for protection against regional threats by US allies (for instance explicitly South Korea and Japan against the Democratic People's Republic of Korea [DPRK] and more implicitly against China; Hahm 2017).

The shift from cold war bipolarity to unipolarity has been the major game changer and that has, in particular, affected the key role of China in all these complexes and sub-complexes: "How China relates to the East Asian region, and how the US and China relate to each other, are deeply intertwined issues which centrally affect not only the future of East Asian, but also global, security". And those depend largely on China's and America's internal developments (Buzan 2003:143). Fifteen years on, this prediction takes on an obvious significance as the policy of President Trump is explicitly returning to a realist geopolitical challenge to China. In parallel, the policy of Secretary General Xi Jinping to move to a more active international role for China has changed the narrative of China as a regional power and potential stakeholder in the international community to one of an explicitly global power on its own terms. The two together may even challenge Buzan's overall assumption about global unipolarity or multipolarity: Buzan argued that the relative autonomy of the RSC is radically different from the rigid bipolarity of the Cold War era and could not be captured either by the idea of globalisation or the 'dismal conclusion' about a world disorder (2003:144). The problem is that he does stick with a focus on the power of the USA and China and the penetration of the RSC by outside powers (of which only the USA is now left: "All that was retained of the extensive Cold War structure of great power intrusion into East Asia was the US position of local containment against China in support of US allies in Northeast Asia" (Buzan 2003:160). Hence, the difficulty of distentangling the global and regional containment strategy if on the both object of containment is China which is itself the key factor in NE Asian security.

This puts the finger also on one of the more problematic issues with Buzan's overall approach of distinguishing a global level of security (and analysis) and a regional one. For NE Asia the usefulness of that distinction is increasingly limited

5 Frazier and Stewart-Ingersoll (2010: 734): "With the exception of the US, however, great powers have had less capability or interest in projecting power globally".

as China is evolving slowly but surely to a global level actor, while the USA is so intricately part of the security complex specifically in NE Asia despite – as Buzan recognises – not being a regional actor. It is hard to disentangle the somewhat abstract global level from the regional level. In any case, capability alone does not determine security orders (Frazier and Stewart-Ingersoll 2010:734), but neither can it then be the same as authors assert (p 737) that the number and relative strength of the regional powers are the major determinants of a regional security order which is simply the translation of an anarchic structure of international relations into a regional level to measure polarity. At the level of (military) capability, it is clear that in NE Asia – with or without the USA – a military conflict would be so costly that it seems a very remote possibility that threats of violence (e.g. China-Taiwan, DPRK-Republic of Korea [RoK]) would actually be carried out. However, small-scale conflict (maritime, airspace and territorial issues) and rollback of spheres of influence, etc. have become the new normal in the last decade or so (ICG 2013, 2014; Hagström 2012). And this new normal is not a function of US-China rivalry, but can be explained by the nationalist dynamics over moralisation gaps in the region (Hahm 2017).

Beyond the US presence in NE Asia and its multiple motives, it is important to uncover the dynamics of conflicted regionness in NE Asia which are not only relevant for security analysis, but also for many other perspectives, economic and environmental governance for instance. Regional economic and environmental cooperation (more than globalisation) require the solving or at least shelving of nationalist conflicts such as during the 1960s–1990s (Hahm 2017). Some of these problems with Buzan's approach can be addressed by considering the RSC as one element in international society that goes beyond security-focused analysis. Beyond the power-related issues, however, international relations analysis in the 21st century has to take account of other realities – the diffusion of power in complexity, the common threats to humanity (climate change) and global and regional economic governance. In all these areas, distinguishing global and regional levels makes only very limited sense, but multilateral cooperation is essential (Wissenbach 2018). I focus here on the internal contradiction of Buzan and Waever's (2003:44) contention that an RSC is a set of units whose security is so interlinked that their security problems cannot be analysed or resolved apart from one another. Thus, I go beyond the distinction between global and the regional levels in NE Asia and focus squarely on the conflicted regionness – that is the very relationships between the 'units' to construct NE Asia as a region.

To understand the evolution of international society in NE Asia to the conflicted regionness today, it is important to examine historical pathways and critical junctures which have shaped the ideological and constitutive institutions of international society and also produced the RSC that Buzan has analysed. The constitutive institutions of international society are sovereignty, international law and the economy; and without focusing on these, it is problematic to analyse NE Asia's regionness. If sovereignty is defined through nationalism, it correlates with a focus on maximising national power over responsibility, on procedural justice and moralisation gaps, constraining cooperation as we can observe in NE Asia. Buzan (2003) only very cursorily addresses this important historical depth as he remains largely focused on explaining the mutation of the RSC in Asia at the end of the Cold War. He mentions nationalism, historical grievances and territorial conflicts, but they are not developed because of his focus on US-China relations as the main (if not only) variable to determine the RSC.

By contrast I argue that nationalism, critical junctures and moralisation gaps at a deeper level need to be taken account of in conflict analysis as independent variables not just informing power relations. Power in this perspective is given meaning by these variables. My analysis is complementary to Buzan's – it 'informs' the RSC and explains its formation and constitution, but also goes beyond to explain other aspects of regionness than security relations (for instance economic issues and regionalisation). I focus on the moralisation gaps between the countries of NE Asia. Some of the reasons for the problems of the RSC in NE Asia are also linked to moralisation gaps between the USA and some of the countries in NE Asia due to the US focus on cold war containment and its failure to settle outstanding territorial issues such as Dokdo/Takeshima and the Diaoyu/Senkaku islets after the Pacific War (Hahm 2017). An example is the gap between North Korea's demand for recognition and a peace agreement concluding the Korean War that would bring some closure to a major historical grievance and the exclusive US focus on North Korea's nuclear programme as a threat to its national security (and to some extent that of its allies – NSS 2017). This is a clear and wide moralisation gap that is not easy to bridge. And it is only one of many in NE Asia.

Nationalism and Realism

This chapter argues that the rise of nationalism in the 19th century shaped international society in NE Asia durably. Key institutions of international society imported from Europe gyrating around national sovereignty then locked nationalism into international society in combination with realism, militarism, war and cold war in the 20th century. NE Asia's RSC (Buzan 2003) has been deeply shaped by nationalism not just US-China rivalry and US-North Korea antagonism. Consequently, nationalism, 'moralisation gaps' and a fierce contest in NE

Asia about the 'correct' version of history are feeding current sovereignty and international law disputes in the region even between US allies. Nationalism has also prevented NE Asia's regionalisation despite theoretically conducive conditions of globalisation, economic interdependence and the regional leadership of ASEAN.

Realism and the early English School cannot explain this pathway because they focus on war and great power balance in a narrow and fairly statist view of power. These concepts were useful to explain European politics from the 18th century to the Cold War (Buzan and Waever 2003) but cannot explain peaceful Confucian International Society or why the EU emerged as an enduring and powerful economic and security community (Wissenbach 2018). The EU was usually and tellingly discarded from theorising in realist accounts (often assuming that sooner or later it would disintegrate). These approaches also fail to convincingly explain today's tensions and conflicts over history, territory and identity in NE Asia that linger below the new US-China rivalry like magma under a rocky surface (Gustafsson 2016).

Hurrell (2007:16) questions the centrality of power more generally rejecting "the view that the international system can be viewed solely in material terms as a decentralised, anarchic structure in which functionally undifferentiated states vary only according to the distribution of power". Instead he underlines the dynamic social and relational structure of international society:

> Central to the 'system' is a historically created, and evolving, structure of common understandings, rules, norms, and expectations. The concepts of state sovereignty, international law, or war are not given by the game of power-politics. Rather, shared and historically grounded understandings of war or sovereignty shape what the nature of the game is, how it is to be played, and, very critically, how it has changed and evolved.

It is precisely how these understandings evolved through critical junctures in the region's historical pathway that I examine in this chapter.

A key point here is to recognise that power politics (labelled 'realism' in the 20th century) is also a socially constructed, ideological institution. While it is often 'objectivised' as the default mode of international interaction, like in the NSS and even by Hurrell (2007:31[6]), it is not a principle like anarchy or hierarchy. It is the simplest, most instinctive but also 'uncivilised' way of ordering a group as described by Hobbes' view of the state of nature which in fact described

---

6 "There is indeed a profound sense in which it is the possibility of war and conflict that continues to define the meaning of 'normal' politics and our understanding of political order".

human behaviour before society formation. And it is intimately linked to ideas of the 19th and 20th century such as nationalism, social Darwinism or colonialism. Those ideas incidentally and disturbingly marked the moral low point of European civilisation. Confucian international society did not rely on this institution to order relationships (Kang 2010). Today, a complex civilising process has come to discredit violent *use* of power as a legitimate social institution to order society, first in domestic society, but ultimately also in international relations (Pinker 2011). As Nye (2011:12) says: "on an increasing number of issues in the twenty-first century, war is not the ultimate arbiter". Nevertheless, threats of force are still commonplace in the rhetoric in NE Asia notably between the DPRK and ROK and the PRC and Taiwan.

In order to explain nationalism as a starting point for a RSC and regionalisation analysis we need historical institutionalism as a tool. This means a focus on historical pathways and critical junctures. The term describes a society moving from one predominant behavioural pattern to another one (Grimm and Schneider 2011:3). That is, for example the case of the breakdown of the Confucian international society at the end of the 19th century which led NE Asian states to adopt the 'Westphalian' state system, or the change in Europe from the 'Westphalian' system of power and war politics to that of European integration after 1945. Another critical juncture, shaping the RSCs globally and in Asia in particular, is the end of the Cold War (Buzan 2003). The concept of critical juncture differs from 'power transition' which is a much narrower concept of (linear or cyclical) change of power distribution within a rigid, unchanged system premised on 'classical' anarchy (Jørgensen 2013). Power transition models ignore the importance of history and emotions (nationalism) and the formation of an international society (not least due to globalisation and multilateralism) by focussing narrowly on material capabilities and rivalry for hegemony as an end in itself.

The first critical juncture that is relevant for my analysis of China's regional neighbourhood and NE Asia's conflicted regionness dates back to the end of the 19th century. The forceful extension of Europe's 'Westphalian state system' and its (partly social-Darwinist) ideas of nationalism and a 'standard of civilisation' to NE Asia irreparably destroyed the Confucian international society with deep consequences until today. 'Westphalian' ideas contributed to China's decline and the birth of Japan's imperialism under the guise of a regional integration project. The violent upheavals over many decades that followed the Western and Japanese imperialism left deep scars of historical justice, victim-perpetrator relations, moralisation gaps and disputes over territories explaining shallow regionalism and tensions about seemingly trivial issues in the region today. China's rise today – at least from a Chinese vantage point – is the reversal of its decline at the hands of external powers (European and American) and its nemesis in the region – Japan.

When Western powers, some of which had earlier blended into the regional international society (the investiture and tribute systems managed by China and Japan; Suzuki 2014; Zhang 2014), turned towards colonising Asia, they destroyed a peaceful and prosperous international society – the Confucian world (Song 2012). NE Asia's traditional regional society imploded. The Western 'modern' logic of anarchy, sovereignty, 'equality' and nationalism overpowered the Confucian logic of cultural homogeneity, hierarchy and harmony through respect for inequality (Mühlhahn 2019). This has had traumatic consequences which are still informing today's international relations (Lovell 2011, Qu 2010; Schmid 2002).

At the end of the 19th century, all 'new' nations in NE Asia found proofs in their often distant past that their nations had not always been 'weak and inferior' as they were portrayed to be in the social-Darwinist climate of the time. Historians quickly noted that past territorial control was not congruent with present-day borders (notably in the frontier lands of Manchuria and the maritime domain; Kang 2010:139–157). Reconfiguring the own nation in the centre was crucial[7]:

> The "Middle Kingdom" was no longer seen as occupying the center but was decidedly on the periphery, both globally and regionally. And as peripheral, China was anything but civilized. This reorientation called into question the full range of practices, texts, and customs that for centuries had been shared by Koreans as part of their participation in the transnational Confucian realm. Formerly accepted as universal, these were increasingly deemed Chinese and thus alien to Korea. (Schmid 2002:11).

This nationalist rejection of a common history continues nowadays and some of the most acrimonious disputes in NE Asia are about history and the moralisation gaps left by it.

The infection with ideas developed in a very specific context in Europe led to extreme violence in the 20th century in NE Asia – including hot wars during the Cold War, which in turn has consequences until today due to the resulting and multiple moralisation gaps – the gap of grievances and historical justice between victims and perpetrators (see below). These have caused both the current conflict fault lines and the region's inability to pursue a region-building project (Gustaffsson 2016; Hahm 2017).

7 Miscievic (2010: 13–5) explains that the moral claim of the centrality of the nation is at the very heart of the nationalist programme.

A short list covering the most salient of NE Asia's moralisation gaps could look like this (and my point is not to argue who is right or wrong or to draw up a complete list of problems and issues; more detail in Wissenbach (2018)):

1) China-Japan: Japan's colonial annexations (Taiwan including the Senkaku/Diaoyu in 1895; Shandong/Tsingtao in 1919; Manchuria in 1931), its invasion of China (1937–1945) and related atrocities (Nanjing massacre; genetic, biological and chemical experiments on humans and many more); the visits of Japanese politicians to the Yasukuni shrine (where class A war criminals are enshrined among the war dead); the comfort women controversy; and controversies over history textbooks, apologies and how they cover or not these subjects (Gustafsson 2016).
2) Korea (both South and North)-Japan: colonisation and abductees – forced labourers (abductees) and comfort women/sex slaves (1910–1945) and related requests for compensation and sincere apologies; Dokdo/Takeshima, the Yasukuni shrine visits; Japan benefiting from the Korean War 1950–1953. Japan vis-à-vis China and Korea deplores a perceived lack of recognition as liberator from Western colonial rule and the economic benefits of its former colonial rule, of its apologies and post-war contributions to peace and prosperity; comfort women often seen as volunteers (Watanabe 2015:25; Selden 2011).
3) China-South Korea: 'ownership' of ethnic and cultural heritage and borders (Yanbian district); the Korean or Chinese character of the ancient kingdom of Goguryo; China's participation in the Korean War saving the North and perpetuating Korea's division (Hahm 2015:19), some maritime disputes.
4) China-North Korea: DPRK stresses ethnic purity and autarky; China's reforms and capitalist ways are seen as betrayal of socialism; China's hegemonic attitude; Chinese irritation at North Korea's ungratefulness towards China after it sacrificed its conquest of Taiwan in favour of helping North Korea fight America and North Korea's destabilising nuclear brinkmanship which undermines Chinese arms control diplomacy and complicates China's relations with the USA.
5) Japan-USA: nuclear bombs, legitimacy of war crime tribunals, comfort women, US-imposed constitution with limited sovereignty and the renunciation of the use of force; perceived lack of recognition for apologies and post-war contributions to peace and prosperity.
6) Japan-Russia: loss of territory (Northern territories/Kuriles in 1945 to the USSR, with the 1956 Joint Declaration between Japan and the USSR making the restitution of two of the four islands conditional upon a peace treaty).

7) North Korea-USA: DPRK poses as victim of US aggression and hostile policy (and US carpet bombing during the Korean War), Japan and North Korea have similar moralisation gaps as South Korea but is even more hostile than ROK on abductees of Koreans to Japan (while for Japan more recent abductions of Japanese citizens by North Korea are a key grievance).
8) North and South Korea: two different accounts over the anti-Japanese struggle and the Korean War. South Korea sees the North as an illegitimate 'other' responsible for the division of the Korean nation, while North Korea sees itself as the true, independent Korea and the South as an American colony. There are issues about abductees and separated families, naval battles along the contested Northern Limit Line (NLL – Roehrig 2009), the DPRK's nuclear programme, attacks on ROK and political assassinations (including former President Park's), military exercises and threats.
9) China-Taiwan and Hong Kong: One China policy, opposite views on the anti-Japanese struggle, the civil war and democracy

Not all moralisation gaps can be covered here, but the list is intended to show the number of the most significant moralisation gaps and regional dynamics. Most tend to be linked to similar critical junctures (the destruction of Confucian international society[8], Japan's imperialism[9], the Cold War). A closer examination

---

8 This destruction of the regional order started with the Opium Wars of the British Empire against the Qing Empire (1839–1842 and 1856–1860) to open up China to Britain's trade (Lovell 2011; but China's internal weaknesses have been obscured by nationalist historiography, Mühlhahn 2019: 129–130). There is no general account of the regional impact of the West on the Confucian world: Kang's (2010) book focuses on the Confucian society and how it worked, not how it was destroyed. Mishra (2012) comes closest, but his book – which also covers the Middle East and India – says very little on Korea for instance. A regional history of 19th- and 20th-century NE Asia remains to be written. See Wissenbach (2018) for a more detailed account.

9 According to Selden (2008:12–13), "Japan broke sharply with the dynamics of center-periphery relations associated with the tributary order. Perhaps most strikingly, in contrast to the protracted peace of eighteenth century East Asia under the earlier tributary order, Japan precipitated successive wars that kept the region in turmoil and ended in defeat for the brash, upstart empire within half a century". Japan forced the Qing through the treaty of Shimonoseki (1895) to cede Taiwan, but the Treaty laid also the groundwork for Japan's subsequent annexation of Korea (Schmid 2002: 26; Oberländer 2012: 272). The Japanese aggression against China is a story that extended over 50 years and that I cannot possibly adequately tell here (Mitter 2014 provides a detailed account). The territories taken by Japan in this period included the nowadays disputed islets like Dokdo/Takeshima and Diaoyu/Senkaku.

of those would corroborate my main argument about the importance of historical grievances, critical junctures and how they relate to moralisation gaps and present distrust and emotionally charged perceptions and decisions, impeding attempts at integration and cooperation despite 'rational' incentives (Wissenbach 2018).

This narrative and list of moralisation gaps are completely different from that of a systemic global challenge such as the Soviet Union presented to the USA or US-China rivalry. Therefore, the conflicted regionness of NE Asia is an important complement to scholarly analysis that focuses on US competition with China.

Nationalism and Regional Conflict Dynamics

The main difference, therefore, of my analysis with realist accounts but also with Buzan's (2003) or authors who build on his pioneering work such as Frazier and Stewart-Ingersoll's (2010) and who combine realist and constructivist analysis is that I go beyond their more narrow focus on power relations (in the region and globally). Where Frazier and Stewart-Ingersoll (2010:732) argue that their regional power approach can help explain the variation in regional dynamics they observe in RSCs globally, I argue that this approach needs to be contextualised and that variations can be better explained by an analysis of historical pathways, critical junctures and moralisation gaps, which do not simply translate into power roles and regional system preferences. This is a synthesis of different theoretical approaches or analytical prisms, rather than a paradigm shift.

Nationalism and the related quest for power and status recognition (Miscevic 2010; Gustafsson 2016) is a crucial 'switch' determining the pathways and institutions of international society in particular at critical junctures. Power relations as such are not the explanation for the conflicted regionness of NE Asia today. Nationalism has produced violent conflict and war in the 19th and 20th centuries and explains rivalry and competition today even between countries and territories sharing liberal-democratic systems (for instance Japan, South Korea, Taiwan or Hong Kong). Nationalism is understood as an interaction between social psychology, history, sovereignty and international law often along potentially conflict-prone moralisation gaps. Bringing nationalism into the concept of international society sheds new light on the acceptability of norms acknowledging different historical trajectories and cultural and political values (or world views; Hurrell 2007:17) within international society. Astonishingly, nationalism is virtually absent in IR literature while anyone watching the news notices its significance. But it is a key variable to explain international relations and conflict in NE Asia in particular (Wissenbach 2018).

Nationalism produces the narratives of national glory and of victimhood at the hands of foreigners. Such narratives are mostly absent in IR scholarship, although they are "the single most decisive mental construct shaping foreign policy" (Ignatieff 2014:2). Moralisation gaps in turn describe the gaps of perception on historical events between victims and victors: the victim emphasises the deliberateness of the perpetrator and the pain and suffering he endures as victim. The perpetrator emphasises reasonableness or unavoidability of the action and minimises the victim's pain (Pinker 2011:537). But each side sincerely believes their version of the story, namely that one is an innocent and long-suffering victim and the other a malevolent and treacherous sadist. The counterpart of too much memory on the part of the victim is too little memory on the part of the perpetrators. All sides of a conflict "are convinced of their rectitude and can back up their convictions with the historical record. That record may include some whoppers, but it may just be biased by the omission of facts we consider significant and the sacralization of facts that we consider ancient history" (Pinker 2011:494). Human psychology distorts our interpretation and memory of harmful events, driven by a desire to present the self in a positive light (Pinker 2011:488–97). Such moralisation gaps are not limited to NE Asia. They are common throughout history and throughout the world as Ignatieff shows under the surface of the Ukraine crisis in 2014: "emotions of volcanic force, two competing genocide narratives – one Russian, the other Ukrainian – that cannot acknowledge each other's truth" (2014:9). In NE Asia, moralisation gaps are key to understand the conflicted regionness (Wissenbach 2018).

Through the European integration process and reconciliation of moralisation gaps after 1945 sovereignty, international law and the 'national' economies were transformed by a gradual shift from nationalism to multilateralism and the forging of a more and more integrated 'European' economy. These transformations were institutionally and legally built up over the last half-century and drawing on intellectual roots of centuries past. Multilateral integration has largely displaced Europe's earlier antagonistic nationalist historic narratives while national identities themselves remain strong. Europe's historical pathway of reconciliation need not be unique. But the EU's deep constitutionalised integration remains an exception in a world of regions while the EU itself is by no means a post-sovereign or post-national polity and hence need not be treated as a 'sui generis' case in international society. Intellectual roots of a shared past also exist in NE Asia, but they are not usually drawn upon for a regional project, although narratives of a renewal of a Sino-centric regional order have surfaced – usually conceived of a Chinese hegemonic bid (French 2017). Nationalist antagonistic narratives undermine attempts at regionalisation. However, the narrative of a shared long peace and of cultural achievement in the Confucian proto-security community is largely absent in today's national narratives of often antagonistic identities. Visions for NE Asian cooperation also largely ignore this past community. Instead the narrative of commonality and harmony is disfigured by projecting the modern nationalist narratives backward in time.

A focus on nationalism brings into the limelight distinct national and regional pathways shaped by historical junctures and narratives which have created specific beliefs and role-relationships for countries in NE Asia. It may be tempting to follow simple explanations such as geopolitics, the rise and decline of great powers, etc. which informs America's NSS. But digging deeper, under this mechanical layer NE Asia's many conflicts reveal underlying moral and emotional positions: historical grievances and demands for recognition which are expressed through nationalism (Gustafsson 2016). Nationalism is therefore not just a domestic issue – it is an ideological belief that deeply structures international relations alongside other factors such as power. Multilateralism, on the other hand, most visibly in the EU, has emerged as a key principle to rein in the zero-sum world of nationalism and is the underlying principle of regionalisation.

Conclusion: Nationalism and the Lack of Regionalisation in NE Asia

The regionness in NE Asia is conflicted and that is undermining conventional regionalism explanations. European experience suggests that regional integration requires a political impulse and institutions. In NE Asia both are missing. Even with approaches to regionalism that discount the need for institutions or political frameworks, such as 'open regionalism' or 'new regionalism' (Telò 2015) it is difficult to explain NE Asia's conflicted relations amidst dense economic networks in which the countries are enmeshed. Not all is gloomy, though: despite this conflicted situation development states in NE Asia have grown very fast based on national competitiveness policies and regional and global value chains and have developed into key players in the global economy (members of G20). Hahm (2017) attributes this precisely to the shelving of nationalist grievances and military expenditure to focus on economic development in the decades up to the new millennium. The countries of NE Asia and the EU are also getting along well with each other (North Korea excepted). They have steadily deepened their political and economic ties (Christiansen, Kirchner and Wissenbach 2019;

Christiansen, Kirchner and Murray 2013). Both the EU and NE Asian countries are active shapers of global governance and emphasise the need for multilateral order. The EU-Japan economic partnership agreement entered into force in February 2019, eight years after the EU-ROK Free Trade Area (FTA).

But regionalisation in NE Asia is confined to an only fledgling and institutionally speaking very weak process of trilateral cooperation. North Korea is completely marginalised, but aggressively pursuing a nuclear missile programme that could spark a nuclear arms race in the region. Nationalism pervades political life and consequently there is no appetite for regionalism apart from loose association with or membership in larger regional organisations (Asia-Pacific Economic Cooperation [APEC], ASEAN, European External Action Service [EEAS], etc.).

Nationalism is the main obstacle to regionalisation in NE Asia. It implies an 'everyone for himself' or 'winner takes all' attitude. That USA has adopted an 'America first' national security strategy which does not support regionalism, but bilateralism is further unsettling the region (Hahm 2017). Buzan builds most of his scenarios on the assumption of Chinese nationalist aggressiveness and different reactions of the USA to that pugnacity, neglecting that the US containment strategy in itself is not benign (Woodward 2017) and that nationalism in other countries may also contribute to conflict situations. Entirely missing is the scenario that US disengagement could actually force the regional powers to address the regional conflicts rather than to rely on the US support. In other words, Japan, for instance could under the US security shield avoid coming to terms with its imperialist legacy and the conflicts with its neighbours about that legacy, which is the main obstacle to realise a scenario of constructing a security regime (not to mention a path to integration) that could effectively address the underlying conflict dynamics (Gustafsson 2016; ICG 2014; Jerdén 2014; Hagström 2012). These dynamics have been suppressed by the narrative of anti-communist containment portraying China into the corner of an uncivilised outcast (Hagström and Hanssen 2016; reminiscent of the discourse on China's backward Confucianism at the end of the 19th century). Where Buzan (2003:168) argues that the US presence enables Japan to remain a civilian power (a label which in 2019 looks increasingly questionable given major changes to Japan's military doctrine and capability including the development of aircraft carriers and attempts to revise the pacifist constitution; Hagström and Hanssen 2016), it also enables it to escape its responsibility for conflict resolution, reconciliation and confidence building with its neighbours. So Buzan's (and many others') conclusion that everything depends on two crucial variables – the USA and China and their respective domestic developments (Buzan 2003:166–7) – is not taking enough account of the regional conflict and security dynamics and the reasons for NE Asia's conflicted regionness which go beyond power transitions before and after the Cold War. The US presence in the region is indeed an important factor, but also a factor that is facing scrutiny in terms of its legitimacy by more than providence (Green 2017). A key lesson from history is that a security order cannot be constructed by leaving a major power out of it (Biscop 2019). Paradoxically, the unpredictability of US policy and its pressure on its allies seem to have pushed the adversaries in NE Asia to resume long-stalled trilateral summits. Maybe the new cold war in NE Asia will not happen after all (Woodward 2017).

References

Buzan, B. (2003). "Security Architecture in Asia: The Interplay of Regional and Global Levels", *The Pacific Review*, 16(2), 143–173.

Buzan. B. and Waever, O. (2003). *Regions and Powers. The Structure of International Security*. Cambridge: Cambridge University Press.

Christiansen, T., Kirchner, E. and Wissenbach, U. (2019). *The European Union and China*. London: Macmillan Red Globe Press.

Christiansen, T., Kirchner, E. and Murray, P. (eds.). (2013). *The Palgrave Handbook of EU-Asia Relations*. Basingstoke: Palgrave.

Frazier, D. and Stewart-Ingersoll, R. (2010). "Regional Powers and Security: A Framework for Understanding Order within Regional Security Complexes", *European Journal of International Relations*, 16(4), 731–753.

French, H. (2017). *Everything Under the Heavens. How the Past Helps Shape China's Push for Global Power*. New York: Alfred A. Knopf.

Gowing, N. and Langdon, C. (2018). *Thinking the Unthinkable*. Melton: John Catt Educational Ltd.

Green, M. J. (2017). *By More than Providence. Grand Strategy and Power in the Asia Pacific since 1783*. New York: Columbia University Press.

Grimm, S. and Schneider, G. (2011). *Predicting Social Tipping Points. Current research and the way forward*. Bonn (DIE) *Discussion paper* 8/2011.

Gustafsson, K. (2016). "Routinised Recognition and Anxiety: Understanding the Deterioration in Sino-Japanese Relations", *Review of International Studies*, January 2016, 1–21. DOI:10.1017/S02602105000546 (accessed on 27.2.2019)

Hagström, L. (2012). " 'Power Shift' in East Asia? A Critical Reappraisal of Narratives on the Diaoyu/Senkaku Islands Incident in 2010", *The Chinese Journal of International Politics*, 5, 267–297.

Hagström, L. and Hanssen, U. (2016). "War Is Peace: The Rearticulation of 'Peace' in Japan's China Discourse", *Review of International Studies*, July 2015, 1–21.

Hahm, C. (2017). "Keeping Northeast Asia 'Abnormal': Origins of the Liberal International Order in Northeast Asia and the New Cold War. Seoul", The Asan Institute for Policy Studies. http://www.theasanforum.org/keeping-northeast-asia-abnormal-origins-of-the-liberal-international-order-in-northeast-asia-and-the-new-cold-war/ (accessed on 30 March 2020)

Hahm, C. (2015). "How China and South Korea Overcame History". In F. Godement (ed.), *How Do Asians See Their Future?*, pp. 17–21. European Council on Foreign Relations. http://www.ecfr.eu/page/-/ECFR130_CHINA_ASIA_REPORT_pdf.pdf (accessed on 27.2.2019).

Hurrell, A. (2007). *On Global Order. Power, Values, and the Constitution of International Society*. Oxford: Oxford University Press.

ICG (International Crisis Group) (2014). "Old Scores and New Grudges: Evolving Sino-Japanese Tensions", *Asia Report* No. 258, 24 July 2014.

ICG (International Crisis Group) (2013). "Dangerous Waters: China-Japan Relations on the Rocks", *Asia Report* No. 245, 8, April 2013.

Ignatieff, M. (2014). *The post-Ukraine world order. The Ditchley Foundation 50th Annual Lecture*. http://secure.ditchley.co.uk/news/post/141-the-post-ukraine-world-order-available-to-view-online (accessed on 18.12.2018).

Jerdén, B. (2014). "The Assertive China Narrative: Why It Is Wrong and How So Many Still Bought into It", *The Chinese Journal of International Politics*, 2014, 47–88.

Jørgensen, K. E. (2013). "Prospects for Multipolarity and Multilateralism in World Politics". In T. Christiansen, E. Kirchner and P. Murray (eds.), *The Palgrave Handbook of EU-Asia Relations*, pp. 45–58. Houndmills: Palgrave Macmillan.

Kang, D. C. (2010). *East Asia before the West. Five Centuries of Trade and Tribute*. New York: Columbia University Press.

Lovell, J. (2011). *The Opium War. Drugs, Dreams and the Making of China*. London: Picador.

Miscevic, N. (2010). "Nationalism". In E. N. Zalta (ed.), *The Stanford Encyclopedia of Philosophy* (Summer 2010 Edition), http://plato.stanford.edu/archives/sum2010/entries/nationalism/ (accessed on 27.2. 2019).

Mishra, P. (2012). *From the Ruins of Empire. The Revolt Against the West and the Remaking of Asia*. London: Allen Lane.

Mitter, R. (2014). *China's War with Japan, 1937-1945. The Struggle for Survival.* London: Penguin Books.

Mühlhahn, K. (2019). *Making China Modern. From the Great Qing to Xi Jinping.* Cambridge, Ma: The Belknap Press of Harvard University Press.

Nye, J. S. Jr. (2011). "Power and Foreign Policy", *Journal of Political Power*, 4(1), 9–24.

Oberländer, C. (2012). "Von den Ungleichen Verträgen zur Großmacht – Japans Weg zum modernen Nationalstaat". In *Geschichte Japans*, pp. 261–331. Stuttgart: Reclam.

Pinker, S. (2011). *The Better Angels of Our Nature: The Decline of Violence in History and Its Causes.* London: Allen Lane.

Qu Congwen. (2010) 中国人与主权观念:从被迫接受到主动建构 ("The Chinese and the Sovereign State: From Passive Receiving to Proactive Construction"), *World Economics and Politics*, 6, 64–78.

Roehrig, T. (2009). "North Korea and the Northern Limit Line", *North Korean Review*, Spring 2009, 8–22.

Schmid, A. (2002). *Korea between Empires, 1895-1919.* New York: Columbia University Press.

Selden, M. (2011). "Small Islets, Enduring Conflict: Dokdo, Korea-Japan Colonial Legacy and the United States", *The Asia-Pacific Journal*, 9(17), https://apjjf.org/2011/9/17/Mark-Selden/3520/article.html (accessed on 27.2.2019).

Selden, M. (2008). "Center and Periphery in East Asia in Three Epochs", *Journal of Northeast Asian History*, 5(1), 5–20.

Snyder, S. (2019). *Is Trump's Hard Bargaining Fraying U.S.-South Korean Ties?*, Washington: CFR, https://www.cfr.org/article/trumps-hard-bargaining-fraying-us-south-korean-ties?utm_medium=email&utm_source=dailybrief&utm_content=022719&sp_mid=58593176&sp_rid=dXdlLndpc3NlbmJhY2hAZWVhcy5ldXJvcGEuZXUS1, (accessed 28.12.2019).

Söderbaum, F. (2015). *Early, Old, New and Comparative Regionalism: The Scholarly Development of the Field.* Berlin: Freie Universität, *KFG, The Transformative Power of Europe, Working Paper* No. 64 (October 2015).

Song, N. (2012). "'Tributary' from a Multilateral and Multilayered Perspective", *The Chinese Journal of International Politics*, 5, 155–182. DOI:10.1093/cjip/pos005.

Suzuki, S. (2014). "Europe at the Periphery of the Japanese World Order". In S. Suzuki, Y. Zhang and J. Quirk (eds.), *International Orders in the Early Modern World. Before the rise of the West*, pp. 76–93. London and New York: Routledge.

Telò, M. (2015). "Three Reasons for Reasserting the Autonomy of a Regionalist and Interregionalist Research Agenda". In M. Telò, L. Fawcett and Fr. Ponjaert (eds.), *Interregionalism and the European Union. A Post-Revisionist Approach to Europe's Place in a Changing World*, pp. 67–83. Farnham: Ashgate.

The White House (2017). *National Security Strategy of the United States of America*. Washington, DC. https://www.whitehouse.gov/wp-content/uploads/2017/12/NSS-Final-12-18-2017-0905.pdf (accessed on 15.02.2019).

Tooze, A. (2018). *Crashed. How a Decade of Financial Crises Changed the World*. Penguin: Random House.

Watanabe, T. (2015). "History as a Diplomatic Tool". In F. Godement (ed.), *How Do Asians See Their Future?*, pp. 23–27. European Council on Foreign Relations. http://www.ecfr.eu/page/-/ECFR130_CHINA_ASIA_REPORT_pdf.pdf (accessed on 27.2.2019).

Wissenbach, U. (2018). *Nationalism versus multilateralism: International Society 2.0 and the diffusion of power in complexity – Europe and NE Asia in a world of issues*. Duisburg-Essen. urn:nbn:de:hbz:464-20181105-093346-4 and https://duepublico.uni-duisburg-essen.de/servlets/DocumentServlet?id=47382, accessed 12.12.2018.

Woodward, J. (2017). *The US vs China. Asia's new Cold War?* Manchester: Manchester University Press.

Zhang, Y. (2014). "Curious and exotic encounters: Europeans as supplicants in the Chinese Imperium, 1513–1793". In S. Suzuki, Y. Zhang and J. Quirk (eds.), *International Orders in the Early Modern World. Before the rise of the West*, pp. 55–75. London and New York: Routledge.

Yuan Feng

Comparative Analysis of the Association of South-East Asian Nations and the Shanghai Cooperation Organisation

The world order is currently moving into a period of greater uncertainty as China and the USA are in the midst of a major rivalry. Rising protectionism, the unclear future for multilateral trade institutions and the unpredictable trends relating to populism are all adding up to a lack of clarity. In this context, the Indo-Pacific region has attracted considerable attention as this is one of the most active regions in the world and is also where there is ongoing competition between China and the USA. As the regionalisation process is developing at an unprecedented speed, there are several subregions in this big area; and these subregions are also interacting and communicating as geopolitical and economic activities interact with one another. Differences in regime types, in economic profiles and diversity in terms of culture are all factors that are influencing the regionalisation of this area. As Mario Telò has pointed out, regionalisation in Asia is quite different from the process in Europe because "private and public forms of economic, trade and societal networking, association and cooperation within a region based on history, regions and geographical contiguity interplay with economic, technological, cultural, and trade globalisation in a positive or negative way according to time and space variations" (Telò, 2017, p. 18).

The Association of Southeast Asian Nations (ASEAN) and the Shanghai Cooperation Organisation (SCO) are both major regional institutions in this area. The two institutions have become more important as regionalism has become more prevalent in the Indo-Pacific region. They share common points in that they are institutions that have been initiated and are regulated by governments (Balassa, 1962). The ASEAN is by far the largest and most institutionalised regional organisation for south-east Asian countries while, after India and Pakistan joined it in 2017, the SCO covers the largest surface area and population out of all the regional institutions.

What we should not neglect is the fact that China plays a major role in both of the institutions. China has grasped the opportunity provided by the post–Cold War period of globalisation to initiate new norms and institutions, and China considers itself as the leader of developing countries and emerging powers (Telò, 2018, pp. 28–29). With the launch of the Belt and Road Initiative (BRI),

China's influences are even more prominent *vis-à-vis* the regionalisation of the whole area.

In this chapter, I would like to provide a comparative analysis of the ASEAN and the SCO in terms of their origins, structure, institutions and development models.

Brief Introduction to the ASEAN and the SCO

The ASEAN

The ASEAN was established in 1967, when the Cold War was at its peak. It was a time when south-east Asian countries had become independent and were robustly embracing nationalism. Its founding members include Indonesia, the Philippines, Malaysia, Singapore and Thailand. The ASEAN Declaration (Bangkok Declaration) has defined the founding ideas and core mission of the ASEAN: "To accelerate the economic growth, social progress and cultural development in the region through joint endeavours in the spirit of equality and partnership in order to strengthen the foundation for a prosperous and peaceful community of South-East Asian Nations". It is interesting to note that, as early as in 1967, the ASEAN Declaration had already pointed out that the current world is "increasingly interdependent" and the ASEAN desires to "contribute towards peace, progress and prosperity in the region" (ASEAN, 1967).

As the ASEAN was created against the Cold War background, and its founding members all had alliances with the USA, it was first considered by Vietnam and China as a political tool of the USA in the Asia-Pacific region (Ren, 2019). After the Cold War, the ASEAN strove to focus on economic cooperation among its member states. The Asian financial crisis in 1997 greatly reinforced the member states' determination to build stronger financial institutions in order to protect their domestic economies against external influences. In 2007, ASEAN member state leaders signed the ASEAN Charter, which greatly reinforced the institutionalisation of the ASEAN.

The Shanghai Cooperation Organisation

The Shanghai Cooperation Organisation (SCO) is an international organisation that covers the largest surface and population in the world. The SCO was established in 2001. It derived from the 'Shanghai Five', an organisation which was founded in 1997 and whose main aim was to provide a platform to discuss security issues (mainly border issues) between China and former countries of the Union of Soviet Socialist Republics (USSR). The founding countries include

Russia, China, Kazakhstan, Kyrgyzstan, Tajikistan and Uzbekistan. Unlike the ASEAN, it started on the basis of security issues rather than on the basis of economic cooperation.

The SCO is the first multilateral institution initiated by China. It is an important step in China's foreign policy history. At the same time, Russia has participated in the SCO although it has differences of opinion with China with regard to this institution's vision. For Russia, the SCO is an institution that can ward off USA's influences in this region, which I will elaborate in the paragraphs on external competition. Neither Russia nor China had been the creator of nor were they leading countries in current institutions when the SCO was founded. Both countries have a vision to revive their glorious historical past and to promote their regional influence. At the same time, both China and Russia are non-democratic countries. The USA's strategy of promoting the 'Coloured Revolution' in central Asia has created a natural tension between the USA and the two regional powers (Rumer, 2006). China and Russia need to justify their legitimacy and also strengthen the centripetal force of central Asian countries through multilateral institutions. Under these circumstances, the SCO has gradually transformed itself into a multilateral institution that seeks to promote regional economic integration by providing public goods. The SCO has developed into an institution that covers politics, economics, culture, military technology, education and public health.

Comparing the Institutional Structures

The ASEAN and the SCO have quite different organisational structures.

The ASEAN

For the ASEAN, the top of its decision-making apparatus is the Secretary General, which is situated permanently in Indonesia. It is then divided into four divisions, whose functions include supporting, evaluating, coordinating and connecting its daily work. There are another four departments, which subdivide into different directorates and divisions (Fig. 1).

The Shanghai Cooperation Organisation

The SCO's structure is much less complicated than the structure of the ASEAN and follows a different logic as to how it organises its work. The highest decision-making body is the Council of Heads of State. The Council of Heads of State meets once every year during SCO summits. Following the Council of Heads of

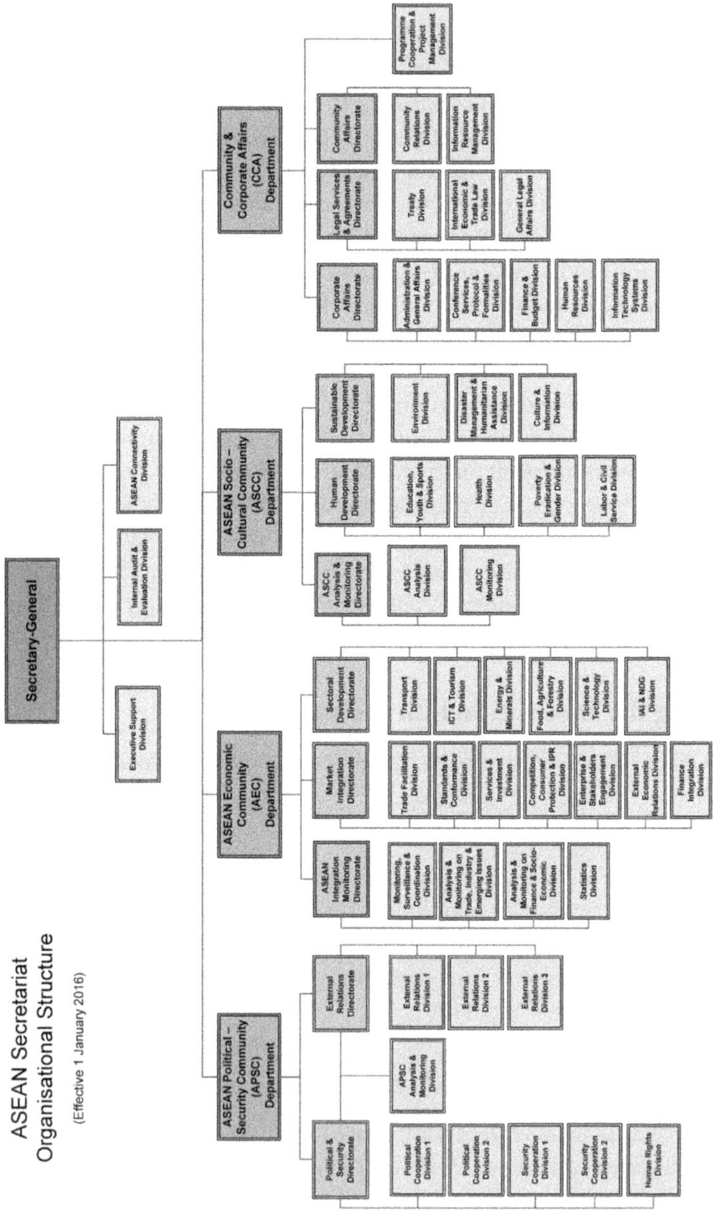

Fig. 1: ASEAN's structure. Source: ASEAN official site

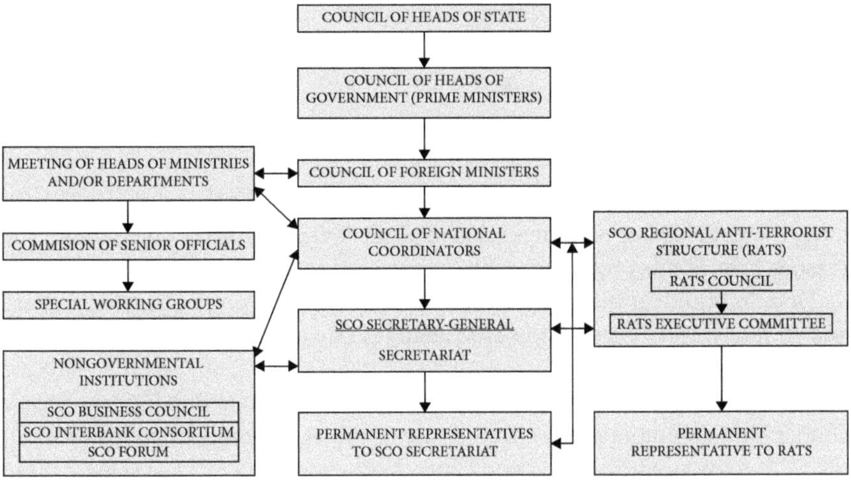

Fig. 2: The structure of the SCO. Source: SCO website

State, the Council of Heads of Government and the Council of Foreign Ministers also hold regular meetings. The Secretary General of the SCO is the executive body and is located in Beijing (Fig. 2).

It is clear that special attention was paid to the anti-terrorism function of the SCO by establishing an anti-terrorist structure (RATS), which is permanently located in Tashkent. By comparison with the relatively balanced structure of the ASEAN, the structure of the SCO still reflects these security functions. The SCO Business Council, SCO Interbank Consortium and SCO Forum are new economic arrangements that are developing.

Although the ASEAN and the SCO are both multilateral institutions and respect the principles that all members share the same rights, there is a distinct difference between the two institutions. Russia and China are two members in the SCO that dominate in terms of their influence. In the case of the ASEAN, there are no members that particularly dominate in terms of their influence.

The dominance of Russia and China is based on their objective conditions and historical legacies. Russia and China surpass other member states of the SCO in terms of surface area, population, economic and military powers.

As the provision of public goods is important in sustaining the development of each institution, the members who are in a position to guarantee the provision of public goods have relatively more influence. There have been many doubts expressed about the SCO's organisational model. The USA has tended to consider it as a military alliance while others express doubts as to whether the SCO is merely a club of heads of state without having anything concrete to achieve.

Comparing the Enlargement Processes

As relatively young international organisations, the ASEAN and the SCO both have the problem of suffering from a weak level of institutionalisation. The reasons behind this problem can be summarised as follows:

First, in both institutions, the member states have strong nationalist feelings and so non-interference in domestic affairs is one of the founding principles of both institutions.

Second, the lack of mutual political trust is still a factor that hinders deeper cooperation among members. In the case of the SCO, competing visions about the SCO harboured by Russia and China have caused the SCO to stagger on in terms of its development. In the case of the ASEAN, the identity of the ASEAN and how the ASEAN can continue to sustain its integrity and solidarity among members is also a major challenge.

However, these difficulties are common to all regional/international organisations. Employing a multilateral institution to try to overcome and sort out these issues also provides opportunities through which the institution can be strengthened.

Enlargement of the ASEAN

Enlargement is an important issue for any international or regional institution since it is an inevitable step as the institution develops and desires to gain more influence. At the same time, enlargement also represents the level of institutionalisation of the institution, its strategic visions and aims.

When the ASEAN was established, it clearly stated that the ASEAN is open to all south-east Asian nations that accept aims, principles and ideas mentioned in the ASEAN Declaration. The ASEAN has undergone four waves of enlargement, respectively, in 1984, 1995, 1997 and 1999, to have reached its current size (Tab. 1).

The ASEAN's enlargement process has experienced several challenges. The division between ideologies brought about by the Cold War certainly had an impact on its first enlargement. During its early years, the ASEAN was considered as a political tool of the USA or of the capitalist camp in south-east Asia.

Tab. 1: The ASEAN's enlargement timeline. Source: Illustrated by the author

Year of establishment/ enlargement	**Members**
1967	Indonesia, Malaysia, the Philippines, Singapore, Thailand
1984	Brunei Darussalam
1995	Vietnam
1997	Laos, Myanmar
1999	Cambodia

As a result, the integration of Vietnam became a controversial issue given that Vietnam is a communist country.

The differences in the types of regime, which emerged during the Cold War, have opened up many issues for debate. And these debates are still very relevant and inspirational for regionalism to this day. First, what is the fundamental basis of regionalism: identity? economic collaboration? regional security? Vietnam invaded Cambodia in 1978, which ran counter to the ASEAN's principle of non-interference in domestic affairs and of not exercising military power. That dealt a huge blow to 'the ASEAN way'. However, the ASEAN never really considered Vietnam as an enemy, but always as a potential member. After the Cold War, Vietnam sought to move closer to the ASEAN after it lost the financial support of the USSR. Finally, in 1995, Vietnam joined the ASEAN.

The same dilemma can be seen in the cases of Laos and Myanmar. Laos adopted a communist regime and Myanmar has been under military dictatorship. Both countries have concerns that the ASEAN may make demands on or criticise their domestic politics.

It has been a great success for the ASEAN to include Vietnam, Laos and Myanmar, which have had hostile relations with existing members. The ASEAN has managed to assimilate these members so that they truly accept the ASEAN's institutions.

It is important to point out that the ASEAN is a geographically defined organisation. With the current members, the ASEAN has already included all the south-east Asian countries. Thus, the ASEAN's future enlargement might encounter legitimate issues in relation to prospective members that are not traditionally considered as south-east Asian countries. Currently, Bangladesh, Fiji, Pakistan, Sri Lanka, Australia, Mongolia, New Zealand, Palau and Turkey are all considering joining the ASEAN.

Enlargement of the SCO

By comparison to the ASEAN, the enlargement of the SCO has been more prudent. Prospective members must first join as an observer. During the 4th Summit of the SCO, Shanghai Cooperation Organisation Observer Regulations were accepted and, at the 8th Summit in 2008, Shanghai Cooperation Organisation Dialogue Partner Regulations were accepted. In 2010 and 2011, the terms of SCO accepting new members and the Memorandum of Application to Shanghai Cooperation Organisation Responsibilities[1] were both adopted. These papers have provided a clear standard and legal process for enlargement. The conditions for any countries who want to join the SCO include:

1. The SCO is open to countries who accept SCO charts.
2. Countries that might become SCO member states should fulfil the following conditions:
   a. Situated in the Euro-Asian region
   b. Have established diplomatic relations with all SCO member states
   c. Have the status of observer or 'dialogue partner' status in the SCO
   d. Have active economic and cultural relations with SCO members
   e. Should not bear any international security responsibilities that are in conflict with other international treaties and documents signed by the SCO
   f. Should not be in military conflict with other countries
   g. Should accept the responsibilities defined by 'The United Nations' Charts and acknowledge international laws and regulations
   h. Should not be under United Nations' Security Council sanctions

The SCO has been quite prudent in its enlargement procedures. India, Pakistan, Mongolia and Iran have been observers since 2005. Afghanistan has had observer status since 2012.

Finally, in the Astana Summit of June 2017, India and Pakistan were formally granted member state status. Enlargement has been an important step for the SCO. This is not only because it has meant the enlargement of the SCO's surface area, population and economic output but it has also meant that, through the SCO, central Asia and south Asia have been connected within one organisation (Bai, 2017).

1 《关于申请国加入上海合作组织义务的备忘录范本》

India and Pakistan have had SCO observer status since 2005 and have had 12 years of contact and interaction with the SCO before officially joining the organisation.

Besides India and Pakistan, Mongolia and Iran have also been observers of the SCO. However, Mongolia did not decide to apply, while possibility of Iran joining has been ruled out due to UN sanctions imposed on the country.

The enlargement in 2017 has had many significant influences over the SCO. According to Li Jinfeng from the Institute of East European, Russian and Central Asian Studies of the Chinese Academy of Social Sciences, the inclusion of India and Pakistan expands the SCO from central Asia to south Asia, which helps to ease the competition between Russia and China in central Asia. As India is also a great nation, it transforms the previous leading pattern of the Russia-China core duo into a core trio of Russia, China and India (Li, 2015).

Indian membership of the SCO is strongly supported by Russia. Russia and India have enjoyed a friendship of more than 70 years under a Treaty of Peace and Friendship, which then turned into a strategic partnership (Indian Embassy to Russia, 2017). Russia is also a major supplier of weapons and energy to India. The two countries are also working together to promote a multipolar world order while India is considered as an important power to counterbalance China's growing influence (Hughes, 2019). As a major regional power in South Asia, India's booming economy and population demand huge quantities of energy. Joining the SCO can provide India with access to safe and cheaper energy resources and also connect India to central Asia (Zou, 2019, p. 35).

Whether or not Pakistan joins the SCO seems to be closely related to China's support. China and Pakistan share a long history of diplomatic relations: Pakistan was one of the first countries to have acknowledged the People's Republic of China (PRC) and had supported China's status in the United Nations. The strategic partnership between China and Pakistan is referred to as an 'All Weather Strategic Cooperative Partnership' while China and India are not bonded together via such a strategic partnership. The possibility of India and Pakistan joining the SCO partially reflects competition between China and Russia in this region and the balance of power between the two powers.

Another important point is that once SCO has admitted India and Pakistan, half of the members of the nuclear club will be within the SCO. This greatly increases the SCO's influence with regard to global strategic stability (Alimov, 2018, p. 3). The SCO has become an institution that links together a large part of Eurasia, but working out how to manage this gigantic area is quite a challenge. There are also concerns that the existing conflicts between India and Pakistan would hinder the SCO in its decision-making efficiency.

Compared to the ASEAN, the SCO has a wider and more ambiguous geographical scope concerning its prospective members. In the SCO charts, it only mentioned the Eurasian region, which could cover quite a large area. Although its original design mainly concerned central Asia, its enlargement to include India and Pakistan is not against its constitution. The SCO is also considering welcoming Iran and Afghanistan as new members. It is also worth mentioning that Armenia, Azerbaijan (Komsomolets, 2012), Bangladesh, Nepal, Sri Lanka, Egypt (TASS, 2015a) and Syria have applied for observer status; and Israel, Maldives and Ukraine have applied for 'dialogue partner' status (TASS, 2015b).

Provision of Public Goods

What are the public goods provided by an institution? How can one provide them? Who would pay for them and who would benefit from them would always be key issues for any institution.

The ASEAN and the SCO share the same issue as their member states have quite divergent political and economic profiles. Neither the ASEAN nor the SCO demand that a member state accepts a certain type of political regime or achieves certain economic standards in order to join. Both institutions support the principle of non-interference in domestic affairs, which also limits them in terms of efficiency of coordination.

The ASEAN

The ASEAN has already launched several infrastructure projects and infrastructure cooperation programmes to promote regional integration and exchanges, which are quite important public goods. These include the Greater Mekong Sub-region (GMS), the Mekong River Commission (MRC), the Brunei-Indonesia-Malaysia-Philippine East Asia Growth Area (BIMP-EAGA) and the Indonesia-Malaysia-Thailand Growth Triangle (IMT-GT) and the pan-Asian Initiative as the Asian Highway and the Trans-Asian Railway (TAR). In the energy sector, the ASEAN Power Grid and the Trans-ASEAN Pipeline are also important energy public goods (Bhattacharyay, 2009).

The most important achievement of the ASEAN is the ASEAN Free Trade Area (FTA). China has initiated the proposition of establishing a China-ASEAN FTA. There is also the Early Harvest plan, which allows different ASEAN member states to work with different products and different tariffs. This is a successful method that means that the FTA actually can put things into practice instead of getting stuck in debates. Following China's model, many countries have established an FTA agreement with the ASEAN, which has greatly boosted the vitality of the ASEAN's international commerce.

In 2015, the ASEAN established the ASEAN Economic Community (AEC). It is by far the most ambitious plan for strengthening the economic integration of this region. From the 2025 blueprint for the ASEAN[2], it is clear that, by providing the public goods of economic integration, the ASEAN is developing into a more coherent regional entity. The ASEAN would like to develop into an integral region, with a specified competitive tariff, regulations, financial tools, institutions and a single market. This indicates that the ASEAN is willing to deepen its institutionalisation process and to compete with non-member states as a whole.

The case of the ASEAN reveals to us a deepening form of regionalisation as nation states are coming together as regions in order to compete for more resources and economic growth.

The financial sources for funding these public goods are quite diverse in the case of the ASEAN. Public and private funding, ASEAN's huge foreign exchange reserves, domestic savings and investments from China, India and Japan are all contributing to the construction of infrastructure in the ASEAN. For example, China has launched China-ASEAN Investment Funding in 2009 to invest in various public projects in the ASEAN[3].

The ASEAN also receives funding from other countries or organisations to promote its regionalisation process. For example, since 2006, Japan has been providing funding to the ASEAN through Japan-ASEAN Integration Funding (JAIF). By 2018, JAIF had already funded 383 projects and another 76 projects were ongoing. These projects cover economic integration as well as cultural and educational exchanges for young people and damage management (Deng and Wang, 2018).

The European Union (EU) also provides specific funds to the ASEAN via the Europe-Asia Connectivity strategy, in order to facilitate the economic integration

---

2 Under the new blueprint, a stronger AEC is envisaged by 2025 with the following characteristics: (a) a highly integrated and cohesive economy; (b) a competitive, innovative, and dynamic ASEAN; (c) enhanced connectivity and sectoral cooperation; (d) a resilient, inclusive and people-oriented, people-centred ASEAN; and (e) a global ASEAN.

3 More information can be found in the website of the China-ASEAN Investment Cooperation Fund: http://www.china-asean-fund.com/index.php.

of the ASEAN. Financial support from Japan and the EU for the integration of the ASEAN shows that the regionalisation of east Asia is a process that attracts different powers attempting to exercise their influence. The regionalisation of east Asia is an inevitable process and the ASEAN is the most important institution that is carrying out this process. Japan's strategy lies in strengthening the recognition of identity between south-east Asian countries and Japan while the EU's strategic consideration lies in strengthening interregional relations with a possible integrated south-east Asia.

The SCO

Unlike the ASEAN, which benefits from external funding, the SCO is mainly financed by China. China has the vision to strengthen economic cooperation and regional economic integration among SCO members, and yet it is a task that is less easily achievable in comparison to security cooperation. Although SCO member states enjoy an abundance of natural resources, they have quite diversified economic profiles and lack economic cooperation.

At the Qingdao Summit of the SCO in 2018, China's President Xi Jinping proposed providing specific loans amounting to 30 billion CNY to the Shanghai Cooperation Organisation Development Bank. These specific loans were designed especially to facilitate regional trade and investment and to promote infrastructure cooperation in the construction of regional energy and transport infrastructure (Xinhua News Agency, 2018). At the same time, the SCO is also strengthening its ties with the Silk Road Foundation, the Asian Infrastructure Investment Bank and the China-Eurasia Economic Collaboration Foundation. Against the backdrop of global economic recession, an efficient form of cooperation that goes beyond national interests has become the way to get through the cooperation bottleneck dilemma. Many Chinese scholars also believe that this is the way that China can contribute to global governance and the building of a 'common fate community of human beings'.

China is the main member that is providing the financial support to get the system up and running.

Internal Conflicts

There are many internal conflicts in both the ASEAN and the SCO.

South-east Asia, central Asia and south Asia are all regions that face conflicts and security challenges. How to tackle these issues is testing the capability of each institution while at the same time also raising new issues.

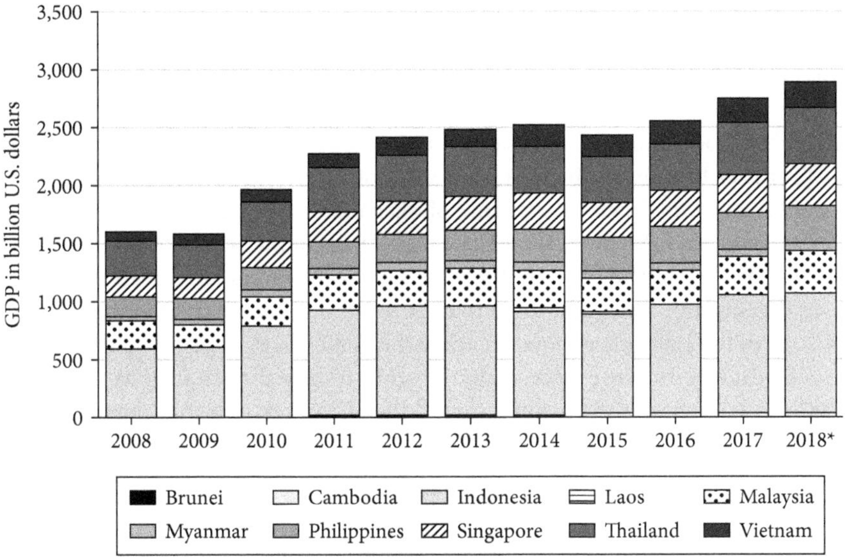

Graph 1: The GDP differences of the ASEAN member states. Source: Statista

The ASEAN

South-east Asian countries have experienced a very strong and stable economic boost in recent years. However, these growing economies have also led to an escalation in social inequalities.

The second challenge is the huge differences among the ASEAN member states' economies. Singapore's GDP is 55 times that of Laos. The differences in economic profile are reflected in differences in infrastructure, public health, anti-corruption levels and social securities (Wen, 2019). This makes it difficult for the ASEAN member states to cooperate within one single standard (Graph 1).

The lack of deeper economic integration hampers the ASEAN in terms of its ability to provide more public goods while the unsatisfied need for public goods would harm the ASEAN's further economic integration.

The SCO

For the SCO, Afghanistan and the escalating India-Pakistan conflicts are both challenging issues.

In Afghanistan, the growth and production of poppy and Taliban's military control are intertwined. After NATO withdrew its army from Afghanistan, terrorism has been closely connected to drug production and the drug business, acting as major destabilising factors in the region. If Afghanistan joins the Shanghai Cooperation Organisation, the SCO would need to make good on its promises to provide the necessary solutions to improve the situation. These would finally boil down to issues of political and economic resources.

For India and Pakistan, the recent escalating conflict in the Kashmir region is another destabilising factor. These two nuclear powers have been in dispute over the Kashmir region for more than 70 years. The recent crisis in the summer of 2019 in the Kashmir region has made the bilateral relationship between India and Pakistan very tense once again. Urgent security threats such as the India-Pakistan crisis have the potential to pull the SCO back into traditional security issues and distract it from its focus on economic integration.

As China envisions reinforcing the economic integration of the member states, the SCO faces the same problem as the ASEAN. There are huge differences in economic development among the SCO members.

External Challenges

The ASEAN

The ASEAN faces competition from other international institutions. This is largely due to the 'spaghetti bowl' effect in the Asia-Pacific region. Different institutions represent different visions and interests, and certainly include different members. Other international institutions include the Asia-Africa Conference (AAC), the Asia-Pacific Economic Cooperation (APEC) body and the East Asia-Latin America Forum.

At the same time, China-US rivalry in the region also poses a dilemma for the ASEAN. Both China and the USA are major trade partners for the ASEAN and yet the ASEAN does not have enough influence to deal with the two giants (Mahmood, 2018). The current US-China dilemma is putting solidarity among ASEAN members and the integrity of the ASEAN to the test and testing whether or not ASEAN can form a common position towards the rivalry between China and the USA (Hirubalan, 2019).

The Shanghai Cooperation Organisation

For the SCO, the greatest challenge lies in the fact that Russia does not fully accept China's development in central and west Asia. The competition between

China and Russia is the main conflict in the SCO (Zhou, 2014). As the SCO developed and China's presence in central Asia strengthened, Russia initiated the collective security treaty and Eurasian Union to maintain its influence over countries in the Commonwealth of Independent States (CIS). Thus, all the SCO member states, except China, are included in the two projects that Russia has initiated. What is special about the Eurasian Union is that it is not only an economic union that aims to achieve united customs, tariff and currency arrangements and free movement of people and merchandise as in the EU, but also a regional integration body that anchors Russia at the center of central Asia and makes the Russian language the dominant language in this region (L. Wang, 2012, p. 34).

China has always expected to promote economic integration among SCO members. As early as in 2003, China proposed establishing an SCO bank and even an SCO FTA. However, these are not priorities for the SCO in Russia's vision. Russia prefers to confine the SCO to security issues and considers the SCO as a tool to contain the USA's influence within central Asia (Chen, 2012). Russia prefers to keep China out of the economic development of central Asia.

At the same time, the USA is also paying considerable attention to central Asia. The USA launched its 'New Silk Road Plan' in 2011, which envisions encouraging central Asian countries to quit the Commonwealth of Independent States, the Collective Security Treaty Organisation and the SCO.

The ASEAN, the SCO and the BRI

As introduced previously, the ASEAN and the SCO are both major regional institutions. Both institutions have developed into sophisticated institutions. Another important aspect not to be neglected is that both the ASEAN and the SCO are concerned with the BRI.

As one of the most important strategies in China's foreign policy, central Asia and south-east Asia have been included in the BRI since the very beginning.

The BRI, which initially stood for the New Silk Road Economic Belt and the Maritime Silk Road respectively, has strategic considerations for the two regions.

For central Asia, the main concerns are:

The Economic Development of Western China

Xinjiang has the largest surface area of all the Chinese provinces. It enjoys an abundance of natural resources and is at the same time the home of many minority ethnic groups. Separatism and terrorism have been an ongoing and sensitive issue in this area. The Chinese government considers that promoting Xinjiang's

Industry	Unit	2007*	2008	2009*	2010	2011	2012	2013	2014	2015*
Steel	10,000 tons	3,500	600	1,691	1,186	2,846	937	884	3,113	957
Ferroalloys	10,000 tons	120	80	162	246	213	326	210	262	125
Iron	10,000 tons	3,000	1,400	2,113	4,100	3,192	1,078	618	2,823	762
Paper	10,000 tons	230	107	51	539	831	1,057	831	547	156
Flat glass	10,000 weight boxes	600	600	600	1,844	3,041	5,856	2,800	3,760	1,109
Coke	10,000 tons	1,000	1,500	1,809	2,533	2,006	2,493	2,400	1,853	600
Cement	1 million tons	50	50	74	140	155	258	106	88	39
Calcium carbide	10,000 tons	50	50	47	115	152	132	118	194	8
Aluminum	10,000 tons	10	15	31	38	64	27	27	51	36
Copper smelting	10,000 tons				25	43	76	86	76	8
Lead smelting	10,000 tons				32	66	134	96	36	49
Zinc smelting	10,000 tons				30	34	33	19		
Printing and dyeing	100 million meters				42	19	33	32	21	8
Chemical fiber	10,000 tons				68	37	26	55	11	
Leather	10,000 pieces				1,576	488	1,185	916	622	245
Lead acid battery	10,000 kvah						2,971	2,840	3,020	738
Citric acid	10,000 tons	2		1	2	4	7	7		
MSG	10,000 tons	5		4	23	8	14	29		
Alcohol	10,000 tons	40		36	85	49	74	34		
Total number of industries		**12**	**9****	**12**	**18**	**18**	**19**	**19**	**15**	**14**

* The 2007, 2009 and 2015 data are planned targets. The remaining are targets that were actually implemented.
** The 2008 data is incomplete. The total number of industries with assigned targets was likely to remain the same with 2007.

Tab. 2: The excessive production level elimination targets set by the Chinese government. Source: Ministry of Industry and Information Technology

economy would be an effective solution to reduce separatism and terrorism in this region. As Xinjiang is adjacent to Kazakhstan, Tajikistan and Kyrgyzstan, reinforcing regional economic collaboration would promote Xinjiang's domestic economy too. Thus, transforming central Asia into an important part of connecting China's economic centre with the European market can be a critical step towards boosting Xinjiang's economy, which conforms to China's 'Westward march strategy' (J. Wang, 2012; Yang, 2012).

1. The need to use up excessive production levels in steel and manufacture

China has noted its excessive production levels of steel and iron and has set the goal of eliminating excessive production levels (Tab. 2). Exporting excess steel and iron to other countries that need to construct infrastructure is an important step towards reaching the goal as it would not pose a risk to domestic employment levels. Thus, the BRI serves the goal of linking the domestic production surplus with the needs of neighbouring countries.

2. An alternative route for energy security for China

China has become a huge consumer of energy, especially petrol and natural gas. Traditionally, petrol reaches China through the Malacca strait, which has been infested with pirates and has been in an unstable regional situation. In order to guarantee a safer route for the transport of petrol, China would like to explore pipelines that can connect central Asian or Iranian petrol to China directly, which would be quicker and safer (Zhang, 2005; Xue, 2010).

For south-east Asia, China's strategy focuses on:

1. The promotion of an Asian identity, which would exclude non-regional powers from regional affairs

This point has become increasingly important since the trade war broke out between the USA and China. China's President Xi Jinping organised the Forum on Asian Civilizations soon after Trump launched the signal for a trade war in early 2019. Together with the BRI, Xi has proposed the concept of 'a common fate community of human beings', and subsequently translated this concept into China's foreign policy strategy. The focus of a 'common fate community' lies in understating the importance of differences in political types, but emphasising the common challenges[4] for human beings in the new era of global governance.

2. The promotion of the regional economic integration of south-east Asia

Economic integration is a key issue in all regionalism. China's promotion of the BRI also focuses on the expansion of bilateral trade between China and the ASEAN, which is very important in shaping a new economic order in east Asia.

3. South-east Asia is a cultural, institutional and geographical hub for the BRI

China considers south-east Asia to be a pivotal hub for the BRI. Besides ASEAN+3, China has also established many mechanisms for dialogue in different areas, and this reaches as far as the local government level. Since 2015, a China-ASEAN Province Dialogue has been held annually. At the same time, the China-ASEAN Expo and Business Development Forum, the Pan-Beibu Gulf Economic Cooperation Forum and the Bangladesh-China-India-Myanmar Economic Corridor (BCIMEC) Working Group Meeting are all providing dialogue platforms for all levels of government. These dialogues and interactions are designed to cultivate social capital among local governments between China and south-east Asian countries and can nurture economic, social and emotional ties among peoples that are promoted by the BRI (Hu and Wang, 2019).

4 This also corresponds to the fact that China has been emphasising 'non-traditional security' in global governance: climate change, cyber security, public health and terrorism.

China has already started cooperation with the ASEAN since 1991 and was accorded full dialogue partner status in 1996 (ASEAN, 2019). There have been many successful stories in this cooperation. As the BRI is developing into a strategy that has the potential to link several subregions, there are as many risks as opportunities. Evidently, there are many unresolved issues between China and ASEAN member states, for example the territorial disputes in the South China Sea with Malaysia and Brunei, while Indonesia and Malaysia pose a religious extremism threat towards China (Jin, 2019, p. 87). According to a survey conducted by Peking University, different ASEAN countries have a very diversified understanding and knowledge of the BRI. Thailand, Laos and Cambodia are enthusiastic supporters while Singapore, Malaysia, Indonesia and Brunei are worried that China's influence might grow in the region (Peking University, 2017).

With its active developing economies, the Asia-Pacific is certainly a region where different institutions are competing. Behind the competing institutions, there is competition for influence in future economic and political structures among great powers. With regard to south-east Asian countries, the Chinese-led Regional Economic Comprehensive Partnership (RECP) and the previously US-led Comprehensive and Progressive Agreement for Trans-Pacific Partnership (CPTPP) are in competition to attract countries in the Asia-Pacific regions to accept different sets of standards and norms. A country such as Vietnam, which is enjoying strong economic development, is also signing new FTA agreements and thus mapping its own FTA partners (Wang, 2019, p. 8). It would be relatively difficult for China to include Vietnam, a growing economy, into the BRI as it can attract enough foreign direct investment for its own development.

Conclusion

In this chapter, we have drawn comparisons between the ASEAN and the SCO.

They are both important regional institutions in Asia, and they have both institutionalised in order to negotiate more advantages from the process of globalisation. The two institutions have quite different starting points, institutions and internal and external issues. Table 3 lists these comparisons.

The ASEAN and the SCO have represented two different kinds of development models in the way that they have flourished. The ASEAN is coordinated mainly by its secretary as there are no dominant large countries in the member states which can exercise a dominant influence, while the SCO is inevitably influenced by China and Russia. The advantages of having great powers within an institution are that decisions are made more efficiently, and financial support is also

Tab. 3: Comparisons between the ASEAN and SCO

Item	ASEAN	SCO
Year of establishment	**1967**	**2001**
Orientation of institution	Starting from economic integration, then developing into security issues	Starting from security issues, then developing into economic integration
Institutions	Secretarial office with different divisions is the highest decision-making body	Council of Heads of State is the highest decision-making body
Enlargements	Geographically defined members, no prospects to enlarge further	Possibility of including Iran and Afghanistan
Provision of public goods	Public and private funding, member states' contributions, Japan-ASEAN Integration Funding, EU-Asia Connectivity Strategy Funding	Member states' contributions
Internal conflicts	Imbalance in economic development, social inequality, differences in regime type	Differences in economic development, different visions between Russia and China
External competition	'Spaghetti bowl' effect in the Asia-Pacific	Eurasia Economic Union, the USA's interference, the 'Colour Revolution'
BRI	Key region in the BRI, yet different countries have different attitudes towards the BRI	Key region in the BRI. Russia has different visions from China concerning this system

arranged more easily. The disadvantages lie in that, when China and Russia have divergences in vision, the institution runs the risk of becoming less efficient or even being left by the wayside.

In an era of rising regionalism, competition between institutions will be a long-lasting phenomenon. In the current regionalised and globalised world, building institutions is therefore the best option if one wants to guarantee member states' collective interests.

The enlargement issue for both the ASEAN and the SCO demonstrates that the institution may have spillover effects as it institutionalises and provides more public goods. Both institutions are expanding beyond their predesignated geographic borders, which indicates that the definition of any given region is not static but is constantly changing.

The ASEAN and the SCO are both and will continue to be important institutions in the big Indo-Pacific region. Nor should we neglect that China is also playing an increasingly important role in regional institution building. Through the BRI and infrastructure projects, China might coordinate with both institutions and play a central role in the regionalisation of central and south-east Asia.

References

Alimov, R. (2018). 'The Shanghai Cooperation Organisation: Its Role and Place in the Development of Eurasia', *Journal of Eurasian Studies*, 9(2), pp. 114–124. DOI: 10.1016/j.euras.2018.08.001.

ASEAN (1967). *The ASEAN Declaration (Bangkok Declaration)*. Thailand.

ASEAN (2019). *Overview of ASEAN-China Dialogue Relations*. Jakarta. Available at: http://www.asean-china-center.org/, accessed 23 August 2019.

Bai, L. (2017). 'Shanghai Hezuo Zuzhi Kuoyuan [Enlargement of Shanghai Cooperation Organisation: New Development Opportunities and Challenges]', *Guoji Wenti Yanjiu [China International Studies]*, pp. 56–69.

Balassa, B. (1962). *The Theory of Economic Integration*. London: Greenwood Publishing Group.

Bhattacharyay, B. N. (2009). *ADBI Working Paper Series Infrastructure Development for ASEAN Economic Integration*. Tokyo: Asian Development Bank Institute, www.adbi.org, accessed 19 August 2019.

Chen, X. (2012). 'Dang E Luo Si Fu Xing Yu Dao Zhong Guo Jue Qi [As Russia's Revival Meets China's Rising]', *Ling Dao Wen Cui [Leaders' Digest]*, https://www.zz-news.com/com/lingdaowencui/news/itemid-954232.html（accessed on 31 March 2020).

Deng, H. and Wang, D. (2018). 'Ri Ben-Dong Meng Yi Ti Hua Ji Jin Gai Kuang Ji Qi Fa Zhan Qu Shi [Japan-ASEAN Integration Fund and Its Development Trend]', *Guo Ji Yan Jiu Can Kao [International Studies Reference]*, 11, pp. 17–23.

Hirubalan, V. P. (2019). 'Thailand Takes up the ASEAN Challenge', *The Diplomat* https://thediplomat.com/2019/06/thailand-takes-up-the-asean-challenge/ （accessed on 31 March 2020).

Hu, J. and Wang, K. (2019). 'Di Fang Zheng Fu Kua Guo He Zuo de Dong Li Ji Zhi yu Yue Shu Tiao Jian: Yi Dai Yi Lu Bei Jing Xia Zhong Guo-Dong Meng de An Li Yan Jiu [The Dynamic Mechanism and Constraints of Local Government's Transnational Cooperation – A Case Study of China-ASEAN under]', *Di Fang Zhi Li Yan Jiu [Regional Management Studies]*, 2, pp. 13–25.

Hughes, L. (2019). *India's Continued Reliance on Russia: The China Factor*. Nedlands, http://www.futuredirections.org.au/wp-content/uploads/2019/03/Indias-Continued-Reliance-on-Russia.pdf, accessed 14 August 2019.

Indian Embassy to Russia (2017). *70 years of India Russia Relations: A Historic Milestone, Indian Embassy to Russia.*

Jin, D. (2019). ['Yi Dai Yi Lu" Chang Yi Xia Tui Jin Zhong Guo-Dong Meng He Zuo de Zheng Zhi Wai Jiao Ce Lue Yan Jiu [A Foreign Policy Strategy Study of China-ASEAN Cooperation under the Belt and Road Initiative]', *He Ping Yu Fa Zhan [Peace and Development]*, 2, pp. 84–101.

Komsomolets, M. (2012). 'Azerbaijan Asks to Join a New Alliance of China and Russia', *Azeri Daily*.

Li, J. (2015). 'Shanghai Hezuo Zuzhi Kuoyuan: Tiaozhan yu Jiyu [Enlargment of Shanghai Cooperation Organization: Challenge and Opportunity]', *Eluosi Zhongya Dongou Yanjiu [Russia, Central Asia and East Europe Studies]*, 6, pp. 36–44.

Mahmood, I. P. (2018). '7 Key Challenges for the Future of ASEAN – and How to Solve Them', *World Economic Forum* https://www.weforum.org/agenda/2018/08/7-challenges-to-business-in-the-asean-region-and-how-to-solve-them/ （accessed on 31 March 2020).

Peking University (2017). *'Yi Dai Yi Lu' Yan Xian Guo Jia Wu Tong Zhi Shu Bao Gao [Five Communicaiton Report of Belt and Road Initiative Countries]*. Beijing.

Ren, S. (2019). 'Dong Meng Yi Ti Hua de Xian Zhuang Yu Wen Ti [The Current Situation and Issues of ASEAN's Integration]', *Shi Dai Jing Mao [Economics and Commerce of the Time]*, 15, pp. 94–94.

Rumer, E. (2006). 'The U.S. Interests and Rules in Central Asia after K2', *The Washington Quarterly*, pp. 145–147.

TASS (2015a).'Egypt Applies to Become Dialogue Partner of Shanghai Security Bloc', *TASS*. https://tass.com/world/806320 （accessed on 31 March 2020).

TASS (2015b) 'Syria, Egypt May Join Shanghai Cooperation Organisation as Observers', *TASS*. https://tass.com/world/799107 （accessed on 31 March 2020).

Telò, M. (2017). *Regionalism in Hard Times: Competitive and post-liberal trends in Europe, Asia, Africa, and the Americas*. Oxon and New York: Routledge.

Telò, M. (2018). 'European and Chinese Multilateralism at Stake: Political and Theoretical Implications'. In Telò, M., Ding, C., and Zhang, X. (eds.), *Deepening the EU-China Partnership: Bridging Institutional and Ideational Differences in an Unstable World*. Oxon and New York: Routledge, pp. 28–42.

Wang, J. (2012). '"Xi Jin": Zhongguo Diyuan Zhanlue de Zai Pingheng [Marching to the West: The Rebalance of China's Geopolitics]', *Huan Qiu Shi Bao [Global Times]*. https://opinion.huanqiu.com/article/9CaKrnJxoLS（accessed on 31 March 2020).

Wang, L. (2012). 'E "Ou Ya Lian Meng" Zhan Lue Ji Qi Dui Zhong E Guan Xi de Ying Xiang [Russia's Eurasian Union Strategy and its influences on Sino-Russia Relation]', *Xiandai Guoji Guanxi [Contemporary International Relations]*, 4, pp. 33–37.

Wang, Q. (2019). '2018–2019 Nian Dong Meng Jing Ji de Fen Xi yu Yu Ce [Analysis and Forecase of ASEAN Economies (2018–2019)]', *Dong Nan Ya Zong Heng [Crossroads: Southeast Asia]*, 2, pp. 3–10.

Wen, S. (2019). 'Dong Meng Ji Chu Gong Gong Fu Wu Di Qu Jian Cha Yi Ji Jun Deng Hua Lu Jing Tan Xi [Analysis of Regional Differences in Public Services in ASEAN and Exploration of Equal Access to the Public Services]', *Chuang Xin [Innovation]*, 2, pp. 64–75.

Xinhua News Agency (2018)? 'Zhong Fang Jiang Zai Shang Hai He Zuo Zu Zhi Yin Hang Lian He Ti Kuang Jia Nei She Li 300 Yi Ren Min Bi Deng Zhi Zhuan Xiang Dai Kuan [China will establish Specific Loaning equal to 30 billion CNY within Shanghai Cooperation Organization Bank Union]', *Xinhua News Agency*, 10 June.

Xue, L. (2010). 'Ma Liu Jia Kun Jing Nei Han Bian Xi yu Zhong Guo de Ying Dui [The Dilemma of Malacca and China's Responses]', *Shijie Jingji yu Zhengzhi [World Economy and Politics]*, 10, pp. 117–140.

Yang, Y. (2012). 'Zhou Bian An Quan Xu Yao Quan Fang Wei Zhan Lue: Jian Yu Wang Jisi Jiaoshou Shangque [The Security of Neighboring Countries Need All-Positioning Strategy: A Discussion with Professor Wang Jisi]', *Huan Qiu Shi Bao [Global Times]*. https://opinion.huanqiu.com/article/9CaKrnJxuJO（accessed on 31 March 2020).

Zhang, J. (2005). 'Zhong Guo Neng Yuan An Quan Zhong de Ma Liu Jia Yin Su [Strait of Malacca in China's Energy Security]', *Guo Ji Zheng Zhi Yan Jiu [International Politics Quarterly]*, 3, pp. 18–27.

Zhou, J. (2014). 'Shanghai Hezuo Zuzhi Neibu Maodun Tanxi [The Analysis of Shanghai Cooperation Organisations' Inner Conflicts]', *Qian Yan [The Front]*, pp. 118–124.

Zou, X. (2019). 'Shi Xi Xin Shi Qi Shang He Zu Zhi de Fa Zhan Kun Jing yu Zhong Guo Ying Dui Fang An [Analysis of Shanghai Cooperation Organisation's Development Dilemma and China's Responding Strategy]', *Zhong Gong Ji Nan Shi Wei Dang Xiao Xue Bao [Study Journal of Jinan Communist Party Committee]*, 1, pp. 34–37.

Jean-François Di Meglio

The China Model and the Specific Case of China within the 'Belt and Road Initiative'

Global visions and regional plans would normally seem two very different sides of development policies for any nation. A standard approach would call for a global ambition or vision to only come after a nation's regional status has taken shape. It may constitute a legitimate and coherent, ascending profile and enable a nation which has built up a regional influence, and in the most positive scenarios, contributed to a region's well-being, status, and recognition to access global institutions and thus play a role in the world's governance.

In many regards, the scheme can definitely match the observations one can easily make in the US case. The best advocates of a strong, influential European Union (EU) entertain a similar version of Europe's future as a more global player and influencer in global governance and the potential process of reforming ailing institutions. In a nutshell, regional integration, cooperation and build-up would logically lead to playing a significant role in interregional and then global order.

Such 'common sense' observations could well stumble on two contradicting and emerging cases, or at least be challenged by them. Both cases crashed into the global scene roughly at the same time, and they are the 'late' Trans-Pacific Partnership (TPP), initiated by President Obama in 2013, which was supposed to shape up before the end of his second term but finally did not outlive his presidency, and the Chinese project now familiar to foreign observers under the name of BRI, Belt and Road Initiative, after being called 'New silk roads' and 'One Belt One Road, OBOR,' while the Chinese name remained unchanged.

As a matter of fact, the American project as well as the Chinese one, the twin and almost simultaneous inventions of which can be explained by each other's rivalry, did not obviously come before the USA and China 'globalized' but quite some time after. The American case needs not to be elaborated, as the USA had become 'the' global power once its various, non-democratic foes or rivals had been defeated in the Second World War then the aftermath of the 'Cold War.' For China, we shall here review how it had actually first arisen to a globally accepted status before it somewhat returned to a project deeply rooted in the region. Possibly, what the question and its potential answers bring up is a new dimension in the 21st-century's international relations, which is the very strong, iterative link between the regional and the international positioning of major powers.

The twentieth-century 'blocks' were not necessarily related to contiguity of the members belonging to the same 'block.' Although members of the Warsaw pact were neighbors, the Soviet block also embraced remote countries like Vietnam and Cuba, in a global chess game. Same could be said about the USA. In the 21st century, it looks like the constitution of the 'Transpacific Partnership,' a coherent geographic area constituted around a 'maritime/oceanic' focus while the 'BRI' would rather be related to a land base straddling the old continent in a continuous manner.

We shall to look into and understand the origins of such a phenomenon, its main and most obvious developments, but also the challenges it may face.

China's Model: "Globalize First, then Look at the National Priorities, the Regional Role Would Follow"

Originally, and while fully consistent with Chinese history which always had been punctuated by opposing sequences of 'openness' and 'closure,' the Chinese path to globalization originated with the burning need to boost the economy after the collapse triggered by the Cultural Revolution, among others. This is why, in 1978, during the famous third plenum of the XIth Congress of the Chinese Communist Party, Deng Xiaoping launched the process of the 'Four modernizations,' the core concept of which was the possibility to partner with foreigners through 'special economic zones' enabling investors from all countries to benefit from generous and attractive conditions. The project was mostly targeting countries belonging to the Western camp, although it did not obviously exclude Japan.

Skipping years and straddling various periods of China's recent history, economic and financial analyses all converge in stating that the eventual and major event in China's rise to the world had been when it joined WTO, in December 2001. This was indeed the incoronation of strenuous diplomatic and political efforts by Chinese leaders to get tolerance first, then acceptance of their unique model which was mimicking the liberal, market-oriented principles while deeply anchored in the post-1949, pragmatic and adaptative ideology. This model was a classical, 'open-door,' low tax scheme which was designed at letting the world come to China, at a time when the surrounding region ('the Tigers and the Dragons of the 1990s') would rather be competitors than partners and members of a regional community.

The goal itself was definitely not to be recognized as a member of an existing, post–Second World War community, rather to take a maximum number of Chinese citizens out of poverty and regain momentum in the economic process of catching up with the world's growth. It was actually 'inward-looking' and purely leveraging globalization in view of domestic development.

Since cooperation with a close neighbor but also old rival, that is Japan, was part of the plan, it is also interesting to consider how Japan actually had successively approached its own rise through the two opposed strategies. Imperial Japan had tragically failed in initially rising through a conquering, regionally expanding approach. The area of 'co-prosperity' was mostly Asia-oriented. Before it collapsed, it was totally similar to other examples of emerging powers trying to ascend to a global role by firming a regional base in the first place. The 'second New Japan,' born again after the Second World War, the surrender and the defeat, was an inspiring model for China: Japan's rise in the 1960s and 1970s was not stressing the importance of a regional role, but rather trying to reap benefits of trade, exchanges and flows of investments with the world and, in the first place, with the most powerful, albeit remote partners, way beyond the region, which still remained backwards and hardly constituting a springboard for Japanese prosperity. At least, the region was less of a priority than the openness to the world.

To a certain extent, one could then define a common, yet differing by some elements, model between Japan and China; and this model would take less into account regional cooperation than benefits earned from a renewed global exposure. Japan had succeeded in becoming a G7 member, reaching the second ranking in the global economies before the 'lost decade.' So this could really inspire China, and contradict well-established previous patterns.

However, such a success would also carry some risks, as two major weaknesses were casting shadows on the future developments: the risk that regional rivals, succeeding too well in following the famous 'wild geese' pattern, could rapidly catch up with the leader, and also the risk that too heavy a reliance on remote economies would expose the country too much to any potential, decorrelated downturn, or a reversal of complacency, or even some acts of retaliation by 'partners' around the world who would feel threatened by a new rival.

Both risks did materialize and affect Japan in a big way, as the Plaza agreement in 1985 led to a violent revaluation of the Japanese currency, thus leading to a sudden loss of competitiveness for Japanese products and, remotely, a need to partially repatriate capital to Japan once the economy slowed down. Yet Japan managed to react and consolidate regional bases, building a subcontracting network, strengthening its own role in Asian Development Bank, the headquarters of which are in Manila but is mostly run by and in favor of Japanese interests. Japan thus did combine an initial success in reaching out to the world and a subsequent reinforced regional role.

As for China, the 1997 'Asian crisis' gave a strong signal that danger from South-east Asia could materialize: deep and breathtaking devaluations by Thailand, Indonesia, and Philippines were both posing a risk to China's competitiveness and also pushing China to follow through and adopt the same devaluation policies in order to keep an edge to China's neighbors vis-à-vis global partners.

China's reaction was totally new and somewhat unexpected. Just like in Japan, and in a similar, bold posture, Chinese leaders decided to 'bite the bullet' and hold firm. Japan had adjusted its labor costs after the Plaza accord and remained competitive. China took the lead and positioned itself as the firewall against contamination by the 'devaluation disease.' It did so first by defending the Hong Kong dollar when the 'peg' (the fixed exchange rate between the currency and the USD) also came under attack. Then Chinese leaders reassured the Asian and global financial spheres, and gave evidence that the Chinese yuan would not devalue. China thus both earned a justification to its imminent entry to WTO as a responsible player and also a new role as a regional leader, able not only to protect the region from unfriendly speculators but also to cooperate and not compete with low-cost countries. Meanwhile, it also earned a top position as the main destination for foreign direct investments, which almost dried down in the direction of south-east Asia and were then rerouted to China, adding an extra 'shot in the arm' to the Chinese economy.

Apart from logical and important reasons for a 'pendulum' approach towards both internationalization and regional cooperation for Japan and China, a common feature can also explain the need and the rationale behind the sequences. Inasmuch as, in the case of the USA, reaching to a global cooperation role (and before them, UK) was logical since the American currency, once it started being used widely beyond US border, was a strong tool helping internationalization of US action; the case is very different for Japan and China. Although pressures on Japan to be more active in internationalizing the usage of the Japanese yen abroad was very strong, especially after the Plaza agreement in 1985, there was no willingness on the Japanese side to say the least. Internationalization of the JPY exists mostly by name, as the currency is indeed convertible, and also through the usage of JPY in some issuances of domestic bonds open for foreign purchases as well as bonds in international markets which were denominated in JPY. Full internationalization of the JPY was basically slowed down deliberately by the Bank of Japan and the Ministry of Finance, in fear that internationalizing would lead to a weaker control of monetary aggregates and policies. Hence regionalization of the JPY, making it a frequent tool for loans to regional borrowers before the Asian crisis (and again, over the last years since the beginning of the decade), had been a useful and efficient tool for cooperation.

For similar reasons, after China confirmed its international role both in the trade and industrial areas, after the 1978 reforms had opened the country, liberalized investments and post-WTO entry, the usage of the Chinese currency, which was far from being fully convertible and even reaching an international status, developed in a big way around the region. While trade had been conducted in foreign currencies, and although the ranking of the RMB rose in 2015 to the seventh position within the universe of currencies used in global trade, loans to foreign countries, development banks abroad, and even participation in the capital of international institutions were conducted in USD.

However, the usage of the 'renminbi' in dealings with lesser developed countries has accelerated with the creation of new bodies by China after 2012, as will be shown below.

'BRI' as a Representation of 'Regionalization within Internationalization'

The first mention of what would then become (in English at least) the 'Belt and Road initiative' (BRI) but at the time was presented as the 'New Silk Roads' was made in 2013 by Xi Jinping in Astana, and then again in Indonesia the same year.

As mentioned, it is worth noting that this is indeed concomitant with the emergence of the 'Transpacific Partnership.' In the time when Chinese commitment into global organizations like WTO obviously but also IMF, a member of which China had become first, before pushing for the inclusion of the renminbi into the special drawing rights (SDR) basket of currencies (effective 2016), the risk that China's rise was also more and more perceived as a challenge to American influence in the region, the invention of the US treaty and the proposal extended by President Obama to Asian and American countries friendly towards the USA showed the path towards new concepts. They were mostly providing a new format for multilateralism. As opposed to the previous 'multilateralist' approaches, where the common goal (be it for UN, World Bank, IMF and other similar institutions) was to gradually aggregate as many participants, stakeholders and partners as possible, this new approach takes stock of conflicting interests which cannot easily be resolved.

There have been many explanations and research on the origins of the 'Belt and Road concept,' first as a 'land-based' alliance for privileged trade and investment relation, as opposed to a 'maritime league' around the Pacific, by which the TPP could have been molded. Unarguably, such a concept could not have appeared without a growing self-confidence that Xi Jinping's regime has expressed.

There would be no such project without China's 'assertiveness.' The new posture taken by China obviously comes from the economic success and the observation also that the existing economic leaders were weakening, be it the region, like in the case of Japan, and worldwide, as was shown by the 2008 and more importantly the 2011 European banking crisis. As China had grown 'global' and dependent on other countries' successes, the risk to be impacted by any slowdown and the need to protect the momentum and create some sort of firewall emerged. While global clients supported the export-based model developed since 1978, the sustainability of growth could possibly be only secured by the creation of a 'China-dependent' region. Both the buffer needed to absorb potential overcapacities and the procurement for some basic goods or ingredients of growth, be they cheap labor force or natural resources, could be found through the creation of 'China-related' zone.

As opposed to theories giving priority to a Chinese geopolitical and strategic ambition, it is highly possible that the 're-regionalization' of Chinese plans just came out the vision that China could not remain too much disconnected from its vicinity, while strengthening links with South and Central Asia as a start (former Soviet Union republics, as well as South-east Asian countries and others like Pakistan for example) would create a better area of comfort for future developments.

Beyond the very specific model proposed by the BRI, which is an 'inclusive' project whereby no specific rules of adhesion are set and where only a 'volunteering' approach is favored, the invention by China of new regional tools of governance are an obvious illustration of the move. The SCO, which unarguably gained momentum since 2010 and enables China to have a very specific role in strengthening the cohesion of countries exposed to political risks but also sharing some 'values,' is the first such tool of China-initiated governance. Obviously, the invention of AIIB, the China-initiated development bank which was probably aimed at counterbalancing Asian Development Bank, perceived as too much Japan-reliant, gives another example of such initiatives.

Meanwhile, China has never stopped running in parallel attempts to gradually involve in the existing global institutions, but the existence of an 'alternative model of governance' and the possibility that regional organizations could grow and gain importance have made the moves to integrate China to the world less critical. Examples of this 'reset' could even be found in more controversial issues: when the South China Sea question grew more sensitive and China was challenged by Philippines through the Hague arbitration under the principles of The United Nations Convention on the Law of the Sea (UNCLOS), which are global, the response was to recourse more and more to 'regional understanding.'

As of now, China is negotiating a regional 'code of conduct' which would apply only for countries involved in potential disputes. China thus demonstrates that global rules could potentially be less efficient than Asia, China-prompted, principles, in the name of the specificity of history, relations, and new links now established between neighbors.

Equally, the possibility that China would manage to create a trade organization in the region which would challenge TPP, as the 'RCEP' (Regional Cooperation Economic Partnership), is a real possibility, matching the ambition to refocus on the region and obviously become again an 'aggregator' for friendly economies.

The very ambiguous role played by the so-called internationalization of the Chinese currency could also illustrate China's approach to an alternative governance, based on regional interests. While the pattern had seemed a classical one to make the Chinese currency an international one, starting with liberalization of trade flows, then the opening of capital flows, full convertibility, which would be needed to achieve such goals, has not yet materialized. Yet the Chinese currency is part of the IMF basket of currencies, the special drawing rights (SDR), as the only member which is not fully convertible. Equally, China has encouraged the circulation of its currency in the region, where cash yuans can be exchanged, for example in South-east Asia, and also bilateral loans can be sporadically extended, like in the recent case of Pakistan which completed its round of refinancing thanks to an additional billion USD-equivalent provided in yuans by China. Internationalization of the yuan could then be a mere 'regionalization,' strengthening the theory according to which priority is now given to making China the center of a loosely defined area of exchanges and cooperation, possibly with concentric circles, the smaller ones being defined by the immediate neighbors cooperating with the BRI and where the major BRI projects have already been developed, an intermediate one encompassing more remote countries which also engaged in the BRI, like eastern European ones, and also South American countries, some of them having also committed in 'currency swap agreements' with the Chinese central bank (as early as 2008 for some of them, which could be the prefiguration of a 'renminbi zone' relying on a region obviously greater than only China's vicinity).

Challenges to the China-Prompted Regionalization

In many regards, risks emerging from the approach apparently taken by China are no less than the risks created by the previous emergences of past regional powers, which aimed at becoming 'global.'

Even through a cautious approach as the one taken by China, the rise of a new power necessarily unsettles the previous order, and the unique way China 're-regionalizes' after going global, in a context where international relations are more and more influenced by the obsessing 'trade war'; and the new deal between the USA and China is now entering a new zone of turbulence. Although the challenging character of the BRI could be seen from the inception, it is now more and more unsettling for several reasons.

The first one arises from the fact that 'inclusiveness,' which is the basic principle on which China has built its initiative, leaves more and more room to the necessity of 'choice.' When Chinese speakers, academics or politicians, invite potential new members to possibly join the BRI, the elements of language gradually switch from pure pragmatic arguments to questions asking what would retain new countries to join. The implicit message could well be: if you do not join, you then oppose. In a nutshell, either you are in or you are out, and if 'you are out,' you would need to clearly explain why.

The second, related, reason is that a potential success of the BRI could also create 'parting lines' and aggravate unwished tensions between Asian countries and former allies. The relative step back by Malaysia when the newly elected PM Mahathir went to Beijing during summer 2018 shows that it is difficult for some Asian economies to put 'all their eggs in the same basket.'

But the real challenges now appearing to the BRI-driven regionalization are rather coming from the risk that China might have stretched the regional ambitions too far, too early and too heavily. While the trade war, together with a managed cool down of the economy and the financing circuits, has brought China's GDP to a slower growth, the difficulty to finance the BRI based on pure Chinese financial resources is growing. Also, the perception by participating countries that financed by China means also an unprecedented growth in indebtedness vis-à-vis GDP and risk severe disappointment in case of restructuring, as has been in seen with the repossession of Sri Lankan assets by China once it had become clear that the debt was not sustainable, contributed to a changing frame of mind.

While re-regionalization has been construed by China as a 'hedge' against the risks posed by a global economy to which China became too much exposed and which was less and less reliable if not steady, the cost of being at the center of this 're-regionalization' appears more and more.

Could solutions be found in a renegotiation of China's position in economic globalization, enabling China and its partners to look at international relations, trade links, security issues which are less potential bones of contention than opportunities to re-think global order? Obviously, the initial steps of the trade war would tend to think the opposite. However, too fast a collapse of Chinese new ambitions in the region, for example if the trade war would continue and weaken China to the point where it would have to repatriate capital, just like Japan did after entering its 'lost decade,' selling assets purchased abroad and drying down loans extended by Japanese banks to south-east Asian countries, could be damaging not only to the region and China, but also to global growth.

It can then be demonstrated that the correlation between global ambitions and regional reach, whichever step is taken first, remains very strong. China has initially chosen a very original path, yet it could not totally avoid the difficulties of managing both dimensions of cooperation, even within the frame of new economic relations, which could be defined as 'coopetition.'

Shiwei Shi

BRI and China's Opening Up Policy: Opportunities and Challenges – from the Perspective of the Global Value Chain

Introduction: Explaining China's Manufacturing Success in the Last 40 Years

China's economy has achieved very rapid growth in the last 40 years. The manufacturing industry is a cornerstone of the national economy. Manufacturing industries are an engine of innovation, of growth in productivity and of exports. On average, one yuan of final demand for manufacturing products generates around 70 fen[1] of value added outside the final producing firm, spread across many countries and economic activities, including to a large extent the service sectors.

How has the Chinese manufacturing sector been able to achieve such success?

It has been mainly through integration into Global Value Chains (GVCs) in line with its dynamic comparative advantages so that Chinese enterprises have been able to benefit from technology transfer from foreign sources to enhance the diversity and quality of its products. In addition, the productivity-enhancing investment in infrastructure and basic industries have, together with the right sequence in the government's opening-up policy, played a major role.

In this chapter, the theoretical framework of GVCs for the analysis of my topic, especially the concept of industrial upgrading along the GVC, will be introduced first of all. The process of participation in the GVCs through the opening up policy will then be reviewed. The consideration given by countries to opening up their economy to the outside world is based on the better use of the benefits of globalisation. I will then try to elaborate on the new aspects of the new round of opening up launched at the 19th Party Congress of the Communist Party and its connection with the Belt and Road Initiatives (BRI) as the response to the economic downturn since 2012. The chapter points out that China's economic Reforms and Opening Up policy both serve the goals of achieving economic development and a better life for Chinese people (recently the leader of China

---

1 1 fen equals 1/10 Chinese Yuan.

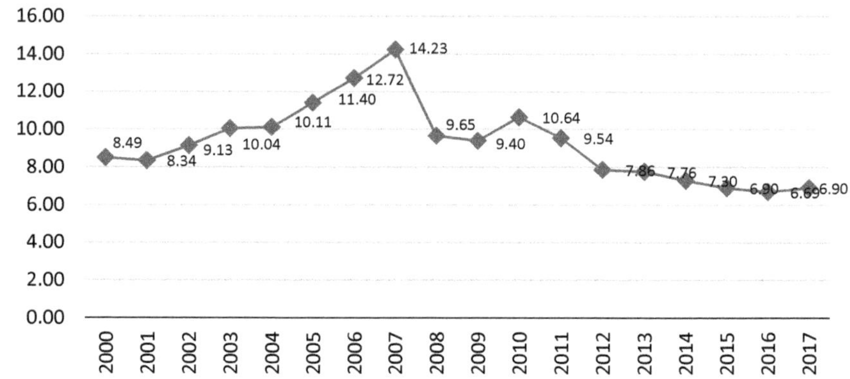

Fig. 1: GDP growth of China. Source: World Bank: https://data.worldbank.org/country

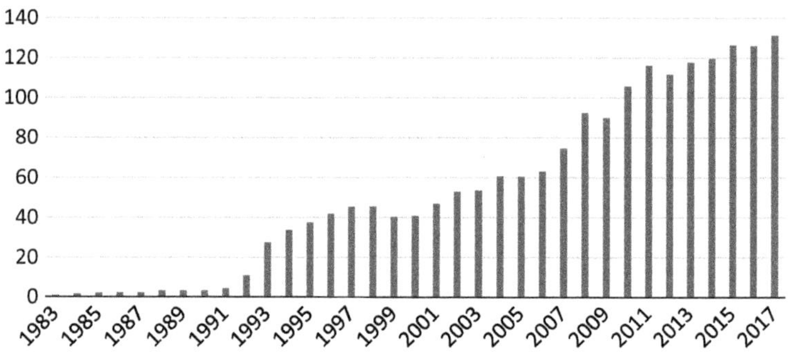

Fig. 2: FDI in China. Source: National Bureau of Statistics of China

has spoken about 'the Chinese dream'), and it has been a proven strategy for Chinese leaders to launch a new round of its opening up policy to overcome economic setbacks since 1978. As a matter of fact, the new round of opening up could describe the essence of BRI more precisely. The main points will be summarised at the end of this chapter.

The BRI and the new round of opening up have certainly had political impacts on the outside world. But I will focus on the economic and domestic aspects of the BRI. Some facts and government documents mentioned in this chapter came from online media and can been found easily. The exact sources for them are not stated.

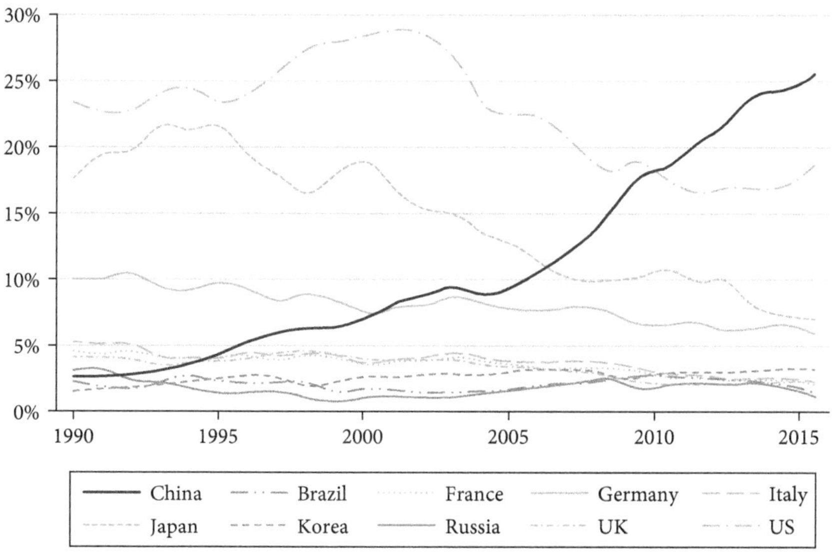

Fig. 3: Percentage share of total world manufacturing value added, 1990–2015

The Framework of the GVC

A GVC means that the production process is broken down into different parts so that different steps can be carried out in different countries. (Global Value Chain Development Report 2017: 2017, 1). It connects globalisation with regionalisation. They complement each other. The key driving force in terms of leveraging GVC is foreign direct investments (FDI) via the offshoring and outsourcing of multinational companies (MNCs).

The involvement of developing countries in the GVC leads to the Flying Geese Paradigm that the Japanese economist Akamatsu Kaname came up with: The idea is that developing countries have achieved more growth and productivity gain through trade, transfer of technology and management methods and have moved up the value chain (industrial upgrading).

The Flying Geese Paradigm viewed Japan as a leading power. It states that manufacturing companies act like migrating geese, flying from country to country as costs and demand change. The second tier consists of the four Asian 'tiger economies' (South Korea, Taiwan, Singapore and Hong Kong) and Malaysia. After these two groups come China and then Thailand, Indonesia and, finally, Vietnam, Laos and Cambodia. It describes not only the movement of

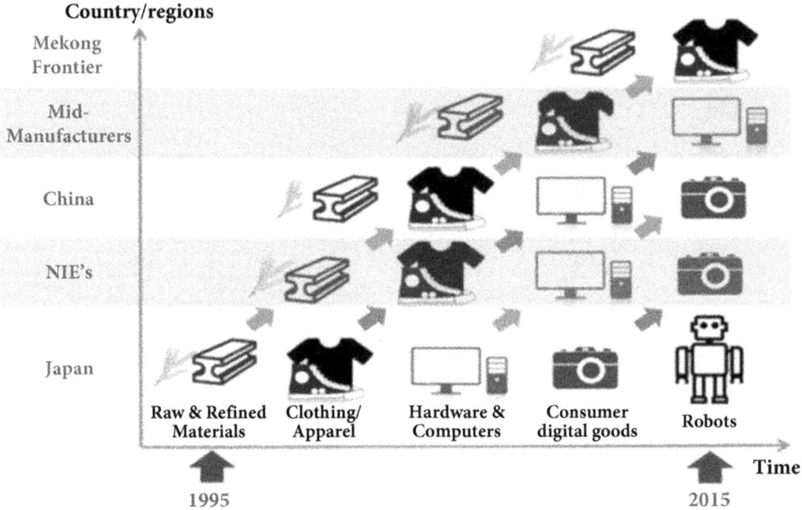

Fig. 4: The Flying Geese Paradigm. Source: Harvard Business Review, May–June 2017

companies from country to country but also a process of industrial upgrading from product to product within each country. The paradigm offers a convincing model as to how Asian economies developed and can be learned by countries in other regions of the world, such as in Africa.

China's Participation in the GVC through Its Gradual Opening Up Policy

Figure 4 hows that the plotted GVC for China's Information and Communication Technology (ICT) exports to the world market looks like a curve in the shape of a smile. China had the largest value-added gain in this GVC (CNH 14). China's ICT industry was located at the low end of the GVC in 1995 and that position did not change much between 1995 and 2009. First of all, it is due to the relatively high share of processing trade in this industry: China's participation in the GVC at an early stage reflects its acceptance of outsourcing tasks such as assembling iPhones. Compared with the traditional production of ICT products, assembly is much more labour-intensive and depends on more foreign parts and components. Secondly, labour costs per hour in current US dollars increased only slightly during this period but not to a very high level because of the abundant labour supply in China. In other words, this choice of participation

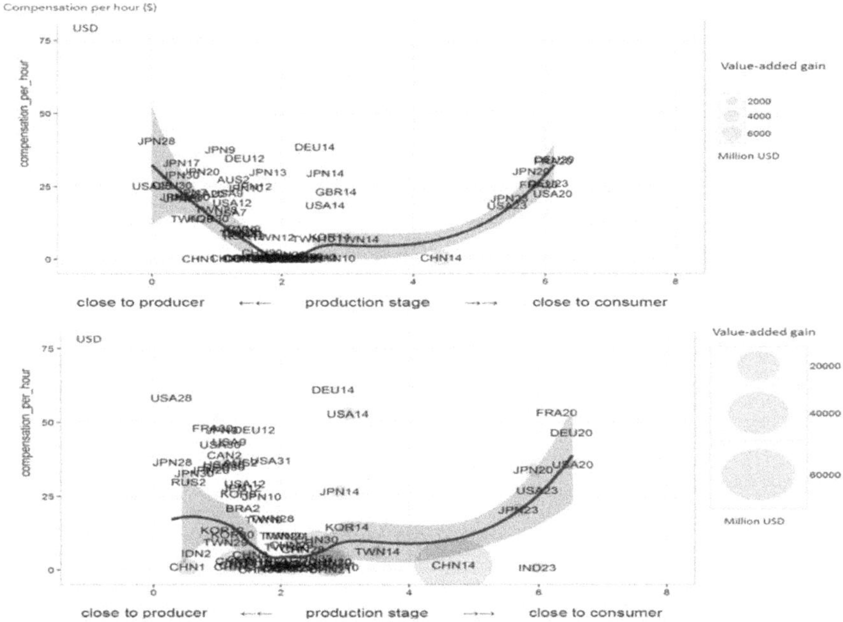

Fig. 5: The estimated curve, in the shape of a smile, for China 's exports of electrical and optical equipment deepened between 1995 and 2009. Source: GVC Development Report 2017: 2017, 55

reflected China's comparative advantage in the target years (Global Value Chain Report: 2017, 54, 56). From the analysis of the facts, we can conclude that the Chinese economy has benefited considerably from integration into the GVC, especially as it created a large number of jobs and drew thousands of millions of people away from the countryside and out of poverty.

But we can see, in Tab. 1 and Fig. 6, that there are several challenges for Chinese manufacturing: most goods from Chinese foreign trade, including high-tech products, stemmed from foreign investment enterprises (FIEs). Chinese manufacturing is still quite dependent on foreign inputs.

Since the financial crisis in 2008, a trend in relation to the world economy has changed. There is a rising tide of protectionism around the globe. Developed countries have turned to protecting their economy more closely. The emerging industrialising countries have narrowed the technology gap by comparison with the developed countries and become their competitors. Major emerging developing economies – including China – have tended to

Tab. 1: Share of FIEs to China´s foreign trade (1987–2017)

Year	Share (total)	Share (exports)	Share (imports)
1987	5.55 %	3.07 %	7.81 %
1991	21.34 %	16.75 %	26.51 %
1992	26.43 %	20.44 %	32.74 %
1995	39.10 %	31.51 %	47.66 %
1999	50.78 %	45.47 %	51.83 %
2005	58.49 %	58.30 %	58.70 %
2008	55.07 %	55.34 %	54.71 %
2011	51.07 %	52.42 %	49.60 %
2012	48.98 %	49.92 %	47.93 %
2013	46.13 %	47.25 %	44.86 %
2015	46.30 %	44.10 %	49.30 %
2016	45.78 %	43.71 %	48.52 %
2017.1–11	44.82 %	43.08 %	46.95 %

Source: Invest in China: Data Service-Statistics http://www.fdi.gov.cn/1800000121_10000177_8.html

substitute imported intermediate inputs with domestically produced intermediate inputs through local learning and forward and backward linkages. On the other hand, developed countries have invested more in technological innovation and tried to become competitive again by reshoring (the process of returning the production and manufacturing of goods back to the company's original country) in the face of challenges from the emerging industrialised countries.

As has been shown, China is currently still dependent on foreign technology. The rise of nationalism and protectionism in developed countries will make it difficult for China to receive the necessary technology for its industrial upgrading from abroad, which will be essential for sustainable growth and employment in the coming decades (e.g. the technology constraints for Chinese enterprises imposed by the USA and the screening of mergers and acquisitions by Chinese firms by the European Union [EU]).

China is also facing several domestic challenges, which make the restructuring of the economy inevitable. China is experiencing demographic change. The population is ageing. This has caused labour shortages. The lack of a proper labour force in some regions, such as Dongguan, has pushed wages

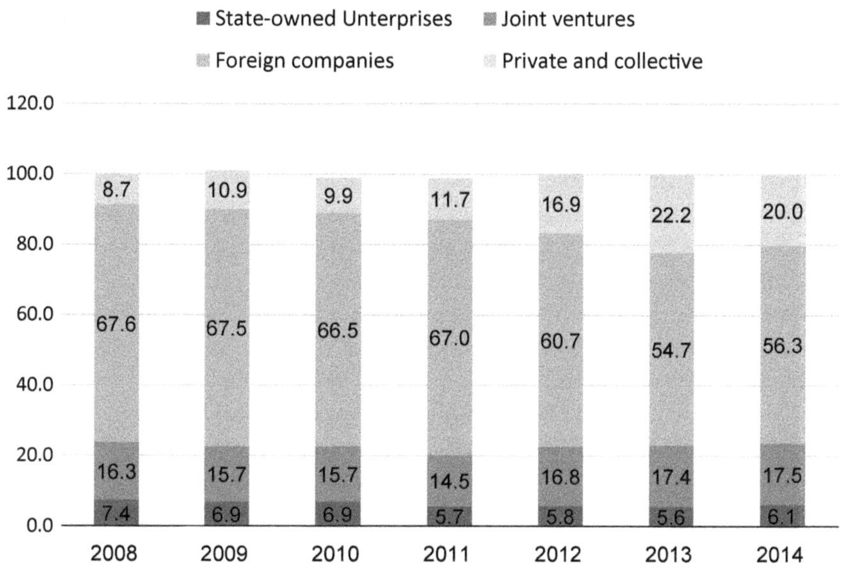

Fig. 6: Structure of high-tech exports according to forms of ownership (%).
Source: Department of Social Technology and Cultural Industry Statistics of National Bureau of Statistics (2017)

upwards to high levels and is posing a threat in the sense that local industries may lose out in terms of competitiveness to countries with lower wages in South Asia and in Africa. Besides, China has suffered from environmental pressures as a result of its extensive development model in recent decades. As a result of those challenges, China's economy has moved to the stage of being 'New Normal', at least in 2012. That means that the growth rate dropped from above 10 % to 6–7 % and FDI has decreased (see Figs. 1 and 2). This has caused huge problems.

What can be done? The Chinese government resorted to the proven strategy: deepening the economic opening-up process that is opening up the economy further, combined with industrial upgrading.

China has experienced four rounds of its opening-up process up until now:

- **First period (1980–1989): Experimental efforts in establishing the Special Economic Zones and opening up the 14 coastal cities to foreign investors.**

The first round is more experimental in nature: The economy was partially opened up whilst the main part of the economy remained under strict state control and therefore has achieved only moderate success.

- **Second period (1991–2001): Further opening up symbolised by the establishment of the Shanghai-Pudong Development Zone and the internationalisation of the Chinese economy with the export boom.** The second round of opening up took place when the economy was facing considerable difficulties after a major democratic demonstration was crushed on 4 June 1989. Chinese politics and society stands at a crossroads. And the Chinese leader decided to continue with the reform and not to revert to the state-controlled planned economy. The combination of the domestic market and the world market led to an export boom.
- **Third period (2001–2008): China's accession to the World Trade Organisation (WTO) – reduction of market access barriers to foreign investors abiding by WTO rules.** In 1999, shaken by the Asian financial crisis, China's economy had stagnated. And accession to the WTO after 14 years of negotiations provided considerable impetus with regard to growth of the Chinese economy. China's economy is integrated with the world economy, not only in terms of material goods flows but also in terms of rules. China has attracted a large amount of FDI since then and has become 'the factory of the world'.
- **Fourth period (2013–): Launching the BRI to promote a new pattern of comprehensive opening up** (全面开放的新格局).

Considering the fourth round of opening up, which began with the BRI, the world economy recovered slowly after the world financial and economic crisis in 2008. Chinese exports went down in absolute terms in 2015 after 2009 (-8 %). On the one hand, Chinese manufacturers have lost their comparative cost advantage (labour costs) to other developing countries such as India, Bangladesh and Vietnam. On the other hand, some Chinese enterprises have improved their competitive edge (e.g. Huawei and Haier) and can operate all around the world. The export share of private enterprises exceeded that of FIEs for the first time in 2015. China leads the world in terms of skill and technology in the high-speed railway and highway sectors after absorbing modern technology from advanced industrial countries and indigenous innovation with massive support from government. That is why China's outbound investment has surged since 2013. Competitive Chinese firms go abroad now not only to source new technology and cooperation partners but also to supply the new markets. We must understand the new situation of the Chinese economy to correctly predict the opportunities that the BRI will provide.

The BRI and Adding Further Depth to the Opening Up Policy

The BRI is a very broad conceptual framework for policies that aim to contribute to greater economic integration within Asia, between Asia and Europe and between Asia and Africa through a diversity of activities and projects. The contours of the initiative have become clearer and more complemented in the last four years and are very closely connected to the new round of the opening up policy.

At the heart of the BRI is a strategic approach to infrastructure development in a very broad sense (telecommunications, pipelines, electricity grids and transport routes). That is why 'connectivity' has become the key word of the BRI and has expanded from infrastructure to four other fields:

- Policy coordination (政策沟通)
- Construction of infrastructure (设施联通)
- Unimpeded trade （贸易畅通）
- Financial integration（资金融通）
- People-to-people ties（民心相通）

The new round of opening up – called a *new pattern of comprehensive opening up* – was announced at the 19th Party Congress of the Communist Party of China in October 2017, four years after the launch of the BRI. The main content of this pattern is listed as follows:

- Combination attracting FDI with the outbound investment of Chinese enterprises, but the 'go aboard' (走出去) has become more relevant;
- Combination of the opening up of coastal regions with the opening up of middle, west regions and border areas;
- Combination of further opening up to manufacturing sectors with opening up to service sectors;
- Combination of opening up to developed countries with opening up to developing countries;
- Combination of promoting the multilateral trade system with promoting regional trade systems.

After viewing the outline of this new round of opening up, one can conclude that the BRI is at the core of it: China will encourage the outbound investment of enterprises – both SOE and private enterprises – particularly in the development countries and neighbouring countries with infrastructure projects. It has been increased and will be increased with the rapid deepening of the BRI. China will not stop attracting FDI, especially high level FDI, even if a shortage of capital is not an obstacle for the development of China. FDI has provided the Chinese economy with advanced technology and management skills, which are essential for moving up the value chain and for structural change to Chinese industries. And if China wants to intensify its foreign engagement and get more acceptance from receiving countries, it must open its markets further, for example heavily protected areas of the service sector such as the financial sector, education, hospital, accounting, retail, etc. China also must reform its economic system significantly and adopt modern rules to regulate the international economy, such as a negative list for market entry. China planned to provide some favourable funding for the BRI projects, particularly in the poor Asian and African countries, to ensure that cooperation will be a 'win-win' deal. But a comprehensive opening up is no less essential for the Chinese authorities if it is aiming to remain a major player in globalisation and is pushing for a greater say in shaping the governance of the world economy.

I mentioned before that the core of the BRI was to build intercontinental-wide infrastructure. But the initiative has a broader interpretation, with five major fields called 5 connectivity. For each initiative, the Chinese government has done something to improve the institutional and political framework in recent years:

- The Chinese authorities do not want to make the decision alone, but to consult with other relevant countries, and they are ready to accept good ideas from others according to the principles of co-construction and sharing (e.g. the Chinese government held a high-level international conference on the BRI in Beijing on 15–16 June 2017 and invited the leaders of the States along the Belt Road to discuss implementation).
- The construction of infrastructure continues to be at the heart of the initiative. As China is the biggest exporter in the world, the Chinese authorities have emphasised the importance of free trade and called for a multilateral trade regime and economic globalisation. The facilitation of transport as a key measure of the BRI serves this goal. But Western countries have some doubt about China's appeals due to some market access barriers in China and are requesting reciprocity. In the past few years, the Chinese government has initiated a number of reforms and changes to the system, emphasising market forces and a liberalisation of several regulations. President Xi announced the further opening up of China's domestic market and an overall improvement in business framework conditions in his speech at the 2017 World Economic Forum in Davos. It was then set down in government policy through a series of documents promulgated by the State Council in 2017 and 2018: international enterprises investing in financial services, automotives, shipbuilding and aerospace had one of their longstanding recommendations accepted,

with announcements that foreign investment caps in those industries would be removed in the coming years. This was followed by the promulgation of the revised Special Administrative Measures on Access to Foreign Investment 2018 (Negative List) (European Chamber of Commerce 2018: 2018, 14). Several measures of this policy have been implemented and some foreign enterprises have benefited from them. For instance, the American E-automotive maker Tesla set up the first wholly foreign owned enterprise (WFOE) for car assembly in Shanghai; big financial groups such as UBS Group AG, Nomura Holdings Inc. and JPMorgan Chase & Co. have taken majority stakes in local securities ventures in China.

- The creation of the Asian Infrastructure Investment Bank (AIIB) and the Silk Road Fund help with this initiative. These measures are welcomed by all participants. China announced that it would increase the fund with an additional 100 billion yuan in 2017. China is seeking to internationalise the renminbi. The Chinese yuan has been a member of the Special Drawing Rights of the International Monetary Fund. The BRI provides an opportunity to accelerate this process. The European Central Bank ECB has increased the amount of yuan it holds as a foreign currency reserve. Two offshore renminbi clearing centres have been set up in London and in Frankfurt. But there was a setback in this field because of the devaluation of the renminbi and recent capital outflow.
- People-to-people ties will improve the understanding of the participating countries in China's history and culture. That will increase mutual trust and facilitate cooperation. (e.g. a high-level governmental dialogue on civil and culture cooperation was started during the visit of Li Keqiang to Berlin in 2017).

By March 2019, China had signed a cooperation agreement, in the framework of the BRI, with 125 countries and 29 international organisations. According to the State Ministry of Commerce (MOFCOM), ca. 1 trillion US dollars was invested in the BRI projects by Chinese enterprises between 2013 and 2018.

Summary

In this chapter, the connection between the new round of opening up and the BRI has been explained from the perspective of the GVC. This gradual and incremental way of opening up has led to the high and constant growth of the economy, overall macroeconomic stability and the creation of hundreds of millions of jobs in the last 40 years. Chinese leaders have been able to use pressures from abroad

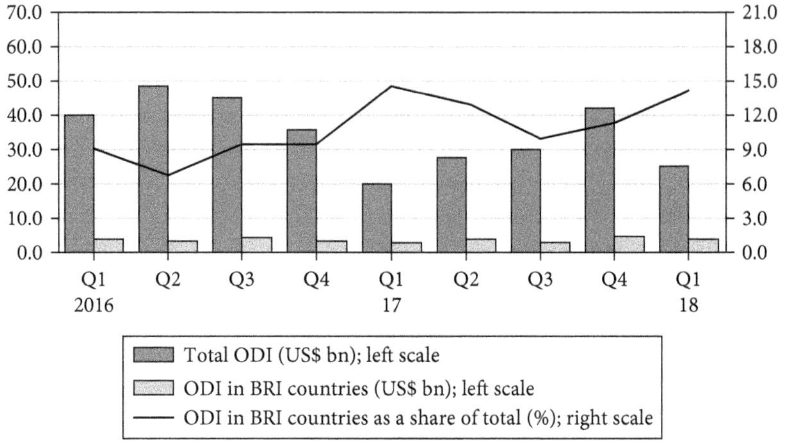

Fig. 7: China's ODI flows to BRI countries. Source: *The Economist*

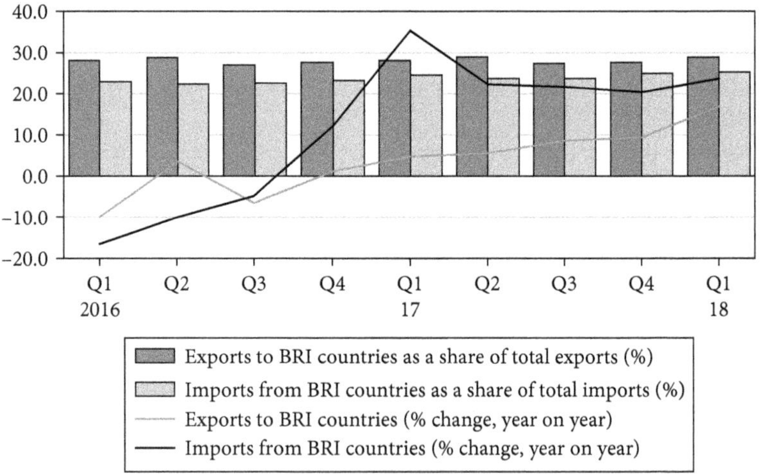

Fig. 8: China's merchandise trade with BRI countries. Source: *The Economist*

for further reforms and structural changes in order to reach their primary goal of growth and have been able to enhance the level of people's life and strengthened the promise of giving markets the decisive role in resource allocation at the third plenary of the 18th Party Congress of the Communist Party in September 2013.

The new round of opening up and the BRI have paved the way for more in-depth cooperation and competition both in China and in the world in an era of globalisation. It is not only Chinese but also foreign enterprises that will benefit from the new round of opening up and the BRI.

References

European Commission, *China: Challenges and Prospects from an Industrial and Innovation Powerhouse*. Brussels, 2019. https://ec.europa.eu/jrc/en/publication/china-challenges-and-prospects-industrial-and-innovation-powerhouse (accession date on 2 April 2020)

European Union Chamber of Commerce in China, *The European Business in China Position Paper 2018/2019*. www.europeanchamber.com.cn (accession date on 31 March 2020)

Hanemann, Thilo, Huotari, Mikko, Kratz, Agatha, *Chinese FDI in Europe:2018 – Trends and Impact of New Screening Polities*. A report by Rhodium Group (RHG) and the Mercator Institute for China Studies (MERICS), March 2019. www.merics.org (accession date on 31 March 2020)

Shi, Shiwei, *Staat, Pfadabhängigkeit, Wechselwirkungen zwischen Wirtschaft und Politik im Transformationsprozeß: politische Ökonomie der Weltmarktöffnung der VR China 1978–1995*. Frankfurt am Main u.a.: Lang, 1998.

Wang, Loulin (ed.), *China's WTO accession reassessed*. London and New York: China Development Research Foundation and Routledge, 2015.

The World Bank, *Global Value Chain Development Report 2017: Measuring and Analyzing the Impact of GVCs on Economic Development*. Washington, 2017.

Zhang, Wenxian, Alon, Ilan, Lattemann, Christoph (eds.), *China's Belt and Road Initiative Changing the Rules of Globalization*. Cham: Palgrave Macmillan, 2018.

Part Three: China Interregional Relations: The Cases of Latin America, Middle East

Jürgen Rüland and Fabricio Rodríguez

Interregionalism, Global Governance and China's Relations with Latin America: A Theory-Guided Analysis

Introduction

The world's institutional architecture changed markedly in the 1980s and 1990s. Globalisation, rapidly growing economic interdependence and the thaw in superpower relations facilitated the rise of an increasingly vertically and horizontally differentiated system of global governance (Rüland 2002). International fora, including regional cooperation arrangements, grew by leaps and bounds (Zürn 2018). After a first wave of regionalism in the 1950s and 1960s, a second wave known in the comparative regionalism literature as 'new regionalism' emerged in the 1990s (Fawcett & Hurrell 1995). Unlike the first wave, when regionalism primarily flourished in Europe and Latin America, the second wave saw regional organisations proliferating in all world regions. By the end of the 1990s, world regions without regionalism no longer existed (Palmer 1991).

As regional organisations increasingly became catalysts for collective action and vehicles to foster 'voice opportunity' (Grieco 1996), they began to interact with each other. The growth of regionalism thus spurred the emergence of interregional relations, which became a new layer of action in global governance and subsequently a research field in its own right (Hänggi, Roloff & Rüland 2006; Rüland 2010, 2014; Doidge 2011; Fehrmann 2014; Ribeiro Hoffmann 2016). By the mid-2000s, Hänggi counted no less than eighty-two interregional fora (Hänggi 2006), a number which may even have increased since then. With the rise of China as a major global actor, Beijing also began to nurture interregional relations as a foreign policy tool. Its Belt and Road Initiative (BRI), launched in 2013 as a gigantic, multi-decade infrastructure and connectivity scheme, linking China with the Eurasian land mass, and by sea with the Middle East, Africa, Europe and even Latin America, opens avenues for China to become a new hub in the world's web of interregional dialogue fora. So far, however, there has been little research on China's role as an agent in interregional relations, a lacuna which this volume addresses. This chapter seeks to contribute to this objective by providing a theory-guided analysis of China as a shaper and driver of interregionalism and global governance exemplified by its relationships with Latin America.

The chapter is structured as follows: After the introduction, it takes, as a *second* step, a closer look at the forms of interregionalism and examines the formats China uses to build its relations with partner regions including Latin America. In a *third* step, the chapter briefly introduces and discusses the functions of interregionalism and probes which of them China activates in its Latin American policy. The next section highlights, *fourth*, key problems of interregionalism such as 'diminished multilateralism' and a profound democratic deficit, which impede its contribution to a nested and inclusive system of global governance (Aggarwal & Fogerty 2004; Rüland & Carrapatoso 2015). The section analyses to what extent China's participation in interregional relations, and in particular those with Latin America, contribute to these problems. The concluding remarks summarise, *fifth*, the main arguments of the chapter and assess China's role as an actor in interregional relations while placing particular emphasis on its interactions with Latin America.

Forms of Interregionalism in China-Latin American Countries Relations

Research on interregionalism has identified three forms of interregional relations: bi-regionalism, transregionalism and hybrid interregionalism (Rüland 2006, 2010; Söderbaum & Stalgren 2010). *Bi-regionalism* denotes group-to-group interactions. Most of these dialogues are grouped in a hub-and-spokes relationship with the European Union (EU) serving as a global reference in the constitution of interregional relations. The EU's dialogue with the Association of Southeast Asian Nations (ASEAN), Mercosur, the South African Development Community (SADC), the Economic Community of West African States (ECOWAS), the Gulf Cooperation Council (GCC) or ASEAN-Mercosur relations are examples of bi-regional cooperation. Bi-regional dialogues rest on the institutional infrastructure of the groupings involved and do not entail specific overarching organs such as a common secretariat. *Transregional dialogues* are more diffuse and emerged later than bi-regional fora. Often they bring together member states of more than two regional organisations. Due to their larger membership and hence greater heterogeneity, they tend to develop overarching organisational arrangements such as a (virtual) secretariat or coordination mechanisms. Examples are the Asia-Europe Forum (ASEM), the Asia-Pacific Economic Cooperation (APEC), the Indian Ocean Rim Association (IORA) and the Forum of East Asia-Latin America Cooperation (FEALAC). Finally, *hybrid interregionalism* refers to fora that are composed of a regional organisation on one side and an individual nation state, usually a major power, on the other side. Examples are the strategic partnerships of the EU and the dialogue relations of ASEAN with major powers including the United States, Russia, China, India and others. The category also involves platforms such as the Africa, Caribbean and Pacific Group of States (ACP), which Holland termed 'imagined interregionalism' (Holland 2006), continental dialogues including the EU-Africa Summit (Cairo Process) (Olsen 2006) and the EU-Latin America Summit (Durán Lima et al. 2014), and what has been called 'interregionalism without regions' (Rüland & Bechle 2010), an institutional arrangement where cooperating regional hegemons unilaterally claim to represent an entire region such as in the India, Brazil, South Africa Forum (IBSA).

In Latin America and the Caribbean, a region dominated by presidential systems and characterised by a relatively weak and heterogeneous landscape of regional organisations (Gardini 2015), leaders have embraced China's growing economic and political presence at different levels, through different formats and with diverse objectives and expectations. The tightening and deepening character of the Sino-Latin American nexus is not only reflected in the remarkable rise of traded goods and thickening flows of capital but also in the quality and frequency of diplomatic contact, which have steadily matured since China's admission to the World Trade Organization (WTO) in 2001. The total value of traded goods rose twenty-two-fold from US$12 billion in 2000 to US$275 billion in 2013. This is a remarkable figure considering that Latin America's trade with all other world regions only experienced a three-fold increase over the same period (ECLAC 2015: 23). Chinese investment in Latin America has also grown at a steady pace since the Global Financial Crisis of 2008/2009. The largest inflow of Chinese foreign direct investment (FDI) was recorded in 2010 with Brazil by far representing the largest recipient. Thereafter, Chinese investments have reached an estimated value of US$9 billion to US$10 billion per annum (*Ibid.*: 34). With a share of 5 to 6 percent of the region's total inward investment, Chinese capital has come to represent a major financial source for Latin American Countries' (LAC) states, thereby offering an additional and alternative source of investment, traditionally dominated by the USA, EU and, to a lesser extent, Japan (*Ibid.*).

China has also gained impressive momentum as a lender to the LAC region with its development banks (mainly the China Development Bank and the China Export-Import Bank) currently providing more loans than their US peers with longstanding presence in the region, as summarised by Gallagher (2016) in the following manner:

> By 2014 Chinese development banks were providing more finance to Latin American governments than the World Bank or the Inter-American Development Bank (IDB). In 2010 and in 2014 China provided Latin American governments more funds than the World Bank, the Inter-American Development Bank, and the US Export-Import Bank (US Ex-Im) combined. (Gallagher 2016: 65)

Since the turn of the century, and as part of its 'Go Out policy', Chinese leaders have indeed cultivated deepening diplomatic relations with Latin American and Caribbean leaders. Between 2000 and 2015, Chinese Presidents and Premiers paid a total of thirty-one bilateral visits to the region (Dussel Peters 2015: 7). The APEC summit held in Lima in 2016 provided President Xi Jinping with an institutional platform to "present himself as a defender of free trade against the protectionist threats of the incoming US president" (Nolte 2018: 2). In the process, China's relationship with Latin America has rapidly evolved under the concept of 'South-South' cooperation (China 2008, 2016), placing a strong emphasis on government-to-government relations, which are in some cases highlighted as 'strategic partnerships' (Feng & Huan 2014; Xu 2016). So far these extend to Argentina, Bolivia, Brazil, Chile, Ecuador, Mexico, Peru, Uruguay and Venezuela (Ellis 2018: 8).

China's strong focus on bilateralism has been progressively complemented by a non-triadic, largely state-centric type of interregionalism, which excludes bi-regionalism and mainly corresponds with transregional formats. Transregionalism hence set the stage for initial interaction in the 1980s and 1990s while hybrid interregionalism has emerged more strongly as a Chinese strategy to engage Latin America and the Caribbean since 2015, thereby complementing other hybrid fora such as the Forum on China-Africa Cooperation (FOCAC), China and the Pacific Island Countries and the China-Arab States Cooperation Forum (CASCF).

The two most important fora providing a platform for early transregional interaction between China and selected Latin American states have been APEC (founded in 1989) and FEALAC (1999). In fact, many of China's rapidly intensifying and diversifying ties with single Latin American states were initially built on bilateral interaction at the sidelines of these transregional fora during the 1980s and 1990s, and have played a crucial role in the signing of free trade agreements (FTAs) as in the case of Chile and Peru.[1]

For Latin American Pacific littorals like Chile and Peru, membership of APEC has played a fundamental role in deepening trade and investment relations with

---

1 Interviews with Peruvian diplomats, Lima, 8 March 2017 and Chile, 8 November 2017.

China. For example, following the signing of Chile's FTA with China in 2005, the Peruvian government was keen to follow up with a similar agreement but initially failed to obtain China's attention. Peru lacked the market size and international weight to engage China in bilateral negotiations for an FTA. Hence the Peruvian strategy consisted of establishing bilateral talks with other APEC members who would potentially increase China's recognition of Peru as an economic partner. The Peruvian leadership thus started bilateral negotiations with Thailand and Singapore, while using APEC as a platform to position Peru as an attractive investment destination for mining activities. This soon led Peru to sign FTA agreements with these countries, and with the USA, which subsequently elicited China's, and later Japan's, interest (Rodríguez 2018).

The Forum for East Asian and Latin American Countries (FEALAC) was founded in 1999 as a diplomatic initiative headed by Singapore's Prime Minister Goh Chok Tong. It was part of a flurry of actions to mitigate the devastating effects of the Asian Financial Crisis of 1997/1998 through the diversification of trade and investment relations. The creation of FEALAC provided an institutional forum for countries like Colombia or Ecuador that as non-members of APEC lacked access to the Pacific and were thus deprived from tapping into the emerging markets of the Asia-Pacific. FEALAC subsequently became an important milestone in bringing Asian and Latin American leaders to discuss issues ranging from economic policy to the management of external conditionalities imposed on the developing world by the US-dominated multilateral financial institutions such as the International Monetary Fund (IMF), the World Bank or regional development banks (Paz 2019: 4025).

With the BRI emerging as China's new flagship for interregional dialogue and cooperation with the LAC region, hybrid forms of interregionalism have become an additional institutional layer of interaction. The new and growing role of regional organisations in China's foreign policy towards Latin America and the Caribbean became most evident on 8 January 2015 with China's President Xi Jinping hosting the first ministerial meeting of the Forum of China and the Community of Latin American and Caribbean States (CELAC) in Beijing. This was reflected in official documents a year later. While cooperation with regional organisations had been mentioned superficially, and mainly as a tool of trade promotion in China's first Policy Paper on Latin America and the Caribbean (China 2008), the second Policy Paper highlighted Beijing's decision to institutionalise a hybrid format of interregional relations with CELAC, stating that:

> The establishment of the Forum of China and the Community of Latin American and Caribbean States (China-CELAC Forum) has provided a new platform for cooperation

> between the two sides, setting the course for simultaneous and complementary development of bilateral and collective cooperation between China and Latin America and the Caribbean (China 2016).

The establishment of the China-CELAC Forum was a significant step in China's strategy to enhance its presence in Latin America and the Caribbean. One of the key objectives was to regain institutional support from its partners in the region, some of which (Argentina, Brazil, Chile, Ecuador, Peru, Uruguay, Venezuela) had been suffering from the negative effects of declining commodity prices resulting from China's 'new normal', that is a new cycle of moderately declining growth rates and shrinking demand for natural resources.[2] Using CELAC as a regional resonance box, China called for the establishment of the China-CELAC package financing facility. This multipurpose fund is furnished with US$35 billion and implemented by way of three complementary mechanisms: the Preferential Loan Program with US$10 billion, the Special Loan Program for China-Latin America Infrastructure Projects with US$20 billion and the China-LAC Cooperation Fund with US$5 billion (China-CELAC Forum 2016: 39).

The establishment of the package financing facility allowed the Chinese government to display its long-term commitment to the region but Beijing refrained from immediately linking this instrument to the BRI. The official invitation for CELAC members to be part of the BRI came from Chinese Foreign Minister Wang Yi during the Second Ministerial Meeting of the China-CELAC Forum held on 21–22 January 2018 in Santiago de Chile. The key message was that China was ready to sign special agreements to integrate the LAC region into its great transformational project which would, according to Wang, open new opportunities for the development of large-scale projects including ports, railways, airports, but also for connecting the region's digital infrastructure to that of China (Aróstica 2018). Yet while LAC may indeed have a strong need to invest in different kinds of regional infrastructure, CELAC lacks both a clear connectivity plan as well as a regionally concerted strategy to engage with China's growing presence and interests in the region. Despite its noteworthy achievements in fostering a minimum of policy orchestration amongst the politically fragmented set of regional organisations in the LAC-region, CELAC remains a thinly institutionalised platform for interregional interaction (Torres Jarrín 2018). It is thus questionable whether CELAC will be an efficient facilitator for China to fulfil its ambitions of building mega-infrastructures in the context of weakly institutionalised regionalism. Such projects may, for instance, include the

---

2 *South China Morning Post*, 14 May 2014.

'Twin-Ocean Rail', which is envisioned to connect Brazil's Atlantic coast to Peru's Pacific coast over a 5,000 km railway, or the 'Two-Ocean Tunnel' envisioned to connect Chile's Pacific coast to Argentina's Atlantic coast (Yu 2015: 1058–1059). These two projects, alongside China's recent bilateral agreement to incorporate the Panama Canal into the BRI, hold crucial value in President Xi Jinping's ambition to maximise economic and political influence in the USA's backyard – and global governance by extension (*Ibid.*).

Another noteworthy case of hybrid interregionalism is that of China-Mercosur relations,[3] which had literally experienced no major movement since 2003. This was partly because the Brazilian governments under President Lula da Silva (2003–2006; 2007–2010) and his successor Dilma Rousseff (2011–2014; 2014–2016) devoted greater strategic importance to the establishment of the Union of South American Nations (UNASUR) from 2004 onward and to the strengthening of the BRICS states from 2006.[4] Traditionally, national development priorities as well as weak institutionalisation at the regional level have stood in the way of regional cooperation and integration within Mercosur (Doctor 2015). Brazilian policies to protect its comparatively large industrial complex from external competition have made it difficult for Mercosur to sign an FTA with the EU for almost two decades (Klom 2003). Additionally, European policies to protect the agricultural sector from external competition have contributed to the long-standing stagnation of interregional trade (Konold 2010) and institutional relations as a result (Doctor 2015). Following paradigmatic changes in favour of political leaders embracing trade liberalisation in Argentina and Brazil, Mercosur resumed its active role in connecting the region with other important markets including interregional negotiations with the EU and China as a new variable in Mercosur's commercial and diplomatic policy.

A major diplomatic driver of Mercosur's trade talks with China was Uruguay's *pro-tempore* Mercosur presidency under President Tabaré Vázquez (June–December 2018). His objective was to enhance Uruguay's bargaining position vis-à-vis Argentina and Brazil while including Paraguay – which maintains diplomatic relations with Taiwan – in a project of significant economic and diplomatic appeal to Beijing. His vocal support of interregional trade provided Vázquez

---

3 The authors thank Andrés Raggio, Universidad de la Republica Uruguay (UDELAR), Uruguay, for valuable insights.

4 Originally, UNASUR included ambitious projects to foster regional cooperation in the fields of security and infrastructure in which Brazilian leadership was key. Today, internal disputes amongst its members have led to the virtual paralysis of the grouping.

with strong domestic support on behalf of Uruguay's meat exporters and agricultural businesses pursuing expanding operations in the EU and Chinese markets. Chinese stakeholders such as the Counselor for Trade and Economic Affairs of the Chinese Embassy in Uruguay welcomed and supported Uruguay's advocacy in favour of a China-Mercosur FTA while keeping all options for bilateral cooperation open.[5] As a result, the 6th China-Mercosur Dialogue Forum was held in Uruguay's capital Montevideo in October 2018 with attendants including vice-ministerial bureaucrats in addition to the subaltern technical teams which had headed previous discussions although failing to achieve noteworthy results in 2003.

A further yet less significant case of hybrid interregionalism in Chinese-Latin American relations is that of China's relations with the Pacific Alliance (Creutzfeldt 2018). This loose regional grouping founded in 2012 is composed of Chile, Peru, Colombia and Mexico – a set of states seeking regional cooperation through an open and long-term commitment to free trade, investment promotion and market liberalisation (*Ibid.*). Like CELAC, the Pacific Alliance also has a network character, although its key objective concerns the commercial integration of its members in the wider economy of the Asia-Pacific (Alianza del Pacífico n.d.). The Pacific Alliance does not have a regional secretariat, and it cannot sign international agreements on behalf of its member states. In practice, the Pacific Alliance represents a platform to promote trans-Pacific trade and to position each of these four states as an attractive destination for foreign investment (Nolte 2016). China is an important stakeholder in this respect but the most important achievements in its relationship with the Pacific Alliance have been crafted bilaterally through FTAs (trade and investment) signed with Chile in 2005 (upgraded to include services in 2017) and Peru in 2009 (including trade, investment and services). A China-Colombia FTA is currently under negotiation, while China's relationship with Mexico faces specific strategic treatment due to the latter's involvement in NAFTA (renegotiated under Trump as the United States-Mexico-Canada Agreement, USMCA), and to the fact that Mexico and China's economies face more competition than complementarities in different manufacturing sectors.

China's relations with all other Latin American and Caribbean regional groupings are less prominent and are likely to lose significance in favour of

---

5 Zhou Quan: "Uruguay, China y el Mercosur", interview with Nuevo Siglo Cable Tv, 24 October 2017, available at: https://youtu.be/VQdqjfQdgmY, (accessed 13 April 2019).

CELAC. This is the case for the Caribbean Community (CARICOM), where China has prioritised a government-to-government strategy by allocating substantial loans and investment to Jamaica. This kind of approach can be seen as a measure to motivate other states from whom Beijing expects more cooperation in the future. The Andean Community (CAN) has lost significance due to internal ideological disputes which led Venezuela to quit the organisation and focus on the creation of the Bolivarian Alliance for the Peoples of Our America (ALBA) in the aftermath of Peru's and Colombia's unilateral initiatives to sign FTAs with the USA in 2005 and 2006, respectively. Another regional organisation of indirect relevance to China's interregional relations with Latin America is the Central American Integration System (SICA), where the Republic of China (Taiwan) has made an effort to maintain a strong foothold, partly collaborating with and supporting the EU in its role of external federator (Torres 2018). Given SICA's institutional weaknesses, it has become increasingly viable for China to gain new allies through bilateral agreements as in the case of Costa Rica, Panama under the BRI umbrella and, more recently, El Salvador.[6]

The previous analysis suggests that bilateral relations between China and single LAC states form the institutional bedrock of interregional interaction, with the sidelines of transnational fora serving as a useful platform for the promotion of bilateral ties. Hybrid interregionalism is a recently emerging and complementary layer, which in practice translates into China-to-region relations. While China advances an increasingly identifiable interregional agenda, especially towards CELAC and, through different mechanisms, towards Mercosur, there is in contrast no clearly identifiable China policy held by any regional organisation in the region. Instead of contributing to the democratisation of global governance – as claimed in China's two Policy Papers on LAC – interregional interaction fosters a particularistic, opportunistic and mercantilist approach to multilateralism. Moreover, the analysis suggests three strategic objectives underpinning China's preference for and Latin American as well as Caribbean actors' approval of advancing diminished forms of interregional cooperation. For China, these motives consist of, *one*, enhancing global power status through the simultaneous expansion of investment frontiers in the Western Hemisphere; *two*, developing an omnilateral and multilevel type of diplomacy in a politically heterogeneous region and, *three*, building contingent capabilities for long-term geostrategic objectives. For regional organisations in LAC, the BRI reinforces incentives for, *one*, attracting capital for infrastructure development following

6 *Diálogo*, 21 September 2018.

the decline of commodity prices; *two*, decentering the regional architecture of development finance through non-conditional loans and, *three*, increasing the space for national leaders to gain political support from domestic and regional business networks in the energy, mining, construction, transport and agricultural sectors.

Functions of Interregionalism in China-LAC relations

The literature on interregional relations distinguishes five functions of interregionalism: 'soft' balancing, institution building, rationalizing, agenda setting and identity building (Rüland 2001; Doidge 2011; Fehrmann 2014). 'Soft' *balancing* describes a strategy by which interregional fora serve as institutional balancing devices. They are formed to balance real or perceived regional or global power disequilibria. Most interregional dialogue fora started as institutional balancing exercises. APEC, for instance, was a response to emerging trade blocks epitomised by the European Single Market and NAFTA. ASEM represented European fears of being marginalised by East Asia's economic miracle and Asian apprehensions regarding US dominance in APEC. The formation of IORA by Australia, India and South Africa was an attempt to counter their omission from ASEM and/or APEC, and the EU-Mercosur bi-regionalism emerged as both partners sought to pre-empt the anticipated US dominance of the Latin American market under the Free Trade Area of the Americas (FTAA), promoted unsuccessfully by Washington (Rüland 1996, 2014).

Institution building refers to the fact that interregional fora constitute a new layer of action and collaboration in the emerging system of global governance. This is complemented in the institutionally more advanced interregional fora by a plethora of subsidiary dialogue platforms, that is regular summits, ministerial meetings, senior official meetings, conventions of business leaders and *ad hoc* working groups. Institutionalists believed that these new dialogue fora would potentially expedite the legalisation, contractualisation and constitutionalisation of international relations. They expected interregional institutions to gradually transform the essentially anarchical character of international relations to approximate the rules-based approach to domestic politics pursued in Western liberal democracies (Abbott & Snidal 2000; Zangl & Zürn 2004). Together with *rationalizing*, that is streamlining overburdened global organisations by shifting unresolved problems downward to interregional or regional fora, and *agenda setting*, that is the advancement of new themes in international negotiations, the institution-building function converges in the concept of 'multilateral utility' (Dent 2004). 'Multilateral utility' denotes a process by which global multilateral forums are strengthened and made more efficient, more democratic, more legitimate and more 'nested' (Aggarwal 1998), that is better integrated into the existing global governance architecture. Yet, as we will demonstrate later, interregional institutions tend to be shallow and examples of effective rationalizing and agenda setting have been rare.

Finally, 'collective identity building' refers to a process of sharpening the notions of the regional self through the process of interaction with regional others (Gilson 2002), a process that Hänggi has felicitously termed 'regionalism through interregionalism' (Hänggi 2003). A good example of such a process is the increasing cohesion among Asian participants in the initial period of the Asia-Europe Meeting (ASEM) (Maull, Segal & Wanandi 1998).

Subsequent research refined the functional approach to interregionalism. In a more recent piece, Rüland (2014) identified open questions related to interregionalism's balancing functions, arguing that the internal dimension of balancing exemplified by the bilateralism and mini-lateralism practiced at the sidelines of interregional fora is largely unexplored. Also, forum shopping (Forman & Segaar 2006) as a case of vertical balancing where weaker actors seek to evade the predominance of rival powers in global multilateral fora by shifting the agenda to interregional fora is as much under-researched as the use of interregionalism for 'hedging' exercises (Kuik 2008, 2016). The concept of hedging refers to the strategy of simultaneously enacting 'soft' balancing measures and policies of engagement to minimise the risks of domination by a hegemon (*Ibid.*).

In a thoughtful contribution, Doidge (2011) linked functions of interregionalism to actorness, which he regards as a key variable moderating the performance of the functions of interregionalism. For him a high level of actorness is associated with a mainly *internally focused, capacity building* interregionalism stimulating institution building in less institutionalised regional organisations. A high level of actorness helps, but is neither a necessary nor a sufficient condition for the *externally focused, globally active* interregionalism which is involved in 'soft' balancing, rationalizing and agenda-setting exercises in global fora.

Less under-researched is the question of to what extent interregional relations serve as channels for the diffusion of norms and policies. While there is widespread agreement that as a 'normative power' (Manners 2002), the EU relies on interregional relations to advance its repository of norms and policies in other world regions (Jetschke & Murray 2012, Jupille, Jolliff & Wojcik 2013), this research is dominated by Eurocentric perspectives which attach to the EU a much greater normative impact than it actually exerts (Allison 2015; Rüland 2014, 2018). An issue that has been largely unaddressed is the extent to which in an 'entangled interregionalism' non-Western regional organisations export norms and policies to the EU and to their non-European partners. This is more than a rhetorical question as the case of ASEAN shows that non-Western organisations are also emulated elsewhere in East Asia and the Global South (Stubbs 2008).

For China, its interregional overtures to Latin America clearly constitute a variant of 'soft' balancing. In the wake of President Obama's Pivot to the Asia-Pacific, regarded by many Chinese strategists as a deliberate attempt to contain, if not encircle, China (Campbell 2016), the extension of bilateralism through a shallow institutional layer of interregional ties is an attempt to build up presence in the immediate neighbourhood of the USA and to challenge the latter's hegemonic position in its own backyard. An enlarged stature in Latin America is undeniably a significant dimension in China's declared goal of changing a US-dominated, largely unipolar world order into a multipolar word order.

For LAC states, interregionalism is clearly dominated by the objective of 'soft' balancing US influence in the region through cooperation with China as in the case of CELAC. However, they also use interregional cooperation with China to put pressure on the EU, as in the case of Mercosur's trade negotiation policies. In addition, LAC states use interregional relations for internal balancing, as exemplified by Uruguay's advocacy role in favor of China, hoping to enhance its position vis-à-vis the regional hegemons Argentina and Brazil. While in the past the USA has tolerated China's economic influence in the region, as it also fosters a higher level of demand for American products and services from the LAC region, more recently the Trump government has responded with threats of hard balancing, especially in the context of the Venezuelan crisis, where Washington perceives China and Russia as perils to regional and national security.[7]

For Beijing, the China-CELAC Forum also gains relevance in terms of institution building as its relationship with Brazil loses political momentum given right-wing populist Jair Bolsonaro's rise to power and his willingness to strengthen strategic cooperation with the Trump administration. It remains open whether the High-Level Coordination and Cooperation Committee (COSBAN), the Global Strategic Dialogue (GSD) instituted bilaterally by China and Brazil, and even the BRICS alliance will retain the same level of significance as they used to

7 "Pompeo: China a 'Corrosive' Presence in Venezuela, Russia 'Escalating' Crisis", *Sputnik Latin America*, available at: https://sputniknews.com/latam/201904121074085306-Russian-Presence-Venezuela-Obvious-Provocation-Pompeo/, (accessed 13 April 2019).

have under Presidents Lula da Silva and Dilma Rousseff. Since their creation in 2006 and 2007, respectively, COSBAN and GSD have formed a key axis of interregional dialogue 'without regions' given China's and Brazil's strategic positions as regional and global actors. With a new hemispheric balance of power in which Brazil is likely to bow to the Trump administration's project to regain influence in the region, this institutional layer of interaction may suffer substantial degradation.

Hence there are many reasons for China to institutionalise relations with CELAC while keeping cooperation channels with all other regional organisations open. *First*, the institutional scope of CELAC offers an all-encompassing, that is omnilateral, space for engaging with the diversity of regional organisations and the thirty-three states of the LAC region on a long-term basis, that is bypassing ideological, economic and foreign policy differences and frictions amongst them. *Second*, while holding high symbolic value as an institutional device devoid of US and Canadian influence, CELAC offers China the opportunity to enhance its radius of influence in the region and its reputation in the Global South as a significant global player. *Third*, given CELAC's weak levels of actorness and China's disproportionately strong financial capabilities, Beijing can enact a highly variable mix of interregional cooperation formats and government-to-government relations according to short-term targets and long-term objectives.

Like in other interregional relations, relieving overburdened global international fora through referring global issues to lower levels of the global governance system for further deliberation ('rationalizing'), so far, has played only a negligible role for China's interregional relations with Latin America. Yet China uses these fora to change the Western-dominated international value system by promoting its BRI agenda of economic interactions devoid of conditionalities and behind-the-border effects. However, as China has so far been unable to effectively promote this objective in the Bretton Woods institutions, it has shifted it to newly formed fora such as the Asian Infrastructure and Investment Bank (AIIB), the New Development Bank (formerly BRICS Development Bank) and interregional fora that it helped to set up. Viewed from this angle, rather than epitomizing the rationalizing function of interregional fora, the institutional promotion of an alternative normative order is more akin to forum shopping and thus vertical institutional balancing (see above).

Unlike 'rationalizing', Beijing uses interregionalism with Latin American countries for 'agenda setting'. One is, as mentioned above, its development agenda, which it seeks to propagate globally. The latter has been dissociated from the Western orthodoxy of development cooperation as specified by the rules of the Development Assistance Committee (DAC). In the Latin American case,

China's concept of development promotion is spelled out in the 1+3+6 strategy of 2014. This agenda stands for cooperation on the basis of '*one* plan', that is the China-LAC Countries Cooperation Plan, 2015–2019, '*three* engines', identifying trade, investment and finance as drivers of cooperation and '*six*' areas, specifying cooperation in the fields of energy and resources, infrastructure construction, agriculture, manufacturing, scientific and technological innovation and information technology (Recavarren 2015). In the wake of the country's energy and natural resource bottlenecks, oversupply of construction materials, determination to internationalise the renminbi and needs for food supplies, this constitutes a much more Chinese than Latin American agenda. As recent research has shown, China's economic agenda poses the risk of keeping LAC at the lowest levels of global production chains while deepening the region's overreliance on resource extraction. This extractive mode of development entails highly adverse political, economic and ecological consequences while it pushes the region back to its historically bitter condition of colonial subalternity (Rosales 2016; Rodríguez 2018). Chinese-Latin American interregionalism also serves the objective of extending the BRI agenda to a strategically significant part of the world, which was originally not included in the scheme. For China, moreover, interregionalism fosters a favorable environment to promote the 'One China' policy in a region where Taiwan, considered by Beijing as a renegade province, maintains its last diplomatic strongholds.

China-LAC interregionalism contributes to 'identity building', as it mutually strengthens the 'South-South' and 'Third Worldist' identity of both partners, which has found expression in cooperation under the aegis of the G77 in the United Nations and other international organisations. It has not necessarily sharpened, but has added collective notions of self for Latin American and Caribbean actors. This corresponds loosely to Hänggi's term of 'regionalism through interregionalism' (Hänggi 2003), although the intensity of the process should not be overestimated. The recent strengthening of the 'LAC' identity is a sub-product of CELAC's interregional dialogue with China that is further nurtured by CELAC's recognition as an interregional actor by the EU (Torres Jarrín 2018: 50) and, later, by Russia and India.[8] These interactions have provided Latin American and Caribbean actors with a sense of common identity which had long proved difficult to promote, even for recognised multilateral institutions

8 Cancillería Ecuador: "CELAC strengthens agreements with India and Russia", available at: https://www.cancilleria.gob.ec/celac-strengthens-agreements-with-india-and-russia/, (accessed 12 April 2019).

like the Economic Commission for Latin America and the Caribbean (ECLAC). One of the main elements leading to such an effect is certainly China's initiative to put substantial financial resources at the disposal of CELAC. While the China-CELAC Forum has provided the LAC region with an emerging notion of collective identity for Latin American and Caribbean states, such a perception of 'regionness' still rests on thin institutional ice, lacking financial contributions from its members and depending on China's thus far unilateral decisions to equip CELAC with substantial levels of funding.

While China uses interregional dialogues to promote its normative agenda, the Beijing Consensus, globally, another facet of this policy is to inculcate these value patterns regionally. At the core is, as explained before, a largely mercantilist economic program and values such as *non-interference* and *non-conditionality*, which denounce Western development policies (e.g., IMF structural programs) as denigrating obstacles to developing countries' own development (Gonzalez-Vicente 2014). While this normative agenda resonates in Latin America, governments are aware that China's policies do have geostrategic strings attached as in the case of their requirement for LAC states to recognise Beijing's One-China Policy. There are, however, recent nuances to this principle. Although the advancement of the One-China Policy is part and parcel of China's core interests in Latin America, Beijing has partly removed this condition from its financial assistance to CELAC members, demonstrating the importance that China's leaders attach to the LAC region. While access to the Preferential Loan Program (US$10 billion) requires LAC states to uphold diplomatic relations with Beijing, the Special Loan Program (US$20 billion) does not. However, evidence is limited given the recent launching of the initiative and the limited number of studies about this issue. Nonetheless, although China has been reluctant to enact political conditionalities, there is recent evidence that recipients might be required or constrained to hire Chinese construction companies or buy Chinese equipment in exchange (Myers & Gallagher 2017: 2). In the absence of detailed empirical studies, it is difficult to evaluate whether China will use interregional channels to enhance collective problem solving in the region or use its financial capacities to forge resistance against Western values among its partners. Nonetheless, the analysis shows that China will use any space available to enhance its economic and political interests in the region, as it provides Beijing with significant material inputs, investment destinations, and the political ground to keep climbing the ladder of global governance.

As far as actorness is concerned, there is little evidence that China promotes what Doidge characterised as internally focused, capacity building interregionalism. Given its disproportionate economic advantage, Beijing enjoys a comfortable position by implementing its regional agenda on a state-to-state basis. There is hence no plausible reason to believe that Beijing will invest decisively in any capacity-building measures seeking to strengthen regional actorness in Latin America and the Caribbean.

Problems and Implications for Global Governance

Most studies conclude that interregionalism has so far contributed little to the teleology of an institutionally deepening and increasingly effective system of global governance as predicted by liberal institutionalists in the 1990s (Yeo 2003; Bersick 2004; Löwen 2004; Robles 2008; Hardacre 2009; Adelmann 2012; Fehrmann 2015; Hulse 2017). By contrast, interregional relations have most frequently been used as 'soft' balancing and hedging devices to respond to real or putative power shifts. With the renewed rise of nationalist, populist and authoritarian regimes and the renaissance of unbridled power politics ending the more cooperative post-Cold War world order, it must be anticipated that interregionalism will continue to be primarily a 'soft' balancing and hedging utility. States merely using institutions for short-term 'soft' balancing purposes cannot be expected to bear the inevitable governance costs associated with deepening interregional relations. Interregionalism thus markedly contributes to entrenching a type of multilateralism that elsewhere has been termed 'diminished' multilateralism (Rüland 2012). The latter denotes international interactions that are characterised by downgrading institutions to arenas of power contests, the relegation of cross-border problem solving to a backseat, flexible, pragmatic, non-binding low-intensity cooperation shaped by 'soft law' and the rise of broad-band institutions that cover a multiplicity of themes. Other properties of 'diminished' multilateralism include widespread forum shopping, the fragmentation and overlapping of fora due to the absence of institutional 'nesting' and the increase of institutional redundancies (Panke & Stapel 2018; Rüland & Michael 2019).

Chinese-LAC relations to a large extent fit these descriptions of 'diminished' multilateralism. They are shallow and pragmatic institutional arrangements, created to 'soft' balance American containment or even encirclement policies under the US Pivot to the Asia-Pacific, or more recently its Indo-Pacific strategy with Japan, Australia and India as major allies in the so-called Quad, and to contest the international normative order. They contribute to forum shopping, institutional overlapping (for instance, with FEALAC) and by not being 'nested' (Aggarwal 1998) with the existing global governance architecture they contribute to institutional redundancies. For many Latin American presidents, the China-driven interregionalism provides an institutional device to respond to domestic pressure from local business networks anxious to expand exports to and attract capital from China. Additionally, the shallow formats of interregional cooperation are actually perceived as a stabilizing mechanism, particularly in the context of Trump's unpopularity in Latin America and the EU's internal problems in managing Brexit.

A second major problem facing interregionalism is its strong executive bias. More than most other international organisations, interregionalism is dominated by governments. While the institutionally more developed interregional fora such as ASEM and APEC have also set up business fora, parliamentary and civil society representation is weak or entirely missing. With the Asia-Europe Parliamentary Partnership (ASEP), only ASEM has developed a feeble parliamentary representation (Rüland & Carrapatoso 2015). Civil society – organised in the Asia-Europe People's Forum – usually organises parallel summits (Bersick 2008) and only since ASEM's Milano Summit in 2014 has it been enabled to briefly meet the heads of government in a largely symbolic exercise (Rüland 2016). Interregional dialogue fora have thus contributed next to nothing to the democratisation of global governance.

Chinese-Latin American interregionalism is representative of many other institutionally shallow interregional dialogues. It is almost exclusively executive driven and entails only a very weak and essentially symbolical nongovernmental dimension. As with virtually all major interregional fora, the China-CELAC Forum also includes a business forum, providing a voice to business representatives interested in the economic interactions agreed by the governments. Yet there is no civil society component to provide social groups affected by the adverse environmental and social effects of interregional projects with a forum to air their apprehensions and objections. The people-to-people interaction promoted by the China-CELAC Forum is hardly more than a corporatist device signifying a semblance of popular participation, which is, in essence, a state-controlled mechanism. The envisaged political party dialogue and legislative interactions, too, are no substitute for a meaningful check-and-balance mechanism in an otherwise strongly top-heavy type of interregionalism. Thus, the China-CELAC Forum also contributes virtually nothing to the badly needed democratisation of executive interregionalism.

Conclusion

This chapter has shown that in its relations with Latin America, China primarily relies on bilateral ties. Yet in the last decade it has extended its web of relations in the region, initially through transregional fora such as APEC and FEALAC and subsequently through hybrid interregional dialogue fora, of which CELAC has become the single most significant case. While the China-CELAC Forum has modestly contributed to international institution building, the two other functions, which are expected to transform interregional fora into 'multilateral utilities', namely 'rationalizing' and 'agenda setting', are widely absent in China's relations with Latin America. As the 'identity building' effect has also been limited, Chinese-Latin American interregionalism is largely confined to institutional balancing and hedging purposes. This is also corroborated by the fact that Chinese-Latin American interregional institutions are essentially shallow, non-binding, pragmatic and soft law-based arrangements. China takes advantage of this loose institutional setting to balance the USA in its own backyard, while LAC use it not only to balance American influence in their hemisphere but also as a way of recalibrating their flagging relationship with the EU. Interacting with China is thus a Latin American, and lately also Caribbean, attempt to carve out better pay offs in its economic and political relations with the USA and with the EU.

China's interregional engagement in Latin America can also be qualified as a particularistic, opportunistic and mercantilist approach to multilateralism. It fosters multilateralism and the constitution of international fora in order to advance its position in the rivalry with the USA and to build up the global presence and status expected of world powers. The particularistic brand of China's approach to multilateralism consists of a strategy to selectively realise short-term advantages, often in glaring dissonance with its official rhetoric. A case in point is China's economic activism in Latin America. Although persistently propagating its commitment to an open global economy and its determined subscription to a rule-based order of trade multilateralism, China relies heavily on state enterprises and mercantilist policies. It thereby accepts that Latin American countries persist in a colonial type of resource-dependent economy, which offers little prospect of climbing the global ladder of value creation through the development of a strong and diversified manufacturing sector. With these economic policies, with its focus on a largely state-centric interregionalism that rests on unpopular governments and elites, and with its heavy reliance on Westphalian values, China's interregionalism entrenches what in this chapter has been termed 'diminished' multilateralism. This particular way of engaging with multilateralism does not necessarily contribute to the strengthening of international institutions for the sake of effectively addressing global problems. Instead, it instrumentalises institutions for the purpose of power contests and facilitates an international order characterised by soft law, forum shopping and institutional redundancy.

Bibliography

Abbott, Kenneth W. & Snidal, Duncan (2000). "Hard and Soft Law in International Governance", *International Organization* 54(3): 421–456.

Adelmann, Martin (2012). *The External Relations of the Southern African Development Community (SADC)*. Freiburg: Arnold-Bergstraesser Institut.

Aggarwal, Vinod K. & Fogarty, Edward A. (eds.) (2004). *European Union Trade Strategies: Between Globalism and Regionalism*, pp. 207–240. London: Palgrave.

Aggarwal, Vinod K. (1998). "Analyzing Institutional Transformation in the Asia-Pacific". In Vinod K. Aggarwal & Charles E. Morrison (eds.), *Asia Pacific Crossroads: Regime Creation and the Future of APEC*, pp. 23–64. New York: St. Martin's Press.

Alianza del Pacífico (n.d.). Abecé Alianza del Pacífico, https://alianzapacifico.net, accessed 23 March 2017.

Allison, Laura (2015). *The EU, ASEAN and Interregionalism: Regionalism Support and Norm Diffusion Between the EU and ASEAN*. Basingstoke: Palgrave Macmillan.

Aróstica, Pamela (2018). China y América Latina: Tiempos de cambios. Blog de Opinión REDCAEM, http://chinayamericalatina.com/china-y-america-latina-tiempo-de-cambios/, accessed 13 April 2019.

Bersick, Sebastian (2004). *Auf dem Weg in eine neue Weltordnung? Zur Politik der interregionalen Beziehungen am Beispiel des ASEM Prozesses*. Baden-Baden: Nomos.

Bersick, Sebastian (2008). "The Democratization of Inter- and Transregional Dialogues. The Role of Civil Society, NGO and Parliaments". In Jürgen Rüland, Gunter Schubert, Günther Schucher & Cornelia Storz (eds.), *Asian-European Relations: Building Blocks for Global Governance?*, pp. 244–269. London: Routledge.

Campbell, Kurt (2016). *The Pivot: the Future of American Statecraft in Asia*. New York: Twelve.

China (2008). *China's Policy Paper on Latin America and the Caribbean*.

China (2016). *Full text of China's Policy Paper on Latin America and the Caribbean*.

China-CELAC Forum (2016). *Basic Information about China-CELAC Forum*, Edited by Department of Latin American and Caribbean Affairs. Ministry of Foreign Affairs of China, http://www.chinacelacforum.org/eng/ltjj_1/P020161207421177845816.pdf, accessed 12 April 2019.

Creutzfeldt, Benjamin (2018). *China's Engagement with Regional Actors: The Pacific Alliance*. Washington, DC: Woodrow Wilson International Center for Scholars.

Dent, Christopher M. (2004). "The Asia-Europe Meeting (ASEM) and Inter-Regionalism: Towards a Theory of Multilateral Utility", *Asian Survey* 44(2): 213–236.

Doctor, Mahrukh (2015). "Interregionalism's Impact on Regional Integration in Developing Countries: The Case of Mercosur", *Journal of European Public Policy* 22(7): 967–984.

Doidge, Mathew (2011). *The European Union and Interregionalism. Patterns of Engagement*. Avebury: Ashgate.

Durán Lima, José, Herrera, Ricardo, Lebret, Pierre & Echeverría, Myriam (2014): Latin America-European Union Cooperation. A Partnership for Development. Santiago de Chile: ECLAC (LC/W.564), https://repositorio.cepal.org/bitstream/handle/11362/37595/S1420618_en.pdf?sequence=1, 13 April 2019.

Dussel Peters, Enrique (2015). *China's Evolving Role in Latin America. Can it Be a Win-Win?* Washington, DC: Atlantic Council.

ECLAC (2015). First Forum of China and the Community of Latin American and Caribbean States (CELAC). Exploring Opportunities for Cooperation on Trade and Investment. Santiago de Chile (14-21103), https://repositorio.cepal.org/bitstream/handle/11362/37578/S1421103_en.pdf;jsessionid=AB1B936131A49EC6B5241D77F3129597?sequence=1, accessed 12 April 2019.

Ellis, R. Evan (2018). "Hacia una asociación estratégica: Las inversiones de China en América Latina". In *Working Paper Series (WPS) REDCAEM* 3, http://chinayamericalatina.com/wp-content/uploads/2019/04/WP3-Mar-2018-REDCAEM.pdf, accessed 13 April 2019.

Fawcett, Louise & Hurrell, Andrew (eds.) (1995). *Regionalism in World Politics. Regional Organization and International Order*. Oxford: Oxford University Press.

Fehrmann, Thomas (2014). *Die Effektivität interregionaler Kooperation. Eine vergleichende Untersuchung der Handlungsfähigkeit von Regionalorganisationen am Beispiel von ASEAN*. Baden-Baden: Nomos.

Feng, Zhongping & Huan, Jing (2014). "China's Strategic Partnership Diplomacy: Engaging with a Changing World". In *European Strategic Partnerships Observatory ESP* (Working Paper 8) http://www.egmontinstitute.be/chinas-strategic-partnership-diplomacy-engaging-with-a-changing-world/ (access on 31 March 2020)

Forman, Shepard & Segaar, Derk (2006). "New Coalition for Global Governance: The Changing Dynamics of Multilateralism", *Global Governance*, 12: 205–225.

Gallagher, Kevin (2016). *The China Triangle. Latin America's China Boom and the Fate of the Washington Consensus*. New York: Oxford University Press.

Gardini, Gian Luca (2015). "Towards Modular Regionalism: The Proliferation of Latin American Cooperation", *Revista Brasileira de Política Internacional* 58(1): 210–229.

Gilson, Julie (2002). *Asia Meets Europe: Interregionalism and the Asia-Europe Meeting*. Cheltenham: Edward Elgar.

Gonzalez-Vicente, Ruben (2014). "The Limits to China's Non-interference Foreign Policy. Pro-state Interventionism and the Rescaling of Economic Governance", *Australian Journal of International Affairs* 69(2): 205–223.

Grieco, Joseph M. (1996). "State Interests and Institutional Rule Trajectories: a Neorealist Interpretation of the Maastricht Treaty and European Economic and Monetary Union". In Benjamin Frankel (ed.), *Realism. Restatements and Renewal*, pp. 261–306. London: Frank Cass.

Hänggi, Heiner (2003). Regionalism through Interregionalism: East Asia and ASEM. In Fu-Kuo Liu & Philippe Régnier (eds.), *Regionalism in East Asia: Paradigm Shifting*, pp. 197–219. London: Curzon Press.

Hänggi, Heiner (2006): "Interregionalism as a Multifaceted Phenomenon: In Search of a Typology". In Heiner Hänggi, Ralf Roloff & Jürgen Rüland (eds.), *Interregionalism and International Relations*, pp. 31–62. London: Routledge.

Hänggi, Heiner, Roloff, Ralf & Rüland, Jürgen (2006), "Interregionalism: A New Phenomenon in International Relations". In Heiner Hänggi, Ralf Roloff & Jürgen Rüland (eds.), *Interregionalism and International Relations*, pp. 3–14. London: Routledge.

Hardacre, Alan (2009). *The Rise and Fall of Interregionalism in EU External Relations*. Dordrecht: Republic of Letters Publishing.

Holland, Martin (2006). " 'Imagined' Interregionalism: Europe's Relations with Africa, Caribbean and Pacific States (ACP)". In Heiner Hänggi, Ralf Roloff & Jürgen Rüland (eds.), *Interregionalism and International Relations*, pp. 254–271. London: Routledge.

Hulse, Merran (2017). *United We Stand, Divided We Fall. Actorness and effectiveness of ECOWAS and SADC in Interregional Negotiations for Economic Partnership Agreements*. Nijmegen: Radboud University Nijmegen, PhD Diss.

Jetschke, Anja & Murray, Philomena (2012). "Diffusing Regional Integration: The EU and Southeast Asia", *West European Politics* 35(1): 174–191.

Jupille, Joseph, Jolliff, Brandy & Wojcik, Stefan (2013). "Regionalism in the World Polity". Paper presented at the International Studies Association Annual Congress, San Francisco, 3–6 April.

Klom, Andy (2003). "Mercosur and Brazil: A European Perspective", *International Affairs* 79: 351–368.

Konold, Dieter (2010). "Farm Interests as Bargaining Chips: France in the EU-Mercosur Free Trade Negotiations", *Journal of Public Policy* 30(3): 321–343.

Kuik, Cheng-Chwee (2008). "The Essence of Hedging: Malaysia and Singapore's Response to a Rising China", *Contemporary Southeast Asia* 30(2), 159–185.

Kuik, Cheng-Chwee (2016). "How Do Weaker States Hedge? Unpacking ASEAN States' Alignment Behavior towards China", *Journal of Contemporary China* 25(100): 500–514.

Löwen, Howard (2004). *Theorie und Empirie transregionaler Kooperation am Beispiel des Asia-Europe Meeting (ASEM)*. Hamburg: Verlag Dr. Kovac.

Manners, Ian (2002). "Normative Power Europe: A Contradiction in Terms?", *Journal of Common Market Studies* 40(2): 235–258.

Maull, Hanns W., Segal, Gerald & Wanandi, Jusuf (eds.) (1998). *Europe and the Asia Pacific*. London, New York: Routledge.

Myers, Margaret & Gallagher, Kevin (2017). *Chinese Finance to LAC in 2016. The Dialogue* (China-Latin America Report), https://www.thedialogue.org/wp-content/uploads/2017/02/Chinese-Finance-to-LAC-in-2016-Web-and-email-res.pdf, accessed 14 April 2019.

Nolte, Detlef (2016). "The Pacific Alliance: Nation-Branding through Regional Organisations". *GIGA Focus Latin America* 4 https://www.giga-hamburg.de/en/publication/the-pacific-alliance-nation-branding-through-regional-organisations （accession date 31 March 2020).

Nolte, Detlef (2018). "China Is Challenging but (Still) Not Displacing Europe in Latin America". *GIGA Focus Latin America* 1, https://www.giga-hamburg.de/de/system/files/publications/gf_lateinamerika_1801_en_0.pdf, accessed 13 April 2019.

Olsen, Gorm-Rye (2006). "The Africa-Europe (Cairo Summit) Process: An Expression of Symbolic Politics". In Heiner Hänggi, Ralf Roloff & Jürgen Rüland (eds.), *Interregionalism and International Relations*, pp. 199–214. London: Routledge.

Palmer, Norman D. (1991). *The New Regionalism in Asia and the Pacific*. Lexington: Lexington Books.

Panke, Diana & Stapel, Sören (2018). "Exploring Overlapping Regionalism", *Journal of International Relations and Development* 21(3): 635–662.

Paz, Gonzalo S. (2018). "Remapping Latin America and East Asia Interregional Relations". In G. L. Gardini, S. Koschut, & A. Falke (Eds.), *Interregionalism and the Americas*. Lanham: Lexington Books: 163–179.

Recavarren, Isabel (2015). "CELAC-China: 1+3+6", *Revista Panoramica*, https://www.panoramical.eu/columnas/opinion-panoramica/celac-china-136/, accessed 12 April 2019.

Ribeiro-Hoffmann, Andrea (2016). "Inter- and Transregionlism". In Tanja Börzel & Thomas Risse (eds.), *Oxford Handbook of Comparative Regionalism*. Oxford: Oxford University Press.

Robles, Alfredo C. (2008). *The Asia-Europe Meeting: The Theory and Practice of Interregionalism*. London: Routledge.

Rodríguez, Fabricio (2018). *Oil, Minerals and Power. The Political Economy of China's Quest for Resources in Brazil and Peru*. Doctoral Dissertation. University of Freiburg.

Rosales, Antulio (2016). "Deepening Extractivism and Rentierism. China's Role in Venezuela's Bolivarian Developmental Model", *Canadian Journal of Development Studies/Revue canadienne d'études du développement* 37(4): 1–18.

Rüland, Jürgen (1996). *The Asia Europe Meeting (ASEM): Towards a New Euro-Asian Relationship?* Rostock: Rostocker. Informationen zu Politik und Verwaltung, Heft 5.

Rüland, Jürgen (2001). *ASEAN and the European Union: A Bumpy Interregional Relationship*. Bonn: Rheinische Friedrich-Wilhelms-Universität Bonn, Zentrum für Europäische Integrationsforschung, Discussion Paper, C 95.

Rüland, Jürgen (2002). "'Dichte' oder 'schlanke' Institutionalisierung? Der neue Regionalismus im Zeichen von Globalisierung und Asienkrise", *Zeitschrift für Internationale Beziehungen* 9(2): 175–208.

Rüland, Jürgen (2006). "Interregionalism: An Unfinished Agenda". In Heiner Hänggi, Ralf Roloff & Jürgen Rüland (eds.), *Interregionalism and International Relations*, pp. 295–313. London: Routledge.

Rüland, Jürgen (2010). "Balancers, Multilateral Utilities or Identity Builders? International Relations and the Study of Interregionalism", *Journal of European Public Policy* 17(8): 1268–1280.

Rüland, Jürgen (2012). "The Rise of 'Diminished Multilateralism:' East Asian and European Forum Shopping in Global Governance", *Asia Europe Journal* 9(2–4): 255–270.

Rüland, Jürgen (2014). "Interregionalism and International Relations: Reanimating an Obsolescent Research Agenda?" In Francis Baert, Tiziana Scaramagli & Fredrik Söderbaum (eds.), *Intersecting Interregionalism. Regions, Global Governance and the EU*, pp. 15–36. Heidelberg: Springer.

Rüland, Jürgen (2016). "Peoples-to-Peoples Connectivity in the Asia-Europe Meeting: 'By the People' Instead 'For the People' ". In Anita Prakash (ed.), *Asia-Europe Connectivity Vision 2015. Challenges and Opportunities. An ERIA-Government of Mongolia Document*, pp. 145–158. Jakarta: ERIA.

Rüland, Jürgen (2018). *The Indonesian Way. ASEAN, Europeanization and Foreign Policy Debates in a New Democracy*. Stanford: Stanford University Press.

Rüland, Jürgen & Bechle, Karsten (2010). "Interregionalism without Regions: IBSA as a Form of Shallow Regionalism". In Jörn Dosch & Olaf Jacob (eds.), *Asia and Latin America. Political, Economic and Multilateral Relations*, pp. 157–176. London: Routledge.

Rüland, Jürgen & Carrapatoso, Astrid (2015). "Democratizing Inter-regionalism. The EU Parliament and its Asia Relations". In Daniela Irrera & Stelios Stavridis (eds.), *The European Parliament and its International Relations*, pp. 197–219. London: Routledge.

Rüland, Jürgen & Michael, Arndt (2019, forthcoming). "Overlapping Regionalism and Cooperative Hegemony: How China and India Compete in South and Southeast Asia", *Cambridge Review of International Affairs* Vol 32, 2019 pp 178-200.

Söderbaum, Frederik & Stalgren, Patrik (2010). *The EU and the Global South*. London: Lynne Rienner Publishers.

Stubbs Richard (2008). "The ASEAN Alternative? Ideas, Institutions and the Challenge to 'Global' Governance," *The Pacific Review* 21 (4): 451–468.

Torres Jarrín, Mario (2018). "EU-CELAC A Multiplayer Interregionalism: Redefining the Atlantic Area". In G. L. Gardini, S. Koschut, & A. Falke (Eds.), *Interregionalism and the Americas*. Lanham: Lexington Books: 37–54.

Xu, Yanran (2016). *China's Strategic Partnerships in Latin America. Case Studies of China's Oil Diplomacy in Argentina, Brazil, Mexico, and Venezuela, 1991–2015*. Lanham: Lexington Books.

Yeo, Lay-Hwee (2003). *Asia and Europe. The Development and Different Dimensions of ASEM*. London: Routledge.

Yu, Lei (2015). "China's Strategic Partnership with Latin America. A Fulcrum in China's Rise", *International Affairs* 91(5): 1047–1068.

Zangl, Bernhard & Zürn, Michael (2004). "Make Law, Not War: Internationale und transnationale Verrechtlichung als Baustein für Global Governance". In Bernhard Zangl & Michael Zürn (eds.), *Verrechtlichung – Baustein für Global Governance?*, pp. 12–46. Bonn: Verlag J.H.W. Dietz Nachfolger.

Zürn, Michael (2018). *A Theory of Global Governance. Authority, Legitimacy, and Contestation*. Oxford: Oxford University.

Sebastian Santander

The Atlantic Triangle in the Era of China's Rising Power in Latin America

Introduction

This chapter focuses on the relations that the European Union (EU), United States (US) and China have developed with the continent of Latin America in the post-Cold War period. It looks at the evolution of each of them, the various different influences they have and their impact on Latin American stakeholders.

US policy on Latin America was for a long time governed by the Monroe Doctrine, based on the mantra of 'America for the Americans'. This explains why for decades Washington had considered Latin America (LA) as its own backyard. Hence the US had a policy that allowed the country to exercise an almost discretionary authority over the continent for most of the 20th century.

Starting in the 1980s, the EU and its Member States took initiatives enabling them to project themselves into the sphere of influence traditionally dominated by the USA. They began to play a role there and to develop their presence there. From the 1990s onwards, this resulted in the establishment of an interregional association between the EU and LA based on institutional and multidimensional relations – which they were quick to describe as 'strategic'. The EU rolled out a strategy that was aimed, for instance, at supporting regional organisations in LA to develop regional group-to-group relations. This strategy was intended to enable the EU to increase its international visibility and recognition, to consolidate its economic and commercial interests and thus to build and establish its role as an actor on the Latin American scene in the face of US power there.

US authorities were aware of this growing European presence in their hemisphere, and developed initiatives in response. Fearing that its companies would lose markets in a context of increased globalisation, the US rethought its strategy towards the continent. The aim was to enhance US trade alliances and to further diversify the country's free trade agreements (FTAs) with LA states.

There emerged what could be called a triangular game in the Atlantic area, where the actors' strategies influenced each other. However, over the past 20 years, the world's pace has accelerated, power has become more diffuse and new powers are emerging and making their presence felt on the international stage. This has only served to increase global competition.

Latin America has watched this new expansion and this increased international rivalry stemming from the new and extra-regional actors taking root on the ground in LA. China is the biggest of these actors, which raises the question as to whether its deployment will likely induce the traditional (the EU and USA) regional actors in the Atlantic Triangle to adapt their own behaviour and strategies. Are China's presence and its appeal to LA transforming the Atlantic Triangle into a strategic space with a quadrilateral rivalry?

EU-LA Relationship as a Soft Balancing against the USA

For over 40 years, the EU and its Member States have been forging multiple relations with Latin American states and regional organisations. Their first approaches were made mainly during the 1980s. This coincided with three specific moments: the revival of the Cold War and Central American armed conflicts, a European desire to exert a more political role on the international scene and the goal of Iberian countries to become an interface between Europe and LA (Santander, 2014a). At that time, the European Community, its Member States and Iberian countries sought to act in concert and to play an intermediary role in the armed conflicts in Central America. However, they soon faced the hostility of the USA, which disapproved of Europe's initiative, especially since the Europeans were dissociating themselves from the USA in terms of interpreting the causes of Central American wars and the best way to respond to these conflicts. The USA advocated an interventionist approach, because it considered these conflicts were the result of East-West rivalry. Yet Europe favoured a regional, peaceful and negotiated approach, believing that these wars arose due to poverty and rampant inequality in the Central American societies (Schumacher, 1995, Crawley, 2006). Unlike the USA, the EU and its Member States played an active role in supporting LA's regional peace initiatives.

This episode, marking a trigger for the development of a future European strategy for the whole of LA in the post-Cold War period, underlines the need to study Europe-Latin American relations by taking into account the US role in the region, especially since LA and Europe see their relations with the USA, for both strategic and economic reasons, as one of their first priorities. To understand the nuts and bolts of these relations and how they change over time as well as the motivation of the actors concerned, we must assess Europe-LA relations in the light of the Atlantic Triangle. This triangle must be viewed in the broader context of globalisation and a multipolar world.

Whatever some experts may claim (Valladao, 1999; Bodemer, Grabendorff, Jung and Thesing, 2002; Arenal and Hirst, 2011; Serbín, 2014), strictly speaking there is no triangular Atlantic relationship fuelled by a 'Western community of values' and by a willingness to cooperate between the triangle's three sides. That is because the Atlantic Triangle exists not as a framework for cooperation with an 'international capacity for action', but is the result of a soft rivalry that has developed between the EU and the USA in relation to LA. This competition is between unequal actors. These actors – to be found in the EU, in LA's countries and regional organisations and the USA – are unequal in power terms. Brussels and Washington both have their own Latin American strategies and they compete with one another, even though the two enjoy a special relationship based on extensive trade and investment as well as considerations of a strategic and military nature as well as political and diplomatic ones. In LA, state and regional actors play with this competition between Europe and the USA as much as possible, in a bid to better balance their relations with the USA and the EU.

When the Cold War ended, the EU came up with a plan for the entire Latin American continent and the USA set about redeploying in this hemisphere by focusing on a more economic and commercial approach. Both strategies were rolled out around the same time and influenced each other. In LA, the US authorities were busily encouraging regional and bilateral relations projects based on the promotion of FTAs (trade but not aid). The idea was to spread the standards and disciplines that underpin the US market economy, and as far as possible to keep outside actors such as the EU at a distance. They set up the North American Free Trade Agreement (NAFTA, 1994). At the initiative of the current Trump administration, this has undergone a facelift and it is now called the United States-Mexico-Canada Agreement or USMCA (2018). They also concluded the Dominican Republic-Central America-United States Free Trade Agreement (CAFTA-DR, 2005). They sought to create a Free Trade Area of the Americas (FTAA) stretching from Alaska to Tierra del Fuego (Argentina). But the failure in 2005 of this initiative pushed the USA to favour a bilateral approach by signing a series of bilateral trade agreements, including with Chile, Colombia and Peru, destabilizing some Latin American regional arrangements and thereby threatening the interregional relations promoted by the EU.

On the European and Latin American side, initiatives were taken to avoid being left behind by US advances in LA. The new expansion of relations between Europe and LA owed much to the many contacts, dialogues and negotiations that took place in the post-bipolar period. These led to an association they called 'strategic'. The association is based on institutional and multidimensional relationships that are themselves based on common principles and interests as well as on numerous themes such as trade, climate, education, energy, gender equality, human rights, democracy, international law and regional integration.

Special attention was paid to regional cooperation and interregional relations, not least because the regional organisations of LA were experiencing a revival from the 1990s. The technical, financial and institutional support for regional integration in LA became a pillar of EU policy on the continent. This regional integration became an 'external federator' for Latin American regional organisations (Santander, 2008). Such support fostered the creation of regional free trade areas, customs unions and common markets, while promoting the adoption of common strategies and institutions as well as the creation of supranational frameworks. Consequently, the interregional phenomenon whereby two specific regional organisations are seeking to interact as a region (Hänggi, Roloff, and Rüland, 2006; Söderbaum and Van Langenhove, 2006) took on greater importance in the relations between the EU and LA.

Relations between the EU and LA would be consolidated with the adoption of over a dozen cooperation programmes funded by the EU (EuroSocial, URB-AL, AL-Invest, Euroclima, Eurosolar, WaterClima-Lac, Ralcea, Alfa, Erasmus+, Copolad, @LIS and LAIF). A series of institutional links were forged and strengthened at governmental level (EU-CELAC biannual summits for heads of state and government; EU-CELAC biannual ministerial summits) and parliamentary level (Euro-Latin American Parliamentary Assembly). In addition, many social actors sought to participate in and influence these relationships. This gave rise to a long series of fora for entrepreneurs, social movements and academics. To facilitate contacts between the decision-makers of this association and civil society, the European Union-Community of Latin American and Caribbean States (EU-CELAC) Foundation was set up. Moreover, the EU successfully concluded different types of agreement with Latin American countries and regional groups (framework agreements, free trade treaties, strategic partnerships, cooperation and political dialogue agreements). These agreements were often concluded more or less at the same time as those negotiated by Washington with the LA actors, examples of this being the bilateral agreements signed individually with Mexico, Chile, Colombia, Peru and Central America. These ever-closer ties enabled the EU to become the second trading partner for LA after the USA, the first development aid provider and the main external investor. According to the European External Action Service (EEAS), in 2016, European investment stock on the Latin American continent reached EUR 825.7 billion, more than the investment stock in China, India and Russia combined (EEAS, 2019).

Consequently, the manner in which Washington moves its pawns in LA has always been viewed with unease in Brussels. The European authorities fear that the way the US deploys its bilateral or regional strategies in LA has the effect of weakening Europe's presence on that continent, while undermining Europe's economic and commercial interests as well as those of its businesses. Many European companies (German, British, Spanish, French, Italian, Dutch and Portuguese) have a presence on that continent and boast significant market shares in the automobile sector (Fiat, Peugeot, Renault and Volkswagen); large retailers (Carrefour, Casino, Jumbo, Makro and Royal Ahold); energy (British Gas, Endesa, Fenosa, Iberdrola, Gas Natural, Repsol, Shell and Suez); telecommunications (Telefónica and Portugal Telecom); banking and insurance (ABN-AMRO, Banco Portugues de Investimento, BBVA, BSCH and Mapfre); aviation (Air Europa, Air France, Alitalia, Ibéria, Lufthansa and TAP) and chemistry (BASF). Latin American governments have always worried about the USA being overly present in their continent and weakening their external relations and ensuring they become locked into overdependence on Washington. This partly explains the failure of the FTAA. As a result, European and Latin American governments typically view their interregional relations as a sort of 'soft balancing' of US influence in the region (Santander, 2008).

The Atlantic Triangle Facing the Shift of Global Power and the Rise of China in LA

During the last 20 years, the shift of global power has become one of the key trends of international relations and particularly of the international political economy. While the 1990s were viewed as a decade when the USA had its 'unipolar moment' (Krauhammer, 1990/1991; Battistella, 2011), the following years saw a growing multipolarisation of the international stage. This spread of power worried the USA and the EU and its Member States, because to some extent it came at the expense of their power and their economic and commercial interests in the world. In particular, this redistribution of power has clearly led to the rise of new powers seeking to increase their presence in world affairs. Their aim is to maximise their interests, diversify their external relations, establish new alliances and encourage changes in international economic and political structures, with a view to rebalancing the new distribution of power to their advantage (Santander, 2009, 2013 and 2014b).

Over the last 15 years, the relations of the EU and the USA with LA have grown weaker. However, as world power has become more diffuse, Asian actors have expanded into LA, notably China, South Korea, Japan and India. This expansion is happening in many sectors and also involves other actors such as Iran and Russia. Actors like these are negotiating agreements with a series of LA countries in fields such as trade, energy and transport. They are also forging political and military alliances and, like Russia, are holding joint military manoeuvres in the region with LA countries, such as Venezuela. Moreover, Russia and its companies are investing billions in this country, in the form of loans or investments (around USD 17 billion) (Mandraud, 2019). Moscow has sold weapons to Venezuela, rescheduled part of the country's debt and supplied bomber aircraft. All of which have only stoked fears in the USA and the EU. Turkey also figures among the extra-regional actors on the Latin American continent. Trade between the two grew substantially from USD 1 to 10 billion between 2000 and 2017. Erdogan's Turkey wants to boost its trade through FTAs, which it is currently negotiating with Colombia, Ecuador, Mexico, Peru and Central America. It is also developing gold trade with Venezuela. Over the last decade, the number of Turkish embassies in LA has more than doubled (from six to 13), and the Turkish Cooperation and Coordination Agency (TIKA) has opened an office in Colombia and Mexico.

The expansion of all these extra-regional actors in LA has been uneven. What concerns Europe and the USA most, economically and commercially, is the presence of China. Its expansion in the region is the most impressive, especially as this has happened in an extremely short period of time. Over the past 15 years, trade between China and LA has multiplied by a factor of 25, from USD 10 to 250 billion. Beijing has negotiated FTAs with several countries on the continent and notably with Chile, Costa Rica and Peru. It is also working on sealing commercial agreements with Colombia, Ecuador and Panama.

For many years, the USA and the EU were, respectively, the first and second trading partners of LA. Today, China is ahead of Europe and in some cases the USA. Indeed, while LA is China's fourth trading partner, the latter has become the second largest partner on the continent and the first for Brazil, Chile and Peru (Müller, Wouters, Defraigne, Santander and Raube: 2017). It is a key customer for LA's raw materials and commodities (crude oil, copper, iron and soybeans), while LA buys mainly high-value-added manufactured products from China (household goods, technologies, appliances, toys, clothing and more) (OECD, 2015). This creates a centre-periphery relationship like the ones sealed by Europe and the USA respectively with LA. Chinese investments have also poured into LA, focusing mainly on sectors such as mining, oil and transport infrastructure (ports, airports, roads, pipelines, gas pipelines and railway lines). According to the ILO, Chinese investments on the mainland reached about USD 200 billion, creating 1.8 million jobs (Dussel and Armony, 2017:47). In the space of a decade, the Chinese government has also made large loans, totalling USD 100 billion, increased the number of high-level political visits to LA and woven a network of political and institutional links, in particular with several regional organisations. To sustain its presence and strengthen its interests within LA, Beijing has joined the Inter-American Development Bank (IDB), whose annual meeting is now also held in China. China also has observer status with the Organization of American States (OAS) and the regional organisation Pacific Alliance (Chile, Colombia, Mexico and Peru), and participates in various multilateral fora. These include the dialogue between China and the Southern Common Market (Mercosur), the Caribbean-China Economic and Trade Cooperation Forum and the China-CELAC Forum.

Recently, the Chinese government has been eager to expand its plans for a 'New Silk Road', known as the 'Belt and Road Initiative' (BRI), to the continent of LA. The initiative aims to reshape the geography of world trade in line with Beijing's vision, so as to promote major infrastructure projects and to further facilitate the delivery of Chinese goods to the four corners of the globe. It is a project with land and maritime parts. The first part seeks to connect China to Europe by land and rail, and the second part makes use of seaways to create an economic zone that would extend westward from south-east Asia to the Mediterranean through the Indian Ocean, The Gulf and the Suez Canal and then to the East by extending its links to LA.

To implement this twin project, the Chinese authorities rely on financial institutions and instruments. They have also set up the Asian Infrastructure Investment Bank (AIIB), which comprises almost 90 countries including Brazil, Bolivia, Chile, Ecuador, Peru and Venezuela as well as a Silk Road Fund with a capital of USD 100 and 40 billion, respectively. The goal is to finance the construction of thousands of roads, ports, bridges, railways, gas pipelines as well as water management facilities and power plants. Panama, which has a strategic commercial positioning thanks to its transoceanic canal, is now becoming the gateway to the Silk Road in LA. In 2017, it even broke off diplomatic relations with Taiwan – a movement started by Costa Rica in 2007 and followed by El Salvador and the Dominican Republic in 2018 – to underline that Panama recognises there is only one China and hence is playing Beijing's game. Washington was deeply disappointed by this, as shown by the recall of its ambassadors from Panama, El Salvador and the Dominican Republic. It disapproved of this relationship and denounced the 'Chinese targets' in Central America and in particular in Panama, a nation until just recently considered a key part of the American zone of influence in the region. By making this highly political decision to break diplomatic relations with Taiwan, Panama has succeeded in winning the favour of Chinese leaders and investors.

This move reflects how, despite the official Chinese line exalting the principle of noninterference in the internal affairs of states, China's international projection strategy still comes with a political mindset. Given that China is expanding, increasing and diversifying its relations and interests in the world, and that since the arrival of Xi Jinping in power (2012) it is abandoning its low-profile diplomacy for a more proactive foreign policy that some have called 'striving for achievement' (Yan, 2014), the country is increasingly likely to get caught up in politics. The Venezuelan crisis is a clear example of this evolution. Beijing – just like Moscow, Tehran and Ankara – has chosen to support Nicolas Maduro as the only legitimate president of Venezuela. This is a political decision because, as some Asian media have reminded us, President Maduro and his predecessor have always been outspoken in their anti-Americanism, thus making them influential political allies for Beijing in its growing rivalry with Washington (Huang, 2019).

Due to this situation, China is in political disagreement with Washington, but also with the vast majority of European and Latin American governments that have taken a stand in favour of the self-proclaimed president, Juan Guaidó, and the presidential elections organisation. This organisation is also advocated by the European External Action Service (EEAS, 2019). China has major economic interests in Venezuela, which boasts the world's largest oil reserves and huge mineral reserves. Various banks, such as China Development Bank and China EximBank, have over the past 10 years granted loans to Caracas of USD 62.2 billion, making Venezuela the biggest Latin American recipient of Chinese loans (Gallagher and Myers, 2017). China is also the main investor in Venezuela's oil production and the chief importer of Venezuelan raw materials. Caracas reimburses its debts to Beijing by sending oil to China on a daily basis. Beijing therefore fears that a regime change would jeopardise China's alliances and interests in the country. However, Maduro's Venezuela is also at the mercy of the dependence it has developed with China.

Chinese authorities are, much more than in the past, engaged in a power policy and intend to defend their interests, including in the geopolitical scene and LA, which the USA seems to continue to regard as its zone of influence. This was notably highlighted by a statement from the US National Security Advisor, John Bolton, who believes that his country has a 'special responsibility' in Venezuela because it is in the USA's hemisphere. In a way, China is gradually moving into LA as a counterweight to the USA and Europe, and is thus inviting itself into the rivalry 'game' that is expanding between the Atlantic Triangle's actors.

It is not surprising then that China's ongoing breakthrough is a worry for both the USA and Europe, especially since China believes it has landed in LA to stay there. In other words, the Latin American continent has acquired strategic importance in the eyes of China, which regularly adopts Policy Papers (2008; 2016) as well as Cooperation Plans and Action Plans (2015, 2017, 2018). Beijing is counting on a long-term relationship with the continent. Growing numbers of senior Chinese officials are visiting the region to consolidate existing links with LA regional platforms, to organise major summits of heads of state and government with all the region's countries, and to intensify its railways diplomacy to interconnect the Atlantic and Pacific coasts. A further goal for China is to accelerate the conclusion of FTAs, with a view to achieving trade with LA worth up to USD 500 billion as well as to invest USD 250 billion on the continent by 2025.

Nevertheless, China is also relying on LA to pursue what it views as a key strategic objective: being recognised as a market economy. Currently, Chinese authorities are in a tussle with Europe and the USA, who deny the country the status of a market economy. As a result, China is looking elsewhere for support and has succeeded in getting countries like Argentina, Brazil, Chile, Peru or Venezuela to recognise it as having a market-economy status. As a result, these countries can no longer impose anti-dumping measures on China.

China's growing presence in LA also partly stems from Europe and the USA paying less interest in the continent over the last decade, plus the fact that Latin American countries have been very enthusiastic about relations with China, paying more attention to this country than have Europe and the USA. Although this relationship has helped to support a series of economies on the continent, it has also been detrimental to LA, since the continent has steadily increased its dependence on the Chinese economy and is therefore more vulnerable. So when China sneezes, LA catches a cold. For instance, when China buys less and commodity prices drop – as happened in 2015 and 2016 – LA's economies feel the effects directly. This dependence also helps to accelerate the process of reprimarisation and de-industrialisation of several economies on the continent (Chaponnière and Salama, 2016) and poses serious challenges to regional integration of LA (Ortíz Velásquez and Dussel Peters, 2016).

One concern is beginning to emerge in several Latin American countries. They see their margin of manoeuvre increasingly reduced by this new dependence on China. As a result, they believe they need to work harder to diversify their economic and commercial relations. Today, the decline of the left due to the arrival of right-wing governments in LA is sometimes accompanied by a certain fear about Chinese power and the sense that relations with the EU should be revitalised as a way to reduce their growing dependence on China. Europe also has concerns about this Chinese presence, as indicated by some representatives of the European institutions who have said that 'we cannot leave Latin America to China'. The President of the European Parliament, Antonio Tajani, has repeatedly expressed views that for years Europe has focused on itself and during that time it has lost ground in LA to the benefit of China. European decision-makers feel that there is a need to inject a new impetus to EU's relations with LA (Santander, 2019).

The Atlantic Triangle at the Time of 'America First' Policy

Responding to a world in turmoil as well as the spread and decentralisation of global power, the Trump administration proposed an external agenda based on the principle of 'America First'. Hence, the USA's international projection policy is notable for challenging the two other sides of the Atlantic Triangle as much the new powers. Indeed, this policy has typically undermined relations with the country's transatlantic neighbours and allies, while allowing the USA to evade its international commitments (acting against the WTO, US withdrawal from several multilateral deals: the Paris agreement on climate change and the Iran nuclear deal, etc.). This is more disruptive to a world order that Washington now views as the one that has supposedly weakened American power and promoted the growth of new powers, particularly the major exporting actors such as the EU and China. From a US viewpoint, the world is a zero-sum game, made up of winners and losers. The 'America First' policy is based on the idea that in order to be one of the winners, a country must have a more nationalistic, unilateralist, and unpredictable policy, and must oppose the multilateral order based on compromise, negotiation, cooperation, and respect for international law.

This conception of international relations based on power relations, the reason of state and the unilateral use of force, has led to the USA strongly contesting the usefulness and effectiveness of international and regional organisations. This has called into question the institutionalisation of multilateralism in all its forms. The Trump administration emphasises force over the law, relies on trade wars, and believes that because the USA is powerful, trade wars are 'good and easy' to win. This approach has also encouraged the USA to bully the other two sides of the Atlantic Triangle and to tackle head on many countries in LA, Asia, and Europe without distinction. Washington has begun to question its traditional alliances, including the one with the EU. While the USA has long supported the construction of Europe, it is now betting on its destabilisation or even its disintegration. In the eyes of the Trump administration, the EU is seen – just like China – as an 'enemy' and a 'competitor' that threatens American economic and commercial interests. The EU is among the main players targeted by the Republican-led government's neo-mercantilist policies, underlining a radicalisation of commercialism freed from reciprocity and multilateralism. Such policies, based on a purely transactional strategy, are designed to benefit the US internal market, to promote its own companies' exports, and to discourage imports by imposing customs barriers (Santander and Vlassis, 2018a).

For the Latin American side of the Atlantic Triangle, the USA has been using aggressive rhetoric and hostile measures. Besides the decisions taken to unravel the Obama administration's legacy of normalising relations with Cuba, the Trump government has taken a radical stance against Venezuela and Nicaragua. With Mike Pompeo, Secretary of State, and John Bolton, National Security Advisor – supported by the influential Republican and interventionist Congressmen Marco Rubio and Mario Díaz-Balart – the Trump administration seems to be increasingly drawn to the theory of 'regime change' in order to confront the Cuban, Nicaraguan, and Venezuelan regimes that Washington has dubbed a 'troika of tyranny' (NSC, 2018) because they supposedly represent a threat to the national security of the USA by spreading anti-Americanism in Latin American societies. The USA has fuelled fears and discontent on the continent and cooled the relationship between Washington and LA. This is due to US controversial comments on Mexico and El Salvador and their respective nationals, attacks on the North American Free Trade Agreement (NAFTA), and withdrawal from the Trans-Pacific Partnership (TPP), plus the adoption of protectionist measures on steel and aluminium. Not to mention the Trump project to build a wall on the border between Mexico and the USA and to end Temporary Protected Status (TPS), which, for example authorises eligible nationals of Central America (El Salvador, Honduras, and Nicaragua) to live and work in the USA for a limited period of time. Paradoxically, the USA's strategy in LA is based on confrontation and unilateral actions, whereas the continent has since 2015 being shifting politically to the right. This shift has resulted in the election of leaders whose agenda is to work for closer relations with Washington. Not since the late 1990s has LA had so many governments in favour of relations with the USA (Santander, 2018b).

However, actors on the international scene are being hassled by the 'America first' policy. LA, the EU, and China have all been the target of the US' confrontational attitude. This has aroused their distrust and encouraged them to diversify their respective external relations and to revalue other alliances. China's presence is being singled out by the US authorities, who say that China is increasingly becoming a 'revisionist power' that seeks to challenge 'the values and interests' of the USA in the world (the White House, 2017:25). This explains Washington's opinion that China's presence in LA is a 'threat to the interests of the countries of the Western Hemisphere'. The US authorities want to take advantage of the coming to power of right-wing governments in Argentina, Brazil, Chile, Colombia, and Peru, in particular because some of them fear the presence of China's power on the continent, as shown by the statements of the Brazilian right-wing president,

Jair Bolsonaro, who has stated: 'The Chinese are not buying in Brazil, they are buying Brazil'. Washington seeks to develop closer relations with these countries in the hope that their right-wing governments could be useful to counter Chinese power in the region. Yet China remains undeterred and has deepened its relations with LA, as shown by the adoption of its second policy paper on LA, published just one week after the election of President Donald Trump. Other indicators include the ramping up of Chinese official visits to the region; accelerated trade negotiations with LA countries; Chinese anchorage in countries historically under American political, economic, and military influence, such as Panama; and extension of the 'BRI to LA'. Beijing is therefore taking advantage of the US attacks on LA countries, with the result that China is increasingly pushing on the door of the Atlantic Triangle, whose shape is constantly changing and increasingly resembles a square.

The EU-LA Relationship: Towards a New Awakening?

The Trump administration's cavalier attitude is also changing the configuration of the EU and LA relationship. Especially since the US government has little interest in developing the kind of relationship with Europe and the LA where everyone listens to each other. Moreover, the USA believes that Europe and LA need it more than the USA needs them. US animosity and unilateral measures are partly responsible for closer relations between the EU and LA, as both these sides view cooperation, free trade, and multilateralism as ways to limit political relations based on power, thus helping to create a world that is less unpredictable and more balanced. Although the 'America first' policy is encouraging closer links between Europe and LA, it should be said that these relations have been grounded in a new context for several years. For in LA and Europe, there has been a political desire to renew their association.

However, over the last 15 years that relationship has sometimes been rocky. During this period, almost all LA and EU summits with heads of state and government were notable for their tension and occasionally even conflicts. The two sides struggled to find common ground at these summits, which were intended to sketch out the general lines of their relationship. When the EU and its Member States proposed to extol respect for multilateralism and human rights, LA's decision-makers criticised the proposal's inconsistency: they pointed to the European governments that had supported the US' illegal intervention in Iraq. When the EU and its Member States defended the need to fight international terrorism, LA countries retorted that this was not a priority for them. When the

EU brought up the issue of social cohesion, several LA governments suspiciously viewed the European proposal as a way to conceal protectionist aims.

Ideological divisions also affected the association. The political left-turn of several LA countries favoured the development of an economic nationalism that was critical of the liberal economic policies promoted by the EU in its relations with LA. In turn, the EU and its Member States disapproved of the protectionist or nationalisation policies of various LA countries' economic sectors and, above all, the strategy of several LA countries to take back control of national energy resources. Moreover, China's growing presence on the continent, plus the ever-intensive policy of extractivism supported by Chinese investments, effectively diverted LA governments' attention during the decade of that left-turn.

Lastly, the fragmentation of LA regionalism and the EU's bilateral strategy further divided the two sides. For many years, the EU has promoted a strategy of relations with the LA regional blocs. However, the difficulties faced by LA regionalism prompted the EU to focus more on promoting individual relations with states. The European institutions were disappointed by the lack of progress in LA integration, and several LA countries were unhappy with the EU's criticism or its change of strategy (Santander, 2009a).

Today there is a more favourable scenario for relaunching relations, especially because of changes within LA and the relative ebb of nationalist and protectionist economic policies there. The return of pro-market policies and open regionalism in the region, alongside concerns about the Trump government's protectionist and unilateral policies, have revived and accelerated regional and interregional cooperation in LA. This trend is seen in a willingness to bring the Pacific Alliance (PA) closer to the Southern Common Market (Mercosur). In Europe, these initiatives are enthusiastically welcomed. The EU has a clear interest in the PA as well as its liberal and economic openness policies. Germany, Spain, and France are pushing for the EU to get closer to the PA. In addition, 21 of the PA's 52 observer states are EU countries. The EU's EEAS has begun to hold meetings with the foreign ministers of the PA countries. According to EEAS officials, the next step will be the signing of a memorandum of understanding with the PA. The EU and European businesses have also welcomed the effort to get closer to MERCOSUR by the 2019 trade arrangement. They would like to see a convergence of the two regional schemes, as this would create economies of scale. Moreover, according to European stakeholders, gradually reducing differences in regulation – such as for rules of origin – would promote the development of global value chains. All the above underlines the European authorities' renewed interest in their relations with LA.

European authorities know that in recent years Europe's attention has been diverted by EU enlargement; geopolitical events in nearby regions (war in Georgia, crisis in Ukraine, annexation of Crimea by Russia, and political conflicts with Moscow); infatuation with the Chinese market; and a series of internal problems (crisis in the Eurozone, social crisis, refugee crisis, growing Euroscepticism, and a crisis of political representation in Europe). They are now trying to pay more attention to LA. This is reflected in the speeches and initiatives taken by the EEAS and the High Representative of the EU for Foreign Affairs and Security Policy, Federica Mogherini. Since starting her duties, she has made many official visits to LA, including more than a dozen to countries such as Argentina, Chile, Colombia, Cuba, and Mexico, and she has visited local multilateral organisations such as the Economic Commission for Latin America and the Caribbean (ECLAC). Europe's official line is intended to be more incisive and proactive, calling for stronger partnerships with LA and the Caribbean (EEAS, 2016a:37). While there is tension in the relations with the USA, European authorities were quick to declare that "transatlantic relations are not confined only to the United States, but also include [...] all of Latin America" (Mogherini, 2017).

This official line has been accompanied by a series of initiatives, among them the strategy to normalise relations with Cuba, which concluded in 2016 with the Political Dialogue and Cooperation Agreement (PDCA) between Brussels and Havana; the resumption of trade negotiations between the EU and Mercosur after several years of stagnation; and initiatives to modernise a series of agreements linking the two sides of the Atlantic and, in particular, the agreements with Chile and Mexico as well as the visa waiver between the EU and Colombia and Peru. As a result, the Europe-LA side of the Atlantic Triangle would appear to be engaged in a new strengthening process, while facing the challenges of Chinese penetration in LA and the 'America first' policies of the Trump administration.

Conclusion

Until the early years of the 21st century, China maintained modest relations with the LA continent. South Korea, Japan, or Taiwan had much deeper relations with LA than did China. However, the power projection strategies of these extra-regional actors remained low key and had no major impact on the strategies deployed by the EU or the USA in LA or the Atlantic Triangle. Consequently, the only external actors with an active strategy to influence LA were the USA and the EU.

Although well aware of the US' dominance and influence in LA, Europe was not afraid to develop, beginning in the 1980s, its presence on that continent. Meanwhile, it maintained close economic, commercial, as well as political and strategic relations with Washington. The relations of both the EU and the USA with LA are not developed separately, nor do they evolve in an international political vacuum. Thus Europe-LA relations and pan-American relations are conditioned by the wider framework of the Atlantic Triangle. Contrary to the prevailing interpretation, this triangle is certainly not a triangular relationship based on a framework of shared values that would allow its actors to act in a concerted manner internationally. Instead, it is a strategic competition environment that determines the play of LA actors and their relations with the EU and with the USA.

With the shift of world power and the rise of new actors, the Atlantic Triangle has become a strategic projection space for other extra-regional actors. This is especially true for China, which is seeking to advance its pawns. Sino-Latin American relations are growing exponentially. In just 15 years, the relationship between China and LA has moved from insignificant to predominant. Powerful China has become an investor and a key economic and commercial partner for the LA continent. By comparison with the other leading players in the Atlantic Triangle, China has emerged as a challenger, because part of the market shares it gains in LA is at their expense. China's increasing weight and presence in LA have made the game and power relations in the Atlantic Area more complex.

In theory, the arrival of new extra-regional actors in LA should be helping to open up the continent. China's presence ought to create opportunities and margins of manoeuvre for LA actors, in their relations with the other leading players in the Atlantic Triangle and in their reciprocal relations. Yet in practice, the opposite has proven true. The relationship between China and LA countries is highly asymmetrical. It perpetuates a pattern of economic and commercial exchange with a strong north-south footprint, like that developed with the EU and the USA. Moreover, LA countries are developing a new dependency, making them vulnerable to upheavals in the Chinese economy. Finally, the close relationship that LA is building with China also has a political fallout. Especially as Beijing is taking advantage of the asymmetrical relations with the continent to stake claims that, whether implicitly or explicitly, it considers to be highly strategic. China's growing economic grip on more and more LA countries has therefore pushed them to recognise China's market economy status or to break their respective diplomatic relations with Taiwan, thus advancing the 'one China' policy. The LA continent has thus become a space to expand Chinese power.

The growth, consolidation, and assertiveness of Chinese power in international relations over the past 20 years have been highly influential on LA actors, offsetting European and American strategies for the continent and transforming the Atlantic Triangle into a strategic space of quadrilateral rivalry.

Literature

Arenal, C. and Hirst, M. (2011). *Las relaciones triangulares: Estados Unidos, Unión Europea y América Latina*. Madrid: Fundación Carolina.

Battistella, D. (2011). *Un monde unidimensionnel*. Paris: SciencePo Les Presses.

Bodemer, K., Grabendorff, W., Jung, W. and Thesing, J. (2002). *El triángulo atlántico: América Latina, Europa y los Estados Unidos en el sistema internacional cambiante*. Germany: ADLAF-Konrad Adenauer Stiftung.

Chaponnière, J.-R. and Salama, P. (2016). 'L'Amérique latine et la Chine: 'je t'aime. . . moi non plus'', *Revue d'économie financière*, Vol. 124, No. 4, 225–242.

Crawley, A. (2006). 'Europe-Latin America (EU-LAC) relations: Towards Interregional Coalition-Building?' In H. Hänggi *et al.* (eds.), *Interregionalism and International Relations*, 167–181. New York: Routledge.

Dussel, E. and Armony, A. (2017). *Effects of China on the Quantity and Quality of Jobs in Latin America and the Caribbean*. Peru: International Labour Organization.

EEAS (2016a). 'EU-CELAC Relations: Factsheets', *European External Action Service*, 26 October, accessed 13 February 2019, https://eeas.europa.eu/headquarters/headquarters-homepage/13042/eu-celac-relations_en

EEAS (2016b). 'A Global Strategy for the European Union's Foreign and Security Policy', *European External Action Service*, June.

EEAS (2019). 'Declaration by the High Representative on Behalf of the EU on the Situation in Venezuela', *European External Action Service*, PRESS RELEASE43/1926/01/2019.

Gallagher, K. P. and Myers, M. (2017). 'China-Latin America Finance Database', *Inter-American Dialogue*, Washington, DC, accessed 15 February 2019, https://www.thedialogue.org/map_list/

Hänggi, H., Roloff, R. and Rüland, J. (2006). *Interregionalism and International Relations*. New York: Routledge.

Huang, C. (2019). 'How China's aid to Venezuela Has Gone from a Win-Win to a Lose-Lose', *South China Morning Post*, February 1.

Krauthammer, Ch. (1990/1991). 'The Unipolar Moment', *Foreign Affairs*, Vol. 70, No. 1, 23–33.

Mandraud, I. (2019). 'Venezuela: l'irréductible soutien de la Russie à Maduro', *Le Monde*, 24 January.

Mogherini, F. (2017). *Speech by Federica Mogherini at the Munich Security Conference*, accessed 18 February, https://eeas.europa.eu/headquarters/headquarters-homepage_en/20832/Speech%20by%20Federica%20Mogherini%20at%20the%20Munich%20Security%20Conference

Müler, G., Wouters, J., Defraigne, J.-C., Santander, S. and Raube, K. (2017). *The EU-Latin American Strategic Partnership: State of Play and Ways Forward*, European Parliament: Directorate-General for External Policies.

The White House (2017). *National Security Strategy of the United States*. Washington, DC: The White House.

NSC (2018, November 2). *Remarks by National Security Advisor Ambassador John R. Bolton on the Administration's Policies in Latin America*. National Security Council.

OECD (2015). *Perspectivas económicas de América Latina 2016. Hacia una nueva asociación con China*. Paris: Organisation for Economic Co-operation and Development.

Ortiz Velásquez, S. and Dussel Peters, E. (2016). 'La nueva relación comercial entre América Latina y el Caribe y China: ¿promueve la integración o desintegración comercial?' In E. Dussel Peters (ed.), *La nueva relación comercial de América Latina y el Caribe con China. Integración o desintegración comercial?*, 13–8. Mexico: UDAL.

Santander, S. (2008). *Le régionalisme sud-américain, l'Union européenne et les États-Unis*. Brussels: Éditions de l'Université libre de Bruxelles.

Santander, S. (2009a). *L'émergence de nouvelles puissances: vers un système multipolaire?* Paris: Ellipses.

Santander, S. (2009b). 'EU-LAC Relations: From Interregionalism to Selective Bilateralism?'. In Ch. Franck, J-Ch. Defraigne and V. de Monriamé (eds.), *The European Union and the Rise of Regionalism: source of Inspiration and Active Promoter*, 263–272. Brussels: Bruylant.

Santander, S. (2013). 'Les puissances émergentes. Portées et limites d'un phénomène international'. In D. Battistella (ed.), *Nouveau manuel de relations internationales*, 523–544. Paris: Ellipses.

Santander, S. (2014a). 'The impact of the Iberian States on European Union-Latin America Interregionalism'. In F. Baert *et al.* (eds.), *Intersecting Inter-Regionalism. Regions, Global Governance and the EU*, 107–127. London: Springer.

Santander, S. (2014b). 'The EU and the Shifts of Power in the International Order: Challenges and Responses', *European Foreign Affairs Review*, Vol. 19, No. 1, 65–82.

Santander, S. and Vlassis, A. (2018a). 'L'UE, une puissance commerciale bousculée', *Diplomatie*, No. 47, 74–77.

Santander, S. (2018b). 'Recomposition régionale à l'heure du tournant à droite et de "l'Amérique d'abord" ', *La revue nouvelle*, No. 5, 56–63.

Santander, S. (2019). 'Latinoamérica y la Unión Europea. Sus vínculos para un nuevo despertar', *Foreign Affairs Latinomérica*, Vol. 19, No. 1, 59–66.

Schumacher, E. (1995). 'Spain and Latin America: The Resurgence of a Special Relationship'. In S. Kaufman Purcell and F. Simon (eds.), *Europe and Latin America in the World Economy*, 113–137. London: Lynne Rienner.

Serbín, A. (2014). 'Squaring the Circle? Transatlantic Relations and New Latin American Regionalism in a Changing Global Environment', *Atlantic Currents. An Annual Report on Wider Atlantic Perspectives and Patterns*, 61–80. Washington, DC: The German Marshall Fund.

Söderbaum, F. and Van Langenhove, L. (2006). *The EU as a Global Player*. Abingdon: Routledge.

Valladao, A. (1999). 'Le triangle atlantique. L'émergence de l'Amérique latine dans les relations Europe-Etats-Unis', *Les notes de l'ifri*, No. 16 https://www.monde-diplomatique.fr/2000/06/HABEL/2327 (accessed on 30 March 2020)

Yan, X. (2014). 'From Keeping a Low Profile to Striving for Achievement', *The Chinese journal of international politics*, Vol. 7, No. 2, 153–184.

Jin Wang

China's Interregional Ties with the Middle East: Concerns, Interests, and Challenges

The role of the Arab States in China's foreign policy is always a debatable topic. Most Chinese researchers highlight the 'traditional friendship' between China and the Arab States, and majorly focus on the bilateral 'friendly communication and exchange'.[1] Meanwhile, researches focus on China's attitudes towards the 'Arab Spring', and try to explain and understand China's policies in Middle East,[2] and China's energy strategies in Middle East.[3] After 2013, China's ties with the Arab States has been encouraged under China's 'Belt and Road' initiative (BRI), and China is attaching more importance towards the Arab world than ever before.

Ancient Historical Roots

China's ties with the Middle East could be traced back to the 2nd century BC when the Chinese emperor sent a diplomatic team to central Asia and west Asia. In the late 1st century AD, another Chinese diplomatic team was sent by the Chinese emperor to central Asia and west Asia, while one unit of the diplomatic team, led by Gan Ying, reached the Gulf region.[4] In the 5th century AD, according to Chinese ancient history literature, some Roman business trading ships emerged

---

1 See, for example, Yang Fuchang, "China-Arab Relations: History and Reality", *China International Studies,* No. 4, 2013, pp. 79–83; Yang Fuchang, "China-Arab Relations in the 60 Years' Evolution", *Journal of Middle Eastern and Islamic Studies*, Vol. 4, No. 1, 2010, pp. 1–15; Yao Kuangyi, "Development of Sino-Arab Relations and the Evolution of China's Middle East Policy in the New Era", *Journal of Middle Eastern and Islamic Studies*, Vol. 1, No. 1 2007, pp. 1–17.

2 Sun Degang, "China's Response to the Revolts in the Arab World: A Case of Pragmatic Diplomacy", *Mediterranean Politics*, Vol. 19, No. 1, 2014, pp. 2–20; Daniel A. Bell, "Why China Wo't Follow Arab Revolt", *New Perspectives Quarterly*, Vol. 28, Issue 2, Spring 2011, pp. 10–13.

3 Xu Xiaojie, "China and the Middle East: Cross-Investment in the Energy Sector", *Middle East Policy,* Vol. 7, No. 3, 2008, pp. 122–136; Steve A. Yetiv and Lu Chunlong, "China, Global Energy and the Middle East", Vol., pp. 199–218.61, No. 2, 2007, Vol. Middle East Journal.

4 According to the Chinese History Book *East-Han History (hou han shu)*, a Chinese diplomatic team led by Gan Ying in 139 BC and 119 BC moved westward until their

near China's coastal areas, while many Chinese trading voyages also reached west Asia by sea. In the 6th century AD, many Chinese businessmen gathered in the coastal area of the Euphrates River while many Arabs and Persians also stayed in Chinese coastal cities such as Guangzhou and Quanzhou. After the Islamic religion emerged in the 7th century AD, on the one hand, the Chinese Tang Empire faced new threats in central Asia, especially when Arab forces defeated the local kingdoms in central Asia that were loyal to the Tang Empire. In 751 AD, the Arab forces defeated Chinese Tang forces in central Asia and many Chinese soldiers in central Asia were taken prisoner and taken to other parts of the Arab empire. One of these prisoners, Du Huan, traveled around the Arab empire for 12 years and came back to China in 763 AD, finishing the book *Trip Memories* (*jing xing ji*) and thereby introducing Arab customs and the Islamic religion to China in the 8th century.

On the other hand, the Chinese Tang Empire also perceived the Arab forces as potentially providing assistance to counterbalance the threat of the rising Tubo Empire in Tibet. Some Chinese ministers noticed the powerful influence of the Arab Empire and even suggested an alliance between the Arab Empire and the Tang Empire.[5] Meanwhile, some Arab businessmen came to settle in China and mosques emerged in some Chinese coastal cities. From 651 to 789, more than 40 diplomatic teams sent by the Arab Empire reached China to communicate with the Chinese Tang Empire. In the early 9th century, more than 100, 000 Arabs and Persians lived in Guangzhou. Many of them married local Chinese people and were perceived by many Chinese Muslims as their ancestors.

From the 9th to the 11th century, the Chinese Song Empire was no longer able to control western China. The sea route therefore became an important channel connecting China with the Middle East. The Chinese emperor encouraged business ties with the Arab kingdoms due to the fact that 'overseas business benefits the national treasury'. At the same time, information about the Middle East was provided in Chinese literature and in many Chinese maps. After the Mongolians occupied China in the 12th century, the connections between China and the Middle East became closer. China's southern coastal city Quanzhou

---

trip was suspended by the "Western Sea" (西海). Most Chinese researchers believe that the "Western Sea" referred to the Gulf.

5 For example, according to the Chinese history book *A General Reflection for Political Administration (zi zhi tong jian)*, one Chinese minister suggested that "the Arab Empire is the most powerful to the west of China, and they have already occupied nearly half of the world. The Arab Empire and India both admire China, and they are the vital enemies of Tubo. I think we should contact them".

became the most important city for foreign ships to China, and Chinese navigator Wang Dalan introduced Arab society through his journey to the Middle East in his book *Foreign Lands* (*dao yi zhi lue*). New Arab and Persian mathematics and astronomy knowledge were introduced into China, and many Arabs and Persians became senior ministers in Mongolian China. After the Ming Empire was established in the 13th century, business ties between China and the Middle East were kept via the sea route and massive maritime ships led by Zheng. He visited the Middle East and south-east Asia seven times from 1405 to 1430 AD. Given that, after the 16th century, China gradually adopted the policy of 'self-separation,' and modern European powers started to dominate the sea, direct communication between China and the Middle East decreased significantly. China-Middle East connections were maintained by Chinese Muslim groups via their religious trips to Mecca and Medina.

After the People's Republic of China (PRC) was established in 1949, the connections between China and the Middle East were restored. Under the newly established communist government, China perceived itself as the representative of oppressed people all over the world and the leader of Asian 'revolutionary people', and hoped to unite all the 'oppressed nations' to revolt against imperialism and colonialism. In April 1956, China and Egypt signed the Cultural Cooperation Agreement between the PRC and the Arab Egypt Republic, and China started to send students to Egypt to learn Arabic. However, given the difference of ideologies and the far distance, China's connections with the Middle East were limited.

After China adopted its reform and opening-up policy in 1978, China's diplomacy withdrew from its left-wing dominated principles and focused on developing friendship and normal ties with all Middle East states. Formal China-Egypt diplomatic relations were established in 1956 and formal China-Saudi Arabia diplomatic relations were established in 1990. China successfully established diplomatic ties with all 22 Arab States. In 1992, China-Israel diplomatic relations were established and China now enjoys diplomatic ties with all Middle East states.

The 'Strategic Partnership' is an important variable measuring China's diplomatic ties with the other states. In 2010 China and the Arab League established the 'Strategic Cooperation' relations, while in 2018 both sides promoted the ties into the 'Strategic Cooperation Partnership', which showed the strong willingness of both sides to further enhance ties with each other. China also established the 'comprehensive strategic partnership' with Algeria in 2015, with Egypt in 2014, with Saudi Arabia in 2016, and with UAE in 2018; and China established the 'Strategic Cooperation' relations with Qatar in 2017, Jordan in 2015, Iraq in

Tab. 1: China's oil dependence on different Arab States in 2015. Source: United Nations, Comtrade Database; China-Arab States Expo Committee

Ranking	Oil imported from	Importing amount (Billion US$)	Dependence ratio
1	Saudi Arabia	20.7	15.47 %
2	Oman	13.9	10.40 %
3	Iraq	12.7	9.43 %
4	Kuwait	5.7	4.25 %
5	UAE	5.1	3.82 %
6	Sudan	2.8	2.14 %
7	Libya	0.94	0.70 %
8	Yemen	0.7	0.52 %
9	Egypt	0.62	0.46 %
10	Algeria	0.16	0.12 %
11	Qatar	0.1	0.08 %
	Total	63.6	47.39 %

2015, Morocco in 2016, Sudan in 2016, Turkey in 2010, Djibouti in 2017, Oman in 2018, and Kuwait in 2018. After 2013, more and more Arab States established different kinds of 'strategic partnership' with China, and the bilateral ties with different Arab States are highlighted by Beijing.

Oil and Economy between China and Middle East

Oil still plays a very important role in China-Middle East business ties while Chinese products are gradually entering Middle East markets. Most Middle East states, especially Arab States, enjoy abundant energy resources; and exporting oil is beginning to account for the largest share of the public revenue of many Arab States. China has become an oil-importing-dependent state ever since 1996, and its oil dependence on Arab States is growing. The leading oil production Arab States include Saudi Arabia, Oman, Iraq, Kuwait, UAE, and Sudan. China cherishes the energy ties with Middle East, especially with Arab oil-producing states. China's oil demand is growing fast during the past decades, while more than half of China's oil is imported from overseas. Meanwhile, China hopes to diversify its oil-importing resources, and therefore, the energy cooperation between China and Middle East oil-producing states become vital for China's energy security (Tab. 1).

Tab. 2: China's industrial goods exported to Arab States in 2015. Source: World Integrated Trade Solution (WITS) Database; China-Arab States Expo Committee

Chinese products exported to Arab States	Export volume (Billion US$)
Transportation goods	5.5
Plastic and rubber products	6.4
Glass and stones	6.5
Metal products	13.9
Textile products	21.9
Machinery and electrical equipment	34.13

Through the BRI, China is starting to encourage closer business connections with the Middle East. Most of the Middle East lacks a complete industrial system and needs manufactured goods from other states. China is an industrial state with high industrial production levels and is able to enter the Middle East markets (Tab. 2).

China is adopting different strategies to develop comprehensive economic and business ties with different Middle East states. To further encourage economic cooperation between China and Arab States, in 2014 China put forward the framework of '1+2+3' to direct future cooperation between China and Arab States under the BRI.[6] The '1+2+3' framework was advocated in accordance with the historical background. The '1', or the core axis of 'energy cooperation', is the cornerstone of cooperation between China and the Arab States. The '2', or investment and infrastructure, is the major potential for cooperation between China and the Arab States in the near future; while the '3', the 'nuclear, new energy and aerospace technology', denotes the 'breakthroughs' for future cooperation. With the development of China-Arab relations, more areas might be included, such as the financial sector, the tourism sector, and the transportation sector. Cooperation between China and the Arab world is dynamic, and new opportunities will emerge with the increasing cooperation (Tab. 3).

Egypt is an important trade partner for China in the Middle East. When Egypt's President Abdel Fattah al Sisi visited Beijing in 2015, China repeated its promise to deepen economic cooperation with Egypt under the BRI while

6 "Xi Jinping Attended the Sixth Ministerial China-Arab Cooperation Forum and Delivered an Important Speech" *(Xi Jinping chu xi zhong a he zuo lun tan di liu jie bu zhang ji hui yi kai mu shi bing fa biao zhong yao jiang hua)*, *Xinhua News*, June 5, 2014, http://www.xinhuanet.com/politics/2014-06/05/c_1111002498.htm.

Tab. 3: China-Arab trade volume from 2009 to 2016. Source: United Nations Comtrade Database

Year	**Trade volume (Billion US dollars)**
2009	101.8
2010	136.8
2011	184.3
2012	222.3
2013	238.8
2014	250.9
2015	205.3
2016	171.0

the New Suez Canal and the China-Egypt Teda Suez Cooperation Zone are becoming major projects in which China has invested in Egypt. During his visit to Egypt in early 2016, China's President Xi Jinping stressed that Egypt should become the 'standing state' (*zhi dian guo jia*) under the BRI.[7]

Gulf states are also showing growing interest in promoting cooperation with China under the BRI. Kuwait is constructing the 'Silk City' project, which includes, as critical features, the massive new port on Bubiyan Island and a $3 billion causeway linking Kuwait city to the current undeveloped north.[8] Kuwait's 'Silk Road' project is an important part of China's BRI in the Middle East. Qatar is another major supporter of China's BRI. In his visit to Beijing in January 2019, Qatar Emir Tamim bin Hamad Al Thani and China's President Xi Jinping signed the Agreement between the Government of PRC and the Government of the state of Qatar in the field of infrastructure, according to which Chinese companies will involve Qatar's infrastructure construction in Qatar's 'vision 2030'.[9]

7 "Three Major Achievements of Xi Jinping's visit to Egypt" *(xi jin ping fang wen ai ji de san da tu chu cheng guo), China News,* January 24, 2016, http://www.chinanews.com/gn/2016/01-24/7730221.shtml.

8 "Kuwait Charts New Path in Changing Region", *Al-Monitor,* July 23, 2019, https://www.al-monitor.com/pulse/originals/2019/07/kuwait-uncertain-path-future.html.

9 China and Qatar signed agreement between the government of People's Republic of China and the government of the state of Qatar in the field of infrastructure, Chinese Ministry of the People's Republic of China, February 1, 2–19. http://www.mofcom.gov.cn/article/ae/ai/201902/20190202832658.shtml.

Tab. 4: China's trade volume with several Middle East states in 2015 (Billion US$). Source: UN Comtrade Database; Ministry of Foreign Affairs of the PRC; Ministry of Commerce of the PRC

State	China's imports from	China's exports to
Saudi Arabia	21.7	30.2
UAE	37.1	11.5
Iraq	7.9	12.7
Oman	2.1	15.1
Egypt	12	0.9
Kuwait	3.8	7.5
Algeria	7.6	0.8
Qatar	2.3	4.6
Sudan	2.6	3.1
Jordan	3.4	0.3
Israel	3.1	6.8
Turkey	9.9	17.3

China established a currency exchange center in Doha in 2015 to facilitate the Chinese currency's internationalisation process. Meanwhile, The Dragon City (龙城) in the Barwa Commercial Avenue of Doha has become a major business center for Chinese products sold in the Gulf Arab region. The UAE is another important state that enjoys close economic ties with China. The UAE perceives itself as an important hub and financial center in Middle East and is interested in promoting bilateral ties, especially commercial and business ties with China. In 2017, the UAE became the second largest economic partner for China in the Middle East, after Saudi Arabia.

Israel, Turkey and Iran are three non-Arab States in Middle East, and China also develops strong ties with these three states. Israel was perceived by China as an important 'start-up nation' with high-tech experiences and strong willingness of cooperation. Chinese firms won the contracts of harbor construction in Israeli coastal cities of Ashdod and Haifa in 2014 and 2015, and several China-Israel research and 'start-up' centers were established in both China and Israel. Turkey's geopolitical importance and market was valued by China, and Chinese construction companies hope to enhance cooperation with local companies to compete for major projects in Turkey, especially the Istanbul Canal and Istanbul's new airport. China supports Iran's resistance against US unilateral sanctions and hopes to develop cooperation with Iran (Tab. 4).

Counterterrorism and De-radicalisation Cooperation

Besides business ties, China also highlights the agreements with and support from the Middle East in connection with Beijing's counterterrorism and counter-extremism policies. Terrorism has become a pressing threat to China's society. On the one hand, several terrorist attacks have been perpetrated both in different provinces of China and in neighboring states against Chinese civilians during the 1990s and the 2000s. These terrorist attacks have deepened Chinese security concerns. On October 28, 2013, eight terrorists launched a terrorist attack against tourists and visitors in Tiananmen Square in Beijing. Five civilians were killed and 38 were injured. On March 1, 2014, 12 terrorists launched an attack against civilians at the Kunming Railway station in southwestern China. In that attack, 29 civilians were killed and more than 130 were injured. Meanwhile, terrorists in Xinjiang from the 1990s to the 2000s launched dozens of terrorist attacks against civilians, mosques, government establishments, and police forces. It is therefore very necessary for China to take measures to prevent attacks in the future.

On the other hand, some Chinese Islamic extremists have constructed networks in the Middle East. China therefore needs help and understanding from Middle East states in relation to China's counterterrorism and counter-extremism movements, especially in Xinjiang. A network connecting Islamic extremists from central Asia and south-east Asia has been constructed. Reports of ISIS recruiters in Hong Kong approaching Indonesians and using Malaysia as a hub for gathering potential fighters are forcing China to become more cautious but also more calculating. The plight of the Uighurs is not new, but what is new is the disenchanted Uighurs who are joining the ranks of ISIS. The threat posed by Uighur extremists became obvious in August 2015 in Bangkok, Thailand, when Uighur Islamic terrorists killed almost two dozen people at the Hindu Erawan Shrine. In July 2013, the leading Chinese media *Global Times* accused Uighur Islamic terrorists of receiving training and support from rebel groups in Syria and Turkey.[10] Beijing pointed out that some Uighur extremists were being recruited by the East Turkistan Islamic Movement (ETIM), working alongside the Istanbul-based exile group the East Turkistan Educational and Solidarity Association (ETESA), and were being sent across the border to train in Syria with al-Qaeda affiliates.

---

10 "Syria Ambassador to China: At Least 30 ETIM members went to Syria". *Global Times*, July 2, 2018, http://world.huanqiu.com/exclusive/2013-07/4081528.html.

In Syria, the Islamic extremists from central Asia and Chinese Xinjiang established their own and independent military groups and organisations, and received training and support from other Islamic extremist groups inside Syria, especially ISIS and Jabhat Fatah al Sham (formerly Jabhat al-Nusra).[11] The most important organisations created by the militants from central Asia include: Jamaat Imam Bukhari, Katibat Seyfullah, and Katibat Tawhid wal Jihad, all of which enjoyed close relations with Jabhat Fatah al Sham and ISIS. Individuals, including many Uighur Islamic extremists from China who previously fought in the ranks of the ETIM and the ETESA, also played an important role in the formation of the above organisations.[12] China's Deputy Minister for Public Security, Meng Hongwei, once warned of the threat of the possible 'return' of Chinese ETIM members from Syria and Iraq.[13] Although the mass return of central Asian militants from Syria is highly unlikely, with a more probable option being their relocation to a new conflict, in the long term, the prospect of an influx of militants to Syria may negatively influence countries in the region, primarily due to the link between the departures of militants for Syria and the growth of radical circles. On the one hand, it was the growth of radical tendencies (mainly a radical form of Salafism) that triggered such a large number of volunteers to go to Syria, whereas, on the other hand, mass participation in the conflict there facilitates further propaganda and recruitment. Radical Salafism and Islamic extremism have become major threats to China's internal security and stability. To provoke dissatisfaction and hatred, many extremists used Islamic extremism and Islamic extremists brainwashed people with the narrowly defined notion of '*Jihad*', helping them to join in violent and terrorist activities against innocent civilians. "All this indicates their denial of modern civilisation, rejection of human progress, and gross violation of the human rights of their fellow citizens".[14]

11 Most Uighur Islamic extremists are in the Idlib province of Syria. See "Turkey's De-escalation Efforts around Idlib Come with Risks", *Al-Monitor,* May 21, 2018, https://www.al-monitor.com/pulse/originals/2018/05/turkey-syria-de-escalation-efforts-around-idlib-risky-1.html.

12 Caleb Weiss, "Uzbek Groups Part of New Offensive in Southern Aleppo", *Long War Journal,* June 7, 2016, http://www.longwarjournal.org/archives/2016/06/uz-bek-groups-part-of-new-offensive-in-southern-aleppo.%20php.

13 "Chinese Islamic Extremists Might Return to China", *Zaobao News,* May 8, 2011, http://www.zaobao.com/special/report/politic/cnpol/story20110508-140335.

14 "The Fight against Terrorism and Extremism and Human Rights Protection in Xinjiang", *The State Council Information Office of the People's Republic of China*, March 2019, http://www.scio.gov.cn/zfbps/32832/Document/1649931/1649931.htm.

China takes harsh measures to prevent and constrain the expansion of both Islamic extremism and terrorism, and some of these measures lead to criticism from the international community. On the one hand, some separatist movements, especially the Eastern Turkmenistan Movement, which advocates the establishment of an independent state in Xinjiang, blame China and describe it as a 'racist regime', while, on the other hand, Washington also hopes to use the Xinjiang issue to isolate China in the Middle East. It is therefore necessary for China to explain its policies in Xinjiang to different states in the Middle East, especially to different Arab and Muslim states in the Middle East.

Saudi Arabia and Turkey are the most important states in the Middle East for China to give explanations to and to earn sympathy from. Saudi Arabia perceives itself as the 'guardian' of all Muslim groups across the world, while Turkey, under the leadership of the Justice and Development Party (AKP), perceives itself as a protector of 'Turkmen groups'. However, Riyadh and Ankara express their support for and understanding of China's counter-extremism and counterterrorism policies in Xinjiang. In September 2018, the Saudi Crown Prince Mohammad bin Salman expressed his understanding towards China's policies in Xinjiang and maintained that extremism is a threat shared by both China and Saudi Arabia. In his visit to China in July 2019, Turkey's President Recep Tayyip Erdogan also expressed his understanding of China's policy to Xinjiang. As a result, although the USA hopes to isolate China in the Middle East through the Xinjiang issue, it is receiving very little support.

Understanding of the Belt and Road Initiative

China hopes to encourage the Middle East to join the 'Belt and Road Initiative' (BRI). The 'BRI' is still a sensitive and controversial topic given that its definition is still far from clear and precise. Although the BRI has become China's major foreign policy since 2013, the intention and detailed concept of the BRI is still under discussion. The BRI derives from the 'Silk Road' expression, which was coined by German traveler, geographer, and scientist Ferdinand Feriherr von Richthofen. The ancient 'Silk Road' traversed east Asia, central and south Asia, the Middle East, and Europe. Some analyse the BRI in a geopolitical context and believe that the initiative aims to break free from the containment of the USA and aims for China to establish new connections with its neighbors in Central Asia. Many believe that the BRI drew inspiration from the 'westward project' put forward by Prof. Wang Jisi of Peking University. In his article published in the *Global Times*, Prof. Wang argued that China should 'look westward' to further cooperation with states in "south Asia, central Asia, the Middle East and Caspian

Sea", largely because of "the long-time threat from the US and the increasingly deepening suspicion from the east".[15] Li Xiguang, a professor at Tsinghua University, views the BRI as a tool with which to break the 'blockade' from the G7 led by the USA: "China breaks the containment of the US by putting forward the Belt and Road Initiative".[16]

Meanwhile, others argue that the BRI is aimed at providing the world with 'public goods' by 'transforming Chinese excessive production capability' to neighbors in central Asia and the Middle East. Wang Yizhou, a professor at Peking University, maintained that the BRI is a process by which China constructs 'public goods' for international society. He differentiates the BRI from 'norms, regulations and system' and suggested that it is aimed at constructing tangible Chinese interests overseas.[17] Wang Yiwei, a professor at China's Renmin University, uses the term 'mutual connectivity' to summarise the initiative. According to Wang, the BRI is aimed at providing the world with 'public goods', connecting each other through Chinese infrastructure and financial support with the aim of promoting the "inclusiveness of globalization and showing the world China's responsibility as a rising power".[18] Jin Canrong, a professor at Renmin University, believes that China has produced too much steel, plate glass, chemicals, solar panels, and other goods for the domestic market and it is therefore necessary to export these goods to the Middle East and Africa.[19] Shi Yinhong, a professor at Renmin University, stresses the risks of the BRI and believes that China should "not speak too loudly about the initiative", instead of being "boaster before constructor". Shi highlights that the BRI may exhaust

---

15 Wang Jisi: " 'Look West', Rethink China's Geographic Balance" *(xi jin, zhong guo di yuan zhan lue de zai ping heng), Global Times,* October 17, 2012, http://opinion.huanqiu.com/opinion_world/2012-10/3193760.html.

16 Li Xiguang, *How to Understand B&R (ru he li jie yi dai yi lu), Guancha, cn,* December 5, 2015, http://www.guancha.cn/culture/2015_12_05_343667.shtml.

17 Wang Yizhou, "Constructing B&R Needs More Specific 'Public Goods'" *(jian she "yi dai yi lu" xu yao ti gong geng jing xi gong gong chan pin), People News,* July 5, 2015, http://world.people.com.cn/n/2015/0705/c397302-27256047.html.

18 Wang Yiwei, *How to Express "B&R" within One Minute (yi fen zhong ru he jiang qing "yi dai yi lu"), huanqiu news,* October 24, 2016, http://opinion.huanqiu.com/1152/2016-10/9589245.html.

19 Jin Canrong, "Both Developing States and Global Governance need 'B&R'" *(fa zhan zhong guo jia he quan qiu zhi li dou xu yao "yi dai yi lu"), Xinhua News,* December 26, 2016, http://news.xinhuanet.com/world/2016-12/26/c_129420647.htm.

China's economic energy given its economic decline in recent years.[20] Yong Wang argues that China is trying to 'contribute to international public goods' through cooperation with Asia, Europe, Africa, and Oceania though the BRI.[21] Yilmaz and Liu believe that the BRI would provide both China and Europe with a new 'identity' through prospects for a new China-led Eurasian integration discourse as an alternative to the US-led Euro-Atlanticism.[22] William Callahan maintains that the BRI is not only a project that "aims to weave neighboring countries into a network of economic, political, cultural and security relations centered around China", but also an ambitious strategy "to re-constitute the Eurasian regional order with new governance ideas, norms, and rules".[23] Liu Weidong and Michael Dunford argue that the BRI shows China's need to "diversify energy sources and routes" and "involves the establishment of a framework for open cooperation and new multilateral financial instruments designed to lay the infrastructure and industrial foundations to secure and solidify China's relations with countries along the Silk Roads and to extend the march of modernization and poverty reduction to emerging countries".[24] Tim Summers also maintains that the BRI "reflects their elevation to the national level more than the creation of substantially new policy content".[25] Zhu Ruixue, Liu Xiuling, and Cai Li reviewed the international and domestic background for BRI and argue that it has strategic significance for China's geopolitical and economic security, energy security, monetary internationalisation, and economic transformation

20 Shi Yinhong, "China Should Talk in Private about B&R" *("yi dai yi lu" zhong guo zui hao guan qi men lai zi ji jiang), US-China Perception Monitor,* August 9, 2015, http://www.uscnpm.com/model_item.html?action=view&table=article&id=5238.

21 Yong Wang, "Offensive for Defensive: The Belt and Road Initiative and China's New Grand Strategy", *The Pacific Review,* No. 3, 2016, pp. 1–9.

22 Serafettin Yilmaz and Liu Changming, "The Rise of New Eurasianism: China's 'Belt and Road' Initiative and its Implications for Euro-Atlanticism", *China Quarterly of International Strategic Studies,* January 2006, Vol. 2, No. 3, pp. 401–409.

23 William Callahan, "China's Belt and Road Initiative and the New Eurasian Order", *Norwegian Institute of International Affairs, Policy Brief,* No. 22, 2016. See also the "Defining the Belt and Road Initiative", *Carnegie Endowment for International Peace,* October 17, 2015, http://carnegieendowment.org/2015/10/17/defining-belt-and-road-initiative/im2h.

24 Liu Weidong and Michael Dunford, "Inclusive Globalization: Unpacking China's Belt and Road Initiative", *Area Development and Policy,* Vol. 1, Issue 3, 2016, p. 323.

25 Tim Summers, "China's 'New Silk Roads': Sub-national Regions and Networks of Global Political Economy", *Third World Quarterly,* Vol. 37, Issue 9, 2016, p. 1828.

and upgrading.[26] Zhang Dongdong views the BRI as "a smart move to potentially achieve co-prosperity by marrying Chinese industrial and infrastructure capacity, which has become excessive due to overinvestment, with the region's rich natural resources and potentially a huge market".[27]

In practical terms, especially if measured against the statements of Chinese leaders, the definition of the BRI is changing. In different speeches and talks, the concept of the BRI covers different states and areas. The evolution of the emphasis on BRI reflects adjustments made to these internal and external concerns. This includes the effort of constructing an open and inclusive platform and making the development of BRI a consultative and mutually beneficial process. The goal set for the BRI can seemingly be largely attributed to China's desire to become a 'public goods provider' through setting up new 'rules' for the existing system of international relations, just as Xi stresses, "we should try to be a leader, not just a follower". China has attempted this approach through involving multilateral lenders, such as the Asian Infrastructure Investment Bank (AIIB), Asian Development Bank (ADB), and World Bank, in investment financing (Tab. 5).

Conclusion

Although China began developing a relationship with the Middle East more than 2,000 years ago, its involvement in Middle East affairs is relatively new by comparison with the USA, France, the UK, and Russia. China's foreign policy has consistently operated from a strategic logic of equilibrium.[28] After the Arab Spring in 2011, China's diplomacy in the Middle East has also been adjusting itself and taking into account recommendations and criticism from both media and academies. China hopes to maintain good relations with all Middle East states via its 'selective engagement' policy to protect its energy security, further economic communications, and contain the expansion of extremism and terrorism in the fragmented Middle East. What should be pointed out is that

---

26 Zhu Ruixue, Liu Xiuling and Cai Li, "Background and Strategic Significance of the 'Belt and Road Initiative' of China", *Journal of Behavioral Economics, Finance, Entrepreneurship, Accounting and Transport,* Vol. 4, No. 3, 2016, 49–53.

27 Zhang Dongdong, "The Making and Implementation of the Belt and Road Policy", *Eaber Working Paper Series,* No. 126, 2016, http://www.eaber.org/system/tdf/documents/EABER%20Working%20Paper%20126%20Zhang.pdf?file=1&type=node&id=25995&force=.

28 John Calabrese, *China's Changing Relations with the Middle East*, London and New York: Pinter Publishers, p. 3.

Tab. 5: Areas of the Belt and Road in China's official documents

	Related foreign states	Areas for cooperation promoted	The role of the Middle East
September 2013, Kazakhstan	Central Asian states	Energy, trade, and financial cooperation	Not mentioned
October 2013, Indonesia	Asian states	Economic cooperation	Not mentioned
June 2014, Beijing	Arab States	Energy, infrastructure, investment, nuclear, space technology, Free Trade Zone	Important cooperators
August 2014, India	South Asia	Economic cooperation and high-tech R&D	Not mentioned
March 2015, Hainan, China	All foreign states	All-round cooperation	Important cooperators
November 2015, Singapore	Neighboring states	All-round cooperation	Not mentioned
January 2016, Egypt	Arab States	All-round cooperation	Viewed as important cooperators in the context of the identity of the Arab world
March 2016, Czech Republic	European states	All-round cooperation	Not mentioned
November 2013, Beijing	All foreign states	Infrastructure	Not especially mentioned
December 2013, Beijing	All foreign states	Infrastructure and economic cooperation	Not especially mentioned
December 2014, Beijing	All foreign states	All-round cooperation	Not especially mentioned
December 2015, Beijing	All foreign states	All-round cooperation	Not especially mentioned
April 2016, Beijing	All foreign states	All-round cooperation	Not especially mentioned
May 2017, Beijing	All foreign states	All-round cooperation	Not especially mentioned

China's role in the political affairs of the Middle East is still a constructive one rather than a leading one. Although China became the world's second biggest economy in 2012, China still lacks the capacity and knowledge to take a full part in Middle East affairs.

China's diplomacy in the Middle East still faces a series of challenges in terms of implementation. First, China has to face an increasingly fragmented Middle East torn between Shiite-Sunni struggles and Iran-Arab competition and other sensitive regional issues. China's strategy is largely based on its 'Making friends with all' principle, which helps China secure its relationship and interests with all Middle East states given its limited military presence. However, China has been compelled at times to take sides between Iran and Arab States competition, between moderate and radical political powers, between democracies and autocracies, between Israel and Palestine, and between Russia and the West. For example, when China called the newly established National Transitional Council (NTC) of Libya in 2011 to protect its projects, the NTC replied with the humiliating words "we have no problems with the West, but may have with China".[29]

Second, based on the principle of 'non-interference in others' internal affairs,' China chooses to cooperate and mediate only with recognised governments with regard to economic and other important areas. However, even if it has strategic partners in the region, such as Algeria, Egypt, and Saudi Arabia, China has no formal allies in the region nor does it have any military presence there to assert its political resolve. Due to a lack of communications with different civil groups and camps inside other states, China's commercial and energy interests would inevitably be harmed once a civil war started, which may significantly influence economic growth and social stability at home.

Finally, China and Middle East states still need time to understand each other. Traditionally, China perceived the Middle East as a whole part under the 'the third world' or 'un-developed' area, and the knowledge towards specific states in the region is still limited. Meanwhile, even supported by government decision to invest some projects in the region, such as the Suez Teda Industrial Zone in Egypt, the real economic profits are difficult to sustain given the poor security environment and differences between Chinese and local social circumstances.[30]

---

29 Ahmed Kandil, *China and the 'Arab Spring': A New Player in the Middle East?*, http://www.iemed.org/observatori-fr/arees-danalisi/arxius-adjunts/copy_of_focus/95-Kandil.pdf.

30 Yang Jian, Qi Xin and Chu Xiao, "Situation, Problems and Suggestion over China's Overseas Economic Zone, An Example from China-Egypt Teda Suez Industrial Zone" *(zhong guo jing wai jing mao he zuo qu fa zhan xian zhuang, wen ti yu jian yi–yi zhong*

Both China and the Middle East need to continue facilitating more understanding and people-to-people exchange with each other, in order to set up more solid foundation of future bilateral ties.

ai tai da su yi shi jing mao he zuo qu wei li), International Economic Cooperation (guo ji jing ji he zuo), No. 1, 2019, pp. 12–21.

Guy Burton

China and Regionalism in the Middle East

What is China's relationship to regionalism and regional entities in the Middle East? What does the form of its engagement with such bodies tell us about the nature of Middle East regionalism and its prospects? Such questions are relevant given China's preferences for bilateral ties with states in the region on one side and wish to improve trade and commercial interests through collaboration on the other. The most notable aspect of the latter was Beijing's development of a China Arab States Cooperation Forum and advocacy of a free trade bloc with the Gulf Cooperation Council (GCC), with which it had stop-start negotiations until 2017.

And yet, despite the Forum and efforts to establish a free trade agreement (FTA) with the GCC, the experience of regionalism and China's contribution towards it has been sparse to date. The chapter explains this by first considering the emphasis on regionalism over regionalisation in the Middle East – but one that has been constrained by a number of factors. The scope for external actors like China to engage at a regional level are limited, as demonstrated by its relations with key regional entities, including the Arab League, the China Arab States Cooperation Forum, the GCC, the Maghreb Arab Union and other extra-regional bodies which have significant representation from the Middle East, such as the oil-producing cartel, the Organization of Petroleum Exporting Countries (OPEC) and the Organization of Islamic Cooperation (OIC). China's interactions with these organisations varies, from nonexistent to information exchange and dialogue to proposals for joint action. But in practice, substantial action has been modest and looks set to persist, especially in the context of regional instability.

Regionalism, Regionalisation and the Middle East

Before considering the concept of regionalism and regionalisation, it is necessary to define what is meant by the Middle East 'region'. As Fawcett and Gandois note, a region may be identified along several lines, including geography, identity or security interdependence.[1] This is challenging in the case of the Middle East as some communities may be included while others are excluded. For instance,

1 Louise Fawcett and Hélène Gandois. "Regionalism in Africa and the Middle East: Implications for EU Studies", *European Integration* 32, No. 6 (2010): 617–636.

in geographic terms Israel and Iran may count as part of the Middle East, but if Arab identity – in the form of language or ethnicity – is used instead, it is often excluded. Similarly, both states may also be excluded on the grounds of security interdependence, as the majority Arab regimes see them as principal threats to their own survival. Additionally, the Middle East may arguably be larger than its geographical region if religious identity is used, to include communities from other regions, for example south and south-east Asia (Pakistan, Bangladesh, Malaysia and Indonesia) as well as the Balkans in Europe (e.g. Albania and Bosnia). For the purposes of this chapter the Middle East 'region' is used synonymously with the Arab world, as the majority of the regional bodies examined have an Arab-based identity. The exceptions to these are extra-regional entities like OPEC and the OIC, which also have a strong Arab component in their membership.

In the context of the Middle East, regionalism arguably trumps regionalisation. Although often referenced together, they are two distinct processes. Fawcett and Gandois distinguish between the former as a top-down political project to achieve cooperation (whether economic or security-related) and the latter as a bottom-up process of economic and social interaction.[2] The grassroots nature of the regionalisation process means that it is less structured or directed from above, owing to the involvement of (sometimes) non-coordinated action by non-state actors. By contrast, regionalism is a more focused activity, being led by state actors with a particular agenda.

Of the two processes, regionalism has been the dominant one – albeit it to a modest and limited degree. The reasons for this were several, and can be explained using theoretical lenses, including realist, liberal (or political economy) and constructivist accounts.[3]

Realist accounts point towards the anarchic state of the region's international politics and the relative weakness of Middle Eastern states to other outside powers. Like much of Africa before 1945, Middle Eastern societies were subject to colonialism and imperialism from the Ottomans, British, French and Italians.[4] That experience may have discouraged the newly independent states from pooling sovereignty, weakening any interest for other forms of authority that might infringe on their freedom of manoeuver and prioritizing states as the

2 *Ibid.*
3 Marc Lynch, "Regional International Relations", in *The Middle East*, 13th ed., ed. Ellen Lust. (Washington DC: CQ Press, 2014), 367–395.
4 Fawcett and Gandois, "Regionalism in Africa and the Middle East".

principal points of reference in the region's international politics.[5] States have been central to the creation of institutions and entities like the Arab Summit, the Arab League and subregional bodies like the GCC, the Maghreb Arab Union and the (defunct) Arab Cooperation Council. Additionally, the emphasis on Middle Eastern states is evident in other forms of extra-regional organisation, including OPEC and the OIC.[6]

Following the colonial period, superpower rivalry continued to subordinate regional differences within the wider Cold War conflict and contained the outbreak and intensity of violence.[7] At the same time, superpower dominance made it difficult for regional powers to project themselves and acquire a regional leadership position during the Cold War and after. That absence may well have discouraged the pursuit or ownership of regional organisations and activities.[8]

In contrast to the realist perspective is the political economy or liberal approach which emphasises domestic factors. This has been dominant since the 1990s, stressing greater integration of markets. Central to this movement has been pressure from business and industry elites who have seen the advantages of greater trade and economic liberalisation for themselves.[9] However, in the case of the Middle East, Kilchevsky et al. noted that the region has largely stood apart. Instead of greater integration, the majority of countries in the region have been isolated both from global and regional markets, trading relatively little with each other.[10]

To explain the Middle East case, Aarts argues that unlike other regions, where private sector actors were relatively autonomous and served as agents of change for economic (and subsequent political) liberalisation, in the Middle East they had limited bargaining power and were in a symbiotic relationship with authoritarian state elites. They were often the beneficiaries of state-led and protectionist economic policies, resulting in a class that served as break on more economically

5 Mohammad-Mahmoud Ould Mohamedou, "Arab agency and the UN project: The League of Arab States between Universality and Regionalism", *Third World Quarterly*, 37, No. 7 (2016): 1219–1233.

6 Lynch, "Regional International Relations".

7 *Ibid.*

8 Fawcett and Gandois, "Regionalism in Africa and the Middle East".

9 Francesco Cavatorta, "International Politics of the Middle East", in *The Middle East*, 13th ed., ed. Ellen Lust (Washington DC: CQ Press, 2014), 396–428.

10 Amichai Kilchevsky, Jeffrey Cason and Kirsten Wandschneider, "Peace and Economic Interdependence in the Middle East", *The World Economy*, 30, No. 4 (2007): 647–664.

liberal reforms.[11] Consequently, business and industry elites did not rock the boat by pressing authoritarian regimes to open up either politically or economically.[12] More recent scholarship has sustained this collaboration between the state and the capitalist class, even as it has acknowledged the greater exposure to regional and global (financial) markets, most notably Hanieh's analysis of 'khaleeji', of Gulf capital.[13]

The authoritarian nature of state elites and their private sector allies also accounts for their mutual suspicion of other states and their own societies.[14] Moreover, the authoritarian nature of most of the region's regimes meant that society had little means to influence the state or pursue bottom-up forms of regionalisation.[15]

Elite suspicion of internal and external threats is evident in what Kliemann has identified as pathologies that discourage cooperation and multilateralism and have failed to build trust.[16] They include a politics of victimisation (e.g. a general Arab trend of criticizing and blaming external actors like Israel or the fate of the Palestinians), a politics of negativism, resentment and revenge (which is demonstrated through regional politics being perceived as a zero-sum game and the need to settle scores) and the politics of scapegoating (by blaming others for their own failings, whether it be conspiracies by imperialists or Zionists, for example).

The high level of elite antipathy may also help explain why constructivist attempts of regionalism failed in the Middle East. Monier, for instance, notes that despite 'Arabness' being a shared identity across much of the region, it was contested by different political elites for their own particularistic advantage[17] – and in so doing led to their failure to achieve regional leadership.

---

11 Paul Aarts, "The Middle East: A Region without Regionalism or the End of Exceptionalism?" *Third World Quarterly*, 20, No. 5 (1999): 911–925.

12 Cavatorta, "International Politics of the Middle East".

13 Adam Hanieh, *Capitalism and Class in the Gulf Arab States* (Basingstoke: Palgrave Macmillan, 2011); Omar Dahi, "Review of Capitalism and Class in the Gulf Arab States", *The Arab Studies Journal*, 20, No. 1 (Spring 2012): 147–151.

14 Lynch, "Regional International Relations".

15 Fawcett and Gandois, "Regionalism in Africa and the Middle East".

16 Aharon Kliemann, "'Middle Easterner': A Regionalism Denied", *Brown Journal of World Affairs*, 15, No. 1 (2008): 305–316.

17 Elizabeth Monier, "The *Arabness* of Middle East regionalism: the Arab Spring and competition for discursive hegemony between Egypt, Iran and Turkey", *Contemporary Politics*, 20, No. 4 (2014): 421–434. This issue was especially notable during the high point of pan-Arabism in the 1950s and 1960s and the attempts by Gamal Nasser in Egypt and the Baathist parties in Iraq and Syria to claim the mantle of leader to the

In sum then, the character of regional interaction in the (Arab) Middle East is limited and constrained, resulting in a primacy of regionalism over regionalisation and to a minimal level possible. The presence of largely authoritarian regimes has dominated the region's politics and in partnership with economic elites have prioritised international security and domestic stability over multilateral cooperation. The results are forms of interaction that are mostly conducted at the state level and which do not encroach substantially on other states' sovereignty.

China's Regional Interactions in the Middle East

Before analysing China's engagement with regionalism, it is worth noting the engagement of other important external actors like the West (especially the USA and Europe). For the West, the Middle East's low level of regionalism and regionalisation has been problematic. They see liberalisation as vital to modernise and develop economies and to achieve stable and representative political systems. At the same time, they have been pragmatic, recognizing the reality of authoritarian leaderships over uncertain democratic outcomes, especially when Islamists won elections in Algeria in 1991 and sectarianism exploded in post-Saddam Iraq after 2003. The EU, for example, has therefore adopted a balancing act on the southern shores of the Mediterranean (i.e. Tunisia, Libya, Egypt, Algeria and Morocco): it has dangled the prospect of greater levels of technical and financial assistance in exchange for greater commitment to human rights and political and economic governance – even though those objectives have not been successful to date.[18] Meanwhile, the USA pursued democracy promotion efforts through its Middle East Partnership Initiative (MEPI) and broader Middle East and North Africa Initiative (BMENA). But in both cases they were downgraded following the victory of Islamists in Egypt and Palestine in 2005 and 2006, respectively.[19]

Unlike the West, Chinese leaders have been largely unconcerned about democracy promotion or working with authoritarian regimes. Like the region's elites, the Chinese leadership has a similar suspicion of external powers owing to its own experience of foreign interference, weak state and civil war in the decades

---

movement. The most notable case of pan-Arabism was arguably the creation of the United Arab Republic between Egypt and Syria in 1958, but which collapsed owing to internal differences and rivalries in 1961.

18 Cavatorta, "International Politics of the Middle East"; Silvia Colombo, Andrea Dessì and Vassilis Ntousas, eds., *The EU, Resilience and the MENA Region* (Brussels: Foundation for European Progressive Studies, 2018).

19 *Ibid.*

preceding the establishment of the People's Republic in 1949. The new revolutionary government set out its Five Principles of Peaceful Coexistence as the basis for its foreign policy in the wider world, which emphasised mutual respect between states over their territorial rights and integrity, nonaggression, noninterference in other states' internal affairs, quality and mutual benefits between states and peaceful coexistence.[20]

Despite their common experience of subordination at the hands of the West, the new Chinese government and political elites in the Middle East had limited contact. With the exception of the nationalist and socialist regimes in Algeria and Egypt in the 1950s and 1960s, the majority of governments in the Middle East were anti-communist and anti-revolutionary, and so viewed Beijing with considerable scepticism. The antipathy was mutual, the Chinese leadership seeing many of the regimes (especially the monarchies) as feudal and reactionary.

Relations between China and the Middle East began to grow from the 1970s. China's entry into the UN in 1971 provided space for the establishment of diplomatic relations and led to further points of contact, including purchases of Israeli-built and supplied weapons and sales of Chinese arms to both sides in the Iran-Iraq war during the 1980s. During these decades, China established diplomatic relations with all countries in the region, Saudi Arabia being the last Arab country to do so in 1990. In the 1990s China became an energy importer and by 2014 was the world's largest net purchaser of oil.[21] After 2000, China had three main concerns: regular and reliable energy supplies (oil and gas), investments in infrastructure and construction projects (especially those associated with its Belt and Road Initiative (BRI) in the region after 2013), and financial investments inside the region and at home.

The 2011 uprisings that broke out across the Arab world were observed with fear by the Chinese leadership. It moved swiftly to shut down any sympathy for them at home and backed established political regimes in the region.[22] Despite

---

20 June Teufel Dreyer, *China's Political System: Modernization and Tradition*, 8th ed. (Boston: Longman, 2012), 338.

21 Andrew Scobell, "Why the Middle East Matters to China", in *China's Presence in the Middle East: The Implications of the One Belt, One Road Initiative*, eds. (Abingdon: Routledge, 2018), 9–23.

22 Jonathan Pollack, "China: Unease from Afar", in *The Arab Awakening: America and the Transformation of the Middle East*, ed. Kenneth Pollack and Daniel Byman (Washington DC: Brookings, 2011), 298–304.

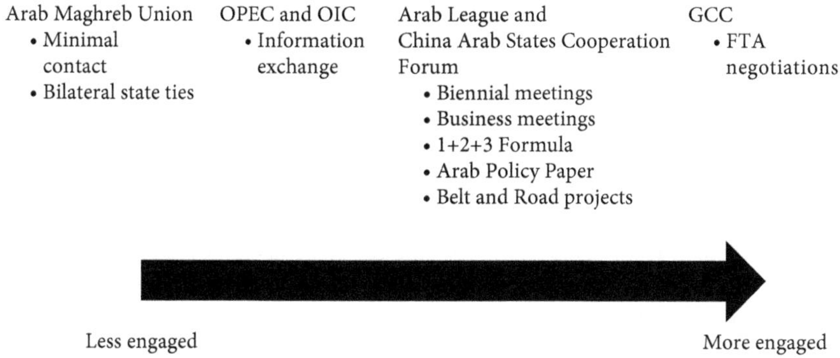

Fig. 1: Range of Chinese interaction with regional and extra-regional organisations in the Middle East

this, the region became more uncertain after 2011, and Beijing has responded by adopting a more reactive and pragmatic hedging strategy to its foreign policy.[23]

While China has largely hedged at the bilateral level with key regional state actors, its relations with regional institutions like the Arab Maghreb Union, OPEC, OIC, Arab League and the GCC has varied, from nonexistent to more engaged (Fig. 1).

At the least engaged end of the spectrum is China's involvement with the Arab Maghreb Union. The Arab Maghreb Union was set up in 1989 between the Arab States in north Africa – Tunisia, Libya, Algeria, Morocco and Mauritania – with the intention to boost economic integration between its members. However, it has been little more than an 'empty shell' owing to the political rivalries and competition within and between its members.[24] These have included civil war in Algeria in the 1990s, border disputes between Morocco and Algeria and the overthrow of political regimes in Tunisia and Libya in 2011. The effect of these differences has meant relatively little integration between its members. A quarter

23 Jonathan Fulton, "Striking a Balance between Security and Economics: China's Relations with the Gulf Monarchies", in *External Powers and the Gulf Monarchies*, eds. Jonathan Fulton and Li-Chen Sim (London: Routledge, 2018); Degang Sun and Yahia Zoubir, "China's Response to the Revolts in the Arab World: A Case of Pragmatic Diplomacy", *Mediterranean Politics*, 19, No. 1 (2014): 2–20.

24 Anouar Boukharis, "Maghreb: Dream of Unity, Reality of Divisions", *Al Jazeera*, June 3, 2018, https://carnegieendowment.org/2018/06/03/maghreb-dream-of-unity-reality-of-divisions-pub-76544.

century after its creation, trade between the five members was equal to 4.8 % of the total volume of trade, each country trading proportionally more with Europe. Were its members able to overcome their differences, the World Bank estimates that each country's GDP should increase by a minimum of 5 %, rising to 24 % for Tunisia, 27 % for Morocco and 34 % for Algeria between 2005 and 2015.[25]

Given the Arab Maghreb Union's internal limits, China's involvement with the organisation has been similarly modest. Beijing appears to have no official or formal relationship with the organisation and like the Europeans operates bilateral relations with its member states. Of the five states, China's interactions are most extensive and deep with Algeria. This reflects longstanding historic ties between the two, which date back to Beijing's support for the nationalist movement in Algiers, and following its independence in 1958, it became the first Arab state to recognise the People's Republic. Additionally, Algeria has the largest and oldest Chinese diaspora in Africa and the Middle East and is involved in a number of important construction projects, including an opera house, grand mosque, airport, government buildings and a major east-west highway.[26]

Further along the regional engagement spectrum, China's relations with OPEC and the OIC have taken the form of information exchange. Although not contained to the Middle East, OPEC and the OIC include member states from inside the region. OPEC was formed in 1960 and consists of 14 member states, of which seven come from within the Middle East (Algeria, Iran, Iraq, Kuwait, Libya, Saudi Arabia and the UAE). The OIC was founded in 1969 and has 57 members, including all the states in the Middle East (except Syria which is currently suspended and Israel).

For Sino-OPEC relations, 2005 was a key year. The two established a formal dialogue, involving high-level technical meetings to exchange views on their respective production and consumption policies. This interaction was not unique: it reflected similar outreach efforts with other key energy markets and actors in the 2005–2007 period, including the EU, Russia, Japan and the International Energy Agency.[27]

25 Wadia Ait Hamza, "The Maghreb Union Is One of the World's Worst-Performing Trading Blocs. Here Are Five Ways to Change That", *World Economic Forum*, June 1, 2017, https://www.weforum.org/agenda/2017/06/five-ways-to-make-maghreb-work/.

26 Djallel Khechib, "One Belt, Different Aims: Beyond China's Increasing Leverage in The Grand Maghreb", *İnsamer*, October 4, 2018, https://insamer.com/en/one-belt-different-aims-beyond-chinas-increasing-leverage-in-the-grand-maghreb_1665.html.

27 OPEC, "Institutionalizing Dialogue", *OPEC Bulletin* (November–December 2005), https://www.opec.org/opec_web/en/press_room/427.htm; OPEC, "Joint Statement of

Dialogue between China and OPEC declined after 2007 but were revived in 2015. They reflected a wish for Chinese and OPEC officials to clarify their respective interests and intentions, especially given Beijing's decision to diversify its oil imports and reduce reliance on OPEC producers after 2010. By the mid-2010s those efforts were beginning to bear fruit as China began increasing its share of purchases from non-OPEC producers like Brazil, Russia and the USA.[28] During this period, China also began to use its currency, the yuan, as a means to price crude oil. This presented a challenge to OPEC producers, the majority who had long based their trade on dollars.[29]

Unlike OPEC, China's relationship with the OIC has been less formally constructed around roundtables and dialogues. High-level meetings have taken place between the OIC secretary-general and prominent Chinese political leaders, including its top congressional leader, foreign ministers and President Xi in 2016. From the Chinese side, the relationship is primarily a means to exchange information, including accounts of Chinese national and religious policies and reports on the economic and social situation among China's Muslim populations and regions – in particular, the far western province of Xinjiang where a sizeable Muslim ethnic minority, the Uyghurs, mostly live.[30]

For the OIC, the Uyghurs and Xinjiang are key challenges. In 2015 the OIC expressed 'deep concern' at news reports claiming that China had banned Muslim Uyghur teachers, students and civil servants from fasting during the month of Ramadan. Its secretary-general appealed to Beijing to investigate the abuses and

---

the 1st China-OPEC Energy Dialogue", No. 24/2005, December 22, 2005, https://www.opec.org/opec_web/en/press_room/1040.htm.

28 Debjit Chakraborty, "China and India Want to Buy More U.S. Oil to Counter OPEC", *Bloomberg*, June 15, 2018, https://www.bloombergquint.com/global-economics/prized-oil-buyers-mull-uniting-on-u-s-crude-to-fight-opec-clout#gs.biYUvCvD; Anjil Raval and Robin Kwong, "How China trimmed its OPEC dependence", *Financial Times*, December 3, 2015, https://www.ft.com/content/7ccb173e-9928-11e5-95c7-d47aa298f769.

29 Kuwait News Agency, "OPEC's Dialogue with China to Stem Yuan's Adoption Impact – Expert", April 3, 2018, https://www.kuna.net.kw/ArticleDetails.aspx?id=2706420&Language=en.

30 Embassy of the People's Republic of China in the Kingdom of Saudi Arabia, "Xi Jinping Meets with Secretary-General Iyad Ameen Madani of Organisation of Islamic Cooperation", January 19, 2016, http://sa.chineseembassy.org/eng/zgyoicgx/t1335506.htm; "Joint Press Release of China's Foreign Ministry and the Organization of Islamic Conference", June 25, 2010, http://sa.chineseembassy.org/eng/zgyoicgx/t711747.htm.

ensure that Muslims were not being persecuted.[31] Then, in 2018, news reports emerged stating that China was adopting an extensive surveillance system and detention policies against the Uyghur population. China claimed it was to prevent extremism and combat terrorism, reflecting a suspicion in leading circles that the Uyghurs were the most susceptible to this.

Despite the media coverage, political leaders in the Muslim world were reticent at criticizing China, owing to their countries' increasing dependence on Chinese investment and trade.[32] Over the summer, pressure began to grow among Muslim groups in Pakistan, Malaysia and Indonesia that their political leaders say something. In December, the OIC took the lead, stating concern at the 'disturbing reports'.[33] By itself, however, the OIC's statement made little difference. For it to have an impact, member states would have to act, whether by demanding an independent investigation into China's policies among the Uyghur population, imposing sanctions or rejecting Chinese finance and capital.[34] Indeed, when Turkey's government became the first to criticise China's actions in Xinjiang in February 2019, they did not follow up their words with any such these actions and the two sides effectively patched up their differences.

While China's interactions with the OIC and OPEC have been focused on dialogue, they have been more involved in the case of the Arab League and its associated China Arab States Cooperation Forum. This engagement has included political dialogues, discussions over economic cooperation and in recent years a blueprint and financial commitments for joint action. These last two are the 2016 Arab Policy Paper and the allocation of $20bn in 2018 to finance projects associated with the BRI.

The origins of the Forum had its roots in the Arab League's decision to strengthen ties with China in 1999. The Arab League's interest reflected interested in the growing ties between China and African governments and businesses, including a Forum on China-Africa Cooperation in October 2000. The Forum led to calls from Arab ambassadors for something similar in their region and

31 *Arab News*, "OIC 'Concerned' over Muslim Situation in China", June 28, 2015, http://www.arabnews.com/saudi-arabia/news/768521.

32 Alexandra Ma, "A Wall of Silence around China's Oppression of Its Muslim Minority Is Starting to Crumble", *Business Insider*, December 29, 2018, https://www.businessinsider.sg/muslim-countries-standing-up-to-china-over-uighur-muslim-oppression-2018-12/.

33 *Ibid.*

34 *Ibid.*

was repeated by Chinese President Hu Jintao during a visit to Cairo in January 2004.[35]

The response was quick. In September 2004, Chinese and Arab ministers held the first Forum, again in Cairo. At this first meeting, China and the parties to the Forum stressed the importance of maintaining and strengthening bilateral ties and using the Forum to achieve this. The Forum would be a biennial ministerial meeting between the foreign ministers of China and those of Arab League member states where action plans would be devised and implemented. Although the focus was primarily commercial and would involve the private sector, chambers of commerce, an entrepreneurs' conference and an economic and trade seminar, the Chinese and Arab leaders also proposed developing other forms of exchange, from cultural and educational to 'civilisational'.[36] The second Forum in 2006 included a communique on environmental protection[37] while the 2010 Forum took place in the wake of the global financial crisis. Chinese and Arab leaders responded by suggesting that they upgrade their relations and set out a joint response to the crisis.[38] Certainly, trade between China and the Arab world did increase and points of cultural and educational contact rose in those years: Confucius Institutes in Lebanon, Morocco, Egypt, Sudan and Jordan were established and around 13,000 Arab students went to study in China.[39] However, the coordinated economic planning for the future did not happen, owing to the uprisings that took place the following year.

The uprisings posed other challenges for China's relations with the Arab States. Following the Assad regime's repression against the opposition, the Arab League suspended Syria's membership in November 2011. The League's action was noteworthy since it was a rare instance when it chose to side with the people rather than with a fellow government.[40]

---

35 Mohammed Numan Jalal, "The China-Arab States Cooperation Forum: Achievements, Challenges and Prospects", *Journal of Middle Eastern and Islamic Studies (in Asia)*, 8, No. 2 (2014): 1–21.

36 Clara Giffoni *et al.*, "The China-Arab States Cooperation Forum (CASCF)" (Rio de Janeiro: BRICS Policy Center, not dated).

37 *Ibid.*

38 Kuangyi Yao, "China-Arab States Cooperation Forum in the Last Decade", *Journal of Middle Eastern and Islamic Studies (in Asia)*, 8, No. 4 (2014): 26–42.

39 *Ibid.*

40 Müjge Küçükkeleş, "Arab League's Syrian Policy", SETA Policy Brief No. 56 (April 2012); Mohamedou, "Arab agency and the UN project: the League of Arab States between universality and regionalism".

China welcomed the Arab League's role as mediator in Syria, but it voted against Qatar's draft resolution to the UN Security Council on behalf of the Arab League. China's veto angered both from the West and the Arab world. Put on the back foot, China justified its veto by expressing its opposition to foreign (i.e. Western) interference in Syria and proposing that government and opposition engage in dialogue.[41]

The schism between China and the Arab League may also have reflected internal changes taking place in Beijing. In 2012, the political leadership had changed from Hu Jintao to Xi Jinping. Over the next few years, Xi began an anticorruption drive at home. Abroad his signature policy was the BRI which was launched in September 2013. The BRI was a continuation of previous governments' efforts to develop the periphery and the surrounding neighbourhood, but also offered Chinese firms and capital opportunities to develop foreign markets to compensate for slowing domestic growth and demand.

The BRI was a key element of Xi's first China Arab States Cooperation Forum in 2014. He proposed a '1+2+3' formula of China-Arab cooperation in energy; trade and investment and the development of new (nuclear, energy and satellite) technology. The 1+2+3 formula pointed towards a more multilateral approach to the region, which was backed up by a similarly broad Arab Policy Paper in January 2016 that stressed political and security concerns alongside long established economic and investment interests.[42]

However, neither the 1+2+3 formula nor Arab Policy Paper led to a substantive change in China's relationship with its Arab partners. Relations remained largely bilateral, as demonstrated by different levels of partnership with individual countries (especially its 'comprehensive strategic partnerships' with Saudi Arabia and Iran and less extensive 'strategic partnerships' with Iraq, Qatar and the UAE).[43] In addition, while Xi pledged $20bn in loans to support reconstruction and employment across the region at the 2018 Forum, it was expected that

41 Yang Fuchang, "Large-Scale Upheaval in the Middle East and China's Diplomatic Relations", *Journal of Middle Eastern and Islamic Studies (in Asia)*, 6, No. 4 (2012): 1–18.

42 Liu Li and Wang Zesheng, "Belt and Road Initiative in the Gulf Region: Progress and Challenges", *China Institute for International Studies*, September 11, 2017, http://www.ciis.org.cn/english/2017-11/09/content_40063037.htm; Manuel Almeida, "China's 'Marshall Plan' for the Arab world", *Arab News*, July 14, 2018, http://www.arabnews.com/node/1338856.

43 Liu and Wang, "Belt and Road Initiative in the Gulf Region".

they would be implemented through the usual channels: through individual projects in specific countries and using selected Chinese firms.[44]

In short, while China and the Arab League member states created a new mechanism for regional engagement in the form of the Forum, it did not challenge the prevailing pattern of interaction. Both sides were broadly comfortable with the bilateral format that predominated, since they provided trade and investment opportunities and without the pressure of democracy promotion and human rights associated with the West.[45]

Arguably the most significant form of regional engagement between China and the Middle East was with the GCC. Created in 1981 by the six Gulf monarchies in response to the security threat posed by the Islamic revolution in Iran (and to a lesser extent Iraqi hegemonic aspirations), the organisation subsequently developed into an economic cooperation and trading bloc. In 2005 it established a customs union between its members and put forward a common electricity grid in 2009 and 2011. A common currency for the bloc was also proposed, but its prospects declined following Oman's withdrawal in 2006 and the UAE's in 2009. A later GCC-wide Value Added Tax (VAT) scheme also failed in 2018: Saudi Arabia and the UAE implemented it while the other members chose not to do so, fearing inflation.[46]

Despite the stop-start nature of the GCC's economic cooperation measures, of all the regional bodies in the Middle East it entailed the greatest level of integration. For that reason, Chinese motives and actions were notable since it pursued an FTA with the GCC at several points after 2004 and then again in 2016–2017. Moreover, China's action was striking since it was the first time that it sought an FTA with a supranational body rather than with individual states.[47]

---

44 Laura Zhou, "China Pledges $23 Billion in Loans and Aid to Arab States as It Boosts Ties in Middle East", *South China Morning Post*, July 10, 2018, https://www.scmp.com/news/china/diplomacy-defence/article/2154642/china-pledges-us23-million-loans-and-aid-arab-states-it.

45 Chris Zambelis and Brandon Gentry, "China through Arab Eyes: American Influence in the Middle East", *Parameters*, 38, No. 1 (2008): 60–72.

46 Dominic Dudley, "Is Time Running Out for the Gulf Cooperation Council", *Forbes*, July 25, 2018, https://www.forbes.com/sites/dominicdudley/2018/07/25/is-time-running-out-for-the-gulf-cooperation-council/#256e234256b8.

47 Gonzalo Villata Puig and Alice Tung Ho Lee, "Challenges and Opportunities of the China-Gulf Cooperation Council Free Trade Agreement", *Hastings International Comparative Law Review*, 40, No. 1 (2017): 123–158.

Chinese interest in an FTA stemmed from the economic importance of the Gulf states to China. Trade between China and the bloc was worth $10bn in 2000. By 2016 it had grown to $115bn. The GCC members were not only key energy suppliers to China, but also an important destination and source of finance and capital. Saudi Arabia was China's largest partner in the Middle East, followed by the UAE in second place. The GCC itself was China's fifth largest import destination and sixth largest export destination.[48] Beyond economic ties, China and Gulf states had begun to deepen their ties to include security cooperation measures and partnerships.[49]

Despite this apparently promising constellation, efforts at forging an FTA failed to flower. The two sides' established forms of engagement with each other due to internal factors in the GCC and China as well as the constraints presented the reasons.

First, there were the difficulties associated with the proposed FTA itself. Initially, it seemed that an FTA with the GCC could be more easily reached with China than the GCC's other trading partners like the EU. This was especially the case following the European Parliament's concern with incorporating human rights conditions into the package and the EU's insistence on high tariffs for petrochemical exports. In 2004–2006 and then again in 2009, an arrangement for most goods between China and the GCC was reached. But a stumbling block was over tariffs for petrochemical exports – just as it had been between the GCC and the EU. The GCC wanted China to remove all import tariffs while China wanted to keep them on petrochemical products, which the GCC suspected was to protect its own petrochemical industry.[50]

The talks had effectively reached a stalemate. Several attempts were made to restart talks through three rounds of strategic dialogue in 2010, 2011, and 2014.[51]

---

48 *Xinhua*, "Strategic partnership heralds new chapter of China, Arab States ties: FM", July 10, 2018, http://www.chinadaily.com.cn/a/201807/10/WS5b44d1fda3103349141e1f3b.html.

49 Theodore Karasik, "The GCC's New Affair with China", Middle East Institute, February 24, 2016, https://www.mei.edu/publications/gccs-new-affair-china; Jonas Parello-Plesner, "China's Gulf Connection", *The American Interest*, January 8, 2019, https://www.the-american-interest.com/2019/01/08/chinas-gulf-connection/.

50 Villata and Tung, "Challenges and Opportunities of the China-Gulf Cooperation Council Free Trade Agreement".

51 Xuming Qian and Jonathan Fulton, "China-Gulf Economic Relationship under the "Belt and Road" Initiative", *Asian Journal of Middle Eastern and Islamic Studies*, 11, No. 3 (2017): 12–21.

Meanwhile, the GCC signed limited FTAs with other actors in this period, including Singapore in 2013 and the European Free Trade Area in 2014.[52] The Chinese leadership was keen to get the FTA talks back on track, and President Xi stressed this point during his regional visit in January 2016.[53] The appeal had some effect. Four rounds of talks took place during 2016. But the hoped-for FTA failed to materialise, prompting Chinese leaders to call for a final agreement again in May 2017.[54] But developments within the GCC the following month would effectively scupper that goal.

The second reason for the FTA's failure was due to internal differences within the GCC itself after June 2017. Rivalries had long existed within the bloc, most especially between Saudi Arabia and Qatar. Saudi Arabia occupied a dominant position, which smaller states like Qatar chafed against and which led to it adopting a 'challenger' role.[55] The Saudi leadership sought to contain Qatari contrariness, leading to border clashes in 1992 and an attempt to reinstate Sheikh Khalifa on the throne following his overthrow by his son, Sheikh Hamad, in 1996.

Saudi-Qatari differences widened during the 2000s and reached crisis point after 2011. Helped in large part by the vast revenues generated by its gas resources, Qatar saw an opportunity to reshape the region in the wake of the uprisings. While the Doha government provided assistance to opposition Islamist groups like the Muslim Brotherhood in Libya, Egypt and Syria, the Doha-based Al Jazeera media network broadcast sympathetic coverage of protests and demonstrators across the region. For a conservative, status quo power like Saudi Arabia and its Emirati allies, this was problematic: they saw the Islamists as a transnational threat and Al Jazeera's reports as threatening to regimes like themselves. They were also concerned that Qatar seemed to be building closer ties with Iran, the Gulf region's chief rival.

In June 2013 Sheikh Hamad abdicated, partly to reduce tensions with Saudi Arabia. But it failed to prevent a Saudi-Emirati-Bahraini boycott during 2014. Although resolved, grievances remained. Following the visit of the recently elected US President Donald Trump to the Gulf in May 2017, his Saudi hosts persuaded him that Qatar constituted a regional security threat. In the absence

---

52 Dudley, "Is Time Running Out for the Gulf Cooperation Council?"

53 Qian and Fulton, "China-Gulf Economic Relationship under the 'Belt and Road Initiative' ".

54 *Xinhua*, "China Calls for Faster Free Trade Negotiation with GCC", May 16, 2017, http://www.xinhuanet.com//english/2017-05/16/c_136288477.htm.

55 Mehran Kamrava, *Qatar: Small State, Big Politics* (Ithaca: Cornell University Press, 2013).

of any American pushback, the Saudis and Emiratis imposed an economic and diplomatic boycott on Qatar and demanded that it renounce support for Islamist groups, turn away from Iran and curb Al Jazeera's reporting.[56] Qatar refused. Instead, it reached out to Iran and Oman to provide ports and trading facilities and began to invest in domestic industries, including a dairy sector, to overcome the loss of imports resulting from the blockade.

The Gulf dispute split the GCC into three: between the Saudis, Emiratis and Bahrain on the one side; Qatar on the other and Kuwait and Oman acting as go-betweens. The first GCC summit following the blockade collapsed after its first day in December 2017.[57] Since then, multilateralism has declined and been replaced by bilateralism: in December 2017 the Saudi-UAE Joint Cooperation Committee was set up, followed by a less extensive Saudi-Kuwait Cooperation Council in July 2018.[58] That same month the Arab League met at Dharan in Saudi Arabia, but Qatar's representatives did not attend. At the end of the year, Qatar announced it was withdrawing from OPEC. Perceived as a snub to fellow members Saudi Arabia and the UAE, it was also an economic decision, Qatar having limited petroleum resources and wanting to maintain its leading edge in the gas industry.[59]

The GCC's breakdown highlights a third problem: How is China to respond to the crisis given its principle and practice of noninterference in foreign policy? Part of China's appeal with states across the region was its refusal to become involved in their domestic affairs. At the same time, this position limited China's ability to help solve local problems. The Chinese foreign minister, Wang Yi, appealed to the two sides to talk to each other and supported Kuwait's efforts at mediation.[60] He also offered Chinese help in any dialogue, but the offer was not

---

56 Kristian Coates Ulrichsen, "Fire and Fury in the Gulf", *Gulf States Analytics*, January 31, 2018, https://gulfstateanalytics.com/fire-fury-gulf/.

57 Naser Al Wasmi, "GCC Summit: Second Day Cancelled amid Qatar Row", *The National*, December 5, 2017, https://www.thenational.ae/world/gcc/gcc-summit-second-day-cancelled-amid-qatar-row-1.681611.

58 Dudley, "Is Time Running Out for the Gulf Cooperation Council?"

59 Steven Wright, "Why Qatar Left OPEC", *Al Jazeera*, December 6, 2018, https://www.aljazeera.com/indepth/opinion/qatar-left-opec-181206102112634.html.

60 *Firstpost*, "Gulf Diplomatic Crisis: China Asks Gulf, Arab Countries to Resolve Standoff within Gulf Cooperation Council", July 21, 2017, https://www.firstpost.com/world/gulf-diplomatic-crisis-china-asks-qatar-arab-countries-to-resolve-standoff-within-gulf-cooperation-council-3839069.html.

taken up – perhaps much to Beijing's relief, since it ensured that it would not have to take sides.[61]

Despite the intra-Gulf split and Chinese inability or unwillingness to mediate, the disputing parties were present at the China Arab States Cooperation Forum in July 2018.[62] At the same time though, Beijing seemed resigned to the fact that an FTA with the GCC was off the table for the foreseeable future. Instead, Chinese leaders declared their intention at the Forum to reach FTAs with each of the Arab League's 22-member states.[63]

Conclusion

This chapter has looked at China's relations with regional bodies in the Middle East. Despite the post-Cold War trend towards regionalism and regionalisation across the world, in the Middle East those processes became largely stuck. Several reasons accounted for this, including the dominance of authoritarian and protectionist political and economic elites which dominate the region's states and their distrust of both other states as well as their own societies. As a result, bottom-up regionalisation by non-state actors was constrained and top-down regionalism was the result, albeit in a limited manner and led by states that were unwilling to pool sovereignty.

Such an environment suited China's leadership. Similarly, wary of interference in domestic affairs, they were willing to build ties with the region's states bilaterally and within established regional institutions. But given the limited scope of most regional institutions, the range of interaction was necessarily limited. This was especially the case in some of the weaker regional bodies, like the Arab Maghreb Union or extra-regional entities like OPEC and the OIC, where states and their interests prevailed over those of the organisations. China's relations were modest, limited to rhetorical support in favour of Maghreb integration while

61 Catherine Wong, "Arab States' Rift with Qatar Clouds China's Plans for Gulf Free-Trade Deal", *South China Morning Post*, June 12, 2017, http://www.scmp.com/news/china/diplomacy-defence/article/2097187/arab-states-rift-qatar-clouds-chinas-plans-gulf-free.

62 Jun Mai, "Top-Level China Forum to Bring Qatar Back to Arab League Table", *South China Morning Post*, July 6, 2018, https://www.scmp.com/news/china/diplomacy-defence/article/2154148/top-level-china-forum-bring-qatar-back-arab-league; *China Daily*, "Highlights of Xi's Speech at China-Arab Forum", July 10, 2018, http://en.people.cn/n3/2018/0710/c90000-9479402.html.

63 Zhou, "China Pledges $23 Billion in Loans and Aid to Arab States as It Boosts Ties in Middle East".

dealing with the states individually and focusing on informational exchange with OPEC and the OIC.

While China and the Arab League created a new form of dialogue and cooperation through the China Arab States Cooperation Forum in 2004, this did not challenge the prevailing pattern of interaction. Beijing's relations with Arab States continued to be largely bilateral. The Forum provided space for joint communiques and the launch of blueprints and finance like the Arab Policy Paper and the funds for the BRI – but they were all proposed by and led by China. In terms of collaboration and partnership on a multilateral level and involving ownership by the Forum rather than by individual states in the region, there has been little evidence of this to date.

Looking forward, bilateralism is likely to be the dominant pattern of relations between China and the Middle East. This seems to be the case, even where Beijing was previously interested in a more multilateral approach – as the case of the aborted FTA with the GCC. The efforts to conclude an FTA with the GCC failed, due in part to Chinese unwillingness to give way on tariffs, but also because of conflict within the bloc. Although China cannot be blamed for the breakdown in the Gulf, its foreign policy stance arguably compounded matters, since it was unwilling to mediate (and thereby compromise its principle of noninterference) in exchange for the prize of an FTA.

Given both the limited state of regional bodies in the Middle East and Chinese aversion to involving itself in domestic matters, it may be argued that Beijing has not served to advance the cause of regionalism. At the same time though, it would be unfair to overly criticise China on this point; it has largely built its diplomatic and economic relations with the region's actors using established patterns. The region has not been especially accommodating to the processes of regionalism or regionalisation.

However, while bilateralism is likely to be the main form of interaction in the Middle East going forward, it is an approach that arguably overlooks important developments across the region and at the subnational level. Since 2011, the old certainties have begun to be questioned as the region entered into a period of convulsion. This new environment arguably requires new practices as a response. However, what these will be is unclear, leading China and other external powers wary of showing their hand. Consequently, the predominant form of international relations appears to be hedging until the constellation of the region's power dynamics begins to crystalise.[64] When it does, we may begin

64 Mehran Kamrava, "Multipolarity and Instability in the Middle East", *Orbis*, 62, No. 4

to see changes in the region's politics at the subnational and national levels, which may have consequences for regionalism and regionalisation in the Middle East. If and when that happens, China's engagement with regional bodies may well change.

References

Aarts, Paul. "The Middle East: A region without Regionalism or the End of Exceptionalism?", *Third World Quarterly* 20, No. 5 (1999): 911–925.

Al Wasmi, Naser. "GCC Summit: Second Day Cancelled amid Qatar Row", *The National*, December 5, 2017, https://www.thenational.ae/world/gcc/gcc-summit-second-day-cancelled-amid-qatar-row-1.681611 (access date 31 March 2020)

Almeida, Manuel. "China's 'Marshall Plan' for the Arab world", *Arab News*, July 14, 2018, http://www.arabnews.com/node/1338856. (access date 31 March 2020)

Arab News. "OIC 'concerned' over Muslim situation in China", June 28, 2015, http://www.arabnews.com/saudi-arabia/news/768521. (access date 31 March 2020)

Boukharis, Anouar. "Maghreb: Dream of Unity, Reality of Divisions", *Al Jazeera*, June 3, 2018, https://carnegieendowment.org/2018/06/03/maghreb-dream-of-unity-reality-of-divisions-pub-76544. (access date 31 March 2020)

Cavatorta, Francesco. "International Politics of the Middle East". In *The Middle East*, 13th edition, edited by Ellen Lust, 396–428. Washington DC: CQ Press, 2014.

Chakraborty, Debjit. "China and India Want to Buy More U.S. Oil to Counter OPEC", *Bloomberg*, June 15, 2018, https://www.bloombergquint.com/global-economics/prized-oil-buyers-mull-uniting-on-u-s-crude-to-fight-opec-clout#gs.biYUvCvD. (access date 31 March 2020)

China Daily. "Highlights of Xi's Speech at China-Arab Forum", July 10, 2018. http://en.people.cn/n3/2018/0710/c90000-9479402.html. (access date 31 March 2020)

Colombo, Silvia, Dessì, Andrea and Ntousas, Vassilis (eds.), *The EU, Resilience and the MENA Region*. Brussels: Foundation for European Progressive Studies, 2018.

(2018): 598–616; Fulton, "Striking a Balance between Security and Economics: China's Relations with the Gulf Monarchies".

Dahi, Omar. "Review of Capitalism and Class in the Gulf Arab States", *The Arab Studies Journal* 20, No. 1 (Spring 2012): 147–151.

Dreyer, June Teufel. *China's Political System: Modernization and Tradition*, 8th edition. Boston: Longman, 2012.

Dudley, Dominic. "Is Time Running Out for the Gulf Cooperation Council", *Forbes*, July 25, 2018, https://www.forbes.com/sites/dominicdudley/2018/07/25/is-time-running-out-for-the-gulf-cooperation-council/#256e234256b8. (access date 31 March 2020)

Embassy of the People's Republic of China in the Kingdom of Saudi Arabia. "Joint Press Release of China's Foreign Ministry and the Organization of Islamic Conference". June 25, 2010, http://sa.chineseembassy.org/eng/zgyoicgx/t711747.htm. (access date 31 March 2020)

Embassy of the People's Republic of China in the Kingdom of Saudi Arabia. "Xi Jinping Meets with Secretary-General Iyad Ameen Madani of Organisation of Islamic Cooperation". January 19, 2016, http://sa.chineseembassy.org/eng/zgyoicgx/t1335506.htm. (access date 31 March 2020)

Fawcett, Louise, and Gandois, Hélène. "Regionalism in Africa and the Middle East: Implications for EU Studies", *European Integration* 32, No. 6 (2010): 617–636.

Firstpost. "Gulf Diplomatic Crisis: China Asks Gulf, Arab Countries to Resolve Standoff within Gulf Cooperation Council". July 21, 2017, https://www.firstpost.com/world/gulf-diplomatic-crisis-china-asks-qatar-arab-countries-to-resolve-standoff-within-gulf-cooperation-council-3839069.html. (access date 31 March 2020)

Fuchang, Yang. "Large-Scale Upheaval in the Middle East and China's Diplomatic Relations", *Journal of Middle Eastern and Islamic Studies (in Asia)* 6, No. 4 (2012): 1–18.

Fulton, Jonathan. "Striking a Balance Between Security and Economics: China's Relations with the Gulf Monarchies". In *External Powers and the Gulf Monarchies*, edited by Jonathan Fulton and Li-Chen Sim. London: Routledge, 2018.

Giffoni, Clara, *et al. The China-Arab States Cooperation Forum (CASCF)*. Rio de Janeiro: BRICS Policy Center, not dated.

Hamza, Wadia Ait. "The Maghreb Union Is One of the World's Worst-Performing Trading Blocs. Here Are Five Ways to Change That", *World Economic Forum*, June 1, 2017. https://www.weforum.org/agenda/2017/06/five-ways-to-make-maghreb-work/.(access date 31 March 2020)

Hanieh, Adam. *Capitalism and Class in the Gulf Arab States*. Basingstoke: Palgrave Macmillan, 2011.

Jalal, Mohammed Numan. "The China-Arab States Cooperation Forum: Achievements, Challenges and Prospects", *Journal of Middle Eastern and Islamic Studies (in Asia)* 8, No. 2 (2014): 1–21.

Jun Mai. "Top-level China Forum to Bring Qatar Back to Arab League Table", *South China Morning Post*, July 6, 2018, https://www.scmp.com/news/china/diplomacy-defence/article/2154148/top-level-china-forum-bring-qatar-back-arab-league. (access date 31 March 2020)

Kamrava, Mehran. *Qatar: Small State, Big Politics*. Ithaca: Cornell University Press, 2013.

Kamrava, Mehran. "Multipolarity and Instability in the Middle East", *Orbis* 62, No. 4 (2018): 598–616.

Karasik, Theodore. "The GCC's New Affair with China", Middle East Institute, February 24, 2016. https://www.mei.edu/publications/gccs-new-affair-china. (access date 31 March 2020)

Khechib, Djallel. "One Belt, Different Aims: Beyond China's Increasing Leverage in The Grand Maghreb", *İnsamer*, October 4, 2018. https://insamer.com/en/one-belt-different-aims-beyond-chinas-increasing-leverage-in-the-grand-maghreb_1665.html (access date 31 March 2020)

Kilchevsky, Amichai, Cason, Jeffrey and Wandschneider, Kirsten. "Peace and Economic Interdependence in the Middle East", *The World Economy* 30, No. 4 (2007): 647–664.

Kliemann, Aharon. ""Middle Easterner": A Regionalism Denied", *Brown Journal of World Affairs* 15, No. 1 (Fall/Winter 2008): 305–316.

Küçükkeleş, Müjge. "Arab League's Syrian Policy". SETA Policy Brief No. 56 (April 2012).

Kuwait News Agency. "OPEC's dialogue with China to Stem Yuan's Adoption Impact – Expert", April 3, 2018, https://www.kuna.net.kw/ArticleDetails.aspx?id=2706420&Language=en (access date 31 March 2020)

Liu Li and Wang Zesheng. "Belt and Road Initiative in the Gulf Region: Progress and Challenges", China Institute of International Studies. September 11, 2017, http://www.ciis.org.cn/english/2017-11/09/content_40063037.htm (access date 31 March 2020)

Lynch, Marc. "Regional International Relations". In *The Middle East*, 13th edition, edited by Ellen Lust, 367–395. Washington, DC: CQ Press, 2014.

Ma, Alexandra. "A Wall of Silence Around China's Oppression of Its Muslim Minority Is Starting to Crumble", *Business Insider*, December 29, 2018, https://www.businessinsider.sg/muslim-countries-standing-up-to-china-over-uighur-muslim-oppression-2018-12/ (access date 31 March 2020)

Mohamedou, Mohammad-Mahmoud Ould. "Arab Agency and the UN Project: The League of Arab States between Universality and Regionalism", *Third World Quarterly* 37, No. 7 (2016): 1219–1233.

Monier, Elizabeth. "The *Arabness* of Middle East Regionalism: The Arab Spring and Competition for Discursive Hegemony between Egypt, Iran and Turkey", *Contemporary Politics* 20, No. 4 (2014): 421–434.

OPEC. "Institutionalizing Dialogue", *OPEC Bulletin* (November-December 2005), https://www.opec.org/opec_web/en/press_room/427.htm (access date 31 March 2020)

OPEC. "Joint Statement of the 1st China OPEC Energy Dialogue", No. 24/2005, December 22, 2005, https://www.opec.org/opec_web/en/press_room/1040.htm (access date 31 March 2020)

Parello-Plesner, Jonas. "China's Gulf Connection", *The American Interest*, January 8, 2019, https://www.the-american-interest.com/2019/01/08/chinas-gulf-connection/ (access date 31 March 2020)

Pollack, Jonathan. "China: Unease from Afar". In Kenneth Pollack and Daniel Byman (eds.), *The Arab Awakening: America and the Transformation of the Middle East*, 298–304. Washington, DC: Brookings, 2011.

Xuming, Qian and Fulton, Jonathan. "China-Gulf Economic Relationship under the "Belt and Road" Initiative", *Asian Journal of Middle Eastern and Islamic Studies* 11, No. 3 (2017): 12–21.

Raval, Anjil and Kwong, Robin. "How China Trimmed Its OPEC Dependence", *Financial Times*, December 3, 2015. https://www.ft.com/content/7ccb173e-9928-11e5-95c7-d47aa298f769 (access date 31 March 2020)

Scobell, Andrew. "Why the Middle East Matters to China". In *China's Presence in the Middle East: The Implications of the One Belt, One Road Initiative*, edited by Anoushiravan Ehteshami and Niv Horesh, 9–23. Abingdon: Routledge, 2018.

Sun, Degang and Zoubir, Yahia. "China's Response to the Revolts in the Arab World: A Case of Pragmatic Diplomacy", *Mediterranean Politics* 19, No. 1 (2014): 2–20.

Ulrichsen, Kristian Coates. "Fire and Fury in the Gulf", *Gulf States Analytics*, January 31, 2018, https://gulfstateanalytics.com/fire-fury-gulf/ (access date 31 March 2020)

Villata Puig, Gonzalo, and Tung Ho Lee, Alice. "Challenges and Opportunities of the China-Gulf Cooperation Council Free Trade Agreement", *Hastings International Comparative Law Review* 40, No. 1 (Winter 2017): 123–158.

Wong, Catherine. "Arab States' Rift with Qatar Clouds China's Plans for Gulf Free-Trade Deal", *South China Morning Post*, June 12, 2017, http://www.

scmp.com/news/china/diplomacy-defence/article/2097187/arab-states-rift-qatar-clouds-chinas-plans-gulf-free (access date 31 March 2020)

Wright, Steven. "Why Qatar Left OPEC", *Al Jazeera*, December 6, 2018, https://www.aljazeera.com/indepth/opinion/qatar-left-opec-181206102112634.html (access date 31 March 2020)

Xinhua. *China Calls for Faster Free Trade Negotiation with GCC*, May 16, 2017, http://www.xinhuanet.com//english/2017-05/16/c_136288477.htm (access date 31 March 2020)

Xinhua. *Strategic Partnership Heralds New Chapter of China, Arab States Ties: FM*. July 10, 2018, http://www.chinadaily.com.cn/a/201807/10/WS5b44d1fda3103349141e1f3b.html(access date 31 March 2020).

Yao, Kuangyi. "China-Arab States Cooperation Forum in the Last Decade", *Journal of Middle Eastern and Islamic Studies (in Asia)* 8, No. 4 (2014): 26–42.

Zambelis, Chris and Gentry, Brandon. "China through Arab Eyes: American Influence in the Middle East", *Parameters* 38, No. 1 (2008): 60–72.

Zhou, Laura. "China pledges $23 Billion in Loans and Aid to Arab States as It Boosts Ties in Middle East", *South China Morning Post*, July 10, 2018, https://www.scmp.com/news/china/diplomacy-defence/article/2154642/china-pledges-us23-million-loans-and-aid-arab-states-it (access date 31 March 2020)

Part Four: The China-EU Multidimensional Interregional Partnership in the Context of the Changing Economic and Political Order

Geoffrey Harris

The Unstable Triangular Relationship between China, EU, and the USA

Three Approaches to Global Power

Since November 2016 the EU has been struggling to find a coherent, united response to the consequences of 'America First.' An era of instability and disruption has begun, leaving the EU sometimes struggling to work out who its friends really are.

In advance of the 2020 US elections, President Trump is not seen as a reliable partner by public opinion and many political leaders in Europe.

As the USA abandons the very concepts of interdependence and multilateralism, the EU has both challenged his approach and looked for partners with which to work towards common objectives. New agreements with Japan, Canada, and Mercosur confirm the EU's readiness to build a stable world trade system. China has the opportunity to contribute to this effort.

The EU, USA, and China represent, however, three approaches to global power, as well as three types of economy. Together they drive the global economy. The current trajectory of US policy towards the UN, the Paris Treaty, the WTO, etc., could push the EU towards greater convergence with China.

In view of the slowness of reform and opening up of China it remains to be seen if the EU can really hope to cooperate with China in support of global governance. Despite a degree of consistency notably absent from US policy, EU-China relations have been relatively stagnant in recent years. Even if on trade and investment EU concerns reflect those of the USA, a common transatlantic strategy towards China seems rather remote. China and the EU may share a common interest in defending globalization but deepening differences on issues of human rights are likely to hamper any such efforts. Events in Xinjiang and Hong Kong confirm the increasingly repressive nature of the regime of President Xi whose image in Europe is not good even if he is considered as less dangerous than Trump.

In view of threats from Russia, most EU countries continue to rely on NATO for their security but even there, Trump has fed doubts about US commitments to European collective security. In their general disdain for liberal democracy and the EU, Trump and Putin seem often to have more in common than with EU leaders.

Whether or not the Trump Presidency marks a permanent shift by the USA away from multilateralism, the EU is set to continue to defend the principles set out in its 2016 Global Strategy.[1] The changes in the EU leadership following the 2019 European Parliament elections are not likely to change the basic approach which was updated in March 2019.

Chinese leaders have faced a similar challenge to that facing the EU in trying to differentiate between rather aggressive language and an insistence by the President that he is a master dealmaker. As the 2020 election approached, he had not achieved deals on trade with either China *or* Europe. The US President remains intent on up-ending what had appeared to be a form of global order dominated by the USA and insisting that *both* China and the EU were taking advantage of US' weakness.

Europe and China also faced challenges to their bilateral relations with growing signs of distrust. They both, however, remained committed to making globalization work.

Writing in the *New Yorker* magazine in January 2018, Evan Osnos considered that "as Donald Trump surrenders America's global commitments, Xi Jinping is learning to pick up the pieces".[2]

Since he took office, NATO summits and the G7 meetings have provided confirmation of a clear trajectory in US policy which has continued *towards* full-scale trade wars with both China and the EU. The President's decisions in relation to the Iran nuclear deal, the Paris Climate Treaty, the US Embassy in Jerusalem, the UN Human Rights Council, UNESCO, and possibly, in due course, the WTO are a straightforward implementation of what he announced as a candidate for office in 2015 and 2016 and which he succinctly described in his inaugural address as putting 'America First.' He is, therefore, not open to accusations of inconsistency in terms of his basic approach. His words, actions, and indeed appointments reflect a coherence to which his domestic and international challengers have difficulty in defining a coherent response.

The fact, however, remains that full-scale conflicts with both China and the EU have so far been avoided with the US President suddenly back-tracking when trade wars seemed imminent.

1 https://eeas.europa.eu/topics/eu-global-strategy/64160/eu-global-strategy-compass-our-action-difficult-times_en

2 https://www.newyorker.com/magazine/2018/01/08/making-china-great-again

Pew research (et. al.)[3] have confirmed that public opinion in Europe is not impressed by the US President. The controversy around his visits to the UK in July 2018 and June 2019 have been damaging to traditional alliances. White House meetings with Macron, Merkel, May, and Rutte have left EU leaders perplexed. In contrast, when the new Italian Prime Minister visited, the two leaders were described by the *New York Times* as 'brothers in nativism.'[4] In the run-up to the 2019 European Parliament elections, the President invited Hungary's Prime Minister Viktor Orban to a coveted White House meeting.

Europe Doubts America

By the middle of 2018 US allies were not hiding their growing concerns. In a historic tweet the President of the European Council Donald Tusk summed up European concerns:

"Looking at latest decisions of @realDonaldTrump someone could even think with friends like that who needs enemies. But frankly, EU should be grateful. Thanks to him we got rid of all illusions. We realise that if you need a helping hand, you will find one at the end of your arm."[5]

This contrast between the President's evident distrust of his G7 allies and his proud expressions of trust in the North Korean leader was remarkable enough and was followed up a few weeks later in July 2018 when Trump met Putin in Helsinki just days after an unhappy NATO summit in Brussels.

At times the President seemed to be joyfully reveling in his increasing isolation seeing it as playing so well with his domestic constituencies. His description of the EU as a 'foe' seemed particularly insulting and his reported encouragement of France to follow Britain out of the EU and strike a bilateral deal with the USA seemed to augur badly for EU-US relations.

As his electoral performances have, so far, confirmed, his detractors underestimate him at their peril. From his support for BREXIT to his playing on East-West divisions in the EU, Donald Trump is a shrewd observer of electoral trends which mainstream leaders may sometimes miss out on. He is clearly aware of his impact on public opinion outside the USA in Western democracies and happily (if somewhat unusually) takes on his challengers via their own media.

---

3 http://www.pewglobal.org/2018/05/29/why-europeans-turned-against-trump/

4 https://www.nytimes.com/2018/08/02/opinion/editorials/trump-conte-italy-immigration.html

5 https://www.euractiv.com/section/enlargement/news/tusk-with-friends-like-trump-who-needs-enemies/

Whether he can assess the long- or even short-term global implications of the impact he is having on opinion in long-standing allied countries is a lot less clear.

It is, however, clear that in Ursula von der Leyen the US President will find a partner with a clear understanding of how the EU should respond to these confusing, sometimes menacing positions. Where Trump has seemed to link NATO members' defense spending with EU trade practices, von der Leyen has been rather blunt.

"I think this is an immature discussion. Therefore, I think we should turn the discussion into a mature discussion which disentangles both topics. They are not related to each other [. . .] We want to remain transatlantic, but we also want to become more European."

Criticizing both Russia and China she has observed that "Donald Trump has to say clearly on which side he is [. . .] Whether he's on the side of the law, peace and democracy, or whether he doesn't care about all that and instead he's looking for a best buddy."[6]

Joseph Borrell, the new EU High Representative for Foreign and Security Policy and Commission Vice-President, had already, before taking office, made clear his ability to take a clear-sighted approach to the new geopolitical situation. Spain has not signed up to the BRI but attending the April 2019 BRI Forum in Beijing he said that while it was too soon to assess the impact of the New Silk Road, the EU shared the US view that China was already a world power, and that European cooperation in the scheme would be based on the premise that certain principles must be respected.

"The novelty now is China promoting alternative governance models abroad or even at the multilateral level. Here is where the commission identifies a systemic rivalry; the debate is not between the EU and China anymore, but worldwide."

He told the *South China Morning Post* that the commission also identified many areas for cooperation between China and the EU. "This is not a paper seeking to heighten tensions between China and the EU, but a document that objectively assesses the relation between both giants with all its pros and cons".

"The EU has always addressed China on the basis that good friends are able to talk frankly about their disagreements and reach compromises at the negotiation table."

6 https://www.politico.eu/article/ursula-von-der-leyen-donald-trump-new-eu-foil-another-strong-female-german-leader/

Summing up his basic approach and confirming the EU's readiness to continue pragmatic, constructive engagement with China, his blunt message was that since joining the WTO in 2001:

"China has entered the world, but the world has not entered in China to the same extent. [The Belt and Road Initiative] is the expression of a new phase in the relationship between China and the rest of the world: China is no longer a developing country, but a world power."[7]

Again, such words are unlikely to be heard in Washington.

USA Pushing Europe into Alliance with China?

Climate change provided an early, clear example of how Trump's insistence on abandoning his predecessor's legacy not only caused outrage in Europe but potentially pushed the EU closer to China. According to leaked minutes from the G7 meeting in Taormina in May 2017, the USA became quite isolated, its partners having failed to persuade Trump to stay in the Paris Climate Agreement.

Der Spiegel reported Chancellor Merkel's warning in Taormina that the Chinese would take advantage of the situation. Xi Jinping is clever, she reportedly added, and would take advantage of the vacuum it created. Resigned to his failure to influence the USA, Macron admitted defeat. "Now China leads," he said.[8]

Welcoming the Chinese President to Berlin, she said:

"It is a great pleasure for us to welcome you here today at a time of turmoil in the world, when China and Germany can make a contribution to calming down this turmoil."[9]

In July 2018 a Trump-Juncker informal agreement headed off an immediate trade war but transatlantic tensions unresolved even if some observers wondered whether this, by itself, would reduce momentum towards closer EU-China understanding on trade issues.

Two years after the fiasco in Taormina, a similar US against the rest scenario played out in Osaka (2019).

7 Belt and Road reflects reality that China is a world power, *SCMP* 23.4.19.

8 http://www.spiegel.de/international/world/trump-pulls-out-of-climate-deal-western-rift-deepens-a-1150486.html

9 http://uk.businessinsider.com/merkel-stands-by-claim-that-europe-cant-rely-on-us-ahead-of-the-g-20-2017-7?r=US&IR=T

China Sees an Era of Strategic Opportunity

At the 19th CPC Congress held in November 2017, President Xi had expressed unbounded confidence in China's potential to seize global leadership and announced his intention to, in effect, abandon the 'low-profile' strategy enunciated by Deng Xiaoping at the end of the 1970s. The Chinese President's speech seemed to herald a more assertive foreign policy with China 'approaching the centre of the world stage.'

According to Xi, "this is a new historic juncture in China's development. It will be an era that sees China moving closer to center stage and making greater contributions to mankind. . . .by 2035 China will have become a global leader in terms of composite national strength and international influence." The Chinese President foresaw that common prosperity for everyone will be basically achieved. Seeking to reassure neighboring counties he added that:

"No matter what stage of development it reaches, China will never seek hegemony or engage in expansion."[10]

In the Osnos article referred to earlier, he reported that:

> In a speech to Communist Party officials last January 20th, Major General Jin Yinan, a strategist at China's National Defense University, celebrated America's pullout from the (TPP) trade deal. "We are quiet about it", he said. "We repeatedly state that Trump 'harms China.' We want to keep it that way. In fact, he has given China a huge gift. That is the American withdrawal from T.P.P." Jin, whose remarks later circulated, told his audience, "As the U.S. retreats globally, China shows up".
>
> For years, China's leaders predicted that a time would come–perhaps midway through this century–when it could project its own values abroad. In the age of "America First", that time has come far sooner than expected[11].

This 'new era' rhetoric has received mixed reactions in the USA and Europe. What is, however, clear is that China has a clearly enunciated strategy to enhance its role in regional and global affairs. This surge of self-confidence comes at a time of division and uncertainty in both Europe and the USA. The latter, until a few years ago, seemed to have established a permanent hegemonic relationship with allies in Europe and across the Pacific. China is now signaling through a series of measures that it sees this era as having come to an end.

As the USA abandons the very concepts of interdependence and multilateralism, the EU needs not only to challenge this approach but also to look for partners with which to work towards common objectives. Trust between China

---

10 http://europe.chinadaily.com.cn/china/2017-10/19/content_33428206.htm

11 Osnos, *op. cit.*

and the EU is by no means sufficient to envisage any kind of alternative alliance. Even the use of such a term has little real significance.

China Trying Divide and Rule in EU?

China has always insisted it wants a more 'democratic' or multipolar world order. It has consistently supported the basic concept of European integration as a step in this direction. The apparent weakening of the transatlantic alliance could lead China to reaffirm this view. On the other hand, China cannot be expected to overlook the strengthening centrifugal forces at work which have led the UK to opt for BREXIT and some leaders from central and eastern Europe to champion 'illiberal democracy' and to see China as an alternative model.

Viktor Orban hosted the November 2017 meeting of the 16+1 group of countries participating in China's Belt and Road Initiative (BRI). In his keynote speech Orban claimed that Europe's most competitive investment environment has come into being in central and eastern Europe.

> There was a time when the modernisation of Asia was only possible if Europe contributed significant technological and financial resources to the process. The situation has been reversed: the star of the East is now in the ascendant, and we live in an era marked by the rise of Asia – and within it China. We are at the beginning of a period in which the further development of Europe will be dependent on the technological and financial involvement of the East. The 16+1 format serves not only the best interests of China, and not only those of our sixteen Central and Eastern European countries: the success of this cooperation also benefits the whole of Europe, and the European Union. We have created a truly win-win situation.[12]

It remains unclear whether the 16 countries concerned or even the four Visegrad countries really do share a common strategy. Orban does not hesitate to present himself as part of a global challenge to liberal democracy but whether China would really play along with his divisive style is by no means clear.

China can take advantage of such gestures as Hungarian (and Greek) opposition to EU criticisms of its human rights record but its leaders are more circumspect about their prospects than Orban, who said in Beijing earlier in 2017 that "globalization is taking a new form dominated by the East" adding "that a large part of the world has had enough of developed countries lecturing it on human rights and the economy."

After 30 years of partnership and dialogue it is also likely that China has developed a greater understanding of European political and economic development

12 https://dailynewshungary.com/china-cee-summit-budapest-opening-ceremony/

than these simplistic comments reflect. Indeed, China needs to look after its reputation in Europe so any close alignment with anti-EU populism (which Trump appreciates) is rather unlikely. Suggestions that China would even be ready to tone down its 16+1 engagement have not materialized and as Lucrezia Poggetti and Jan Weidenfeld put it:

> The EU should seize the moment. Rather than second-guessing Beijing's motives for changing its 16+1 policy, decision-makers in Brussels and in EU member states, like France and Germany, should seize the moment and seek greater alignment of EU member states' China policies. Expediting the implementation of existing plans in Brussels for a new EU connectivity initiative for Europe seems a timely venture, as more CEEC come to terms with the sobering realties of China's economic engagement in the region. Brussels also needs to popularize the message among opinion multipliers in CEE EU member states and EU neighborhood countries that so far China has not lived up to its ambitious financing and investment rhetoric and that Chinese activities are a long way away from matching what the EU has put on the table to date.[13]

In Dubrovnik in April 2019 Greece became the 17th European country to join this framework. This came a few weeks after Italy became the first western European country to sign up to a 'Memorandum of Understanding' with China on participation in the BRI. After the new leadership of the EU was chosen in June 2019 the failure of any CCEC country to achieve any leading position was noted but still China insists that such BRI cooperation does not mean that China is joining in American or Russian attempts to undermine the EU. Yixiang Xu has[14] written that seven years after the partnership was launched reality has met the fanfare with "rather underwhelming results for most CEE partners. Rather than building infrastructure to suit local needs, Beijing only supports projects it deems strategic, including steel mills, chemical plants, highways, and railways. While multiple projects are underway in Serbia and Montenegro, Chinese infrastructure projects have hit a wall inside the EU."

Can the EU Really Aspire to Cooperate with China in Defense of Global Governance?

During preparations for the 2018 EU-China Summit in Beijing it was reported that China was somehow ready to form an alliance with the EU to challenge

13 China seems to tone down its 16+1 Engagement, MERICS March 14th, 2018.

14 https://www.aicgs.org/2019/04/from-161-to-171-the-eus-challenge-from-the-rebranded-china-ceec-initiative/

Trump's approach particularly in view of the apparent outbreak of trade war which the USA had, hitherto, appeared rather gleeful about.[15]

Talk of any kind of alliance is exaggerated as Europe and China do not share any common security structures or interests but they do both have an urgent need to try to keep the USA, as far as possible, within the structures of the rules-based international economy.

The Economist sees the Europeans flirting with China to show America that they should not be taken for granted but it is clear that "without common values, co-operation is likely to remain limited. The Europeans are far more worried about Mr. Xi's authoritarian ways than about Mr. Trump's tendencies–and they share Mr. Trump's objections to China's own mercantilist policies."[16]

Clearly the EU and China share concerns as to the impact of the US abandonment of multilateralism and the consequent profoundly destabilizing effects in China and Europe, possibly leading to economic difficulties or even a global recession. The real question is whether the EU will find China a genuinely reliable partner in developing its response to Trump policies. Trump may have created an opportunity for Xi, but he also has set a test of the Chinese leader's ability to emerge as the kind of statesman he clearly aspires to be.

Can Europe Really Trust China?

China insists it can be trusted and considers that its ambitions are sometimes willfully misunderstood in western countries. As an article in the Party Newspaper the *Global Times* put it in October 2017:

> China will not only be a strong nation with and a first-class army, but will focus on its continued pursuit of harmony, balancing an ecological environment, and democracy. . . .. Peaceful development and achieving a win-win result are the driving ideas behind the creation of the country's modern socialist power. If we can maintain these principles, China will be able to maximize its resources and energy required for this type of progress, thus ensuring steady development [. . .] China is reviving the concepts of post-modernity for a new global era. The past examples set by foreign superpowers are not applicable.[17]

---

15 https://www.euractiv.com/section/economy-jobs/news/china-presses-europe-for-anti-trump-alliance-on-trade/

16 https://www.economist.com/international/2018/08/02/countries-team-up-to-save-the-liberal-order-from-donald-trump

17 http://www.globaltimes.cn/content/1071834.shtml

China is, however, a close ally of Russia which appears less of a target for the US President even if it is the primary security concern for Europe and indeed the US Congress. As G7 leaders were meeting in Charlevoix, Quebec, and failing even to agree on the need to save the rules-based international order, President Xi was with President Putin and others in Qingdao, China, for a summit of the Shanghai Cooperation Organization (SCO).

Russian media was happy to report that:

> In a robust show of unity, leaders of eight SCO member states, including Russia and China, arrived for a get-together to talk security and trade, and hail expansion of the bloc – in sharp contrast with the calamitous G7 meeting [. . .] Chinese President Xi Jinping gave the leaders of Pakistan and India a "special welcome" to their first SCO summit, while Russian leader Vladimir Putin said the new members made the alliance look as it should be. "Regarding the enlargement [of the body], we agreed that the current structure is optimal", Putin said, as cited by TASS, adding, "we must see how the organization will work in an enlarged mode".
>
> "If we calculate. . . per capita, the seven countries are wealthier, but the size of the SCO economies [combined] is larger. And the population is of course much bigger – half of the planet", Putin stated.[18]

The USA may be underestimating the depth of the China-Russia relationship because the partners in this alliance do not go out of their way to trumpet it. Indeed, among the reasons the alliance between Russia and China is not widely recognized for what it is, reflects the extraordinary lengths to which both powers go to deny the fact of its existence. As Jamil Anderlini has pointed out "the most important unifying factor between the two is ideological. Mr. Xi and Mr. Putin are strongmen, autocrats who share an aversion to representative government."[19] Both are each other's best friend, a reality Europe should not overlook as the state of its relations with each develop in different directions.

In spite of a degree of consistency notably absent from US policy, EU-China relations had until very recently been stagnating with differences on trade and investment issues, EU concerns which reflect those of the USA.

Towards Global Triangulation?

On July 17, 2018, in Beijing the 20th EU-China Summit seemed to signal an end to a stagnant period in EU-China relations. The coincidence of dates was well

18 https://www.rt.com/news/429324-sco-expansion-summit-qingdao/

19 https://www.ft.com/content/1b4e6d78-9973-11e8-9702-5946bae86e6d

noted by EU Council President Donald Tusk who referred explicitly to the 'other' summit under way in Helsinki.

> Today, on the same day as Europe meets China in Beijing, American President Trump and Russian President Putin will talk in Helsinki. We are all aware of the fact that the architecture of the world is changing before our very eyes. And it is our common responsibility to make it a change for the better. Let us remember, here in Beijing, and over there, in Helsinki, that the world we were building for decades, sometimes through disputes, has brought about peace for Europe, the development of China, and the end of the Cold War between the East and the West. It is a common duty of Europe and China, America and Russia, not to destroy this order, but to improve it. Not to start trade wars, which turned into hot conflicts so often in our history, but to bravely and responsibly reform the rules-based international order.[20]

For the first time in three years an EU-China Summit was able to close with a joint statement[21] in which it was announced that:

"the EU and China will reinforce the global dimension of their partnership to promote peace, security and sustainable development. Both sides reaffirmed their commitment to multilateralism and the rules-based international order with the United Nations at its core."

Reiterating their common commitment to the JCPOA Iran Nuclear Agreement they confirmed their challenge to a major plank of US policy. The text agreed also confirmed a readiness to defend global trade rules and work together through a new working party on WTO reform.

In a global context in which the US leaders did seem to be putting China in a strong position, Trump also provided an example of what the EU can achieve if it remains united.

EU: A Positive Influence on China and the USA?

On the key, long-term issue of WTO reform the EU had already in July 2018 succeeded in getting Trump onto the same page as itself and China. At a White House meeting Juncker impressed Trump enough for the EU and USA to agree to work together on energy and intellectual property issues, the latter being at the heart of conflicts between China and both the EU and the USA.

---

20 https://eeas.europa.eu/delegations/china_ko/48419/Press%20Statement%20by%20European%20Council%20President%20Donald%20Tusk%20following%20the%2020th%20EU-China%20Summit

21 https://eeas.europa.eu/delegations/china_en/48424/Joint%20statement%20of%20the%2020th%20EU-China%20Summit

In the age of multipolar global trade diplomacy, the EU had been able to rise to the challenge without giving too much away to either the USA or China.

As Bart Oosterveld, director of the global business and economics program at the Atlantic Council think tank, in Washington explained “the avoidance of a disaster is not a success. Juncker and Trump agreed to continue to talk and take a joint approach to Chinese trade practices, it’s significant. . . . To see them make joint statements on the WTO, is a positive but those of us who care about a rules-based order on global trade shouldn’t run a victory lap just yet.”

Trade remains just one of numerous recent differences between the USA and EU, ranging from the Paris climate accord to the Iran nuclear deal, so it is by no means clear that Trump has really changed course to any significant extent.

China could not help but notice that Trump and Juncker claimed to be ready to work together to reform the global-trade system, and to act together in the face of the threats from Chinese protectionism. In their joint statement the two Presidents announced that:

> we agreed today to join forces to protect American and European companies better from unfair global trade practices. We will therefore work closely together with like-minded partners to reform the WTO and to address unfair trading practices, including intellectual property theft, forced technology transfer, industrial subsidies, distortions created by state owned enterprises, and overcapacity.[22]

As in Beijing a few days earlier, the EU had got its partner to agree to work on WTO reform. It remains to be seen what the next steps will be in both partnerships. China and the EU are not under the same domestic political pressure to achieve instant results as Trump is ahead of mid-term elections. The US President talks of love with his erstwhile foe whereas China and the EU have overcome the stagnation of their relationship. In a period of geopolitical turbulence created by Donald Trump, the EU is not going in for the same kind of rapid changing of partners that the USA might hope for.

EU Does Not Have to Take Sides

It seems unlikely that concerns about China will lead to any strengthening of understanding between Washington and the new EU leadership in Brussels. As Michael Romanowski has put it:

---

22 https://eeas.europa.eu/delegations/united-states-america/48861/joint-us-eu-statement-following-president-junckers-visit-white-house_en

> The grievances that divide Europe and China draw the former closer to the United States. In theory, the common understanding of issues such as values, trade, investment, and the geo-economic significance of Beijing's Belt and Road Initiative could be a solid foundation for a fruitful cooperation. Yet to forge a new transatlantic deal on China, the United States, embodied by President Donald Trump, must become less arrogant and Europe less lethargic and naïve concerning the future of multilateralism. . . . .
> The European Union, with the world's largest trade surplus, is the only power that could potentially balance the scale between Washington and Beijing. However, Europe is unwilling to pick a side just yet. The internal divisions towards China do not help. In 2016 Hungary and Greece – major recipients of the Chinese capital – blocked a strong EU Council declaration on Beijing's operations in the South China Sea.
> Hypothetically, the European Union could emerge as a winner in the conflict of its two major partners. The composition of EU exports suggests economic opportunities both in China and the United States with the greater gains to be expected in the latter. Although Europe now exports across the Atlantic twice as much as to China in the long-term, Beijing is envisioned to call the shots not only in the global economy but also in technology – with quantum computing or bullet trains – and politics where the recent trend, also observed in Europe, has favored a model of a strong centralized government. [. . .] Europe is still uncertain whether China is an opportunity or a strategic threat. Washington has made up its mind in this regard, but has not come up with a comprehensive policy, instead focusing largely on trade.
> For now, Europe carefully maneuvers the murky international waters in which Trump's Twitter torpedoes occasionally diminish the transatlantic bond and the Chinese lifeboat could appear as a rescue only at first glance. In mid-term, however, the United States and the European Union should side with each other in order to present a truly effective China agenda.[23]

At the G20 meeting in Osaka in June 2019, Trump and Xi postponed the trade war and the US President suddenly dropped his own hard line position on Huawei participation in European's 5G network construction and announced a resumption of trade talks with China. Whilst this undermines the credibility of his threats it also raises the possibility that Trump will look for grand bargain with China before the US votes in November 2020. This might be at the expense of the EU, but it could reduce the risk that Europe will become a front line in conflict between the USA and China over the creation of 5G networks and cybersecurity in general. In a worst-case scenario, the anti-globalists in the USA could get the upper hand leading to forms of de-globalization with China happy to separate its own cyberspace from that of others.

In the course of the early months of 2019 the EU showed it was thinking hard about how to resolve or at least come to terms with this continuing dilemma.

---

23 https://yaleglobal.yale.edu/content/will-china-save-transatlantic-relations

Asia Is More Than China

As the EU moves to consolidate its global strategy and advance its defense policy, it should confirm its interest in peace and cooperation in the Asia-Pacific region.

With Trump in office China can more easily advance its own ideas of 'Regional Globalism.' As Mireya Solis, a Brookings expert, put it after the 2017 APEC summit:

> President Xi moved once again to occupy, rhetorically, the space the United States vacated as champion of multilateralism and free trade. Addressing the same audience right after President Trump, he delivered a starkly different message. He defended the value of international trade as a win-win proposition and tool for development, and portrayed globalization as an unstoppable yet moldable force that could be more inclusive and balanced.... But leadership in free trade may be China's last frontier because it hinges on the supply of a commodity in short supply in Xi's vision for China: liberalization. The 19th Party Congress did not set China on a path to become a free trader.[24]

The presence of European Council President Donald Tusk at the ASEAN summit in Manila in Autumn 2017 (which President Trump skipped) was an important signal as clearly the EU has an enormous direct interest in the peaceful resolution of conflicts such as those on the Korean Peninsula and in Myanmar. The Asia-Europe (ASEM) summit in Brussels in 2018 was another opportunity to advance in this direction. China and the EU share a common need for regional stability, but it is by no means clear that the EU can approach China with any meaningful geopolitical strategy.

Europe should continue to work with China to safeguard and build upon such major global achievements as the Paris Climate Treaty and the agreement on preventing Iran from developing nuclear weapons. The EU is developing a role in China's neighborhood. Seoul and Brussels have cooperated in efforts to support the new situation on the Korean peninsula. EU messages on human rights or the South China Sea have, however, been cautious. This partly reflects internal differences of approach as well as some countries' sensitivity to Chinese economic interests.

Interdependence is a concept with which the EU and its leaders feel much more comfortable than the USA.

In October 2018, the 12th Asia-Europe meeting was held in Brussels and the EU took the opportunity not only to reassert its readiness to cooperate with Asia as a region but also to present a meaningful vision of infrastructure cooperation

---

24 https://www.brookings.edu/blog/order-from-chaos/2017/11/15/the-new-geopolitics-of-trade-in-asia/

linked to but not undermining China's own BRI strategy.[25] Critics insisted that this strategy was insufficient without deeper cooperation with China but the EU had made its point clear to India, Japan, and others that Asia is much more than China.

EU 2019: New Leaders Same Strategy

In the course of the early months of 2019, the EU showed it was thinking hard about how to resolve or at least come to terms with the continuing dilemmas of dealing with China in the current global situation.

In April 2019, the European Council held a rare exchange of views on overall relations with China in the global context after which President Tusk stated that "Our aim is to focus on achieving a balanced relation, which ensures fair competition and equal market access. In this context, we hope to persuade China to include industrial subsidies as a crucial element of the WTO reform."

This discussion was based on a document from HRVP Mogherini which reaffirmed the 2016 strategy and confirmed that the EU was adopting:

> a more realistic, assertive, and multi-faceted approach. This will ensure that relations with this strategic partner are set on a fair, balanced and mutually beneficial course. China is, simultaneously, in different policy areas, a cooperation partner with whom the EU has closely aligned objectives, a negotiating partner with whom the EU needs to find a balance of interests, an economic competitor in the pursuit of technological leadership, and a systemic rival promoting alternative models of governance. This requires a flexible and pragmatic whole-of-EU approach enabling a principled defense of interests and values. The tools and modalities of EU engagement with China should also be differentiated depending on the issues and policies at stake. The EU should use linkages across different policy areas and sectors in order to exert more leverage in pursuit of its objectives.

The EU's response should be based on two objectives:

- Based on clearly defined interests and principles, the EU should deepen its engagement with China to promote common interests at global level.
- The EU should robustly seek more balanced and reciprocal conditions governing the economic relationship.[26]

25 https://ec.europa.eu/transport/sites/transport/files/2018-07-13-eu-china-connectivity-platform-action-plan.pdf
26 please refer to HRVP 12.3.2019 JOIN (2019) 5 final.

In short, the EU would stick to a pragmatic engagement with China without the aggressive rhetoric coming from the USA. The EU knows that China's expansionism in the South China Sea has the same meaning as Russia's annexation of Crimea but according to Sven Biscop of the Egmont Institute:

> the EU message remains that it prefers to work with and not against China. But for that course to be pursued, the EU has to see concrete actions that prove that China is willing to be an effective partner. The EU approach can be summarized as: cooperate when you can, push back when you must.[27]

A few weeks later the 21st EU-China Summit took place in Brussels at which the EU got China to reaffirm its commitments to the UN, including on human rights. They reaffirmed their commitment to work together on 5G issues and WTO reform. On the Paris Climate Agreement and the JCPOA on Iran they restated their common approaches. Since then the EU has continued despite internal divergences to speak out on human rights in Xinjiang. The EU also reminded China that it is ready to cooperate on all aspects of EU-Asia connectivity, without subsuming everything for China's own BRI plan. President Macron had received President Xi in March 2019 along with President Juncker and Chancellor Merkel. He had made his position clear in advance, welcoming the fact that the EU had woken up to the threat of an assertive China. By dispensing with the almost xenophobic language of Donald Trump it is just possible that Macron helped to get Europe's message across to China.

China Gets the EU Message?

Evidence soon emerged of a new realism on the side of China which has, in effect, given up on insisting that after 15 years in the WTO they should be recognized as having achieved 'Market Economy Status.' In June 2019 it emerged in Geneva that China had accepted a WTO disputes panel adjudication which means that Beijing must accept continued EU and US 'anti-dumping' levies on cheap Chinese goods. This had been a controversial issue for the EU but explosive for the USA, with President Donald Trump regularly threatening to quit the WTO if the organization did not 'shape up.'

It is interesting to note that another of the key new leaders of the EU institutions Christine Lagarde has taken a relatively optimistic view of the extent to which China might be ready to learn how to address Western concerns over its ability to integrate into genuine forms of interdependence. Gillian Tett of the

27 Sven Biscop, *The puzzle of the EU's China strategy is falling into place*, July 2019.

Financial Times reported that at a conference in Los Angeles in May 2019 she was asked about the BRI, producing an unexpected flash of optimism saying that the IMF had been working with the Chinese "for weeks and weeks to explain how debt sustainability matters." She noted that President Xi Jinping had pledged at the BRI summit to create a new framework to make the hundreds of billions of dollars of debt it has extended for BRI projects more 'sustainable,' in both a fiscal and environmental sense.[28]

China has, in effect, showed signs that it is ready to change key aspects of its approach and set a test of its credibility the response to which the EU will be able to judge the potential for deeper cooperation on the key BRI and WTO issues.

The EU has not suddenly noticed the idea of 'win-win' cooperation. Unlike the former USSR, the People's Republic of China has always supported the idea of European integration, even though it started under US hegemony. Unlike Trump and Putin, China's leaders have offered no encouragement to populist, nationalist, and anti-EU forces which do threaten stability in the EU.

On substance both China and Europe have shown a common ability to follow long-term strategic goals which are in both sides' interests. China and the EU have both followed relatively consistent approaches for over 40 years.

They both accept that multilateral structures are as important as bilateral relationships.

The crisis of multilateralism is certainly an opportunity for China and the EU to show that there is an alternative to nationalism and conflict.

As uncertainty and maybe constitutional chaos continues in the USA, China and the EU both face huge internal challenges.

China may also be entering a difficult period. President Xi has centralized power in a way which may provoke challenges to his leadership inside the Communist Party and in civil society on which he continues to clamp down.[29] Partly because of the US disruptive trade measures, the economic outlook is less positive than for some time. President Xi likes to present an aura of stability but as Minxin Pei put it "politics has a nasty habit of surprising us – especially in a country like China."[30]

---

28 Belt and Road Initiative lacks 'Chinese characteristics.' *Financial Times*, May 21, 2019.

29 https://www.theguardian.com/world/2018/aug/04/cracks-appear-in-invincible-xi-jinpings-authority-over-china

30 https://www.project-syndicate.org/commentary/china-trade-war-risks-to-xi-jinping-by-minxin-pei-2018-08

Europe's new leadership has the experience and opportunity to show both China and the USA that it can offer stable, productive partnership as an alternative to instability and conflict. The EU now has to show that it has recovered the unity and sense of purpose to do so and to bring the other two global powers along the road to genuine interdependence.

Ruixia Jia

The '16+1' Cooperation in the Context of the China-EU Innovation Partnership

Introduction

International scientific and technological cooperation is an important way to promote global peace and prosperity. Innovation is the current trend. Expanding the space for innovation and enhancing the level of scientific and technological cooperation is the focus of major actors of the present day, including the EU and China.

In 1998, China and the EU signed the EU-China Science & Technology Agreement. After several renewals, this bilateral scientific and technological innovation cooperation continues to deepen. The EU's research framework programmes (Framework Programme 4 (FP4)-Framework Programme 7 (FP7) and Horizon 2020) and China's major national science and technology plans are open to each other. Scientific researchers from China and Europe have more platforms for close exchanges and common promotion of technological innovation and development.

The report of the 19th National Congress of the Communist Party of China proposed that China must speed up the construction of an innovative country. In the 40 years of its reform and opening up process, China has made considerable progress in terms of scientific and technological innovation but it requires more scientific and technological innovations of high quality and high efficiency to constantly meet the new needs of economic and social development. As one of the leading players in innovation, the EU has always held an advanced position in the world in this area, and there are many aspects where lessons can be learnt from the EU. In the future, on the basis of deepening mutual understanding, the two sides should open a new era of the China-EU Innovation Partnership, face challenges together and make responsible contributions to the sustainable peace and prosperity of mankind. This should become a new consensus for China-EU innovation cooperation and the basis of the China-EU innovation partnership.

The CEECs' Innovation Progress in the EU

Since 2004, Central and Eastern European Countries (CEECs) have been gradually joining the European Union and have reshaped their countries within the

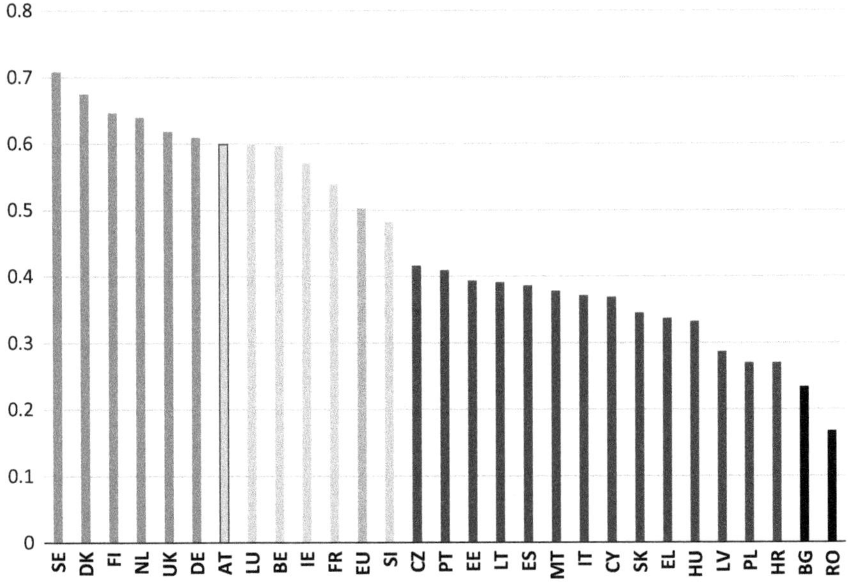

Fig. 1: Summary Innovation Index (SII), 2016. Source:Internal Market, Industry, ntrepreneurship and SMEs. http://ec.europa.eu/growth/industry/innovation/facts-figures/scoreboards/

context of European integration. Most of the CEECs have achieved remarkable results in the area of scientific and technological innovation and expanded the space and area of innovation for the integration of the European Union by catching up and through convergence.

The Summary Innovation Index

The European Union measures the innovation performance of various countries through a Summary Innovation Index (SII). Member countries are divided into four different levels of innovators: innovation leaders, strong innovators, moderate innovators and modest innovators (Fig. 1).

The EU Innovation Scoreboards (EIS) 2017 Report pointed out that, compared with 2010, EU innovation performance has progressed, but its pace has slowed down and the gap between member states is still wide. Compared to 2010, 15 member countries have improved their innovation capabilities and 13 countries have reduced their innovation capabilities (see Tabs 1 and 2).

Tab. 1: Growth of innovation performance. Source:http://ec.europa.eu/growth/industry/innovation/facts-figures/scoreboards/

Member States	Growth rate (%)
LT	21
MT	12.2
UK	11.7
NL	10.4
AT	8.9
LV	8.5
IE	3.5
FR	2.8
SE	2.3
PL	2
BE	1.4
LU	1.4
EL	0.7
BG	0.1

Tab. 2: Reduced innovation performance growth rate. Source:http://ec.europa.eu/growth/industry/innovation/facts-figures/scoreboards/

Member States	Growth rate (%)
SI	-0.2
IT	-0.2
HR	-1.4
ES	-1.8
PT	-2.4
DK	-2.8
HU	-3.5
CZ	-3.5
EE	-3.6
DE	-3.7
FI	-5.1
CY	-12.7
RO	-14.1 %

The ultimate goal of the EU's evaluation of the innovation capabilities of its member states is not the scores themselves. Rather, the ultimate goal is to make each member understand the strengths and weaknesses of its own progress in terms of innovation through the dynamic and static measurement of each indicator so as to clarify the direction of its efforts. The EU has also continuously improved its evaluation system for many years in order to create a better innovation environment. At present, the EU is increasingly concerned about the role of digital use and entrepreneurship in driving innovation.

Innovation in CEECs

At present, 11 CEECs belong to the latter three innovation groups: Slovenia is ranked in the strong innovator group and is the only member of the CEECs to have joined the second group since 2010; the Czech Republic, Estonia, Lithuania, Slovakia, Hungary, Latvia, Poland and Croatia rank in the moderate innovator group. Romania and Bulgaria have been in the last group since they joined the EU (see Tab. 3).

Strong innovators: Slovenia. According to EU statistics, Slovenia is the only CEEC to have been listed in the strong innovation group since 2010. Slovenia's economic structure is dominated by agriculture, mining and manufacturing and the working population is concentrated in these fields. Slovenia's small- and medium-sized enterprises and small and microenterprises account for a large proportion of enterprises while the number of large enterprises is relatively small. There are many foreign enterprises. At present, the economic growth rate is relatively low. The population is also growing slowly. Slovenia currently has good innovation framework conditions, such as human resources and innovation environment, which are higher than or equal to the EU average level. In terms of investment in innovation, the index of investment in innovation activities is also higher than the EU average. However, there is obviously a lack of public funds to support innovation. In addition, Slovenia also needs further improvement in the two dimensions of 'impacts'.

Moderate innovators: the Czech Republic, Estonia, Lithuania, Slovakia, Hungary, Latvia, Poland, Croatia and Serbia. This group can be divided into the three Baltic states (Estonia, Lithuania and Latvia), the 'Visegrád 4' (the Czech Republic, Slovakia, Hungary and Poland) and two western Balkan states (Croatia and Serbia) based on their regions.

Three Baltic states. The economic structure of Estonia is dominated by its manufacturing industry. However, high-level and intermediate-level technical manufacturing industry accounts for a relatively small proportion of its

Tab. 3: Four Main types of indicators and ten innovation dimensions. Source: based on the data from http://ec.europa.eu/growth/industry/innovation/facts-figures/scoreboards/

	Framework conditions			Investments		Innovation activities			Impacts	
	Human resources	Attractive research systems	Innovation-friendly environment	Finance and support	Firm investments	Innovators	Linkages	Intellectual assets	Employment impacts	Sales impacts
EU-28 Ave.	121	111.8	114.3	83.7	113.6	85.8	95.3	100.4	100.1	102.9
SI	172.9	101.6	114.3	40.4	141	76.6	105.7	93.6	74.3	75.7
CZ	97.4	82.6	94.2	77.5	114.6	73.7	63.0	60.8	95.4	95.0
EE	122.1	93.6	112.8	124.4	76.3	23.6	57.7	96.9	69.9	64.4
LT	124.0	34.6	138.9	97.2	100.3	79.4	108.6	52.9	66.6	33.5
SK	96.5	52.5	70.4	72.4	69.4	28.6	62.4	38.6	111.8	105.6
HU	64.8	55.5	93.4	44.4	88.9	14.4	60.4	46.9	126.7	98.0
LV	93.2	37.6	160.1	75.9	44.0	11.9	41.4	49.8	84.5	46.7
PL	77.4	33.0	83.7	51.2	85.1	2.2	26.8	77.9	88.0	55.2
HR	77.3	40.2	47.9	50.9	107.6	61.7	50.8	39.7	62.0	24.9
RS	76.8	44.1	37.0	43.9	130.2	81.2	42.6	22.7	94.0	65.3
BG	71.8	28.6	66.4	16.1	59.0	11.6	17.7	99.2	97.9	33.5
RO	49.8	30.0	89.8	18.1	11.9	0.0	29.4	24.9	37.0	62.2
MK	49.3	25.3	61.7	2.8	67.9	66.2	41.2	13.9	8.7	70.6

manufacturing industry. Employment is concentrated on the public sector and the construction industry. There are many microenterprises and small- and medium-sized enterprises but only a few large enterprises. The country's economic growth is fast. In recent years, the demographic growth rate of Estonia has been low, with negative growth, and its population density is also low. Lithuania and Latvia are very similar. The agricultural and mining sectors of the two countries account for a large number of employees, while the levels of employment in high-tech and medium-high-tech manufacturing industries are relatively small. Small- and medium-sized enterprises dominate, while there are few large enterprises. There are a relatively large number of foreign enterprises. Economic growth is fast but the population growth is low (with negative growth) and population density is low.

The three Baltic states share similar advantages in terms of innovation capability, such as human resources, the innovation environment and public funds to support innovation. The Latvian and Lithuanian research systems are not attractive due to a lack of innovation capability. Latvia is far below Estonia and Lithuania in terms of levels of company investment in R&D.

The Visegrád 4. The Czech manufacturing industry is well developed and employment levels in agriculture and mining are relatively small. In addition, the proportion of people employed in the public sector and the construction industry is also relatively large. Economic growth is fast, but population growth is low and population density is low. Slovakia's economic structure is similar to that of the Czech Republic and its economic growth rate is relatively fast. However, Slovakia's public administration has also absorbed more jobs and there are fewer foreign enterprises. Slovakia also faces the dilemma of low population growth. Hungary's employed population is concentrated in manufacturing and public administration. The proportion of foreign enterprises is high, while the proportion of R&D expenditure is low. Economic growth is high but population growth is low. Poland's labour force is concentrated in agriculture, mining and manufacturing. The proportion of people employed in high-tech manufacturing and service industries is low, while the proportion of foreign enterprises is high. There are only a few enterprises with a high proportion of R&D expenditure. Economic growth is slow, as is population growth. The Czech Republic has a robust capacity for innovation and performs well in all dimensions. However, its enterprise innovation activities need to be strengthened. Slovakia, Hungary and Poland do not perform well as innovators and in the area of 'need to cultivate innovative enterprises'. The three countries also lack attractiveness in terms of their research systems. Slovakia and Hungary also need to catch up in the area of intellectual property.

Two western Balkan states: Serbia and Croatia. Croatia's agricultural and mining sectors account for large numbers of the working population while the proportion of those employed in the high-tech manufacturing industry and the medium and high-tech manufacturing industry is relatively low. Foreign companies account for a large proportion of employees, the economy is growing slowly, the population is also growing slowly or is even experiencing negative growth and the population density is low. Croatia's innovation advantage lies in its enterprise investment, its human resources and the impact of employment levels. It is relatively weak in the areas of intellectual assets, its research system and as an innovator. The comparative advantages of Serbia's innovation progress lie in the areas of enterprise investment, impact of employment levels and as an innovator. Its relative weakness lies in the areas of intellectual assets, innovation environment and contact.

Modest innovators: Bulgaria, Romania and North Macedonia. Bulgaria, Romania and North Macedonia are far below the EU average in terms of innovation capability. However, the three countries also have their own unique features. Bulgaria is dominated by agriculture, mining and manufacturing, with a low proportion of employment in high-tech, medium-and-high-tech manufacturing and knowledge-intensive service industries. Small and microenterprises and small- and medium-sized enterprises dominate, whilst there are few large enterprises. Economic growth is fast, but population growth is low and population density is low. Romania is dominated by agriculture and mining, and the proportion of people employed in high-tech and medium-and-high-tech manufacturing industries is low. With its knowledge-intensive enterprises accounting for a high proportion of employment, Romania's economic growth rate has been among the highest in the EU in recent years, but its population growth rate is low and its population density is low. Romania's service industry has developed rapidly in recent years, with the information and communication technology industry performing well. North Macedonia's labour force is concentrated in the industrial sector while the service industry is underdeveloped. Its economic growth is fast, population growth low and population density low. The common problems shared by the three countries lie in the lack of attractiveness of their research systems and insufficient financial support for innovation from the public sector.

A country's economic structure affects its innovation capability, while the development of innovation capability in turn affects the country's economic structure. The EU did not evaluate the innovation performance of Albania, Montenegro and Bosnia and Herzegovina. The economic transformation of these three countries is progressing slowly. By comparison with other CEECs, their economic development is relatively backward and the basic environment for innovation is yet to be vigorously cultivated.

On the whole, the innovation capabilities of CEECs are still at the stage of catching up with the average level of the EU. The economic structure of a country has an impact on the ability of each country to innovate and, at the same time, the innovation capacity growth bears, in turn, on the economic structure of each country. For example, Slovenia has good conditions for innovation frameworks, its human resources and innovation environments are higher than or equal to the EU average level and, in terms of innovation investment, the country's investment in innovation activities also exceeds the EU average level. The Baltic countries have similar advantages in terms of innovation capabilities, such as human resources, innovation environment and public funds to support innovation. However, there are also some nation's innovation performances that are declining, such as Croatia, Hungary, the Czech Republic, Estonia and Romania. These CEECs have innovation cooperation with China.

The Case of Poland

Poland is a big country in central and eastern Europe and its innovative development is of great significance. Since Poland joined the EU in 2004, its R&D innovation system has undergone significant changes. The Polish government has reformed the systems for science and higher education, focusing on improving the quality and effect of R&D and increasing support for R&D. Poland's SII shows an overall upward trend and the country is among the moderate innovators.

Poland's Innovation Capability

The ten dimensions of the EU's Innovation Scoreboard can also provide a detailed understanding of Poland's innovation progress. Tables 4 to 13, respectively, list Poland's scores in these dimensions from 2010 to 2016.

The area of human resources takes into account a country's newly graduated doctoral students, the population of 25–34-year-olds with a higher education degree and lifelong learning. In this area, Poland is showing an upward trend but occasionally slips back, slightly increasing its gap with the EU average.

The area relating to the attractiveness of research systems takes into account international cooperation and the publication of Polish R&D institutions (professionals), the publication of papers in world-renowned scientific publications and the training of non-EU doctoral students. Table 5 shows that Poland is far below the EU average.

Tab. 4: Human resources. Source: http://ec.europa.eu/growth/industry/innovation/facts-figures/scoreboards/

	2010	2011	2012	2013	2014	2015	2016
Poland	69.4	65.5	69.6	74.6	75.6	74	77.4
EU-28 average	100	102.5	105	115.3	118.8	120	121

Tab. 5: Attractive research system. Source: http://ec.europa.eu/growth/industry/innovation/facts-figures/scoreboards/.

	2010	2011	2012	2013	2014	2015	2016
Poland	22.7	24.8	25.7	25	26.6	31.5	33
EU-28 Average	100	101.9	104.9	108.4	107.2	109.5	111.8

Tab. 6: Innovation-friendly environment. Source: http://ec.europa.eu/growth/industry/innovation/facts-figures/scoreboards/.

	2010	2011	2012	2013	2014	2015	2016
Poland	44.8	44.8	45.8	45.7	50.8	61.9	83.7
EU-28 Average	100	99.6	96.7	96.4	94	102.7	114.3

The area of innovation-friendly environment takes into account the popularity of broadband and the innovation motivation of entrepreneurship. Poland's innovative and friendly environment is approaching the EU average. According to the data in Tab. 6, Poland developed well in this area in 2015 and 2016.

This area covers R&D expenditure in the public sector and the overall support from venture capital for Polish innovation. From 2010 to 2016, Poland's public sector R&D spending and venture capital investment and innovation generally declined but approached the EU average. The government's public R&D support is the main force driving innovation in Poland. In 2015, Poland's expenditure on public funds to support innovation accounted for 0.48 % of its GDP. The EU average for the same period was 0.72 %. Venture capital is one of the major sources of funds for the new business model. When enterprises want to develop new but risky technologies, venture capital is the safest source of funds. In 2015, Poland's venture capital accounted for 0.017 % of its GDP, while the EU average for the same year was 0.062 % (Tab. 7).[1]

1 *EIS 2016 Data Base*, http://ec.europa.eu/DocsRoom/documents/17823

Tab. 7: Finance and support. Source: http://ec.europa.eu/growth/industry/innovation/facts-figures/scoreboards/

	2010	2011	2012	2013	2014	2015	2016
Poland	46	49.3	52.9	58	52.1	49.7	51.2
EU-28 Average	100	99.8	93.6	90	86.2	85.4	83.7

Tab. 8: Firm investments. Source: http://ec.europa.eu/growth/industry/innovation/facts-figures/scoreboards/.

	2010	2011	2012	2013	2014	2015	2016
Poland	71.8	71.8	62.1	65.6	67.8	74.7	85.1
EU-28 Average	100	100	95.5	96.7	107.3	110.1	113.6

Tab. 9: Innovators. Source: http://ec.europa.eu/growth/industry/innovation/facts-figures/scoreboards/.

	2010	2011	2012	2013	2014	2015	2016
Poland	25	25	15.7	15.7	7.9	7.9	2.2
EU-28 Average	100	100	99.6	99.6	86.8	86.8	85.8

This area shows that the R&D support for Polish firms is on the rise and is approaching the EU average. After joining the EU, Poland's investment by firms in innovative R&D has been increasing year by year, approaching the EU average (Tab. 8).

The innovator dimension comprehensively measures the proportion of small- and medium-sized enterprises that carry out product, process, marketing and organisational innovation in all small- and medium-sized enterprises. From the data, Poland deviates considerably from the EU average in this dimension (Tab. 9).

This area indicates the external cooperation and innovation of small- and medium-sized enterprises in Poland and public-private cooperation. As can be seen from the data in Tab. 10, Poland is declining in this area and there is a big gap between Poland and the EU average here.

This area covers patent application, trademark application, design application and other fields. It can be seen from Tab. 11 that the Polish intellectual assets' index has been increasing year by year, approaching the EU average

Tab. 10: Linkages. Source: http://ec.europa.eu/growth/industry/innovation/facts-figures/scoreboards/.

	2010	2011	2012	2013	2014	2015	2016
Poland	37.4	40.9	35.8	29.6	28.4	29.1	26.8
EU-28 Average	100	99.7	94.2	93.1	97	96.8	95.3

Tab. 11: Intellectual assets. Source: http://ec.europa.eu/growth/industry/innovation/facts-figures/scoreboards/.

	2010	2011	2012	2013	2014	2015	2016
Poland	56	57.7	60.3	63.2	71.8	77.6	77.9
EU-28 Average	100	101.1	102	102.9	102.2	100.9	100.4

Tab. 12: Employment impacts. Source: http://ec.europa.eu/growth/industry/innovation/facts-figures/scoreboards/.

	2010	2011	2012	2013	2014	2015	2016
Poland	92.2	93.3	96	95.4	97.1	83.9	88
EU-28 Average	100	101.1	101.6	101.6	102.2	106.6	100.1

Tab. 13: Sales impacts. Source: http://ec.europa.eu/growth/industry/innovation/facts-figures/scoreboards/.

	2010	2011	2012	2013	2014	2015	2016
Poland	68.5	67.1	59	57.6	52.5	53.3	55.2
EU-28 Average	100	99.4	98.9	99.3	95.4	97.2	102.9

The area of employment impacts measure the employment ratio of knowledge-intensive enterprises and the employment ratio of fast-growing enterprises in innovative sectors. Poland is generally on the rise in this area and is very close to the EU average (Tab. 12).

The sales impacts' index measures the proportion of medium-and-high-tech products, knowledge-intensive services' exports and newly listed and newly developed products in sales. Poland's sales dimension is showing a downward trend, with the gap between Poland and the EU average widening (Tab. 13).

According to Tab. 8, Poland has developed well in its financial support for innovation. Poland is paying attention to the protection of intellectual property rights, and innovation has a positive impact on employment. However, there are still some imbalances in terms of Poland's innovation and development that need to be addressed, especially 'innovators', 'attractiveness of research system', 'linkages' and 'human resources', 'innovation-friendly environment' and 'sales impacts'. Poland still has a long way to go to catch up with and converge with the EU in the field of innovation.

Driving Forces of Innovation in Poland

In light of the high risks related to innovation, state support is particularly important. Real innovation is based on cooperation between research, business and government and the government should play an important role here. Poland's central and local governments actively support R&D projects and enterprises engaged in innovation. The science budget reached a high in Polish history in 2015, with a 1.747 billion euro plan[2]. In October 2015, Poland held parliamentary elections. The new government continued the existing policies and took new measures to continue encouraging innovation. Reindustrialisation is an important task for the current administration and achieving this goal depends on technologies independently developed by Poland. The current problems facing Poland are: no funding for good research projects, gaps between research results and commercial applications and large enterprises' reluctance to invest in R&D. In January 2016, the government set up the Innovation Committee, with Polish Deputy Prime Minister and Minister of Development Morawiecki as its chairman. The Deputy Prime Minister and the Minister of Culture, the Deputy Prime Minister and the Minister of Science, Technology and Higher Education, the Minister of Treasury and the Minister of Digitalisation are all members of the Innovation Committee, which is responsible for coordinating about 16 billion euro of investment in innovation by 2020. In 2016, the Polish government issued a White Paper on Innovation and published legislative and organisational proposals to promote an innovative business environment.

Since Poland joined the EU, its R&D and innovation have been developing within the context of European integration. Public financial support for R&D is increasing year by year. In 2007, Poland's R&D intensity was 0.6 %, which rose to 1 % by 2015. Of course, this level is still lower than that of the EU Average

---

2 Krzysztof Klincewicz, Katarzyna Szkuta, Rio country report 2015: Poland, 2016, p. 13

Index. Although Poland's R&D investment has been increasing in recent years with the support of EU funds, it still lags far behind EU standards. The government has promised that Poland's R&D investment will account for 1.7 % of its GDP by 2020 but, in the current financial situation, it is difficult to achieve this goal even with the support of EU funds. The government requires that the management of Poland's large state-owned enterprises significantly increase investment in R&D to resolve this contradiction. Poland's military industry is the area of state-owned enterprises with the most potential to increase R&D investment.[3]

Although Poland's R&D innovation system is mainly supported by public funds, the role of private funds is also growing, mainly from large foreign-funded companies and multinational companies for now. In 2013, there were 2,467 business enterprises engaged in R&D in Poland, focusing on industry and information technology.[4] The R&D momentum of small- and medium-sized enterprises is also improving.

Poland's business environment, which provides the necessary basis to encourage innovation, is also improving. The current Polish government should strive to take measures to simplify business procedures and support enterprises to increase investment in R&D through tax policies. In addition, in response to the global trend towards using industrial intelligence, Poland is also accelerating its construction of infrastructure and use of smart applications. However, there is still a bottleneck in relation to key facilities and the facilities and technologies of railway departments are ageing. The economy is still driven by coal energy, with high emissions and pollution. Power station facilities, most of which are thermal power stations with high levels of demand for electricity, are ageing. These are all areas in which Poland should vigorously improve through innovation.

At present, growing regional importance is an important feature in the changes in Poland's R&D system. The central government still has an advantage in terms of allocating R&D funds, but new regulations will also promote the development of local innovation systems. The administration capacity of the government, including local governments, needs to be further improved.

Strengthening the internationalisation of innovation is very important for Poland. The innovation cooperation between Poland and China on the Belt and Road Initiative (BRI) and the '16+1' platform has a very promising future. The role of research and innovation is crucial to Poland's development and there are

---

3 The Chinese Economic and Commercial Counsellor's Office in Poland, "State-owned Enterprises in Poland Will Invest More R&D Funds", January 18, 2016.

4 GUS (Central Statistics Office of Poland), 2015.

many '16+1' cooperation opportunities in the future, including cooperation between China and Poland.

'16+1' Innovation Cooperation Promotes China-EU Innovation Partnership

Since the '16+1' cooperation process was launched in 2012, good progress has been made in many fields and at many levels. The deepening mutual understanding between China and the CEECs has provided a good environment and opportunity for China and the CEECs to carry out innovation cooperation. '16+1' innovation cooperation has also provided a new driving force for the improvement and development of the China-EU innovation partnership.

In Poland, for example, in 2004, China and Poland established a friendly and cooperative partnership. In 2011, China and Poland established a strategic partnership. In 2012, the '16+1' cooperation mechanism was established. In 2013, China put forward the BRI, and the '16+1' cooperation mechanism has increasingly become an integral part of the BRI. Cooperation between China and Poland in the area of science and technology innovation has also gained a broader platform. The levels of cooperation and exchange between the two countries in traditional fields such as agriculture, mining safety, chemical industry, machinery, electronics, communications and medicine are deepening. Cooperation and exchanges in new fields such as green mobile, biomedicine, new materials and clean energy and space are being further expanded. In July 2013, the China Great Wall Industry Corporation won the bid to undertake Poland's small satellite launch project, which is the first cooperation project between China and Poland in space.[5] On the basis of the intergovernmental cooperation mechanism, China and Poland are actively exploring new mechanisms to further deepen bilateral scientific and technological cooperation. In particular, they have reached a consensus relating to jointly funding R&D projects integrating production, teaching and research and promoting the industrialisation of research results. According to the Bucharest Guidelines, China's Ministry of Science and Technology successfully held the first China-CEEC Seminar on Innovation, Technology Cooperation and International Technology Transfer in Shanghai. The Polish National

---

5 http://www.chinaembassy.org.pl/chn/ywzn/kjhz/zbkjhz1/t1191267.htm (accessed on 30 March 2020)

Research and Development Centre and Jagiellonian University sent two representatives to attend the meeting.[6]

From 23 to 27 November 2015, Andrzej Duda, the President of the Republic of Poland, paid a state visit to China and attended the '16+1' summit. Strengthening cooperation in high-tech fields was one of the themes for President Duda's visit to China. China and Poland have signed several major cooperation documents, such as the memorandum of understanding to jointly promote the BRI. On 20 June 2016, China's President Xi Jinping held talks with Poland's President Andrzej Duda. Both sides agreed to establish a comprehensive strategic partnership between China and Poland. Huawei Technologies Co. Ltd. and Warsaw University signed an agreement to jointly build an innovative scientific data centre. The aim of the innovative scientific data centre is to cooperate in the fields of big data, cloud computing, efficient computing and data analysis. LiuGong DRESSTA Machinery Co. Ltd. has signed a memorandum of cooperation with Poland's National Research and Development Centre, and Liugong has set up a European research and development centre in Poland.[7]

With sound China-Polish relations and expanding economic and trade cooperation between the two countries, the cooperation between the two governments and local governments is increasingly close. Poland's development strategy to build an innovative economy and its policy to promote innovation and entrepreneurship coincide with China's innovation-driven development strategy. The two sides have great potential for cooperation in research and innovation.

From the previous overall analysis of the CEECs' innovation capability and case studies, we can see that the innovation cooperation between China and the CEECs has a certain basis. Since 2012, China and the CEECs have worked on cooperation in many fields under the '16+1' framework mechanism, achieving good results, and '16+1' local cooperation is also in the ascendant. In the future '16+1' cooperation mechanism, innovation cooperation should become a new bright spot, laying a new foundation for the implementation of the BRI. With regard to '16+1' innovation cooperation, new opportunities can be explored along the following paths:

International scientific and technological cooperation is one of the important ways to promote global peace and prosperity. Innovation is the current trend, while expanding the space for innovation and improving the level of scientific and technological cooperation are the focuses of major actors, including the EU

6 http://pl.chineseembassy.org/chn/kj/zbkjhz/t1263895.htm (accessed on 30 March 2020)

7 http://pl.chineseembassB.org/chn/kj/zbkjhz/t1383931.htm

and China. With the development of globalisation, exchanges and cooperation concerning scientific and technological innovation between countries or regions have become increasingly close and new opportunities have also been put forward for cooperation in the area of scientific and technological innovation among developing countries or countries in transition and developed countries.

Opening a New Era in the China-EU Innovation Partnership

Since China and the EU signed the China-EU Science and Technology Cooperation Agreement in 1998, cooperation in the area of science and technology innovation between the two sides has continued to deepen after the agreement for cooperation was renewed several times. The EU's R&D Framework Programme and China's major national science and technology plans are open to each other, and Chinese and European researchers have more platforms for close exchanges and joint promotion of scientific and technological innovation and development.

Firstly, faced with many challenges, the EU will pay more attention to the guidance of innovation in relation to integration, closely combine innovation with social and economic development and identify a new route for integration. Secondly, the development of the CEECs in the area of innovation also needs to be further deepened. The CEECs have lagged behind the EU during the transition period. Now they have to work hard to overcome the aftermath of the 2008 financial crisis. Support for innovation from various countries needs to be further improved to boost the attractiveness of the research system. In addition to increasing the government's provision of funds for the construction of innovative 'infrastructure', it is also necessary to create a good environment to attract more enterprises and funding for investment in innovation. The most crucial point is that, under the guidance of the spirit of the 19th National Congress of the Communist Party of China, China will pay more attention to the development of an innovative country. China's more open attitude has provided new opportunities for '16+1' innovation cooperation and created a new space for the sustainable and green development of China and CEECs while providing a new driving force for the improvement of the China-EU Innovative Partnership.

Increasing Cooperation on the Construction of '16+1' Innovation Capability 'Infrastructure'

In October 2018, the '16+1' local leaders' meeting was held in Bulgaria and the topic of innovation undoubtedly became the focus for all the participants. China and the CEECs can carry out a variety of cooperation projects at the central and local levels to lay solid foundations for their respective innovation and cooperation activities.

Carrying Out '16+1' Cooperation in Higher Education

The scale of student exchanges with 16 CEECs should be increased and the period of studying abroad extended. Chinese and CEEC universities should be encouraged to strengthen exchanges and cooperation. Intercollegiate student exchanges and research and innovation cooperation can be carried out on the '16+1 Local Cooperation' platform. Students should be encouraged to learn each other's languages, understand each other's national conditions, other talents should be taught together with language and professional skills and human resources should be built up for '16+1' cooperation.

Building A '16+1' Network Platform to Encourage Seamless Connection. Online platforms should be available to offer nodes for sharing knowledge so that people in China and CEECs can understand each other online, find new business opportunities and develop e-commerce. Language translation on the internet platform requires a large amount of human resources and the human resources mentioned in point 1 can be fully utilised.

Promoting '16+1' Research Institutions to Jointly Apply for Participation in Various International Research and Development Cooperation Projects and Jointly Publishing and Applying Cutting-Edge Innovations. China's cooperation with 16 CEEC research institutions based on international frontiers or advantages of all the parties should be increased, with results published to enhance the international influence of scientific research. Meanwhile, research institutions and enterprises are being encouraged to cooperate to actively translate research results into practical applications. Research cooperation opportunities should be sought within the existing cooperation mechanism between China and central and eastern Europe and local or higher education institutions be encouraged to actively participate. All parties are encouraged to jointly apply for EU scientific and technology research projects.

Promoting '16+1' Cooperation on Information and Communication Technology (ICT) and Consolidating E-Commerce Broadband Facilities. The popularisation and application of ICT technology and broadband are one of the important foundations for a country's innovation and development and also an important prerequisite for the development of e-commerce. China and CEECs should, provided that the corresponding legal restrictions of the EU are noted, carry out ICT infrastructure cooperation, increase the speed of broadband, strengthen network security and lay good foundations for the development of '16+1' cooperation in connection with e-commerce and the big data industry.

Strengthening Research on Central and Eastern Europe and the International Situation and Closely Monitoring the Risk Assessment of '16+1' Cooperation

We should pay attention to changes in CEEC presidents, parliaments and governments as well as their positions, attitudes and policies towards China so as to come up with timely responses. In particular, the mutual restrictions between the prime ministers and presidents of some governments from different political parties may have an impact on '16+1' cooperation.

At present, many young political figures born in the 1970s, 1980s and 1990s in central and eastern Europe have entered the political arena or taken on big responsibilities who have no personal experience of the traditional friendship between China and the CEECs. When these young politicians grew up, China was generally 'absent' from the CEECs. This gap is highlighted with the passing away of the old generation of central and eastern Europeans who are familiar with and friendly to China. Therefore, we suggest strengthening cultural exchanges between young people in China and central and eastern Europe and to strengthen various exchanges at the various levels of parliament, political parties, government and local governments so as to lay a solid foundation for long-term friendly relations between China and the CEECs.

We should also pay attention to the impact of EU policies on China and the CEECs. Attention should be paid to the recent measures or motions within the EU to restrict foreign investment, which would have adverse effects on the promotion of '16+1' cooperation.

As international terrorism spreads across Europe, the Balkan region is also exposed to the risk of extreme Islamic terrorism. Geopolitical security is still a core issue for the European continent, especially with regard to relations between the EU, the United States and Russia. These are all unavoidable safety factors in '16+1' innovation cooperation.

Conclusion

Innovation is an important core element in the BRI and some of the EU member states support this initiative. The China-EU Innovation Partnership should help the development of the BRI. The '16+1' cooperation can improve the China-EU Innovation Partnership and the BRI in many fields.

- Facing many challenges, the EU will pay more attention to innovation and combine innovation closely with socioeconomic development, identifying new routes for its integration.
- The innovation and development of the CEECs needs further in-depth development. In the transition period, the CEECs have lagged behind the EU. Since 2008, they must also work harder to overcome the consequences of the global financial crisis. The support of CEECs for innovation activities has yet to be improved to enhance the attractiveness of the research system. In addition to increasing government fiscal aid for the construction of the innovation 'infrastructure', a better environment, which is capable of attracting more private companies to invest in innovation, should be created.
- According to the guidance of the 19th National Congress of the Communist Party of China, China will pay more attention to the construction of an innovative country. China's more open attitude has provided new opportunities for '16+1' innovation and cooperation, creating new space for sustainable and green development in both China and the CEECs. It has also provided a new driving force for the improvement of the China-EU Innovation Partnership.

References

1. https://ec.europa.eu/growth/industry/policy/innovation/scoreboards_en
2. EU, European Innovation Scoreboard 2017.
3. European Commission, Innovation Union progress at country level.
4. The website of the Chinese Economic and Commercial Counselor's Office in the CEECs.
5. Krzysztof Klincewicz, Katarzyna Szkuta, Rio Country Report 2015. Poland, 2016.
6. GUS (Central Statistics Office of Poland), 2015.
7. World Economic Forum (2016), Global Competitiveness Report 2016–17.
8. OECD, Economic Surveys.
9. European Commission, Country Report.
10. Eurostat.

Min Zhang

The New Developments in China-European Scientific and Technological Innovation Cooperation

Introduction

In recent years, China's attention to science and technology innovation-driven development has risen to unprecedented strategic heights. In the past 40 years of its reform and opening up process, China has achieved remarkable economic development results and become the second largest economy in the world. However, there are many problems in its high-speed economic growth model, such as low quality and efficiency of development, serious damage to the ecological environment, weak innovation ability and the need to improve the level of the real economy. China's average annual economic growth rate has been unable to maintain the high-speed growth rate of nearly 10 % in the past 40 years and has fallen to a medium-high-speed growth rate of about 7 %. The economic growth pattern has entered a transitional period, objectively requiring a change in the driving force of economic growth, from 'factor-driven' and 'investment-driven' to 'innovation-driven'.

In this context, the Central Committee of the Chinese Communist Party and the State Council issued the Outline of an Innovation-Driven Development Strategy in May 2016, which put forward the strategy of innovation-driven development. In the report of the Nineteenth National Congress of the Communist Party of China, the General Secretary of the Chinese Communist Party, Xi Jinping, once again emphasised that "innovation is the first driving force for development and the strategic support for the construction of a modern economic system" and put forward clear goals and tasks for the establishment of an innovative country[1]:

1 In the fifth part of the report of the 19th National Congress of the Communist Party of China, "Implementing the new development concept and building a modern economic system", it is clearly pointed out that China's economy has changed from a period of high-speed growth to a period of high-quality development, and is in the critical period of transforming the mode of development, optimising the economic structure and transforming the driving force of growth. Building a modern economic system is a breakthrough. There is an urgent need of strategic goal of China's development.

1. Emphasising that innovation is the first driving force for development and the construction of a modern economy and the strategic support of the system.
2. Aiming at becoming one of the world's scientific research innovation leaders, strengthening basic research, focusing on forward-looking, leading and breakthrough research.
3. Strengthening the construction of the national innovation system and building a technology innovation system with deep levels of cooperation between industry, universities and researchers;
4. Training and cultivating international-level strategic scientific and technological talent and scientific and technological teams. Relying on an innovation-driven development strategy and the goal of building an innovative country have created new opportunities for cooperation between China and the EU in the field of scientific and technological innovation and generated higher standards.

A large number of existing studies have confirmed that the reason why scientific and technological innovation has become the driving force of economic growth is that it can continuously innovate the mode of economic growth, create and improve new productivity, accelerate the upgrading of traditional industries and comprehensively boost economic competitiveness.

> In the strategy of innovation-driven development, scientific and technological innovation capability, as an important support of national core strength, has promoted the evolution of national economic development to a stage of more detailed division of labour, more rational structure and higher form, and then crossed the 'middle-income trap'. Breakthrough technologies brought about by basic research and scientific explorations are constantly emerging. It reshapes the world competition pattern and the comparison of national strength and provides a window of opportunity for the late-developing countries. Through innovation and the cultivation of new economic growth points, it provides a basis for maintaining medium and high-speed economic growth and striding toward the 'double goals' of industries at the high and middle levels.[2]

Recently, China has become a country in a position of technological catch-up.

In the process of technological development, first of all, it relies on opening up, introducing, digesting and absorbing advanced foreign technology. In order

---

Accelerating the construction of an innovative country is a key element in building a modern economic system.

2 Liu Xielin, Gao Yuchen and Ding Xuechen, "Searching for New Theoretical Thinking of Innovation-Driven Development – Based on New Schumpeter's Growth Theory". [J] Managing the World, No. 12, 2017.

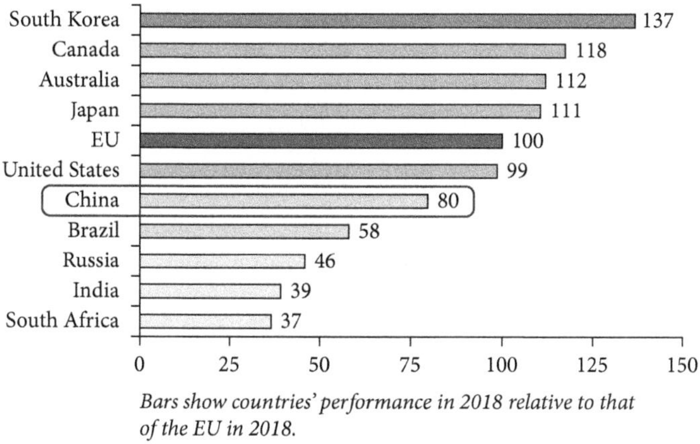

Fig. 1: Global innovation performance in 2019. Source: Authors based on European innovation scoreboard 2019 report https://ec.europa.eu/growth/industry/policy/innovation/scoreboards_en (accession 31 March, 2020)

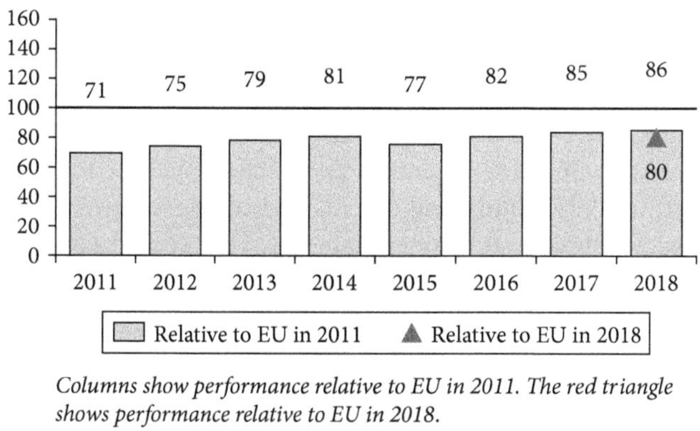

Chart 1: China performance relative to EU. Source: Authors based on European innovation scoreboard 2019 report https://ec.europa.eu/growth/industry/policy/innovation/scoreboards_en (accession 31 March, 2020)

to realise the 'innovative national strategy' proposed in the report of the 19th National Congress, China should, nowadays and in the future, increase its openness to the outside world in the field of scientific and technological innovation and continue to support the pace of international cooperation. By comparison with the United States and Japan, China's scientific and technological cooperation with Europe has more strategic value. This is because China-EU scientific and technological cooperation is the core content of the comprehensive strategic partnership between China and Europe. The EU is the main source of technology transfer in China. In recent years, China-EU scientific and technological cooperation has become increasingly active; and it has become more and more active with the EU, its member countries and other European countries. Establishing an innovative partnership has become a new direction via which to promote Sino-EU scientific and technological cooperation. Sino-EU scientific and technological cooperation has gradually shifted away from traditional technical cooperation towards scientific and technological innovation cooperation. The new highlights and progress of China-EU cooperation in science and technology innovation are described from three perspectives.

Scientific and Technological Innovation: A New Bright Spot in China-EU Relations

Transforming from Scientific and Technological Cooperation to Innovative Cooperation

China-EU science and technology cooperation has become a core part of the China-EU comprehensive strategic partnership. So far, the important moments in the process of Sino-EU scientific and technological cooperation are as follows: First, in 1998, China and the EU signed the Sino-EU Agreement on Scientific and Technological Cooperation. The EU's R&D framework plan and China's high-tech research plan, the basic research plan (i.e. the '863' plan and '973' plan), are open to each other, which offers precious opportunities for cooperation for scientists from both sides. So far, the Agreement on Scientific and Technological Cooperation has been renewed three times, respectively, in 2004, 2009 and 2014. Secondly, in May 2009, China and the EU signed the China-EU Science and Technology Partnership Plan, and the relationship between China and the EU in science and technology cooperation has gradually shifted away from being European-oriented towards seeking an equal partnership. The two sides jointly decide, select and fund research projects in mutually reinforcing priority areas. At the same time, the China-EU Scientific and Technological Cooperation Working Group has been upgraded and renamed the Steering Committee for China-EU Scientific and Technological Cooperation. Through regular meetings, the coordination and management of scientific and technological cooperation between China and EU branches such as the General Research

Department, the General Energy Department and the General Information Department have been strengthened. Thirdly, during the 15th China-EU Summit in 2012, China and the EU signed the Joint Statement on a China-EU Innovation Cooperation Dialogue and held the first China-EU Innovation Cooperation Dialogue in Beijing on 21 November 2013. The two sides discussed how to optimise and how to adjust the innovation governance system and promote effective innovation support measures in order to create a better environment for innovation and other issues and in order to strengthen communication and consultation[3]. Fourthly, in 2015, China and Europe established a joint funding mechanism for scientific research and innovation (CFM). This is one of the results of the annual China-EU Innovation and Cooperation Dialogue. On 7 September 2015, at the 'Pursuing Excellence – Promoting the Exchange and Cooperation of Scientific Research Personnel between China and Europe' conference, the two sides announced the launch of a new China-EU Joint Funding Mechanism for Scientific Research and Innovation.

The innovative element of this kind of cooperative model is that the joint funding mechanism was set up by the Chinese Ministry of Science and Technology and the European Commission's Research and Innovation Directorate respectively. In order to implement the joint funding mechanism highlighted in the joint statement of the 17th China-EU Summit, the mechanism relies on the EU's research and innovation plan Horizon 2020 and China's relevant research and innovation funding plan for five years (2016–2020). The European Commission plans to continue to invest about 100 million euro annually from Horizon 2020.[4] The Horizon 2020 plan supports institutions established in Europe in taking part in joint projects with Chinese institutions. The Chinese side will support the establishment of institutions in China to take part in joint projects with European partners in the framework of the Horizon 2020 plan. This mechanism has greatly increased the proportion of Chinese scientific researchers taking part in the EU's R&D framework plan as project hosts and has transformed China's participation in the EU's R&D framework plan from its previous decentralised application status to a centralised and unified declaration through the National Science and Technology Management Information

3 Delegation of the EU to China, https://eeas.europa.eu/delegations/china/15394/china-and-eu_en.

4 Launching a new joint funding mechanism for scientific research and innovation with China, International Online, http://news.cri.cn/gb/42071/2015/09/08/8011s5094725.htm

System of the Ministry of Science and Technology, thus facilitating scientific and technological cooperation system between the two sides. As a result, our initiative in China-EU scientific and technological cooperation has been strengthened to deliver 'win-win' results for mutual benefit. This model has been given high praise by both China and Europe.[5]

Innovative Highlights of China-EU Scientific and Technological Cooperation

The Transformation of the Governance System of Scientific and Technological Cooperation

The management mode of Sino-EU scientific and technological cooperation has gone through three stages: 'one to many' centralised management,[6] multi-head management and collaborative management. The improvement of the management mode effectively integrates the existing resources of Sino-EU scientific

---

5 "Scientific and technological cooperation is an important part of China-EU comprehensive relations, and science and innovation will inject momentum into economic growth and social development", said Minister Wan Gang. "The establishment of a joint funding mechanism will have a significant impact on the strategic partnership between China and Europe, and scientific research and innovation has become an important part of this partnership", said Carlos Moedas, member of the Council of Europe for Scientific Research and Innovation.

6 Before the signing of the Agreement on Science and Technology Cooperation between China and Europe, the 'one to many' centralised management model was applied (1981–1998). The 'one to many' centralised management model refers to the fact that, during this period, China was under the unified responsibility of the then National Science and Technology Commission for scientific and technological cooperation with foreign countries, while the energy, information and development departments of the European side were equal. Given the functions of decision-making and management of science and technology, it is necessary to expand the functions of this department by developing cooperation in relevant fields of science and technology after the establishment of diplomatic relations between China and Europe. During this period, China and the EC mostly adopted the aid and demonstration mode in their scientific and technological cooperation. As the EC had the leading role, China was in a passive position and the cost of personnel training and expert visits were basically borne by the EC. Most of the Sino-European cooperation projects are related to projects under China's '863' plan. Although China is relatively weak in cooperation, it has also improved the research level of domestic researchers and accumulated international cooperation research experience.

and technological cooperation and makes cooperation between the two sides develop in the direction of high efficiency and equality.

After the signing of the China-EU Agreement on Science and Technology, the model of China-EU cooperation has been a typical multi-head management model (1998–2015). The 1998 agreement clearly states "China will continue to participate in EU research activities for development as a developing country". This provision guarantees that China can, not only participate as an equal partner in the main part of the EU Framework Plan, but also continue to enjoy the assistance treatment of developing countries in the International Cooperation Specific (INCO) of the Framework Plan. Since then, China's scientific research institutions and personnel have not needed to use the National Science and Technology Commission (Ministry of Science and Technology) as an intermediary. As long as they can find EU research partners, they can directly establish links with them to apply for the funding from the framework plan.[7] This agreement at the national level has transformed the 'one-to-many' model of Sino-EU cooperation into a 'multi-to-many' multi-head management model, and the Sino-EU scientific and technological cooperation has entered a stage where it is in full bloom.

Since 2015, it has entered the collaborative management mode stage. In accordance with the China-EU Joint Initiative to establish a Joint Funding Mechanism (CFM), from 2016, the Ministry of Science and Technology of China will provide financial support for Chinese institutions to take part in the research and innovation projects of the Horizon 2020 Project and the exchange of research personnel. During the period from 2016 to 2020, China and Europe will raise 1.5 billion euro and 500 million euro, respectively, for the joint funding scheme. Since then, the EU R&D framework projects hosted by China have been submitted to the website of the Ministry of Science and Technology and the proportion of projects hosted by Chinese researchers will be greatly increased. In the past, the Chinese decentralised application procedure has been adjusted to the unified application procedure through the National Science and Technology Management Information System of China and the European Union Scientific Research Information Network. This mode of scientific and technological cooperation effectively integrates the existing resources of China-EU scientific and technological cooperation, changes the decentralised state of previous

7 Gao Jie and Liu Li: "Evolution and Prospect of China-EU Science and Technology Cooperation Path", http://www.sohu.com/a/158869656_468720

multi-pronged cooperation and promotes efficient and equal development of bilateral cooperation.

The main reasons for adopting a cooperative management system are as follows: Firstly, a multi-head management mode promotes the cultivation of scientific research teams on both sides, but it does not prevent unnecessary competition and does not prevent resources from being wasted. When Chinese scientific research teams directly apply for EU projects, they cannot obtain the direct support of the Ministry of Science and Technology, and the Ministry of Science and Technology cannot grasp the situation and the actual progress of project cooperation. There is a gap between the scientific and technological cooperation management agencies and the specific project executing departments. Secondly, in the Horizon 2020 plan, which will be implemented in 2014, China and other emerging economies will no longer automatically receive Horizon 2020 project funds. Chinese participants must provide funds or assistance in kind as financial contributions for project participants. Therefore, China-EU scientific and technological cooperation is carried out with government-led participation and the fact that the Chinese Government provides research funds is the basis for promoting the establishment of a partnership between China and Europe for scientific and technological innovation (Tab. 1).

Cooperation Between China and the EU Within the R&D Framework Plan

The EU's R&D Framework Plan (FP) has been fully open to China since 1998[8]. Cooperation between China and the EU in the FP has been the main channel for China-EU scientific and technological cooperation. The year 1998 coincided with the implementation period of the Fourth Research and Development Framework Plan of the EU.

> In the fourth R&D framework plan of the European Union, China participated in 81 projects, 52 of which are the Cooperation Plan for Developing Countries (INCO-DC), which receives 25 million euros from the European Union, and is the developing country with the largest amount of projects and funds in the INCO-DC plan. In the fifth R&D framework plan, China participated in 110 projects altogether, in which 44 are

8 In 1998, the fourth EU R&D framework plan included cooperation with third countries (INCO) for the first time. The sub-plan of INCO, i.e. the Cooperation with Developing Countries (INCO-DC), emphasises the participation of developing countries, which provides the possibility for China to participate in the EU's scientific research programme.

China	2011	2018	2011-2018
Doctorate graduates	13	11	-2
Tertiary education	35.2	40.4	5.1
International co-publications	36.1	43	7
Most cited publications	62.4	79.6	17.2
R&D expenditure public sector	62.9	72.6	9.7
R&D expenditure business sector	114.9	126.7	11.8
Product/process innovators	n/a	n/a	n/a
Marketing/organisational innovators	n/a	n/a	n/a
Innovation collaboration	n/a	n/a	n/a
Public-private co-publications	116.9	106.5	-10.4
Private co-funding public R&D exp.	8.5	5.4	-3.1
PCT patent applications	66.9	91.7	24.8
Trademark applications	234.3	296.6	62.3
Design applications	212.7	202.6	-10
Medium & high-tech product exports	96.5	91.9	-4.6
Knowledge-intensive services exports	91.8	72.4	-19.4

Tab. 1: China Performance in 2011 and 2018 relative to EU in 2011. Source: European innovation index official site (2019) https://ec.europa.eu/growth/industry/policy/innovation/scoreboards_en (accession 31 March, 2020)

> from INCO-DC Projects. In the sixth R&D framework plan, China participated in 239 projects and received about 35.19 million euros of EU research funds, accounting for 10.88 % of the total EU project funds received by third countries (non-EU countries), second only to Russia. In the seventh framework plan, China successfully applied for 410 projects.[9]

At present, China is the largest partner of the EU Horizon 2020 project, focusing on cooperation in food, agriculture and biology, energy, water, information and communication, nanotechnology and space and polar research. The China University of Science and Technology, Tsinghua University, Peking University, Shanghai Jiaotong University and other universities have joined the programme. The EU also encourages Chinese personnel to apply for scholarships and exchange schemes provided by the European Commission for scientific research and the Marie Curie Action Plan.

9 Zhang Min: "New Trends of EU Horizon 2020 Scientific Research Program", [J] *Xinhua News Agency "Outlook" Weekly*, No. 1, 2018.

New Development Opportunities for China-EU Innovation Cooperation

During the third China-EU Dialogue on Innovation Cooperation (2 June 2017), China and the EU signed the Agreement between the Ministry of Science and Technology of China and the European Commission on the Implementation of the Sino-EU Flagship Cooperation Plan for Research and Innovation and Other Research and Innovation Cooperation Projects in 2018–2020 through the Joint Funding Mechanism, in order to create intergovernmental scientific research for follow-up by China and the EU. The new cooperation framework provides guidance and a basis for cooperation.

At the end of October 2017, the European Commission officially announced the allocation of innovative R&D funds in the last three years of the EU Horizon 2020 (2018–2020)[10]. According to this plan, the EU will invest up to 30 billion euro in the Horizon 2020 project in the period from 2018 to 2020, of which 2.7 billion euro will be used to launch the European Innovation Council, the EU's new research management institution. As soon as the scheme was announced, it attracted considerable attention from the outside world by focusing on society-related and market-driven frontier scientific research with large-scale funds and significant breakthroughs. The new round of project cooperation has the following three new characteristics: (1) EU funding in the field of R&D will be more concentrated on changing the broad coverage of the past, funding projects, almost in a 'pasta noodles' funding mode; (2) Focus on supporting innovative research that leads to technological breakthroughs and is market-driven, seeking a linkage and balanced development between technological breakthroughs and market-driven results and (3) To adjust and reform the European Research Council system and to establish and launch the European Innovation Council. The paths for project funding, key breakthroughs and governance of scientific and technological innovation have been adjusted and changed, which provides new opportunities for more effective innovation cooperation between China and the EU.

Nevertheless, it is noteworthy that the Horizon 2020 project, which features reciprocal openness, two-way cooperation, fund allocation and sharing as the new rules and trends of Sino-European cooperative research projects, sets out

---

10 EU Horizon 2020, the eighth EU R&D framework, has a total budget of 77 billion euro. It is the largest R&D framework in the field of scientific and technological innovation in the EU so far. The total funding of the seventh R&D framework program is 55.8 billion.

higher requirements in relation to research priorities, fund requirements and intellectual property ownership of research results. This makes it possible for Chinese scholars to participate in R&D projects. The objective is very challenging.

According to the latest plan announced in this report, during the period 2018–2020, the European Commission will allocate 3.3 billion euro for future research on low-carbon, climate change adaptation; 1 billion euro for circular economy research; 1.7 billion euro for the digitalisation and transformation of EU industry and services; 1 billion euro for EU security research and 200 million euro for immigration research. In addition, 2.2 billion euro will be allocated to projects in four related areas of clean energy: renewable energy, energy-efficient buildings, transportation of electricity and storage of electricity. Out of these 2.2 billion euro, 200 million euro is being used to support the development and production of the next generation of batteries.

According to the above-mentioned R&D funding priorities in the next three years, China can jointly tackle key issues with the EU in the research and development of low-carbon and green development technologies and provide new technologies, new programmes and new practices for China in the areas of green development and low-carbon growth. Strengthening R&D cooperation between China and the EU in low carbon, digitalisation and clean energy technology will help China and the EU jointly contribute to a new era of low carbon and green development for mankind.

Sino-British Scientific and Technological Innovation Cooperation Has Entered an Era of Co-consultation and Decision-Making

The cooperative management system between China and the EU and its member countries is divided into the supranational level and the member country level. China and EU member countries have signed scientific and technological cooperation agreements and established scientific and technological cooperation committees. Scientific and technological cooperation with major EU member countries such as France and Germany is getting closer and closer. However, scientific and technological funding schemes at various national levels are very important. After all, China's openness is limited. At present, Britain is negotiating to leave the EU but the bilateral scientific and technological cooperation between China and the UK has continued to advance and has made breakthroughs. Sino-UK cooperation in the field of scientific and technological innovation is unique and worthy of attention and research.

From 31 January to 2 February 2018, the UK's Prime Minister Teresa May made her first visit to China during her term of office, announcing the opening of a new journey in the 'golden age' of Sino-British relations, which has injected new vitality into the achievement of strategic docking between the two countries and the strengthening of pragmatic cooperation in various fields. It has become a hot topic to build an enhanced version of the 'golden age' of Sino-British relations. China's President Xi Jinping has elaborated it as follows: to jointly create an 'enhanced golden age', we should constantly enhance and highlight the strategic, pragmatic, global and inclusive nature of Sino-British relations.

Sino-British Scientific and Technological Cooperation Has Always Been at the Forefront of the World

In 2015, China's President Xi Jinping visited Britain, creating a 'golden age' of Sino-British relations. In recent years, China and the UK have been moving on an established track and their willingness to cooperate has been growing. They are drawing up grand blueprints. Deepening cooperation in the field of scientific and technological innovation has become a highlight in the development of Sino-British relations. So far, scientific and technological cooperation between the two countries has been fruitful and unique in terms of global scientific and technological cooperation. Sino-British scientific and technological cooperation is characterised by being pragmatic, pioneering, strategic, forward-looking and global. It has become one of the most important areas of cooperation with 'golden texture' and a 'strategic connotation' in the 'golden age' of Sino-British relations. In the current international situation, Sino-British scientific and technological cooperation is in line with the strategic vision of a 'Globalised Britain' and a 'Globalised China' and is committed to the long-term goal of building a new type of cooperative relationship between the East and the West, between major developing countries and developed countries.[11]

In 1950, Britain became the first Western power to recognise the 'new' China with a strategic vision of facing the world and embracing both East and West. Since the establishment of diplomatic relations in 1972, the two sides have achieved fruitful results in cooperation in various fields. The development and deepening of a series of bilateral relations set out in this way vividly illustrates every historic moment in which Sino-British scientific and technological

11 Zhang Min: "'Golden Age' Enhanced relation: Two Points of Sino-British Science and Technology Innovation Cooperation", [J] *World Affairs*, No. 4, 2018.

cooperation has always been at the forefront of the world. In November 1978, China and Britain signed the Intergovernmental Agreement and Protocol on Scientific and Technological Cooperation. After the smooth handover of Hong Kong's regime in 1997, bilateral relations entered a new stage of all-round development. In 1998, Sino-British relations were upgraded to a comprehensive partnership. In September of the same year, the agreement on scientific and technological cooperation was revised, the high-tech field was identified as the focus of cooperation and the regular mechanism of joint scientific and technological committees was established, which endowed bilateral scientific and technological cooperation with a deeper strategic connotation. In 2004, the two countries established a comprehensive strategic partnership. In January 2009, the UK government published the first strategic document on China, entitled the UK-China Cooperation Framework, which further strengthened the comprehensive strategic partnership between China and Britain. Then, in 2012, the high-level human-cultural exchange mechanism between China and Britain was launched and the exchange of scientific and technological talent became a major trend. President Xi Jinping's state visit to Britain in October 2015 ushered in the 'golden age' of Sino-British relations and formally established the Sino-British Innovation Partnership, thus bringing Sino-British scientific and technological cooperation into a new era of scientific and technological innovation cooperation. Up to now, the two countries have held eight ministerial level meetings of the Joint Committee on Scientific and Technological Cooperation (renamed the Sino-British Joint Committee on Scientific and Technological Innovation and Cooperation after 2015).

The Newton Fund and The Research and Innovation Bridges Project Have Achieved Fruitful Results

Within the framework of the China-UK comprehensive strategic partnership, scientific and technological cooperation between the two countries has developed steadily along the path of equality, mutual benefit and reciprocity. Attention should be paid to the innovative R&D activities of basic theory and applied science and joint action in relation to major scientific research activities should be carried out. For example, the Sino-British Innovation Programme, the Sino-British Science Bridge Programme, the China Tomorrow Programme and the Fudan-Tyndall Center for Global Environmental Change Research have enhanced the innovative R&D capabilities of China and Britain. We should build innovative partnerships; emphasise the training of talent, cooperative research and technology transfer; stimulate innovative vitality and deliver the industrialisation of innovative achievements. The Newton Fund and Research Innovation Bridges Project and other innovative research funding methods and cooperative research relationship models represent a robust path in the process of Sino-British scientific and technological innovation cooperation.

The Newton Fund, known as the Sino-British Joint Research and Innovation Fund, was officially launched in 2014. It plans to invest 200 million pounds of joint funding by China and the UK in five years to carry out scientific research and innovation cooperation in seven key areas: health, environmental science and technology, food and water security, urbanisation, energy, education and the creative economy. The implementation of the Newton Fund series of projects has promoted a strong alliance between the Chinese and British intergovernmental science and technology departments, with the participation of relevant authorities, scientific research institutions and non-governmental organisations in both countries. So far, the Newton Fund has supported about 460 cooperative projects. China's Vice Premier Liu Yandong spoke highly of it, calling it 'a masterpiece of innovation and cooperation between the two countries'. Talent projects under the Newton Fund project: Newton Senior Scholars Foundation, Newton International Scholars Foundation and so on, are becoming boosters for training top talent in the field of scientific innovation in China and Britain.

During Vice Premier Liu Yandong's visit to Britain in September 2015, the two sides signed a plan to launch the Sino-British Joint Scientific Innovation Fund, Research and Innovation Bridge. The plan aims to support innovative cooperation between China and the UK in the field of the transformation of scientific research achievements and to provide solutions to specific challenges facing the two countries in their development process. The Bridge of Research and Innovation project has built a bridge between the two countries for the cooperation of industry, education and research and the transformation of scientific research achievements, with a planned investment of 350 million pounds. Through a series of projects, the scientific researchers of the two countries are being encouraged to carry out a series of cross-disciplinary, comprehensive and high-level scientific innovation cooperation research.

The Research and Innovation Bridges initiative advocates technology transfer cooperation in which higher education institutions in China and Britain play an important role. British universities are keen on scientific and technological cooperation with China and promote technology transfer between China and the UK through personnel training and technological exchanges. For example, the Oxford University Technology Transfer Company has promoted technology transfer to China in an orderly way. At present, four joint ventures have been set up in Changzhou and other places. Bradford University and Sichuan University have jointly established the China-UK Advanced Materials Research Centre.

The Bridges of Research and Innovation programme promotes the innovation and diversification of the mode of industry-university-research cooperation. The two sides have established long-term scientific and technological cooperation or regular exchanges with scientific research institutions, universities or enterprises. The one belt, one road (OBOR) initiative encourages Chinese enterprises to 'go out'. In addition to directly acquiring and developing strong R&D companies, Chinese enterprises are cooperating with universities and research institutes in the UK to set up R&D centres and to make use of advanced international scientific and technological resources to carry out industrial R&D and personnel training. For example, the China Aviation Industry Group has jointly established R&D centres with the Imperial College of Technology and Nottingham University; China National Car Group and Birmingham University, Imperial College of Technology and Southampton University are planning to establish a joint R&D Centre for rail transit technology between China and Britain, aiming at R&D cooperation in high-speed rail and other fields. The centre will focus on the key areas of rail transit vehicle dynamics, structural strength, vibration reduction and noise reduction, with new technologies, new materials, new structures and new processes as the starting point, and will focus on the study of international rail transit 'interconnection' technology and standards and a normative system, so as to build a research and development base for new high-speed rail technology in Europe. These future achievements of industry-university-research cooperation will enhance the international R&D level of the two countries and lay a solid foundation for China to build an innovative country.

Sino-UK Scientific and Technological Innovation Leaps to a New Level

The year 2018 will mark the 40th anniversary of Sino-British scientific and technological cooperation and cooperation in scientific and technological innovation between the two countries will be enhanced. This started with the intergovernmental agreement on scientific and technological cooperation, which laid the foundation for the two countries to move towards an era of innovative partnership. Not long ago, China and Britain jointly formulated the Sino-British Strategy for Scientific and Technological Innovation Cooperation for the first time, which marked a leap in terms of bilateral scientific and technological cooperation. On 6 December 2017, China and the UK signed the Memorandum of Understanding on Science and Technology Innovation Cooperation, formally promulgating the China-UK Strategy for Science and Technology Innovation Cooperation. This is the first bilateral science and technology innovation cooperation strategy jointly formulated by China and other countries. China and Britain foresee that today's scientific and technological revolution and industrial change are in the making, which is a major opportunity for the future prosperity and development of every country in the world. Jointly formulating the strategy of scientific and technological innovation cooperation will further tap the potential for cooperation, enhance complementarity and promote the development of cooperation in a multi-field, deep-seated, all-round and high-quality direction.

This joint strategy will open a new chapter in Sino-British cooperation, which is a concrete reflection of the enhanced version of the 'golden age' of Sino-British relations. In accordance with the objectives and requirements of the Sino-British Strategy for Scientific and Technological Innovation Cooperation, China and the UK are both responsible big powers. They will lead international scientific and technological innovation cooperation by raising the level of cooperation between the two countries. By gathering global intellectual resources, we can jointly meet global challenges with all countries in the world and build a community of human destiny for the benefit of all mankind. In the future, the achievements of scientific and technological innovation in China and Britain will shine brightly as we make progress in the construction of a China-UK global partnership.

Innovation Strategic Partnership between China and Switzerland

In April 2016, China-Switzerland relations were upgraded to innovative strategic partnerships, which became a major initiative in the development of China-EU relations and highlighted the 'innovation highlights' of China-Switzerland relations. Switzerland has become China's first innovative strategic partner country and the first foreign relations country named after China's five major development concepts. The development process of Sino-Swiss relations on the 67th anniversary of the establishment of diplomatic relations shows that Sino-Swiss cooperation can be regarded as a model of friendly cooperation among countries with different social systems, at different stages of development and of different sizes, and it has become a new benchmark for Sino-European bilateral scientific and technological innovation cooperation.

The Development of Sino-Swiss Relations Has Created Many First Places

Switzerland has set many 'world records' in its contacts with China: Switzerland was one of the first European countries to recognise the founding of the new China and formally established diplomatic relations with China on 14 September 1950. Switzerland is one of the Western countries that is actively participating in the process of China's reform and opening up, and the Swiss Schindler Group has become the first joint venture to enter the Chinese market. By contrast with the EU's reluctance to recognise China's market economy status, Switzerland took the lead in recognising China's full market economy status in 2007. Switzerland attaches great importance to cooperation with China in a more open attitude at a time when economic growth in European countries is weak and trade protectionism is rising. Switzerland became the first continental European country to sign a free trade agreement with China in 2013. In April 2016, China and Switzerland established a strategic partnership for innovation, which is the first time that China has established a partnership going by the name of 'innovation' with a foreign country. This series of milestones will set an example for the opening, inclusive and win-win cooperation between different systems in the East and the West, and provide positive energy for pragmatic cooperation between China and the EU in various fields.

Innovative Cooperation: Highlighting the Strategic Relationship Between China and Switzerland

Cooperation between China and Switzerland in the field of scientific and technological innovation is playing a leading role. In April 2016, Article 5 of the Joint Statement on the Establishment of the Innovation Strategic Partnership between China and Switzerland clearly stated that bilateral cooperation in all fields, from basic scientific research to scientific and technological innovation, had achieved remarkable results. The two sides have established a joint working group mechanism for scientific and technological cooperation between China and Switzerland to provide a platform for China's innovation-driven development strategy and Switzerland's docking of innovation advantages. We will work together to enhance innovation capabilities and support and actively promote innovative cooperation between the enterprises, universities and scientific research institutions of the two countries.

Compared by land area, *per capita* GDP level and international innovation capability ranking, China and Switzerland are, among big innovative and developing countries, complementary in terms of their cooperation and their advantages in their efforts to achieve the long-term goal of science and technology innovation-driven development. Switzerland is a small country in Europe, with only 40,000 square kilometres of surface area, but it is based on highly developed industries such as machinery and electronics, metals, medicine and the chemical industry, clocks and watches, finance and so on. Switzerland is ranked in the top 20 countries in the global economy and is ranked first in the world in terms of the *per capita* wealth of its residents. Switzerland attaches great importance to innovation. Its annual investment in scientific and technological innovation-related R&D accounts for more than 3 % of GDP. Swiss clocks and watches, Swiss military knives and other industrial innovation achievements with the Swiss label are well known all over the world. In the global competitiveness rankings issued by the World Economic Forum, Switzerland has ranked first in the world competitiveness rankings of the World Economic Forum for nine consecutive years[12], has ranked first in the Global Innovation Index issued jointly by the World Intellectual Property Organisation for seven consecutive years and is known as the 'country of innovation'.[13]

China is a large developing country. In 2017, the *per capita* GDP was equivalent to US$8,583[14] (in terms of market exchange rates), which is about one tenth of Switzerland's[15]. As the second largest economy in the world, China is ranked second in the world for its GDP and R&D investment. In 2017, the total R&D investment was 1.75 trillion yuan, accounting for 2.12 % of GDP.[16] Our country's

---

12 In the Global Competitiveness Report 2017–2018 issued by the World Economic Forum, Switzerland was ranked first in global competitiveness for nine consecutive years.

13 On June 15, 2017, the World Intellectual Property Organisation (WIPO) released its tenth edition, Global Innovation Index 2017: Innovation Feeding the World. Through 81 indicators, the report assesses the innovation capacity and measurable results of 127 economies worldwide. Switzerland continues to lead the global innovation list with a high score of 67.69, which is the seventh consecutive year that Switzerland has been ranked first in the global innovation index.

14 IMF, World Economic Outlook Database, October 2017.

15 Switzerland's GDP *per capita* in 2017 is equivalent to US$80,837 (at market exchange rates).

16 According to the preliminary results of the annual report of comprehensive science and technology statistics, the total investment in R&D in China in 2017 was 1,750 billion yuan, an increase of 11.6 % over the previous year and a percentage point higher than the previous year, according to the data released by the National Bureau of Statistics on 13 February 2018. At present, the total investment is second only to the United States, ranking second in the world. In addition, the intensity of R&D investment (the ratio of R&D expenditure to GDP) in China is 2.12 %, which is 0.01 percentage points higher than the previous year.

Global Innovation Index 2019 rankings

Country/Economy	Score (0–100)	Rank	Income	Rank	Region	Rank	Median 33.86
Switzerland	67.24	1	HI	1	EUR	1	
Sweden	63.65	2	HI	2	EUR	2	
United States of America	61.73	3	HI	3	NAC	1	
Netherlands	61.44	4	HI	4	EUR	3	
United Kingdom	61.30	5	HI	5	EUR	4	
Finland	59.83	6	HI	6	EUR	5	
Denmark	58.44	7	HI	7	EUR	6	
Singapore	58.37	8	HI	8	SEAO	1	
Germany	58.19	9	HI	9	EUR	7	
Israel	57.43	10	HI	10	NAWA	1	
Republic of Korea	56.55	11	HI	11	SEAO	2	
Ireland	56.10	12	HI	12	EUR	8	
Hong Kong, China	55.54	13	HI	13	SEAO	3	
China	54.82	14	UM	1	SEAO	4	
Japan	54.68	15	HI	14	SEAO	5	
France	54.25	16	HI	15	EUR	9	
Canada	53.88	17	HI	16	NAC	2	
Luxembourg	53.47	18	HI	17	EUR	10	
Norway	51.87	19	HI	18	EUR	11	
Iceland	51.53	20	HI	19	EUR	12	
Austria	50.94	21	HI	20	EUR	13	

Fig. 2: China in Global Innovation Index 2019 rankings. Source: Global innovation index Official Site (2019) https://ec.europa.eu/growth/industry/policy/innovation/scoreboards_en (accession 31 March, 2020)

innovation ability does not match the world's second largest economy, R&D investment is less than half that of the United States and science and technology innovation ability has a low ranking in the world. In 2017, China was ranked three places higher in the Global Innovation Index and 23rd in the world. Although it was the first middle-income country to enter the top 25 countries in the world rankings, there was a huge gap between China and Switzerland. Switzerland was ranked first for seven consecutive years. In the future, strengthening innovation cooperation between China and Switzerland will help to improve China's manufacturing level and innovation capability and gradually narrow the income gap between China and developed countries (Fig. 2).[17]

17 Zhang Min: "Innovative Spotlight of Sino-Swiss Relations", [J] *Xinhua News Agency "Outlook" Weekly*, No. 4, 2017.

Connecting 'Made in China 2025' with 'Swiss Industry 4.0'

From 15 to 18 January 2017, China's President Xi Jinping visited Switzerland for the first time in the new century. During his visit to Switzerland, the two countries signed ten Sino-Swiss cooperation agreements. In the field of scientific and technological innovation, the most important practical cooperation is to establish a practical cooperation platform for Sino-Swiss scientific and technological innovation docking, strengthen the docking between 'Made in China 2025' and 'Swiss Industry 4.0' and to further highlight the innovative meaning of the Sino-Swiss strategic partnership for innovation. This is also an important innovation platform for technological docking with European countries, which has been clearly put forward by China and Germany.

'Made in China 2025' is the first ten-year action plan for China to implement the strategy of strengthening the country. In the future, manufacturing capacity will be comprehensively enhanced in ten key areas. The 'European Industrial 4.0' Industrial Revolution will provide strong technical support for the transformation from Made-in-China to Created-in-China and from Chinese products to Chinese brands. 'Swiss Industry 4.0' is embodied in: Switzerland giving full play to its advantages in its traditional fine manufacturing of machinery, textiles, tools and watches; vigorously promoting intelligent manufacturing; transferring information via machines, raw materials and products through the Internet of Things and cooperating to complete production tasks.

In the future, 'Made in China 2025' and 'Swiss Industry 4.0' will effectively achieve docking. Through a series of technical cooperation activities in intelligent manufacturing, the digital economy, environmental protection and energy, we will absorb and draw lessons from Switzerland's 'craftsman spirit' and 'brand awareness', which will help build a 'golden signboard' of Chinese manufacturing enjoying a global reputation.

Concluding Remarks

The above three levels represent the latest developments in and direction of scientific and technological innovation cooperation between China and Europe. They have strategic, forward-looking and breakthrough characteristics. China-EU scientific and technological cooperation emphasises an 'R&D innovation' nature and plays a leading role in cooperation between China and other European countries in the field of scientific and technological innovation. China-EU relations will be upgraded to a China-EU Comprehensive Innovative Strategic

Partnership in the future[18]. Making full use of external scientific and technological innovation resources is one of the major ways to enhance the driving force of innovation in China. Strengthening cooperation in scientific and technological innovation between European countries and different member countries will help China catch up with the latest frontier of world scientific and technological development, accelerate the upgrading of scientific and technological innovation capacity and provide theoretical and practical guidance for the construction of innovative power. Therefore, at this stage and in the future, we should learn from the experience of China-EU scientific and technological innovation cooperation to provide theoretical and practical support for the construction of a modern economic system and realise the strategic goal of China's innovative power.

18 The basic orientation of China-EU relations is the China-EU Comprehensive Strategic Partnership established in 2003. In 2013, the two sides signed the Strategic Plan for China-EU Cooperation 2020, which identifies the common goals of strengthening cooperation in the fields of peace and security, prosperity, sustainable development and cultural exchanges, and promotes the deepening development of the China-EU comprehensive strategic partnership. In 2014, China and Europe will jointly build four major partnerships of peace, growth, reform and civilisation.

Gerhard Stahl

China-EU Cooperation in a Period of Fundamental International Changes: Review of the Past and Suggestions for the Future

The International Changes

We live in a time of rapid and fundamental changes. The globalisation of living conditions and the increasing internationalisation of the economy are having an impact all over the world. Poverty in developing countries is falling, and innovation and new technologies are accelerating structural changes.[1]

We are at the beginning of the Fourth Industrial Revolution (FIR), a new era of technological development based on digital transformation. The Internet of Things (IoT), the development of artificial intelligence and cloud computing will generate wide-ranging economic and social consequences. By 2025, it is estimated that 26–30 billion of devices in the home and workplace will be equipped with sensors, processors and embedded software, and connected to the IoT. These objects can operate autonomously based on the data they collect or exchange with each other.[2]

Overall, the heavyweight of the global economy shifts to Asia, where more than half of the world's population lives. While the USA and the EU accounted for more than 60 % of global economic output in 1990, its share has now fallen to 40 %. Calculated in purchasing power, China has already become the biggest economy.[3]

These changes pose major challenges to our societies. New skills are needed for the digital economy and numerous existing jobs might disappear in industry and administration. Historically grown norms governing the reconciliation

---

1 In the following documents different aspects of the globalization process are analysed: World Trade Report (2013), Factors Shaping the Future of World Trade, WTO, Geneva. Thomas Palley (2018), "Three Globalizations, not two, rethinking the history and economics of trade and globalization", *FMM working paper*, No. 18, Hans-Böckler-Stiftung.

2 European Patent Office (2017), fourth industrial revolution, study in cooperation with Handelsblatt, p. 10.

3 Compare IMF (2017), world economic outlook, data base.

of interests of different parts of the society in the developed Western democracies are undermined by globalisation. This is true of national tax legislation, given the mobility of capital and the location of Internet companies. This applies to national social legislation and national environmental standards, given the relocation of production and international supply chains. New distributional conflicts arise between winners and losers of globalisation. In the USA, in China and other countries the inequality of income and wealth has increased. In the US, in the UK and Italy, the stagnation of real income of the middle class prepares the ground for populist movements favouring protectionism and disengagement from international cooperation.[4]

The traditional liberal market idea about the functioning of the economy, shaped by national experiences and the role of the state in Western democracies, no longer provides sufficient guidance for the challenges of a tightly knit international economy: for international competition where private companies compete with state-owned enterprises and where different political and regulatory systems meet.

The system of international financial institutions that emerged after the Second World War, with the International Monetary Fund, the World Bank and the dollar as the dominant international reserve currency, is also changing. China and other emerging countries demand more influence and participation in decision-making. New international financial institutions such as the Asian Infrastructure and Investment Bank and the BRICS Bank were created to support investment and economic development especially in Asia, Africa and Latin America.

The new Silk Road or One Belt One Road Initiative (BRI) of China is a mayor investment program. It will connect parts of Europe, Asia and Africa with the big Chinese market, reshaping the economic geography and giving China a central place.[5]

In the international economy, not all currencies are equal. Despite the multipolarity of today's world economy, the US dollar remains the main international currency. The euro that has been introduced in 2002 already comes second. But its further ascent was hindered by the aftermath of the international financial

4 A historical overview is given by: Thomas Piketty (2014), *Capital in the Twenty-First Century*, Cambridge. For the USA, different aspects of the hollow-out of the middle class are analysed in: John Komlos (2018), "Reagonomics: a Historical Watershed", *CESifo working paper*.

5 The study of Rand Europe: Hui Lu, Charlene Rohr *et al.*, (2018), *China Belt and Road Initiative*, gives an overview and tries to measure the impact on international trade.

crisis, starting as sub-prime crisis 2007 in the USA and becoming later a sovereign debt crisis. This sovereign debt crisis affected very much the EU and exerted pressure to reform further the European Monetary System.

The international role of the Yuan is still in an infant state. Its international use is hampered by capital controls and the limited integration of the Chinese financial system into the international financial market. But China is changing quickly and opens further also in the financial sector. Hong Kong is already a leading international financial centre, connected to all parts of the world. Its role will be strengthened by the close integration into the big bay area. This macro-regional pilot project for 70 million people will increase Hong Kong's economic and financial links with one of the most dynamic parts of mainland China. Cross-border lending, foreign portfolio holdings and presence of foreign banks and insurance companies will increase. New fin-tech services and special rules for this pilot regions will be developed and tested to prepare the step by step opening of the Chinese financial market in general.

The American government uses the US-dollar dependency of the international financial system to force companies to submit to American political goals.[6] The exterritorial effects of American sanctions lead to increased political tensions. The EU and China, therefore, increase its efforts to reduce the dependency on the US dollar and to further develop the international role of their currencies.[7]

Two Conflicting Policy Answers: My Nation First versus Multilateral Rules-Based Cooperation

These fundamental changes unsettle many people and lead to very different political answers. On the one side, the American administration under President Trump falls back to a policy of national interest first. Also in the past the USA was prudent not to accept too easily that American policy is constrained by

6 One of the most striking examples is the US sanction against Iran. This forced the EU to establish a mechanism, INSTEX, to enable companies to engage in economic exchanges with Iran partners without requiring direct transfer of money between the EU and Iran.

7 For more details, see: Communication by the EU-Commission (2018), Towards a stronger international role of the Euro: https://ec.europa.eu/info/files/communication-towards-stronger-international-role-euro_en

international rules and institutions.[8] But under the Trump administration and with the slogan 'America first' this policy got a new dimension. The USA withdraws from international agreements and reduces its support for international organisations and multilateral policies. The argument of national security is used to create new protectionist barriers.[9] More and more commentators fear that US policy makers perceive the changes as a geopolitical conflict between the USA as the leading international political and economic power against a rising China. A White House spokesman has recently criticised the BRI as 'made in China, for China'.[10] The 2018 US National Defence Strategy builds on the 2017 National Security Strategy's qualification of China as a 'revisionist power' and defines China as "a strategic competitor using predatory economics to intimidate its neighbours while militarizing features in the South China Sea".[11]

On the other side, the EU is uniting countries and establishes common legislations for all members. Instead of a policy based on national sovereignty the EU's legal framework forces member states to share sovereignty by accepting common rules and to break down barriers protecting national markets. The EU has an economic focus and supports the multilateral international system. It is a major driving force in negotiating wide-ranging free trade agreements (FTAs).[12] China is not perceived as a geopolitical rival, but as a partner and competitor on the international market, that poses a specific challenge because of its unique political system.[13]

---

8 This can be seen in the case of the International Criminal Court in The Hague. Whereas the Clinton Administration signed the Rome Statue that founded the International Court, the USA withdrew later its support and did not ratify the agreement.

9 Report to the Congress (2017), on China's WTO compliance, presented by the US trade representative in January 2018. This report has a long list of complaints towards Chinese policies and it is stated, e.g. on page 25: "The United States is determined to use every tool available to address harmful Chinese policies and practices [. . .]".

10 See G. Rachman, "The US, China and the Return of a Two-Bloc World", *Financial Times*, 11 March 2019.

11 See https://dod.defense.gov/Portals/1/Documents/pubs/2018-National-Defense-Strategy-Summary.pdf, p. 1.

12 One recent example is the EU-Japan Economic Partnership Agreement, which entered into force on 1 February 2019.

13 In the Communication of the Commission "EU–China – A strategic outlook", 12.3.2019, the following description of the relationship is given on page 1: "China is, simultaneously, in different policy areas, a cooperation partner with whom the EU has closely aligned objectives, a negotiating partner with whom the EU needs to find a balance of interests, an economic competitor in the pursuit of technological leadership, and a systemic rival promoting alternative models of governance".

China's leadership is also committed to a multilateral international system. This can be seen by its support to international institutions, whether it is the UN, IMF, World Bank or WTO.[14]

President XI stated in his speech in Davos at the World Economic Forum 2017: "We should adhere to multilateralism to uphold the authority and efficacy of multilateral institutions. We should honour promises and abide by rules".[15]

Nevertheless, concerns are raised not only in the USA but also in Europe about the readiness of China to engage in multilateral cooperation on equal terms and to accept that international rules and international institutions might limit China's national sovereignty.

The Rise of China: A Major Driving Force for Globalisation

The rise of China is closely linked to the globalisation of recent decades and these changes. For China, internationalisation has led to a unique economic success story that began when Deng Xiaoping opened the country 40 years ago. When the first special economic zone was created in 1979 in Shenzhen, just outside Hong Kong, the People's Republic was an impoverished, agriculturally dominated developing country. Meanwhile, the majority of Chinese lives in cities. The former fishing village of Shenzhen has become an attractive and modern metropolis that has more inhabitants than Paris. There are 180 of the Fortune 500 companies represented there. There is a vibrant start-up scene in Shenzhen, as well as Chinese companies like Huawei and Tencent, which have become international market leaders. Many of the Chinese metropolises have become the intersections of an internationally intertwined economy. China has become the workbench of the world and has set itself the goal of becoming the market leader in future technologies. Meanwhile, the services sector generates more than 50 % of gross domestic product and the adaptation of a heavily export-oriented industrial sector is making significant progress. The current account surplus has fallen from over 9 % of GDP in 2007 to less than 2 %. in 2018. In 2019 there might be even the risk of a small current account deficit. Thousands of new companies are founded, and more and more of them are start-ups in the high-tech sector. The

14 This support is visible by the fact that China has become one of the biggest provider of UN peacekeeping forces, by its signature of the Paris Climate Agreement and by the acceptance of WTO dispute settlements.

15 See http://www.china.org.cn/node_7247529/content_40569136.htm

wealthy urban Chinese middle class covers nearly 400 million people, more than the population of the United States.[16]

European Integration: It Has Helped EU Countries to Integrate Further into the Global Economy

But for Europe too, the internationalisation of the economy has brought many changes and great advantages. In Europe, globalisation was shaped by the EU and the creation of the Single European Market for more than 500 million people. Medium-sized companies have also become increasingly international. Many companies now regard the European domestic market as their home market and have been able to build cost-saving value-added chains and supplier structures beyond national borders. In the internal market, not only goods and capital are mobile, but also the mobility of workers has increased. This increased the supply of labour in the industrial centres and in booming regions. The common EU trade policy protects individual EU countries from bilateral demands from trading partners for concessions. The creation of the euro has reduced the exchange rate risks and guarantees a favourable exchange rate for some of the export-oriented EU-economies. Labour migration and EU policies contributed to the international competitiveness of European companies. To present just one example: Studies confirm that Germany has become one of the most integrated countries in the global economy.[17] Based on the European home market, major German companies have strengthened their international presence and invested heavily in research and innovation. Siemens alone has built 20 research centres in China. The 128-year-old, traditional insurance company Allianz also shows the extent to which German companies have adapted to the international economy. Most of the economic activities are now taking place outside Germany. This is also reflected in the ten-member board. Only three of the board members are from Germany; others are from Italy, Spain, South Africa and Sri Lanka. The

16 See Gerhard Stahl (2018), "Forty Years of China's Opening: Changing the Post World War II International Order" in EU-China Observer, issue #2.18, College of Europe.

17 See McKinsey Globalization report 2016, Digital Globalization, the new era of global flows. The report calculates an MGI Connectedness Index. This index offers a comprehensive look at how countries participate in inflows and outflows of goods, services, finance, people, and data. The MGI Index shows that Germany is one of the most globalized countries, see page 56.

high – some say too high – competitiveness of the German export industry is also reflected in one of the world's highest current account surplus of 230 billion euros or approximately 8 % of GDP.

Comparing the Benefits for Europe and China Obtained from the Globalisation Process

It is interesting to look into some recent quantitative studies that tried to calculate the benefits of globalisation for different countries. The Globalisation Report of the Bertelsmann Foundation analyses the situation of 42 countries. It tries to answer the question: Which country has benefitted most from the globalisation? The study is based on a globalisation index covering the period from 1990 to 2016.[18]

It can be seen that the integration into the global economy and the achieved openness of the markets of European countries had created the biggest per capita globalisation benefits for European countries. Even if China has been because of its size and export performance a key player in the globalisation process of the last decades, its per capita benefits are smaller. This is explained by the fact, that the opening up process of China is a cautious step-by-step approach. Taking the Bertelsmann study as a reference, it can be concluded that the further opening of the Chinese market could create big economic benefits for Chinese citizens.[19] But one remark of caution might be necessary towards this conclusion. The quantitative methods and regression analysis used to analyse the empirical data of the past have its limits for forecasting future developments if big disruptions in the international economy will happen. The consequences of new protectionist measures related to the US-China trade dispute and the dynamic aspects linked to the innovation competition to master the FIR must be also considered to make a final judgement about the appropriate scale of market opening.

State of Play of EU-China Cooperation

The EU and China have since 1975 diplomatic relations and agreed in 2003 to *a comprehensive strategic partnership.* Over 60 regular expert meetings and one

18 Globalisierungsreport 2018, Wer profitiert am stärksten von der Globalisierung, Bertelsmann Stiftung.

19 See Globalisierungsreport 2018, p. 9.

Tab. 1: EU-China trade in goods *in euro billion*

Year	2015	2016	2017
Imports from China	350.85	344.91	374.30
Exports to China	170.36	169.66	198.25
Trade Balance	-180.49	-175.25	-176.04
Total Trade	521.20	514.58	572.55

Tab. 2: EU-China investment flows *in US-dollar billion.* Source: EU-Commission, fact sheet for the EU-China Summit, 16 July 2018

Year	2015	2016	2017
EU into China	11	8	6
China into EU	23	40	32
Balance	-12	-32	-25

annual EU-China summit took place to implement this agreement. The partnership includes annual dialogs on numerous areas like foreign and security policy, economy, trade, financial markets, competition policy, regional policy, research and innovation.

Over the last decades the trade and investment relations between China and the EU were very successful and became a pillar of the international economy. The EU is now the biggest trading partner of China. China is the second biggest partner for the EU behind the USA. The trade in goods between the two partners is around 1.5 billion euros per day.

The Federal Republic of Germany is by far the largest European trading partner for China. For some German companies in the automotive sector China has become an important production location in the context of joint ventures with Chinese partners and even the largest sales market.

More than 1800 European companies are located in China and the number of Chinese companies being directly present in the EU is increasing rapidly. This can be seen by the positive development of foreign direct investment (FDI). Traditionally, the EU was a big source for FDI, contributing to the Chinese economic development. But recently the dynamics of FDI has changed. While Chinese investment in the EU reached record highs, EU investment in China weakened (Tabs. 1 and 2).

Perspectives for the Future of EU-China Cooperation

Even if there are some complaints about unequal treatment and a persisting trade deficit of the EU, the general appreciation of the EU-China cooperation is positive. This cooperation was a major driving force for increased international trade and investment with all its benefits over the last decades. But what will the future bring? Will EU-China cooperation be hampered by increased protectionism and deglobalisation?

The future of EU-China cooperation will depend very much on an open international economy and the answers to the FIR. The FIR will affect all parts of economy and society. With the help of artificial intelligence and big data new methods of production will be developed, new services will be delivered and as a consequence restructuring of economies will take place.

China has outlined with its Made in China 2025 strategy and its five years plan priorities its ambition to master the FRI.[20] The EU still has to elaborate a comprehensive approach. It has to combine national innovation strategies with European instruments like competition policy, trade policy, regional policy and R&D financing.

It will be important that the implementation of the FIR strategies is not based on the concept of technological autarky and national preferences. It would undermine an open international economy if each of the big economic blocs tries to set its own standards for the digital economy and creates its own national FRI champions.

In this context, this year's 21st EU-China summit was of special importance. In an international climate where the American government questions the benefits of free trade and the globalised economy, where trade disputes degenerate into geopolitical conflicts articulated as fight for innovation – and technology supremacy – where more and more experts advocate for protectionist measures, where populist movements want to create new barriers between people and countries, the cooperation between the EU and China is more important than ever to keep the world economy open. It was reassuring that – after intensive preparations and tough negotiations – the Chinese delegation headed by Premier Li Keqiang and the European delegation under the leadership of EU-Commission President Juncker could agree on an ambitious program for the future, covering a broad area of economic and political measures. Both sides confirmed their firm support to the rules-based, transparent,

20 Zenglein, Holzmann (2019), "Evolving Made in China 2025", *Merics* No. 8, July, https://www.merics.org/en/papers-on-china/evolving-made-in-china-2025

nondiscriminatory, open and inclusive multilateral trading system with the World Trade Organization (WTO) at its core. They confirmed the cooperation on the WTO reform based on the work of a joint working group.[21]In light of the trade disputes it was of specific importance that both agreed to achieve in the course of 2019 the decisive progress required for the conclusion of an ambitious EU-China Comprehensive Investment Agreement in 2020.

The successful conclusion of the comprehensive EU-China investment agreement would be a strong signal that common rules can be established between the socialist market economy of China and the social market economy of the EU. This agreement would demonstrate that a common understanding about access to markets, investment rules, competition policy and state aid can be developed between different political and economic systems.

It would be also a solid basis to reinforce cooperation in other areas of common interest.

- Measures against climate change

A sustainable economic model has to be developed to fight climate change. In the words of Chinese leadership: an ecological civilisation has to be built. Without fundamental changes in the economy, global warming will have dramatic effects on the ecosystem, biodiversity and human livelihoods. The fight against climate change cannot succeed by national measures alone, a coordinated international policy is needed. The EU was a frontrunner in climate policy and environmental legislation. It established, for example the first big international CO2 emission-trading scheme to reduce the emission of Greenhouse gases. China is also committed to an ambitious environmental policy. This could be seen by China's signing of the Paris Climate Agreement of December 2015. Also, the last G20 meeting on the 28th and 29th of June 2019 confirmed China's engagement by supporting together with the European countries the commitment to an ecological paradigm shift.[22] The USA, which has withdrawn its support to the Paris agreement, also objected to this commitment in the G20 Osaka declaration. Cooperation to fight climate change should address very concrete measures. Best practices can be exchanged between European and Chinese experts

21 See EU-China joint summit statement, Brussels: https://www.consilium.europa.eu/media/39020/euchina-joint-statement-9april2019.pdf

22 See the declaration of the Osaka G20 meeting and especially paragraph 35 and 36: https://www.consilium.europa.eu/media/40124/final_g20_osaka_leaders_declaration.pdf

about sustainable city planning, public transport, circular economy and waste disposal, energy-saving and green energy. There are already very interesting exchanges between Chinese and European cities and regions on these issues.

- Develop an open and fair international economy

A common position is needed against trade- and investment-barriers and rising protectionism. Reciprocity has to be achieved in investment rules, by taking into account some specific conditions linked to different institutional systems and development objectives. EU and China should cooperate on the reform of the WTO.[23]

The system of international financial institutions that emerged after the Second World War has to be adapted to the changes in the international economy. This reform should help developing and emerging countries to get their fair share in the global governance and international economy.

It is a promising sign of EU-China cooperation that major European countries supported the creation of the Asian Infrastructure Investment Bank and have been amongst the founding members.

- Support the economic development of Africa

Looking at the demographic developments of the world population, further changes will happen. Especially Africa's economic importance should increase, based on a growing and young population and plenty of natural resources. EU-China cooperation could support and facilitate economic development in Africa and its integration into the international economy. Chinese companies are major investors in more than 20 African countries; Africa-China trade increases quickly and China has become the biggest trading partner of Africa. The BRI provides support and financing to build the necessary infrastructure for further economic development. But there are also close and longstanding economic relations between African and European Countries. The EU remains an important trading partner of Africa, and is by far the biggest donor for development assistance. Cooperation between the EU and China could create synergies, improve the efficiency of financial assistance programs and could extend beyond economic questions, for example supporting measures to improve security in conflict regions.

23 A more detailed discussion of different aspects and positions regarding the reform of the WTO and the future of free trade can be found in *ifo Schnelldienst*, No. 11 (2018), "Handelskrieg und seine Folgen: Ist die WTO am Ende?", 14.6.2018.

Conclusion

We are in a historical moment where conflicting concepts are presented concerning the future of international relations and the international economy. Successful EU-China cooperation could be essential to safeguard a globalised economy and to reject a return to national power politics that was so devastating in the 20th century.

Published Books

N° 1 – Catherine Lanneau, *L'inconnue française. La France et les Belges francophones (1944-1945)*, 2008

N° 2 – Frédéric Dessberg, *Le triangle impossible. Les relations franco-soviétiques et le facteur polonais dans les questions de sécurité en Europe (1924-1935)*, 2009

N° 3 – Agnès Tachin, *Amie et rivale. La Grande-Bretagne dans l'imaginaire français à l'époque gaullienne*, 2009

N° 4 – Isabelle Davion, *Mon voisin, cet ennemi. La politique de sécurité française face aux relations polono-tchécoslovaques entre 1919 et 1939*, 2009

N° 5 – Claire Laux, François-Joseph Ruggiu & Pierre Singaravélou (dir./eds.), *Au sommet de l'Empire. Les élites européennes dans les colonies (XVIe-XXe siècle) / At the Top of the Empire. European Elites in the Colonies (16th-20th Century)*, 2009

N° 6 – Frédéric Clavert, *Hjalmar Schacht, financier et diplomate (1930-1950)*, 2009

N° 7 – Robert JAblon, Laure Quennouëlle-Corre & André Straus, *Politique et finance à travers l'Europe du XXe siècle. Entretiens avec Robert Jablon*, 2009

N° 8 – Alain Beltran (ed.), *A Comparative History of National Oil Company*, 2010

N° 9 – Sarah Mohamed-Gaillard, *L'Archipel de la puissance ? La politique de la France dans le Pacifique Sud de 1946 à 1998*, 2010

N° 10 – Marie-Anne Matard-Bonucci, Anne Dulphy, Robert Frank & Pascal Ory (dir.), *Les relations culturelles internationales au vingtième siècle. De la diplomatie culturelle à l'acculturation*, 2010

N° 11 – Yves-Marie Péréon, *L'image de la France dans la presse américaine, 1936-1947*, 2011

N° 12 – Léonard Laborie, *L'Europe mise en réseaux. La France et la coopération internationale dans les postes et les télécommunications (années 1850-années 1950)*, 2010

N° 13 – Catherine Horel (dir.), *1908, la crise de Bosnie cent ans après*, 2011

N° 14 – Alain Beltran (ed.), *Oil Producing Countries and Oil Companies. From the Nineteenth Century to the Twenty-First Century*, 2011

N° 15 – Frédéric Dessberg & Éric Schnakenbourg (dir), *Les horizons de la politique extérieure française. Régions périphériques et espaces seconds dans la stratégie diplomatique et militaire de la France (XVIe-XXe siècles)*, 2011

N° 16 – Alya Aglan, Olivier Feiertag & Dzovinar Kévonian (dir.), *Humaniser le travail. Régimes économiques, régimes politiques et Organisations internationale du travail (1929-1969)*, 2011

N° 17 – Pierre Journoud & Cécile Menétrey-Monchau (dir./eds.), *Vietnam, 1968-1976. La sortie de guerre / Vietnam, 1968-1976. Exiting a War*, 2011

N° 18 – Louis Clerc, *La Finlande et l'Europe du Nord dans la diplomatie française. Relations bilatérales et intérêt national dans les considérations finlandaises et nordiques des diplomates et militaires français, 1917-1940*, 2011

N° 19 – Yann Decorzant, *La Société des Nations et la naissance d'une conception de la régulation économique internationale*, 2011

N° 20 – Lorenz Plassmann, *Comme dans une nuit de Pâques ? Les relations franco-grecques 1944-1981*, 2012

N° 21 – Alain Beltran (dir./ed.), *Le pétrole et la guerre / Oil and War*, 2012

N° 22 – Valentine Lomellini, Les relations dangereuses. *French Socialists, Communists and the Human Rights Issue in the Soviet Bloc*, 2012

N° 23 – Martial Libera, *Un rêve de puissance. La France et le contrôle de l'économie allemande (1942-1949)*, 2012

N° 24 – Séverine Antigone Marin, *L'apprentissage de la mondialisation. Les milieux économiques allemands face à la réussite américaine (1876-1914)*, 2012

N° 25 – Claire Sanderson & Mélanie Torrent (dir./eds.), *La puissance britannique en question. Diplomatie et politique étrangère au 20e siècle/ Challenges to British Power Status. Foreign Policy and Diplomacy in the 20th Century*, 2012

N° 26 – Elena Gretchanaia, *« Je vous parlerai la langue de l'Europe… ». La francophonie en Russie (XVIIIe-XIXe siècles)*, 2012

N° 27 – Alfred Wahl, *Histoire de la Coupe du monde de football. Une mondialisation réussie*, 2013

N° 28 – Catherine Fraixe, Lucia Piccioni & Christophe Poupault (dir.), *Vers une Europe latine. Acteurs et enjeux des échanges culturels entre la France et l'Italie fasciste*, 2013

N° 29 – Danièle Fraboulet, Andrea M. Locatelli & Paolo Tedeschi (eds.), *Historical and International Comparison of Business Interest Associations. 19th-20th Centuries*, 2013

N° 30 – Annie Guenard-Maget, *Une diplomatie culturelle dans les tensions internationales. La France en Europe centrale et orientale (1936-1940 / 1944-1951)*, 2014

N° 31 – Catherine Horel (dir.), *Les guerres balkaniques (1912-1913). Conflits, enjeux, mémoires*, 2014

N° 32 – Bruno Dumons & Jean-Philippe Warren (dir.), *Les zouaves pontificaux en France, en Belgique et au Québec. La mise en récit d'une expérience historique transnationale (XIXe-XXe siècles)*, 2015

N° 33 – Pierre Chabal (dir.), *Concurrences interrégionales Europe-Asie au XXIe siècle*, 2015

N° 34 – Florent Pouponneau, *La politique française de non-prolifération nucléaire. De la division du travail diplomatique*, 2015

N° 35 – Alain Beltran (ed.), *Les routes du pétrole / Oil Routes*, 2016

N° 36 – Pierre Chabal (dir.), *L'Organisation de coopération de Shanghai et la construction de la « nouvelle Asie »*, 2016

N° 37 – María Luisa Azpíroz, *Public Diplomacy. European and Latin American Perspectives*, 2015

N° 38 – Massimo Bucarelli, Luca Micheletta, Luciano Monzali & Luca Riccardi (eds.), *Italy and Tito's Yugoslavia in the Age of International Détente*, 2016

N° 39 – Michel Dumoulin & Catherine Lanneau (dir.), *La biographie individuelle et collective dans le champ des relations internationales*, 2016

N° 40 – Sebastian Santander, *Concurrences régionales dans un monde multipolaire émergent*, 2016

N° 41 – Alain Beltran, Éric Bussière & Giuliano Garavini (dir.), *L'Europe et la question énergétique. Les années 1960/1980*, 2016

N° 42 – André Straus and Leonardo Caruana de las Cagigas (eds.), *Highlights on Reinsurance History*, 2017

N° 43 – Vincent Genin, *Incarner le droit international. Du mythe juridique au déclassement international de la Belgique (1914-1940)*, 2018

N° 44 – Catherine Horel & Robert Frank (eds.), *Entrer en guerre, 1914-1918 : des Balkans au monde*, 2018

N° 45 – Clotilde Druelle-Korn, *Food for Democracy ? Le ravitaillement de la France occupée (1914-1919). Herbert Hoover, le blocus les neutres et les Alliés*, 2018

N° 46 – Thomas Meszaros (dir.), *Repenser les stratégies nucléaires. Continuités et ruptures. Un hommage à Lucien Poirier*, 2019

N° 47 – Amélie Zima, *D'ennemi à allié. L'adhésion de la Hongrie, de la Pologne et de la République Tchèque à l'Alliance atlantique (1989-1999)*, 2019

N° 48 – Michel Dumoulin, Vincent Genin & Sabina Gola (eds.), *Autour de l'année 1866 en Italie. Echos, réactions et interactions en Belgique*, 2020

N° 49 – Mario Telò & Yuan Feng (eds.), *China and the EU in the Era of Regional and Interregional Cooperation*, 2020

www.peterlang.com

www.ingramcontent.com/pod-product-compliance
Ingram Content Group UK Ltd.
Pitfield, Milton Keynes, MK11 3LW, UK
UKHW021921120926
8556IPUK00042BA/1110

9 782807 613966